Debugging by Thinking

A Multidisciplinary Approach

Debugging by Thinking

A Multidisciplinary Approach

Robert Charles Metzger

ELSEVIER
DIGITAL
PRESS

Amsterdam • Boston • Heidelberg • London • New York • Oxford
Paris • San Diego• San Francisco • Singapore • Sydney • Tokyo

Library of Congress Cataloging-in-Publication Data
Metzger, Robert C.
    Debugging by thinking : a multidisciplinary approach/Robert Charles Metzger.
    p. cm.
    ISBN: 1-55558-307-5
    1. Debugging in computer science. I. Title.

QA76.9.D43M48 2003
005.1'4–dc22

2003055655

British Library Cataloguing-in-Publication Data
A catalogue record for this book is available from the British Library.

The publisher offers special discounts on bulk orders of this book.
For information, please contact:

Manager of Special Sales
Elsevier
200 Wheeler Road
Burlington, MA 01803
Tel: 781-313-4700
Fax: 781-313-4882

For information on all Digital Press publications available, contact our World Wide Web home page at: http://www.digitalpress.com or http://www.bh.com/digitalpress

10 9 8 7 6 5 4 3 2 1

Printed in the United States of America

For my family – Marcia, Erika, and Benjamin – who make it all worthwhile.

Contents

Preface

Why I Wrote This Book

When I first learned to program, I found the process of testing and debugging very frustrating. I can remember slamming my fist down on the hard metal shell of the Selectric typewriters we used to interact with the time-sharing system at the amazing speed of 15 characters per second. The bugs didn't disappear any more quickly for the beating. None of my professors taught me anything about testing and debugging that I can remember.

During the nearly 30 years that I have worked in software development, many aspects of the profession have changed. Languages have become popular and gone out of favor. Better development methodologies have been introduced, only to be replaced by yet more sophisticated methodologies. Microprocessors have become ubiquitous, and software has become the driving force behind many new products. The laptop computer that I wrote this book on has a faster processor, more memory, and more disk space than the multimillion dollar IBM™ mainframe on which I learned to program.

Some things have not changed, however. Software products still contain far too many bugs. Software developers still spend far too much time finding and fixing those bugs. People who are learning to program spend far too much time struggling to learn by trial and error.

I wrote this book because I wanted to introduce a systematic approach to debugging to a wide audience. If you learn something from this book that enables you to find and fix bugs more quickly, then I will have succeeded.

Who Should Read This Book

This book was written with both students and professional programmers in mind. Any student who has completed a course in computer programming and a course in data structures and algorithms should be able to understand and apply the material in this book. Professional programmers should find new ideas to make them more productive, along with new twists on old ideas they have been using for years.

The case studies were done in C++ and Java because they were the most popular programming languages in use when this book was written. I refer to other popular languages, particularly C and Fortran, when they are relevant to a particular topic. Since this book focuses on how to think about debugging, rather than on specific platforms, almost all of the material is relevant to all programming languages. If your primary language is not Java or C++, you should still be able to apply at least 90 percent of the material in this book.

How to Read This Book

There are several reasons that this book takes a multidisciplinary approach to debugging. One reason is that people are unique, and different people have different preferred modes of learning. Some people need to see things to learn, others prefer to hear new material, and others have trouble understanding unless they can work something with their hands. In a similar way, some people will relate to some of the lessons of certain disciplines better than others.

When the material in this book was presented in classes for computer science graduate students, I found a wide difference in which disciplines the students found most interesting or helpful. Some absolutely loved the analogy to detective literature. Others were uninterested. Some were fascinated by the study of human error. Others had trouble seeing how it was relevant to them. If you have problems relating to the analogy of one particular discipline, move on to another one, and come back later to the first one.

An undergraduate student who wants to develop debugging skills quickly should probably read chapters 1–4, 7–9, 5, 10, 11, and 15, in that order. Graduate students in computer science should add chapters 12–14 after that.

A professional programmer with years of experience may not feel the need to read the case studies (chapters 5 and 10). If you aren't sure whether a chapter will be of use to you, read the review at the end of the chapter first.

The material in chapters 6 and 12 is more theoretical than the rest of the book. Chapter 6 gives the rationale for the organization of chapters 7–9.

Chapter 12 applies ideas from cognitive psychology that attempt to explain how programmers create bugs.

Make sure that you read chapter 15, and make a plan for applying what you have read.

Typographical and Grammatical Conventions

Italics are used to emphasize a point and identify the names of publications and products.

Boldface is used to introduce new terms, which are collected in the glossary, and to distinguish programming language keywords and commands from the text.

Example material that is computer generated, such as command-line entries and source code listings, is set in the following typeface:

```
This is a computer listing
```

Example material that isn't computer-generated, such as algorithm descriptions and debugging logs, is set in the following typeface.

```
This is a debugging log
```

Choosing the right third-person singular pronoun is a difficult task these days. In this book, unknown software developers are referred to as "he or she."

Acknowledgments

Thanks to my wife Marcia for encouraging me to finish a book I had been talking about for 10 years. She suggested that I read the Lord Peter Wimsey mysteries, and the result is apparent in this book.

Thanks to Dr. Lawrence Rauchwerger, Dr. Nancy Amato, and their graduate students at Texas A&M University for giving me opportunities to present an early version of this material to them and for giving me valuable feedback on their classes.

Thanks to my managers at Hewlett-Packard, Betty van Houten, Steve Rowan, and Ty Rabe, who gave their permission for HP Books to publish this book.

Thanks to all the programmers I have worked with and managed at I.P. Sharp Associates, Convex Computer Corporation, and Hewlett-Packard. I learned both from your successes and failures in debugging complex systems.

Thanks to Ken Robinson and the technical support people at Parasoft, who gave me lots of help working with Insure++.

Thanks to my editor, Pam Chester, for taking on this project enthusiastically and carrying it through to completion professionally.

Thanks to my technical reviewers, Steve Heller, Piotr Findeisen, and Richard Goldhor, whose helpful suggestions greatly improved the quality of this book.

Any errors that remain are purely the responsibility of the author.

Permissions

The quote in chapter 1 is used by permission of Gerald M. Weinberg.

Quotes in chapter 1 from Grady Booch, *Object-Oriented Analysis and Design with Applications* © 1994 Benjamin Cummings Publishing Company, Inc., are reprinted by permission of Pearson Education, Inc.

Quotes in chapter 1 from *The Art of Software Testing* by Glenford J. Myers © 1979 John Wiley and Sons, Inc., are reprinted by permission of John Wiley and Sons, Inc.

Quotes in chapter 3 from *The Unpleasantness at the Bellona Club* by Dorothy L. Sayers © 1928 by Dorothy Leigh Sayers Fleming, copyright renewed 1956 by Dorothy Leigh Sayers Fleming, are reprinted by permission of David Higham Associates.

Quotes in chapter 3 from *Strong Poison* by Dorothy L. Sayers © 1930 by Dorothy Leigh Sayers Fleming, copyright renewed 1958 by Lloyd's Bank, Ltd., executor of the estate of Dorothy L. Sayers, are reprinted by permission of David Higham Associates.

Quotes in chapter 3 from *Have His Carcase* by Dorothy L. Sayers © 1932 by Dorothy Leigh Sayers Fleming, copyright renewed 1960 by Lloyds Bank, Ltd., executor of the estate of Dorothy L. Sayers, are reprinted by permission of David Higham Associates.

Quotes in chapter 3 from *Gaudy Night* by Dorothy L. Sayers © 1936 by Dorothy Leigh Sayers Fleming, copyright renewed 1964 by Anthony Fleming, are reprinted by permission of David Higham Associates.

Quotes in chapter 3 from *Busman's Honeymoon* by Dorothy L. Sayers © 1937 by Dorothy Leigh Sayers Fleming, copyright renewed 1965 by Anthony Fleming, are reprinted by permission of David Higham Associates.

Quotes in chapter 4 from *How to Find Lost Objects* by Michael P. Solomon © 1993 Top Hat Press are reprinted by permission of Top Hat Press.

Quotes in chapter 6 from George Polya, *How to Solve It,* copyright renewed 1973 by Princeton University Press, are reprinted by permission of Princeton University Press.

Quotes in chapter 6 from *Mathematical Problem Solving* by Alan Schoenfeld © 1985 by Academic Press, Inc., are reprinted by permission of Academic Press.

Quotes in chapter12 from *Human Error* by James Reason © 1990 Cambridge University Press, are reprinted by permission of Cambridge University Press.

Quotes in chapter 13 from *Invention by Design* by Henry Petroski © 1996 by Henry Petroski, are reprinted by permission of the publisher, Harvard University Press.

Quotes in chapter 13 from *Flying Buttresses, Entropy, and O-Rings* by James Adams © 1991 by the President and Fellows of Harvard College, are reprinted by permission of the publisher, Harvard University Press.

Quotes in chapter 13 from *To Engineer Is Human* by Henry Petroski are reprinted by permission of the author.

Introduction

If builders built buildings the way programmers wrote programs, the first wood-pecker that came along would destroy civilization.

—Gerald Weinberg

1.1   The nature of the problem

I don't believe that the story of a moth found in a relay of one of the first digital computers adequately explains why software defects are commonly referred to as bugs. Books on debugging often begin with a recitation of how Adm. Grace Hopper found a moth, which had shorted out an electronic relay, in the Mark II computer. While the story may be true and although there are many variations told, the aptness of the term goes far deeper than this incident.

The word "bug" is commonly used to refer both to insects and arachnids. In the natural world, bugs are often the chief competitors of humankind. Scientists speculate that if humans became extinct, bugs would become the dominant life form on the planet. According to the Bible, three of the ten plagues that God visited on Egypt, to free the Israelites from slavery, were visitations of bugs (gnats, flies, and locusts). Bugs bite us, sting us, destroy our houses, consume our food, and transmit to us many of the worst diseases that afflict humanity.

Software bugs afflict people in very similar ways. Like natural bugs, they're everywhere. Almost all interesting software has bugs, and most interesting software has far too many bugs. Like natural bugs, they cause irritation and even pain when we encounter them. Now that computer chips are embedded in so many devices, software bugs can threaten human life and property. Calling software defects "bugs" resonates with us at a deep level.

This is because software defects are becoming as troublesome as insects and arachnids have been in the past.

There are many reasons why today's software has so many defects. One reason is that many programmers aren't very good at debugging. Some programmers look on the debugging phase of the software life cycle with the same enthusiasm they show for filling out their income tax forms.

The purpose of this book is to reduce the effort programmers expend to diagnose software bugs. If the time available to debug remains constant in a project, this efficiency improvement will reduce the total number of bugs in a software program. If the number of outstanding bugs remains constant in a project, this efficiency improvement will reduce the time it takes to deliver that software. Either way, the person who benefits is the ultimate user of the program.

1.1.1 Definitions

It's important to use a consistent set of terms when studying a subject. We will use the term **symptom** to mean an observable difference between the actual behavior and the planned behavior of a software unit. The IEEE94 Software Engineering Standards [IEEE94] refer to this as a **failure.**

We will use the term **defect** to mean that aspect of the design or implementation that will result in a symptom. The IEEE94 Software Engineering Standards refer to this as a **fault**. We will use the term **bug** interchangeably with defect.

1.2 The six ways of thinking

This book explores methods for debugging, organized according to six intellectual disciplines:

1. The way of the detective
2. The way of the mathematician
3. The way of the safety expert
4. The way of the psychologist
5. The way of the computer scientist
6. The way of the engineer

Each way has an analogy, a set of assumptions that forms a worldview, and a set of techniques associated with it. We follow a multidisciplinary approach, in which we seek the best methods for solving intellectual problems.

When we follow the way of the detective, we use an analogy between the search for the culprit in a murder mystery and the search for a software defect in a program. The defect is treated as a crime, and the programmer is the detective. A detective who wants to solve a crime must determine the answers to several important questions:

- Who did it?
- How did the culprit do it?
- When did the culprit do it?
- Why did the culprit do it?

We seek similar answers for software defects.

When we follow the way of the mathematician, we use an analogy between developing a proof of a mathematical proposition and developing a diagnosis of a software defect in a program. In the past several centuries, mathematicians have developed numerous methods for constructing proofs. These methods, however, have only recently been organized and taught in a way that the average student can learn and apply as effectively as the mathematically gifted.

When we follow the way of the safety expert, we use an analogy between accidents or critical events and failures of software to behave as expected. The defect is considered a critical event, and the programmer is the safety analyst. The safety expert seeks to prevent future problems by analyzing the causes of significant events, such as accidents, near misses, and potential problems.

When we follow the way of the psychologist, we recognize that software defects are the result of human error. Human error has recently become an area of study for cognitive psychologists. The information-processing model used by many psychologists provides a means to explain how humans make mistakes.

When we follow the way of the engineer, we use an analogy between the design of reliable material objects and the design of reliable immaterial software. Engineers follow a standard process for creating physical objects. We can leverage the methods that can prevent or identify defects that are introduced during phases of the software-development process. Engineers design useful objects by following standards, and we suggest ways to prevent software defects by following standards.

When we follow the way of the computer scientist, we treat defective software as processes that fail to manipulate symbols correctly. Computer scientists study symbol manipulation by digital electronics. Some of the theoretical concepts of computer science for classifying and analyzing information can be applied to the process of debugging. Computer scientists advance their discipline by inventing layers of tools that can be composed into larger systems. When we follow the way of the computer scientist, we look for tools that can automatically diagnose software defects.

1.3   The two eras of software engineering

The craft of software engineering has gone through several eras. One way we can identify them is by the books published that promoted the main ideas of each particular era. In each era, the basic concepts were applied to the various phases of the software-development life cycle.

1.3.1   Structured development history

The following is a representative list of the popular books published during the era of structured development:

- Structured programming
    - *Techniques of Program Structure and Design*—Yourdon, 1975
    - *The Elements of Programming Style*—Kernighan and Plauger, 1974
    - *Top-Down Structured Programming Techniques*—McGowan and Kelly, 1975
- Structured design
    - *Structured Systems Development*—Orr, 1977
    - *Structured Design*—Constantine and Yourdon, 1979
    - *Composite/Structured Design*—Myers, 1978
- Structured analysis
    - *Structured Systems Analysis*—Gane and Sarson, 1979
    - *Structured Analysis and System Specification*—DeMarco, 1979
    - *Structured Requirements Definition*—Orr, 1981

- Structured testing

  - *Software Testing Techniques*—Beizer, 1982
  - *A Structured Approach to Systems Testing*—Perry, 1983

While there is some overlap, from this data we can identify the phases of the structured era as follows.

Structured programming, 1974–1975

Structured programming produces source code. It has two distinguishing characteristics:

1. Modules are decomposed hierarchically.

2. Modules are composed using only flow-of-control constructs that have a single entry and a single exit.

Structured design, 1977–1978

Structured design produces a functional design. It has three distinguishing characteristics:

1. Graphic tools display the hierarchy and communication between modules of a system.

2. Evaluation criteria distinguish between good and bad designs at the modular level.

3. Implementation strategies determine the order in which to code and implement modules.

Structured analysis, 1979–1981

Structured analysis produces a functional specification of a software system. It has three distinguishing characteristics:

1. Data-flow diagrams

2. Data dictionaries

3. Structured English

Structured testing, 1982–1983

Structured testing produces a test design. It has three distinguishing characteristics:

1. Behavioral tests are generated from requirements.

2.   Structural tests are generated from implementation of the software.

3.   Both behavioral and structural tests can be created. The appropriate aspect of the software is represented as a graph, and the inputs that will traverse the arcs of the graph are identified.

Structured documentation, 1985

Structured documentation produces user documentation. It has three distinguishing characteristics:

1.   Documents are hierarchically decomposed into two-page modules, one of which is text and the other is graphics.

2.   Forward and backward references (**goto** statements) between modules are eliminated.

3.   Module text is written in easy-to-read language.

The basic concepts of the structured development era were top-down decomposition and the use of a small set of simple and safe control-flow constructs. These concepts were successfully applied to everything from coding to documentation. A book that discusses structured debugging, whatever that might be, is notably lacking.

1.3.2   Object-oriented development history

The various structured disciplines were concerned with organizing computation with respect to actions. In contrast, the object-oriented disciplines are concerned with organizing computation with respect to data. Actions aren't things that stand on their own; they're attributes of information that corresponds to an entity in the real world.

The following is a representative list of the popular books published during the era of object-oriented development:

- Object-oriented programming
  - *Object-Oriented Software Construction*—Meyer, 1988
  - *The C++ Programming Language, 2nd ed.*—Stroustrup, 1991
- Object-oriented design
  - *Object-Oriented Design with Applications*—Booch, 1991
  - *Object-Oriented Modeling and Design*—Rumbaugh et al., 1991
  - *Design Patterns*—Gamma et al., 1995

- Object-oriented analysis
  - *Object-Oriented Analysis and Design with Applications*—Booch, 1994
  - *Object-Oriented Systems Analysis*—Shlaer and Mellor, 1989
- Object-oriented testing
  - *Object Oriented Software Testing*—Siegel, 1996
  - *Testing Object-Oriented Systems*—Binder, 2000

While there is some overlap, from this data we can identify the phases of the object-oriented era as follows.

Object-oriented programming, 1985–1991

Object-oriented programming produces source code. Booch [Bo94] defines it as follows:

> Object-oriented programming is a method of implementation in which programs are organized as cooperative collections of objects, each of which represents an instance of some class, and whose classes are all members of a hierarchy of classes united via inheritance relationships.

Object-oriented design, 1991–1995

Object-oriented design produces a functional design. Booch defines it as follows:

> Object-oriented design is a method of design encompassing the process of object-oriented decomposition and a notation for depicting both logical and physical as well as static and dynamic models of the system under design.

Object-oriented analysis, 1994

Object-oriented analysis produces a functional specification of a software system. Booch defines it as follows:

> Object-oriented analysis examines requirements from the perspective of the classes and objects found in the vocabulary of the problem domain.

Object-oriented testing, 1996–2000

Object-oriented testing produces a test design. It deals with the numerous issues raised by object-oriented programming that weren't previously issues: inheritance, polymorphism, and so forth.

Once again, a book addressing object-oriented debugging, whatever that might be, is notably lacking.

1.4 Debugging and development methodologies

The other phases of software development were amenable to the structured and object-oriented approaches. Why wasn't the same true of debugging?

There are at least three reasons.

1.   There is a big difference between constructive versus cognitive activities.

2.   Debugging is widely confused with testing.

3.   The supporting disciplines needed for structured and object-oriented debugging developed much later.

1.4.1 Constructive versus cognitive activities

Coding, designing, analyzing, and testing are all constructive activities. They each produce a tangible result. Coding produces source code. Designing produces design documents. Analysis produces a variety of documents, depending on the methodology used. Testing produces test cases and reports on the success or failure of tests.

In contrast, debugging is primarily a cognitive activity. The end result is knowledge of why there is a problem and what must be done to correct it. There will be a source change, but it may only involve adding or deleting a single character or word. The constructive output of debugging is often disproportionate to the effort expended.

1.4.2 Confusing testing and debugging

Most books and papers written in the 1960s and 1970s confuse debugging with testing. When they talk about debugging, they're really discussing testing.

One of the earliest books to properly define testing was Glenford Myers's [My79] *The Art of Software Testing*:

Testing is the process of executing a program with the intent of finding errors.

In his book, Myers was concerned with debunking definitions such as the following: "Testing is the process of demonstrating that errors are not present."

This definition, and other similar ones, all define testing negatively, in terms of the absence of errors. It's impossible to prove the absence of anything in general. In the particular case of software, it's even more pointless because large useful software systems all contain defects.

Myers defines debugging as follows:

Debugging is a two-part process; it begins with some indication of the existence of an error . . . and it is the activity of (1) determining the exact nature and location of the suspected error within the program and (2) fixing or repairing the error.

Following Myers's lead, we further refine the definition of software testing to contrast it with software debugging.

Testing is the process of determining *whether* a given set of inputs causes an unacceptable behavior in a program.

Debugging is the process of determining *why* a given set of inputs causes an unacceptable behavior in a program and *what* must be changed to cause the behavior to be acceptable.

The lack of a clear definition of the goals of the testing and debugging processes prevented the development of a discipline of structured or object-oriented debugging.

1.4.3   Supporting disciplines developed later

The cognitive psychology of human error, induction, and deduction did not become widely understood until the early 1990s. The following are some key texts in each of these areas:

- *Human Error,* James Reason, 1990.

- *Induction: Processes of Inference, Learning, and Discovery,* J. H. Holland et al., 1989.

- *Deduction,* P. N. Johnson-Laird and R. M. J. Byrne, 1989.

Books that documented the mathematical problem-solving process did not become widely available until the mid-1980s. The key text in this area is

- *Mathematical Problem Solving*, Alan H. Schoenfeld, 1985.

These disciplines provide important insights into the debugging process. It wasn't possible to develop a general theory of debugging prior to the publication of research in these areas.

1.4.4   Uncommonly common sense

If you're an experienced programmer, some of what follows will seem like common sense to you. If you're a novice, it may seem like great words of wisdom. The odd thing about common sense is that it's so uncommon. If you have professional programming experience, we hope that we will state some principles that you're already following.

Most people who read this book will already have had at least some success in computer programming, if only in passing several computer science courses. Unfortunately, plenty of people can't pass an introductory programming course. Inability to debug programs is a major reason that people don't pass such courses.

The inability to learn to debug software can be, and often is, simply due to a lack of aptitude for this type of work. In some cases, however, the difficulty students have in learning to debug is due to the lack of adequate instruction in how to do this task and the lack of any kind of systematic approach to debugging. This book can make the difference for some students who have some aptitude but aren't receiving the instruction they need to succeed.

1.4.5   Debugging by thinking

Where did the title for this book come from? Consider some of the other methods that people use for debugging.

Debugging by editing: This is often the first approach to debugging that programming students try. If their first effort doesn't work, they make some changes and try executing the program again.

The student will probably achieve some success with this approach. Introductory programming courses usually assign trivial programs, and the number of possible changes to a partially correct program is relatively small.

Debugging by interacting: This is usually the next approach that students learn. The programming student will inevitably be told by an instructor or a fellow student that he or she should try using a debugger. This is reasonable, since interactive debuggers that work with high-level languages are almost universally available.

This is an improvement over the previous phase in at least one respect. The programming student will use the debugger to observe some aspect of the program's behavior before making a change.

Debugging by repeating: As the programming student uses an editor and a debugger, he or she will inevitably hit upon certain sequences of actions that prove useful. Without fully understanding the assumptions or limitations of a particular method, the programmer will apply the action set to every problem. Sometimes the actions will prove useful, but at other times they won't help. Given a sufficient number of trials, this approach will winnow down a large number of actions to a "bag of tricks" of manageable size.

This method of developing debugging skills is nearly universal. It's probably the reason for magazine articles and books with titles like "The Black Art of Debugging." The programmer can't explain scientifically the assumptions, limitations, or relationships between the techniques he or she has learned to use, so they seem similar to a set of sorcerer's incantations.

There are problems with this approach. It takes longer than necessary to produce a highly developed set of debugging skills. The time used by the trial-and-error evaluation of methods is determined by the random order in which the programmer encounters bugs. In addition, programmers often waste time when faced with debugging problems for which nothing in their bag of tricks is helpful.

Debugging by Thinking as a methodology has the following characteristics that distinguish it from the other ways of debugging described above:

Explicit methodology: It's much easier to teach a skill to people when you make the steps of the methodology explicit. The alternative is to expose them to lots of examples and hope that they will discern the steps by induction. Debugging by thinking means using techniques whose steps are explicitly described.

Multidisciplinary approach: It's much easier to understand debugging as primarily a cognitive process, rather than as a constructive process, like the other phases of the software life cycle. Once we recognize this, we can leverage the insights that people who work in other problem-solving disciplines have developed. Debugging by thinking means actively seeking methods from intellectual disciplines that solve analogous problems.

Self-awareness: It's much easier to find problems in software if you know the kinds of problems that are possible and the ways in which people make mistakes. Debugging by thinking means understanding our assumptions, our methodologies, and our tendencies to make mistakes.

1.5   Review

This book explores methods for debugging, organized according to six intellectual disciplines:

1.   The way of the detective

2.   The way of the mathematician

3.   The way of the safety expert

4.   The way of the psychologist.

5.   The way of the engineer

6.   The way of the computer scientist

Each way has an analogy, a set of assumptions that forms a worldview, and a set of techniques associated with it. A **symptom** is an observable difference between the actual behavior and the planned behavior of a software unit. A **defect** is that aspect of the design or implementation that will result in a symptom.

Testing is the process of determining *whether* a given set of inputs causes a nonacceptable behavior in a program. **Debugging** is the process of determining *why* a given set of inputs causes a nonacceptable behavior in a program and *what* must be changed to cause the behavior to be acceptable.

The craft of software engineering has gone through several eras. These eras can be identified by the books published promoting the main ideas of each particular era. In each era, the basic concepts of that era were applied to the various phases of the software-development life cycle. The various structured disciplines were concerned with organizing computation with respect to actions. In contrast, the object-oriented disciplines are concerned with organizing computation with respect to data.

There are no books addressing structured debugging or object-oriented debugging. This seems odd, since the structured and object-oriented approaches have been applied to every other facet of the software-development life cycle.

Coding, designing, analyzing, and testing are all constructive activities. Debugging is primarily a cognitive activity. The cognitive psychology of human error, induction, and deduction did not become widely understood until the early 1990s. Books that documented the mathematical problem-solving process did not become widely available until the mid-1980s. These disciplines provide important insights into the debugging process.

Programming students start with debugging by editing, then move on to debugging by interacting, and then graduate to debugging by repeating. *Debugging by Thinking* is different from all of these approaches because it provides an explicit methodology that uses a multidisciplinary approach and makes the programmer self-aware as he or she works.

2

Sherlock Holmes

You know my methods. Apply them!

—Sherlock Holmes

2.1   Preview

This chapter makes an analogy between finding a perpetrator or a missing object and finding the cause of a defect.

The first section of this chapter explains how the literature of detection and investigation can be applied to the field of software debugging. The section begins by explaining the worldview of the detective. It presents an analogy in which the software defect is considered a crime, and the programmer is the detective. The second part of this section explains why most famous detective fiction is useless for understanding ways of debugging software.

The second section of this chapter explains the methods of the great Sherlock Holmes and how they can be applied to debugging software. This section begins by reviewing the life and character of Sherlock Holmes. It summarizes the points of Holmes's methodology that apply to software debugging and expands on the analogy of a software defect as a crime. It concludes by identifying techniques that Sherlock Holmes employs in his detective work, with quotes from the Holmes stories for each technique.

2.2   Worldview of the detective

One of the world's most popular forms of fiction is the detective novel, particularly the murder mystery. There are all kinds of detectives found in this genre. There are police professionals, private detectives, and avocational dabblers in detection. There are modern detectives and detectives from historical settings, all the way back to ancient Rome. Literary critics believe that the appeal of the murder mystery is the combination of the clear delineation of right and wrong and the intellectual challenge of identifying a villain.

What does all of this have to do with finding software defects? We can make an analogy between the murder mystery and the search for a software defect. The defect is considered a crime, and the programmer is the detective. A detective who wants to solve a crime needs answers to the following questions:

- Who did it?

- How did the culprit do it?

- When did the culprit do it?

- Why did the culprit do it?

Here, we're interested in observing the thought processes and methodologies of these literary detectives.

2.3   **Detective fiction**

Most famous detective fiction is useless for the purpose of understanding ways to debug software. The world's most popular writer of detective fiction is Agatha Christie. She wrote dozens of highly entertaining novels and dozens more short stories as well.

Her characters, however, aren't helpful in teaching us about the process of detecting. Miss Marple is an acute observer of human behavior and a cunning eavesdropper, but her methods of mental association are baffling. Hercule Poirot is always talking about how he uses "the little gray cells" to solve crimes, but he never tells us how those gray cells operate.

Other writers of detective fiction pose similar problems. Raymond Chandler and Dashiell Hammett wrote beautiful prose, but their detectives find the villain mostly by beating up and shooting people. While some may find this entertaining, few will find it educational. To find wisdom for debugging software, we focus on two erudite fictional detectives. These two detectives not only solve baffling mysteries, but they also often explain how they do it in the process.

2.4   The character of Sherlock Holmes

We begin our study of the way of the detective by investigating the career and philosophies of the greatest of all detectives in literature, Sherlock Holmes.

2.4.1   The life of Sherlock Holmes

Let's start by considering what we know about Sherlock Holmes the character. He was born in January 1854 and entered Oxford or Cambridge in 1872. He moved to London to start a career as the world's first consulting detective in 1877. He shared a suite of rooms with Dr. John Watson, who had retired from the army, starting in 1881. Holmes was believed to have died in a fight with his archenemy, Dr. Moriarity, in 1891. After three years in seclusion, he returned to detection in 1894. He finally retired to farming in 1903. All of these facts can be gleaned from reading the Holmes corpus or consulting any of several Holmes encyclopedias.

2.4.2   The literature about Sherlock Holmes

What books do we use as sources in understanding the methods of Sherlock Holmes? The following books by Sir Arthur Conan Doyle document his cases:

- *A Study in Scarlet*—1888
- *The Sign of the Four*—1890
- *The Adventures of Sherlock Holmes*—1892—anthology
- *The Memoirs of Sherlock Holmes*—1893—anthology
- *The Hound of the Baskervilles*—1902
- *The Return of Sherlock Holmes*—1905—anthology
- *The Valley of Fear*—1915
- *His Last Bow*—1917—anthology
- *The Case-Book of Sherlock Holmes*—1927—anthology

The books noted as anthologies contain a total of fifty-six short stories. The other works are complete novels. If you want a scholarly edition of these works, complete with explanatory notes, you will appreciate the nine-volume edition *The Oxford Sherlock Holmes*.

Jeremy Brett starred in the definitive video rendition of many of Holmes's adventures. They originally aired in the United Kingdom and subsequently in the United States on PBS's Mystery! series and later on the A&E cable network. They are available on videocassette.

2.4.3   The author behind Sherlock Holmes

It is just as important to consider the life of Holmes's creator, Sir Arthur Conan Doyle. He was born in Edinburgh, Scotland, in 1859. He received a Jesuit education from 1868 to 1876. He attended medical school in Edinburgh from 1877 to 1880. Doyle served as a ship's surgeon from 1880 to 1882. After that, he started a medical practice in Southern England. He married Louise Hawkins in 1885. She died several years later, and in 1907 he married Jean Leckie. Doyle served as a volunteer doctor in the Boer War in South Africa from 1900 to 1903, and he died in 1930. Besides his Holmes stories, he wrote twenty-four other books of fiction and ten other books of military history, medical studies, and other nonfiction.

There are a couple of important points to observe about Sir Arthur Conan Doyle. He was an educated man, he was a man of science, and he was an historian. In these respects, the detective that he created was made in his own image.

2.5   The methods of Sherlock Holmes

We can summarize the points of Holmes's methodology that apply to software debugging under the following categories:

- Use cross-disciplinary knowledge

- Focus on facts

- Pay attention to unusual details

- Gather facts before hypothesizing

- State the facts to someone else

- Start by observing

- Don't guess

- Exclude alternative explanations

- Reason in both directions
- Watch for red herrings

2.5.1 Applying Holmes to debugging

To apply the wisdom of Sherlock Holmes to debugging software, we must consider the analogy between software defects and crime. We must answer the following questions:

- Who did it?—suspect
- How did the culprit do it?—means
- When did the culprit do it?—opportunity

Our approach to motive is somewhat different, since we assume that all defects were caused accidentally. We are interested in an answer to the question, why did this problem happen? We treat the why question the way an accident investigator would, rather than the way a detective would. The detective seeks to assign guilt for a crime. The investigator seeks to find contributing causes, to prevent the accident from occurring again.

Detectives don't need to find a motive either, although juries are more easily convinced when a motive is given. If the prosecution presents an ironclad case that only one person had both the means and opportunity to commit a crime, a rational jury should convict the defendant. By analogy, if only one possible piece of code had both the means and opportunity to cause an observable failure, the programmer should focus on that code segment as the cause of the defect.

2.5.2 Use cross-disciplinary knowledge

In *The Valley of Fear* [Do15], Holmes is called in to assist in the investigation of a grisly murder in the country. As the police are pursuing a man who fits the general description of the suspect all over the country, Holmes tells them to give up the chase. They want an explanation. He describes some interesting features of the ancient manor house where the body was discovered. The police inspectors complain that he's making fools of them, and he replies, "Breadth of view . . . is one of the essentials of our profession. The interplay of ideas and the oblique uses of knowledge are often of extraordinary interest."

In *The Five Orange Pips* [Do92], a young man asks Holmes to help him. His uncle and father have died from unusual accidents, and he has received the same mysterious threats that they did. After the man leaves 221B Baker Street, Holmes and Watson discuss the meager evidence:

> Problems may be solved in the study which have baffled all those who sought a solution by the aid of their senses. To carry the art, however, to its highest pitch, it is necessary that the reasoner should be able to utilize all the facts which have come to his knowledge; and this in itself implies, as you will readily see, a possession of all knowledge, which, even in these days of free education and encyclopedias, is a somewhat rare accomplishment.

When developing applications software, it's as important to understand the application as the software to be able to diagnose defects. Back in the bad old days, corporate information technology (IT) departments were referred to as data processing (DP). Those DP departments employed an artificial separation of tasks between systems analysts and programmers. Systems analysts talked with the users, understood their requirements, and translated them into specifications for programmers to implement.

Nowadays, most development methodologies encourage programmers to work closely with users to develop prototypes, create specifications, and the like. The Extreme Programming movement, not surprisingly, has taken this trend to its logical conclusion [Be99]. It advocates daily feedback from the users on what the programmers created the previous day. Not every project can be developed using the Extreme Programming approach, but the advocacy of close interaction with the client is a good idea.

Domain-specific knowledge makes it possible to identify problems in logic that are plain to the user of the application. At a minimum, you should learn enough about the application domain to master its jargon and fundamental concepts. If you're using the object-oriented analysis and design methodology, you will be identifying entities in the real world that should be modeled by objects in your program. This is difficult without having some understanding of the application domain.

2.5.3 Focus on facts

In *The Adventure of the Copper Beeches* [Do92], a young woman asks Holmes's advice. She wants to know whether she should take a position as a governess, which has some unusual requirements. She decides to take the job and promises to telegraph Holmes if she needs help. As Holmes waits for an update on her situation, Watson observes him muttering, "Data! Data! Data! I can't make bricks without clay."

In *A Study in Scarlet* [Do88], we're first introduced to the characters of Dr. Watson and Sherlock Holmes. Inspector Gregson of Scotland Yard asks Holmes to help him with a baffling case of murder. Holmes and Watson review the scene of the crime, and Holmes makes a number of deductions about the murderer. Holmes and Watson then head off to interview the policeman who found the corpse. On the way, Holmes remarks, "There is nothing like first-hand evidence."

One of the fundamental tenets of modern science is that results must be reproducible to be accepted. Holmes understood this principle well. The police he worked with were often convinced that a suspect was guilty based on their view that the suspect had a motive. Motives are purely subjective. They can't be observed or measured.

Holmes focuses on facts. He seeks to establish that a suspect has access to the means used to commit the crime and opportunity to commit the crime. These criteria are objective and can be proved or disproved with facts.

Don't accept defect reports unless you're given sufficient data to reproduce the problem. If you don't have sufficient data to reproduce the problem, you only have second-hand evidence that a problem exists. You can get very frustrated attempting to debug an alleged defect without sufficient data.

Just because someone is technically adept, don't assume that person is capable of providing a reproducible defect description. Some of the most useless defect reports we have ever received were written by experienced programmers.

2.5.4 Pay attention to unusual details

In *A Case of Identity* [Do92], Holmes is visited by a young woman who wishes to find her fiancé, who disappeared shortly before they were to be married. As she describes the man, Holmes remarks on the value of the details she is providing: "It has long been an axiom of mine that the little things are infinitely the most important."

In *The Boscombe Valley Mystery* [Do92], Holmes requests that Watson take a few days away from his practice and his wife. He wants a companion to journey with him to investigate an unusual murder case near the Welsh border. Holmes describes the murderer in great detail to police detective Lestrade, after observing the scene of the crime. Lestrade leaves to pursue his own methods. Holmes then explains to Watson how he came to be certain of the details of his description: "You know my method. It is founded upon the observance of trifles."

In *The Man with a Twisted Lip* [Do92], Watson discovers Holmes in disguise in an opium den. Watson is helping a woman who believes she saw her husband looking out the window on the second floor of that same building. The husband seems to have disappeared, and evidence indicates that he may have been murdered. When Holmes and Watson visit her home, she receives a letter indicating that he's alive. Holmes observes several interesting characteristics of the letter and envelope and observes, "It is, of course a trifle, but there is nothing so important as trifles."

In *A Study in Scarlet* [Do88], Holmes solves a case of revenge murder, which had taken the victims and their pursuer across the Atlantic. Holmes reviews how he solved the case with Watson: "I have already explained to you that what is out of the common is usually a guide rather than a hindrance."

In *The Reigate Puzzle* [Do93], Sherlock Holmes accompanies Dr. Watson to the country estate of one of the officers Watson served with in India. The purpose of the trip is a holiday to restore Holmes's strength. He had exhausted himself with a very important case of financial fraud. When a series of burglaries results in a murder, the local constabulary calls Holmes in for assistance. After nearly getting killed himself when he identified the villain, he later explains to Watson and his friend how he came to the solution: "It is of the highest importance in the art of detection to be able to recognize out of a number of facts, which are incidental and which vital. Otherwise your energy and attention must be dissipated instead of being concentrated."

To know what is unusual, you must know what is common. What should be common in an operational piece of software is correct behavior.

Correct behavior is defined by an external reference. Some common external references include the following:

- A standards document

- A functional specification document

- A prototype system

- A competitive product

The correct behavior of some software is defined by a document issued by a standards group, such as ANSI/ISO or the IEEE. Compilers for programming languages, for example, must accept as valid all programs that the standard for the language defines as valid. They must also reject as invalid all programs that the standard for the language defines as invalid. If you're working with a product whose behavior is defined by a standards document, you should always compare bug reports against the standard.

The correct behavior of most software is defined by a functional specification document. This document defines what the software should do when presented with both valid and invalid inputs. It doesn't define how the software should achieve this result. This is normally done in an internal design document. If you're working with a product whose behavior is defined by a functional specification, you should always compare bug reports against the specification.

The correct behavior of some software is defined by the behavior of other software. In the case of a prototype, the customer or sponsor agrees that the behavior of the prototype is how the final product should work. In the case of a replacement product, the customer or sponsor mandates that the behavior of a competitive product is how the final product should work. If the purpose of your product is to replace software that comes from another source, you may even choose to be "bug-for-bug" compatible.

Without an external reference that defines correct behavior, trying to resolve a defect report is like flying blind. You only know you're done when you hit the ground.

2.5.5 Gather facts before hypothesizing

In *A Study in Scarlet* [Do88], Inspector Gregson of Scotland Yard asks Holmes to help him with a baffling case of murder. On the way to the scene of the crime, Watson is puzzled by Holmes's lack of attention to the matter at hand. Holmes replies, "No data yet. It is a capital mistake to theorize before you have all the evidence. It biases the judgment."

In *A Scandal in Bohemia* [Do92], Watson reads aloud a letter that Holmes has just received. It announces that Holmes will receive a visit from an unnamed visitor of great importance. Watson wonders what it all means, and Holmes says, "I have no data yet. It is a capital mistake to theorize before one has data. Insensibly one begins to twist facts to suit theories, instead of theories to suit facts."

In *The Adventure of Wisteria Lodge* [Do17], Holmes is visited by an upset young man who has had an unusual visit with an acquaintance in the country. Just as he's about to tell the story, police inspector Gregson visits Holmes looking for this very man as a suspect in a murder. After the man tells his story, and the police take him to their station, Holmes and Watson review the case. As Holmes begins to formulate a hypothesis, he comments, "If fresh facts which come to our knowledge all fit themselves into the scheme, then our hypothesis may gradually become a solution."

The five steps of the scientific method are as follows:

1.   State the problem.

2.   Form a hypothesis.

3.   Observe and experiment.

4.   Interpret the data.

5.   Draw conclusions.

You shouldn't be experimenting (collecting data) unless you're trying to confirm a hypothesis. The probability that you will generate a correct program by randomly mutating your source code is much lower than the probability that you will be hit by lightning next year.

The best way to ensure that you have a hypothesis is to write it down. If you take the trouble to record hypotheses, we recommend that you also record the corresponding problems and observations. There are several ways to do this.

- *You can keep a notebook in which you write as you work.* The benefit of doing this is that you can walk away from the computer and read and review your notes.

- *You can keep an open editor window, in which you type as you collect information.* The benefit of having this data online is that you can search it quickly. Instead of saying, "I think I've seen this before," while scratching your head, you can execute a search and know for sure. The drawback of this approach is that if ignorant or unscrupulous authority figures find out about the existence of your information, they may use it in ways that you never intended. In addition, your employer may not allow you to take this information with you to another job.

■ *You can use a hand-held computer to record your notes as you work.* This approach combines the benefits of the notebook and the editor window. The drawback is the investment in the hardware. If you bear the cost on your own, of course, you're more likely to be able to walk away with information when you change jobs. You also have to pick up and put down the hand-held, which some people find disrupts their efficient use of the keyboard.

2.5.6 State the facts to someone else

Silver Blaze [Do93] begins as Holmes and Watson depart by train for the scene of a murder in the country. As is often the case, Holmes rehearses the facts for Watson and explains why he does so.

> At least I have got a grip of the essential facts of the case. I shall enumerate them to you, for nothing clears up a case so much as stating it to another person, and I can hardly expect your cooperation if I do not show you the position from which we start.

Describing a problem to someone else is one of the oldest ways programmers have used to uncover defects. Weinberg was one of the first computer scientists to document and recommend its use [We71]. It has been rediscovered for the umpteenth time by the Extreme Programming movement [Be99].

Since the chief benefit of this method is to get the viewpoint of another person, the place to start is by giving your viewpoint. Try to answer the following questions:

■ What do I know for sure? (What have you observed?)

■ What do I believe to be true? (What have you inferred?)

■ What do I not know?

2.5.7 Start by observing

In *The Adventure of the Cardboard Box* [Do93], Inspector Lestrade requests assistance from Holmes in solving the riddle of a box containing two human ears, which was sent to a woman in the suburbs of London. After determining who was responsible, Holmes turns the information over to the inspector and reviews the case with Watson back at their home. He explains his method thus: "Let me run over the principal steps. We approached the case, you remember, with an absolutely blank mind, which is always an advantage. We had formed no theories. We were simply there to observe and to draw inferences from our observations."

In *A Scandal in Bohemia* [Do92], Dr. Watson has married and moved away and returns to visit Holmes. Holmes delights Watson with his deductions about Watson's life and work, based on trivial details. Watson remarks that Holmes always baffles him with these deductions, even though his eyesight is just as good as Holmes. Sherlock replies, "You see, but you do not observe. The distinction is clear."

Detecting and debugging differ in the extent to which we can create additional evidence. Detectives can take things from a crime scene and have them analyzed and identified. All forensic analysis, however, is after the fact.

When we debug software, we can repeat the defective behavior and observe what we want to see. For a detective, it would be the equivalent of going back in time and planting a video camera at the scene of the crime.

When collecting data, consider not only what to observe, but also what point of view to observe it from. It is helpful to consider how application performance analysis tools collect data. They observe one aspect of a program's behavior. The alternative approaches they use to collect data are analogous to either manual or automatic collection of information related to software bugs.

First, performance information can be collected either when an event occurs, such as a subroutine call, or at fixed time intervals. The former approach is referred to as event-based, while the latter is called sampling.

Second, the collected information can be accumulated as discrete records, or it can be summarized as it's generated. The former approach is called tracing, while the latter is referred to as reduction.

Since there are two axes of choice, and two options on each axis, there are four possible ways to apply these approaches. When you're instrumenting a program to collect data, consider all four approaches. Each has its benefits and drawbacks.

1.   Event-based data collection is precise, but can take longer.

2.   Sampling-based data collection is an approximation, but can take less time.

3.   Trace-based data collection is complete, but can use lots of storage.

4.   Reductionist data collection loses details, but uses much less storage.

Another way to look at point of view is the difference between **synchronic** and **diachronic** approaches. A synchronic ("with time") approach takes a snapshot of a static situation at a given instant. A diachronic ("through time") approach observes the evolution of a situation over some period. Make sure you use both viewpoints when observing the behavior of a program.

2.5.8   Don't guess

The Sign of the Four [Do90] begins with Holmes in a cocaine reverie. He is waiting for a problem to challenge his intellect, expounding to Watson on various aspects of the science of detection. After Holmes outlines the life of Watson's brother, based on observing a watch that the brother owned, Watson is astonished. He wonders whether Holmes was just lucky at guessing certain facts. Holmes replies, "I never guess. It is a shocking habit—destructive to the logical faculty. What seems strange to you is only so because you do not follow my train of thought or observe the small facts upon which large inferences may depend."

If you ever hear yourself saying, "let's see what this will do," or "maybe this will fix the problem," it is time to go home. If you don't know what effect a change will have, you have no business making the change. You can undo weeks of work in a few minutes of desperation. There are many definitions of hacking, some positive, some negative. Hacking at its worst is making changes without being sure of what effect they will have.

A hypothesis isn't the same thing as a guess. A hypothesis includes a means of verifying the correctness of the proposition. Guessing is symptomatic of inadequate knowledge of the software. If you find yourself guessing, you need to spend more time understanding the software you're working on. You may need to study the application domain, the programming language, or the system design before you will be able to generate hypotheses that include means of verification. Taking time to learn these aspects of the software will reduce your total debugging time.

2.5.9   Eliminate impossible causes

In *The Adventure of the Beryl Coronet* [Do92], Holmes is called upon to solve the disappearance of jewels entrusted to a banker as security on a loan to a member of the royal household. After he returns the jewels to the banker, he explains how he solved the case. In the middle of this explanation, he offers this nugget of logic: "It is an old maxim of mine that when you have excluded the impossible, whatever remains, however improbable, must be the truth."

In *The Sign of the Four* [Do90], Holmes and Watson are called upon to aid a young woman whose father, an infantry officer, disappeared mysteriously and who had been receiving valuable treasure in the mail from an even more mysterious benefactor. After meeting with one of her benefactors and finding the other one dead, Holmes and Watson review what they know about the case. As they consider how the murderer committed his crime, Holmes rebukes Watson: "How often have I said to you that when you have eliminated the impossible, whatever remains, 'however improbable,' must be the truth?"

In computer software, causation isn't a matter of probability. Either a code segment caused a problem or it did not. Something may be a logically possible cause until we have sufficient information to make a yes or no determination.

Try to eliminate as many possible causes and culprits as you can with a single observation. Eliminating possible causes isn't quite as simple as it sounds. For example, you can't eliminate a procedure as a possible cause because it isn't executed. The lack of execution may have the side effect of causing default values not to change, resulting in an incorrect computation. The same goes for loops that aren't executed and conditional branches that aren't taken.

Defects that are difficult to locate are often caused by a conjunction of several conditions, each of which isn't sufficient to cause the problem on its own. While you may be able to eliminate each individual condition as a cause of the defect, you should be careful not to eliminate also the conjunction of the conditions from your list of suspects.

2.5.10   Exclude alternative explanations

In *The Adventure of Black Peter* [Do05], Holmes is called to help a local police detective solve the grisly murder of a former ship's captain. After setting a trap for the culprit and apprehending a suspect, Holmes reviews the case with Watson. Holmes expresses disappointment with the work of the policeman and states, "One should always look for a possible alternative and provide against it. It is the first rule of criminal investigation."

In *The Hound of the Baskervilles* [Do02], Holmes is consulted by Dr. Mortimer, the executor of the estate of Sir Charles Baskerville; he's concerned about the manner of Sir Charles's death and the potential for harm to the heir, Sir Henry Baskerville. After hearing all of the relevant facts, Holmes asks for twenty-four hours to consider the matter. Holmes asks Watson to obtain tobacco for him to smoke and begins the process Watson describes as follows: "He weighed every particle of evidence, constructed alternative theories, balanced one against the other, and made up his mind as to which points were essential and which immaterial."

When you formulate a hypothesis, consider if you already have evidence in hand that disqualifies the hypothesis. This is much easier to do if you're keeping a log of your observations and hypotheses.

It takes less time to disqualify a hypothesis in this way than to perform yet another experiment. After you have performed an experiment, consider brainstorming a list of all the hypotheses that this experiment disqualifies.

2.5.11 Reason in both directions

In *A Study in Scarlet* [Do88], Holmes explains to Watson how he was able to capture the criminal in three days:

> "In solving a problem of this sort, the grand thing is to be able to reason backward. That is a very useful accomplishment, and a very easy one, but people do not practice it much. In the everyday affairs of life it is more useful to reason forward, and so the other comes to be neglected. There are fifty who can reason synthetically for one who can reason analytically."
>
> "I confess," said I, "that I do not quite follow you."
>
> "I hardly expected that you would. Let me see if I can make it clearer. Most people, if you describe a train of events to them, will tell you what the result would be. They can put those events together in their minds, and argue from them that something will come to pass. There are few people, however, who, if you told them a result, would be able to evolve from their own inner consciousness what the steps were that led up to that result. This power is what I mean when I talk of reasoning backward, or analytically."

In *The Five Orange Pips* [Do92], a young man whose uncle and father have died from unusual accidents asks Holmes to help him when he receives the same mysterious threat that they did. After the man leaves 221B Baker Street, Holmes and Watson discuss the meager evidence. "'The ideal reasoner,' he remarked, 'would when he had once been shown a single fact in all its bearings, deduce from it not only all the chain of events which led up to it but also all the results which would follow from it.'"

The *American Heritage Dictionary of the English Language* defines *deduction* as, "The process of reasoning in which a conclusion follows necessarily from the stated premises; inference by reasoning from the general to the specific." The same dictionary defines *induction* as, "The process of deriving general principles from particular facts or instances."

As Holmes suggests, programmers almost always work on debugging inductively, rather than deductively. It is possible to reason through a non-trivial bug without touching a keyboard. You need a lack of disturbances and a thorough knowledge of the software you're working on. You mentally enumerate the possible causes of a given effect and then prune them with the knowledge you have.

Many software systems are too big for any one person to have enough knowledge of the system to do deductive debugging. Deductive analysis is possible for medium-sized systems, particularly if a single author created them. If you're working on such a system, we encourage you to try it sometime.

2.5.12   **Watch for red herrings**

In *A Study in Scarlet* [Do88], when a suspect in the first murder turns up dead himself, Holmes tries an experiment, and after he sees the results, comments, "I ought to know by this time that when a fact appears to be opposed to a long train of deductions, it invariably proves to be capable of bearing some other interpretation."

In *The Boscombe Valley Mystery* [Do92], Watson is traveling with Holmes by train to Herefordshire to investigate a murder case in which the circumstantial evidence seems to point overwhelmingly to the son of a murdered man. Watson opines that the facts seem to be so obvious as to make the endeavor pointless. Holmes retorts, "There is nothing more deceptive than an obvious fact."

Red herring is fish cured by smoke, which changes its color. It has a very persistent odor. Dog trainers use red herring for training a dog to follow a scent. A dog that gets a good whiff of red herring will lose any other scent that it has been following. The English idiom "red herring" means a piece of information that distracts or deceives.

Where there is one defect, there are likely to be more. When you come upon a fact that seems to bear upon your investigation, consider all of the interpretations of the fact. The ability to recognize red herrings in a debugging investigation improves with experience. You can quicken your acquisition of this experience by keeping a debugging log.

2.6   Review

When developing applications software, it's as important to understand the application as the software to be able to diagnose defects. Domain-specific knowledge makes it possible to identify problems in logic that are plain to the user of the application.

One of the fundamental tenets of modern science is that results must be reproducible to be accepted. Don't accept defect reports unless you're given sufficient data to reproduce the problem.

To know what is unusual, you must know what is common. What should be common in an operational piece of software is correct behavior. Correct behavior is defined by an external reference.

You shouldn't be experimenting unless you have a hypothesis you're trying to confirm. The best way to ensure that you have a hypothesis is to write it down.

Describing a problem to someone else is one of the oldest ways programmers have used to uncover defects. Since the chief benefit of this method is to get the viewpoint of another person, the place to start is by giving your viewpoint.

Detecting and debugging differ in the extent to which we can create additional evidence. When collecting data, consider not only what to observe, but what point of view to observe from.

If you don't know what effect a change will have, you have no business making the change. A hypothesis includes a means of verifying the correctness of the proposition.

Try to eliminate as many possible causes and culprits as you can with a single observation. Defects that are difficult to locate are often caused by a conjunction of several conditions, each of which isn't sufficient to cause the problem on its own.

When you formulate a hypothesis, consider whether you already have evidence in hand that disqualifies the hypothesis. It takes less time to disqualify a hypothesis in this way than to perform yet another experiment.

Programmers almost always work on debugging inductively, rather than deductively. It is possible to reason from an observation to the causes for medium-sized systems, particularly if a single author created them.

The English idiom "red herring" means a piece of information that distracts or deceives. When you come upon a fact that seems to bear upon your investigation, consider all of the interpretations of the fact.

Lord Peter Wimsey

Does it occur to you that what's the matter with this case is that there are too many clues?

—*Lord Peter Wimsey*

3.1   Preview

This chapter explains the methods of the amateur sleuth Lord Peter Wimsey and how they can be applied to debugging software. This section begins by reviewing the life and character of Lord Peter. It summarizes the points of Wimsey's methodology that apply to software debugging and expands on the metaphor of a software defect as a crime. It concludes by identifying techniques that Lord Peter Wimsey employed in his detective work, with quotes from the Wimsey stories for each technique.

3.2   The character of Lord Peter Wimsey

In this chapter we turn our attention to the life and wisdom of the amateur sleuth Lord Peter Wimsey.

3.2.1   The life of Lord Peter Wimsey

It is useful to start by considering what we know about Lord Peter as a character. The following bibliographic entry, written in the style of the Who's Who directories of the time, comes from his creator:

WIMSEY, Peter Death Bredon, D.S.O.; born 1890, 2nd son of Mortimer Gerald Bredon Wimsey, 15th Duke of Denver, and of Honoria

Lucasta, daughter of Francis Delagardie of Bellingham Manor, Hants.

Educated: Eton College and Balliol College, Oxford (1st class honors, Sch. of Mod. Hist. 1912); served with H. M. Forces 1914/18 (Major, Rifle Brigade). Author of "Notes on the Collecting of Incunabula," "The Murderer's Vade-Mecum," and so forth. Recreations: Criminology; bibliophily; music; cricket.

Clubs: Marlborough; Egotists'. Residences: 110A Piccadilly, W.; Bredon Hall, Duke's Denver, Norfolk. Arms: three mice courant, argent; crest, a domestic cat couched as to spring, proper; motto: As my Whimsy takes me.

3.2.2 The literature about Lord Peter Wimsey

What stories do we use as sources in understanding the methods of Lord Peter? The following books by Dorothy L. Sayers document his cases:

- *Whose Body?*—1923
- *Clouds of Witness*—1926
- *Unnatural Death*—1927
- *The Unpleasantness at the Bellona Club*—1928
- *Lord Peter Views the Body*—1928—anthology
- *Strong Poison*—1930
- *The Five Red Herrings*—1931
- *Have His Carcase*—1932
- *Murder Must Advertise*—1933
- *Hangman's Holiday*—1933—anthology
- *The Nine Tailors*—1934
- *Gaudy Night*—1935
- *Busman's Honeymoon*—1937
- *In the Teeth of the Evidence*—1939—anthology
- *Thrones, Dominations*—1998—with J. P. Walsh
- *A Presumption of Death*—2002—J.P. Walsh & D. L. Sayers

The books noted as anthologies contain twenty-one short stories about Lord Peter and some about other characters of Dorothy L. Sayers's invention. The other works are complete novels. The last two novels were completed by completed by Jill Paton Walsh based on material from Sayers.

Ian Carmichael starred in video versions of five of the Lord Peter adventures. These were originally aired in the United Kingdom and subsequently in the United States on PBS's Masterpiece Theater. Edward Petherbridge starred in video versions of three other Lord Peter Mysteries, which were aired first on the BBC and later on PBS's Mystery! series. Both of these series have recently become available on videocassette and DVD.

3.2.3 The author behind Lord Peter Wimsey

Dorothy L. Sayers was born in Oxford, England, in 1893, the daughter of a clergyman. She was fluent in Latin, French, and German and was one of the first women to earn an Oxford degree in 1915. She was a scholar of medieval literature. After World War I, she worked for the largest British advertising firm. In 1926, she married the famous World War I correspondent, Capt. O. A. Fleming. After writing the last Lord Peter novel, she spent the rest of her life translating medieval literature and writing plays and academic studies. She died in 1957.

There are a couple of important points to observe about Dorothy L. Sayers. She was educated at Oxford, a scholar of history and of literature. Despite her academic training, she was capable of earning her living first in the business world and later as a writer. In these respects, the detective that she created was made in her own image.

3.3 The methods of Lord Peter Wimsey

We can summarize the points of Lord Peter's methodology that apply to software debugging under the following categories:

- Use alibis as clues
- Eliminate impossible causes
- Exercise curiosity
- Reason based on facts
- Enumerate possibilities

- Use the power of logic
- Use a system for organizing facts
- Exercise caution when searching
- Use gestalt understanding
- Show how something could be done

3.3.1 Applying Wimsey to debugging

Once again, we apply the analogy of viewing software defects as crimes to be solved. We must answer the following questions:

- Who did it?—suspect
- How did the culprit do it?—means
- When did the culprit do it?—opportunity

Our approach to motive is somewhat different, since we assume that all defects were caused accidentally, as we explained previously. We are interested in an answer to the question, why did this problem happen? We treat the why question the way an accident investigator would, rather than the way a detective would. The detective seeks to assign guilt for a crime. The investigator seeks to find contributing causes, to prevent the accident from occurring again.

3.3.2 Use alibis as clues

In *Have His Carcase* [Sa32], Lord Peter works with the mystery writer Harriet Vane. They search for the murderer responsible for a body Harriet found on a beach while on holiday. After a serious investigation, Lord Peter works his way through a long chain of deductions while conversing with one of the suspects:

> "Always suspect the man with the cast-iron alibi"—was not that the very first axiom in the detective's book of rules? And here it was—the cast-iron alibi which really was cast-iron; meant to be scrutinized; meant to stand every test—as how should it not, for it was truth!

Later on in *Have His Carcase*, Lord Peter realizes that the time of death wasn't what the inquest determined, and the alibis of the suspects pointed to the correct time.

> "Yes," he said when he'd recovered himself a little, "but here's a snag. If he might have died at any time, how are we to prove he did at twelve o'clock?"
>
> "Easy. First of all, we know it must have been then, because that's the time these people have an alibi for. As Sherlock Holmes says somewhere: 'Only a man with a criminal enterprise desires to establish an alibi.'"

An alibi has three components: time, place, and corroboration. Detectives attempt to break alibis with questions like the following:

- Was the time of the alibi actually the time of the crime?
- Did the suspect have time to move from the place of the alibi to the place of the crime within the time period that the crime was committed?
- Could the corroboration be accidentally or deliberately wrong?

A program that has side effects has no alibi for the time a problem occurred or the place it occurred. A side effect causes a change in the state of computation outside the context in which it's presently occurring. Software side effects come in several forms. Some languages, such as C and C++, have pointers. Pointers allow a program to modify memory at any address to which they point. Other languages, such as Fortran, have aliases. Aliases, like pointers, make it possible for a module to modify storage in places far removed from the immediate context. Some languages, such as C++ and Java, support exceptions. Generating an exception that isn't handled in the immediate context can cause code in arbitrary parts of the system to be executed.

The debugging equivalent of an alibi is the assertion that a given system component can't be the cause of a problem. Software engineers break alibis when they search for bugs with questions like the following:

- Was the time the defect occurred distant from the time it was manifested due to side effects?

- Was the location of the defect distant from the location it was manifested due to side effects?

- Is the information giving a component an alibi misleading or incorrect?

3.3.3 Eliminate impossible causes

In *The Unpleasantness at the Bellona Club* [Sa28a], Lord Peter is asked to investigate the circumstances of the death of the ancient General Fentiman. The inheritance of a large fortune depends on determining precisely when he died. After an exhumation and autopsy determine that the general did not die naturally, Lord Peter has the following conversation with his friend Detective-Inspector Parker:

"What put you on to this poison business?" [Parker] asked.

"Aristotle, chiefly," replied Wimsey. "He says, you know, that one should always prefer the probable impossible to the improbable possible. It was possible, of course, that the General should have died off in that neat way at the most confusing moment. But how much nicer and more probable that the whole thing had been stage-managed. Even if it had seemed much more impossible I should have been dead nuts on murder."

In *Strong Poison* [Sa30], Lord Peter Wimsey first encounters the mystery writer, Harriet Vane. She's on trial for murder, and he's determined to find evidence to clear her. As he interrogates some of her friends, one of them suggests an alternative suspect, based on the following reasoning:

"I merely proceed on the old Sherlock Holmes basis, that when you have eliminated the impossible, then whatever remains, however improbable, must be true."

Lord Peter agrees with the principle, but disagrees with its application, and notes that the quote actually originates with Auguste Dupin, a fictional detective created by Edgar Allen Poe.

3.3.4   **Exercise curiosity**

In *Unnatural Death* [Sa27], Lord Peter decides to investigate the death of an aged and ailing woman, after the country doctor who attended her suspects something other than a natural death. After hearing the doctor's story, he says the following:

> "Do you know," he said suddenly, "I'm feeling rather interested by this case. I have a sensation of internal gloating which assures me that there is something to be investigated. That feeling has never failed me yet—I trust it never will. . . . I always make it a rule to investigate anything I feel like investigating. I believe," he added, in a reminiscent tone, "I was rather a terror in my nursery days. Anyhow, curious cases are rather a hobby of mine."

Exercising curiosity is one way we leverage the labor of finding the cause of a defect. Leveraging investigation work across several problems is an important way to increase programmer productivity. Software-development methodologies and tools are several decades behind hardware-development methodologies and tools. As a result, software developers must look for innovative ways to improve their productivity. People who understand economics know that productivity improvements are the only noninflationary way to increase wages. Most programmers are interested in increasing their wages, so exercising curiosity should be important to them.

We use curiosity when we investigate potentially related problems, even before they're reported. The quality of software products in comparison to hardware products is so pathetic that software developers must find "force multipliers" if the gap is ever to be closed.

Answering the following questions will help you exercise your curiosity:

- Is there another defect of the same root cause:
  - In this section of code?
  - In this procedure?
  - In closely related procedures?
- Is there another kind of defect:
  - In this section of code?
  - In this procedure?
  - In closely related procedures?

3.3.5   **Reason based on facts**

In *Clouds of Witness* [Sa27a], Lord Peter investigates the death of his sister's fiancé. Lord Peter's brother stands accused of the murder and refuses to account for his movements at the time of death. After sending some evidence to a chemist for analysis, Lord Peter has the following conversation with his extremely efficient butler:

> "Must have facts," said Lord Peter, "facts. When I was a small boy I always hated facts. Thought of 'em as nasty, hard things, all knobs. Uncomprisin'."
>
> "Yes, my lord. My old mother . . . she always says, my lord, that facts are like cows. If you look them in the face hard enough they generally run away. She is a very courageous woman, my lord."

Facts aren't complete without qualification. "It doesn't work" is the most useless of error reports. The following information should be included with a basic defect report for a programmer to diagnose the problem most effectively:

- Who observed the defect?
- What was the input?
- Where was the software run (hardware platform, operating system)?
- When did the defect occur?
- How often does the defect occur? (always, sometimes, once)

3.3.6   **Use the power of logic**

In *Have His Carcase* [Sa32], Lord Peter works with the mystery writer Harriet Vane to find the murderer responsible for a body Harriet found on a beach while on holiday. While interviewing one of the people who had a motive for killing the victim, Lord Peter has this Boolean revelation:

> Mr. Weldon grappled for some moments with this surprising logic, but failed to detect either the petitio elenchi, the undistributed mid-

dle or the inaccurate major premise which it contrived to combine. His face cleared.

"Of course," he said. "Yes. I see that. Obviously it must have been suicide, and Miss Vane's evidence proves that it was. So she must be right after all."

This was a syllogistic monstrosity even worse than the last, thought Wimsey. A man who could reason like that could not reason at all. He constructed a new syllogism for himself.

"The man who committed this murder was not a fool."

"Weldon is a fool."

"Therefore Weldon did not commit this murder."

Aristotle originally codified the principle of noncontradiction, which says that nothing can both be and not be at the same time in the same respect.

If you believe that a phenomenon observable by the human senses is both true and false, you're going to have a hard time using the scientific method. All classical reasoning methods depend on this principle.

If you don't know what the law of noncontradiction is, or you don't know how to apply the rules of logic to everyday discourse, you need to upgrade your thinking skills to be an effective bug finder. There are a number of excellent books that teach critical-thinking skills, including the proper use of logic. See the bibliography for recommended reading in developing your critical-thinking skills.

3.3.7 **Enumerate possibilities**

In *Whose Body?* [Sa23], Lord Peter is asked to investigate the accusations against an acquaintance of his mother's who found an unidentified naked man dead in his bathtub one morning. As he discusses Scotland Yard's analysis of some evidence with Detective Parker, Lord Peter describes the situation as follows:

Then Possibility No. 3 is knocked on the head. There remain Possibility No. 1: Accident or Misunderstanding, and No. 2: Deliberate Villainy of a remarkably bold and calculating kind. . . .

Following the methods inculcated at that University of which I have the honor to be a member, we will now examine severally the various suggestions afforded by Possibility No. 2. This Possibility may be again subdivided into two or more Hypotheses.

The trick with enumerating possibilities is knowing when you're done. You can enumerate possibilities by using the principle of noncontradiction and a binary tree. Repeatedly divide the logical possibilities that describe the situation into two alternatives. Place one possibility on the left-hand side of the bottom branch, and place the other possibility on the right-hand side. When there are no more logical possibilities, look at the leaves of the tree. They are the possibilities.

3.3.8 Use a system for organizing facts

In *Have His Carcase* [Sa32], after several days of fact-finding, Lord Peter and Harriet Vane decide that it's time to bring some order to what they have learned.

> At ten o'clock Wimsey and his collaborator sat down before a neat pile of scribbling paper. Harriet was inclined to be brief and business-like. "What system are we going to adopt about this? Do you favor the Michael Finsbury method by double entry as in 'The Wrong Box'? Or one of those charts, made out in columns, with headings for 'Suspect,' 'Alibi,' 'Witnesses,' 'Motive' and so on, worked out in percentages?"
>
> "Oh, don't lets have anything that means ruling a lot of lines and doing arithmetic. Let's behave like your Robert Templeton, and make a schedule of Things to Be Noted and Things to Be Done. That only means two columns."

In *Gaudy Night* [Sa35], the mystery writer Harriet Vane attends a reunion at her Oxford alma mater and finds herself in the midst of a campaign of intimidation and murderous threats being waged against the faculty, staff, and students. When Lord Peter shows up to visit his hospitalized nephew, Miss Vane asks him to join in her search for the culprit.

> Harriet handed him the loose-leaf book and an envelope containing the various anonymous documents, all endorsed, where possible, with

the date and manner of publication. He examined the documents first, separately and carefully, without manifesting surprise, disgust, or, indeed, any emotion beyond meditative interest. He then put them all back in the envelope, filled and lit a pipe, curled himself up among the cushions and devoted his attention to her manuscript. He read slowly, turning back every now and again to verify a date or a detail. At the end of the first few pages he looked up to remark, "I'll say one thing for the writing of detective fiction: you know how to put your story together; how to arrange the evidence."

There are lots of good ways to organize a search for the explanation of a defect, but few programmers use any system. Here are several different systems for describing a software defect:

- Input, output, deviance
- Observation, hypothesis, experiment
- Who, what, where, when, how much, how many
- Test case, reference, delta

The first method describes the problem in terms of a "black box." First, it describes the particular input that caused the problem. Next, it describes the output or behavior that resulted from this input. Finally, it describes the deviance from what was expected. This method is useful when the person reporting the problem is unaware of how the software works.

The second method describes the defect in terms of the scientific method. It begins with an observation of how the software is behaving. This is followed by a hypothesis that attempts to explain why the observed behavior is occurring. It concludes with an experiment that should verify or falsify the hypothesis.

The third method might be called "the reporter's method." It describes the problem by answering the questions posed by the standard interrogative pronouns. It is also useful when the person reporting the problem is unaware of how the software works.

The fourth method could be called "the tester's method." It describes the problem by referring to a test case that is failing, the document that is the basis for the test case, and the difference between the reference document and the behavior shown when processing the test case.

3.3.9 **Exercise caution when searching**

In *Whose Body?* [Sa23] Lord Peter is asked to investigate the accusations against an acquaintance of his mother's who found an unidentified naked man dead in his bathtub one morning. After running down a number of possible leads to dead ends, Lord Peter goes to visit his friend Detective Parker at his home.

> Peter took up the book his friend had laid down and glanced over the pages.
>
> "All these men work with a bias in their minds, one way or other," he said; "they find what they are looking for."
>
> "Oh, they do," agreed the detective; "but one learns to discount that almost automatically, you know. When I was at college, I was all on the other side—Conybeare and Robertson and Drews and those people, you know, till I found they were all so busy looking for a burglar whom nobody had ever seen, that they couldn't recognize the foot-prints of the household, so to speak. Then I spent two years learning to be cautious."
>
> "Hum," said Lord Peter, "theology must be good exercise for the brain then, for you are easily the most cautious devil I know."

The obvious advice to give is, don't make assumptions. Unfortunately, this is easier said than done. Here is a method for minimizing the effect that assumptions will have on your search for the cause of a bug:

- List all the assumptions you know you're making.

- List assumptions you have made in the past that turned out to be false. Keeping a notebook of your debugging efforts will help here.

- List a procedure to validate each assumption, in case you run out of hypotheses and still haven't found the defect.

- Don't start with the following emotionally comfortable hypotheses:
  - The defect is in code written by someone else.
  - The defect is in a tool you're using.
  - The defect is in the operating system or hardware.
  - The defect was a fluke and won't happen again.

3.3.10 Use gestalt understanding

In *Whose Body?* [Sa23] Lord Peter is asked to investigate the accusations against an acquaintance of his mother's who found an unidentified naked man dead in his bathtub one morning. As he stayed up late one night, trying to put the pieces of the puzzle together, he had the following experience:

> And then it happened—the thing he had been half unconsciously expecting. It happened suddenly, surely, as unmistakably, as sunrise. He remembered—not one thing, nor another thing, nor a logical succession of things, but everything—the whole thing, perfect, complete, in all its dimensions as it were and instantaneously; as if he stood outside the world and saw it suspended in infinitely dimensional space. He no longer needed to reason about it, or even think about it. He knew it.

The *American Heritage Dictionary of the English Language* defines *gestalt* as "a configuration or pattern of elements so unified as a whole that its properties cannot be derived from a simple summation of its parts."

The human brain performs many types of visual pattern matching far more effectively than any software system available today. If you're working with large amounts of data, display it graphically. This will enable your brain to recognize larger patterns you might not recognize from looking at numerical values.

Excessive reliance on interactive debuggers limits your ability to see the big picture. Even the largest monitor can only display on the order of ten thousand characters. While the debugger can provide a window on extremely large data aggregates, the scrolling and paging required to see the entire collection limits the pattern-recognition ability of the human brain.

You can see some patterns only by covering a desk or conference room table with diagnostic output. Younger programmers may tend to be more oriented toward looking at information on a video display. Those of us who can remember times before high-capacity bitmapped video terminals may tend to make more use of paper listings. Don't be bound to just one medium—choose the medium that helps you see patterns.

Color-coding items in a listing is an effective way to make your brain pick out patterns. Some sophisticated debugging tools provide array visualization tools, which convert large amounts of program data into color-coded display, such as isobar charts and temperature charts. Use these tools if they're available to you.

3.3.11   **Show how something could be done**

In *Busman's Honeymoon* [Sa37], Lord Peter and the mystery writer Harriet Vane are on their honeymoon in a quaint country house they have just purchased. Unfortunately, someone decides to murder one of the locals and deposit the body in their basement, right before they take possession of their home. Naturally, they must help the local constabulary investigate this mystery.

> "You have no idea," said Peter, irrelevantly, "how refreshing it is to talk to somebody who has a grasp of method. The police are excellent fellows, but the only principle of detection they have really grasped is that wretched phrase, 'Cui bono'? They will hare off after motive, which is a matter for psychologists. Juries are just the same. If they can see a motive they tend to convict, however often the judge may tell them that there's no need to prove motive, and that motive by itself will never make a case. You've got to show how the thing was done, and then, if you like, bring in motive to back up your proof. If a thing could only have been done one way, and if only one person could have done it that way, then you've got your criminal, motive or no motive. There's How, When, Where, Why, and Who—and when you've got How, you've got Who. Thus spake Zarathustra."

There are several ways you can use to show how a defect could occur.

- Write a list of cause-and-effect pairs that show a logical chain of events that could lead to the symptom of the defect.

- Draw a series of diagrams of a data structure showing how it could come into its current erroneous state.

- Draw a tree showing the control-flow decisions that could result in the undesired behavior.

3.4 Review

An alibi has three components: time, place, and corroboration. A program that has side effects has no alibi for the time a problem occurred or the place it occurred. The debugging equivalent of an alibi is the assertion that a given system component can't be the cause of a problem.

Exercising curiosity is one way we leverage the labor of finding the cause of a defect. We use this curiosity when we investigate potential related problems, even before they're reported.

Facts aren't complete without qualification. Use the reporter's questions—who, what, where, when, how often—to qualify the facts of a defect report to make it useful.

If you believe that a phenomenon observable by the human senses is both true and false, you're going to have a hard time with the scientific method. All classical reasoning methods depend on this principle.

The trick to enumerating possibilities is knowing when you're done. You can enumerate possibilities by using the principle of noncontradiction and a binary tree.

There are lots of good ways to organize a search for the explanation of a defect, but few programmers use any system. Some possible approaches include the black box, the scientific method, the reporter's method, and the tester's method.

In many disciplines, we're told, don't make assumptions. Unfortunately, this is easier said than done. You can follow a method that minimizes the effects that assumptions have on your search.

If you're working with a large amount of data, display it visually so that your brain can recognize larger patterns you might not recognize from looking at numerical values. Color-coding items in a listing is an effective way to make your brain pick out patterns.

Use one of several diagram types to show how a defect could occur.

4

Professor Solomon

Maybe you're ready, after all these years, to become a Finder, not a Loser.

—Professor Solomon

4.1   Preview

This chapter explains the methods of the master of finding lost things, Professor Solomon, and how they can be applied to debugging software. Professor Solomon's work purports to be nonfiction, so the treatment is different from that of Holmes and Wimsey. Part of Professor Solomon's work contains twelve principles for finding lost things. This chapter applies those principles to finding the causes of bugs.

4.2   The methods of Professor Solomon

4.2.1   How to find lost objects

Professor Solomon isn't a professor, nor is he a detective. His advice on how to find lost objects is nonetheless in the best tradition of Sherlock Holmes and Lord Peter Wimsey. They spend little of their literary lives looking for lost objects. Real detectives, however, are often hired to find missing persons and sometimes missing objects as well.

Most of Professor Solomon's book is devoted to his twelve principles for finding lost objects:

1.   Don't look for it.

2.   It's not lost—you are.

3.   Remember the three c's.

4.   It's where it's supposed to be.

5.   Look for domestic drift.

6.   You're looking right at it.

7.   The camouflage effect.

8.   Think back.

9.   Look once, look well.

10.   The eureka zone.

11.   Tail thyself.

12.   It wasn't you.

4.2.2   Applying Professor Solomon's method to debugging

Our approach to applying the professor's method is to make an analogy between lost objects and unknown causes of defects. The lost object is instead an action or lack of action occurring in an unknown location in a program. The visibility of an object is instead the understanding of how a piece of code causes the symptom.

4.2.3   Don't look for it

Professor Solomon explains this somewhat cryptic advice with the following suggestion: "Wait until you have some idea where to look."

Professor Solomon's approach fits perfectly with ours. After all, we advocate debugging by thinking, not debugging by playing around in an interactive debugger or debugging by hacking source code. Professor Solomon advocates finding things by thinking.

The first thing not to do when you have found or received evidence of defect is to start looking at source code. The second thing not to do when you have found or received evidence of defect is to start running the application and looking at output.

Here are some things you should do when you first start thinking about a bug:

■ Make a list of criteria you will use to qualify modules or procedures for or disqualify them from investigation.

- Make a list of similar defects you have seen before, particularly in this application.

- Make a list of root causes of those defects and choose the ones that are possible hypotheses.

Once you have created the first list, you can start applying your criteria and eliminating parts of the application from further consideration. Once you have created the second list, you can select those parts that remain that have demonstrated similar problems in the past. Once you have created the third list, you can start thinking about how to collect information from these parts to prove or disprove your hypotheses.

4.2.4   It's not lost, you are

Professor Solomon expands on this observation with the following qualification: "There are no missing objects. Only unsystematic searchers."

Lost objects are objects whose location is currently unknown to you, not objects whose location is unknowable. In the same way, a bug is a behavior that is as yet unexplained. It isn't impossible to explain it; it's just not yet explained.

We suggest a number of different ways to search systematically for the causes of defects. To a surprising degree, it doesn't matter which system you use, so much as whether you use any system at all.

A systematic searcher can tell you what he or she has already searched, what he or she is currently searching, and what remains to be searched. Some people search systematically, but have never put their thought processes into words. You can assess whether you're searching systematically by writing down the details of your search. When you read the journal at a later time, you should see the system you're using, even if you weren't conscious of it at the time.

4.2.5   Remember the three c's

"To find a lost object, you must be in the proper frame of mind.

Comfort

Calmness

Confidence"

There are several aspects of comfort when programming. Your eyes should be comfortable looking at the display. Your body should by comfortable sitting in the chair. The posture you must take to reach the keyboard and mouse should be comfortable from the chair. The work area should be comfortable to rest your hands on as you type or move the mouse.

Why does Professor Solomon recommend getting comfortable before tackling a difficult search? The most obvious reason is that the physical tension caused by squinting, sitting in unnatural positions, and so forth translates into mental tension. This tension isn't conducive to thinking.

Young programmers, particularly students, are more likely to think that they're immune to ergonomic problems. This is foolish. There are people who have been programming since their early teens who have done permanent damage to their hands by their mid-twenties.

If a bug has never put you in a frantic state of mind, either you haven't been programming long or you're a rare individual. Whether it's a live customer demonstration or a project deadline, bugs manifest themselves at the most inconvenient times. You won't be effective in finding a difficult bug if you're in a state of panic.

There are several ways to get yourself back into the right frame of mind. Perhaps you or your spouse have learned breathing exercises as a part of a natural childbirth course. They are very effective outside the delivery room as well. Some people also find prayer or meditation an effective means of relaxing.

You can also listen to music that is relaxing while you debug. Just because you enjoy a particular genre of music doesn't mean it will relax you. For example, if you like symphonic music, composers who wrote prior to 1800 will probably be the most helpful. If you like popular music, some New Age music may prove helpful. You want composers who soothe emotions, rather than stir them.

When a bug shows itself in code that you thought you had thoroughly tested, it can shake your confidence. When you spend fruitless hours trying to track it down without success, this feeling is only compounded.

If you use the methods suggested in this book, you can restore your confidence. First, you're using methods that have proven effective for thousands of programmers. Second, you need to put the bug that is currently tormenting you into perspective. Finding the cause of a defect isn't as hard as finding the answer to life, the universe, and everything. It is also likely that no matter how terrible this problem may seem to you, a year from now, or five years from now, you probably won't even remember it.

4.2.6   It's where it's supposed to be

"Believe it or not, things are often right where they're supposed to be."

To apply this concept, we have to stand it on its head. We aren't supposed to be putting any bugs in our software, so we certainly don't have a standard place to put them.

So, now the question becomes, where is a defect not supposed to be? Here we have to work backward.

1.   *The defect shouldn't be in the code that shows the defective value.* So, start by verifying the code that formats or writes the output that is incorrect. You may trust system libraries that do the conversion, but check the control inputs you provide to those libraries. You can't determine where the problem is until you can trust the code that is indicating a problem exists.

2.   *The defect shouldn't be in the code that computes the value.* So, you must verify the code that calculates the values. Do you own a calculator or hand-held computer? You should. They are quite valuable in manually checking complex calculations.

3.   *The defect shouldn't be in the code that reads in the values that are used as input to the calculations.* So, you must verify the code that reads and converts the input, and then verify the input values themselves. No paranoia goes unrewarded.

4.2.7   Look for domestic drift

"Many objects do have a designated or customary place where they are kept. But the reality is that they aren't always returned there. Instead, they are left wherever last used."

The customary place for a bug to occur is the last place that was modified. The place where an incorrect value is created is often not the place that it's observed.

Defective values tend to drift down the data-flow graph. A data-flow graph is a collection of arcs and nodes in which the nodes are either places where variables are assigned or used, and the arcs show the relationship between the places where a variable is assigned and where the assigned value is subsequently used.

To find the source of a defective value that has drifted down the data-flow graph, work backward from the manifestation to the definitions. The difficulty of performing this analysis depends on the scope of the variable. If it's a local variable on the stack, your search can be more limited. If it's a global variable, you may have to review many procedures to develop a graph that shows the chain of values.

There are several ways to develop a data-flow graph. If you have a compiler or tool that generates cross-reference tables, it will do much of the dirty work for you. Failing that, a simple text search with a tool like the UNIX™ command *grep* can help you identify the places where a variable is assigned or used. A slicing tool, explained in Chapter 14, is most helpful.

4.2.8   You're looking right at it

"It is possible to look directly at a missing object and not see it. This is due to the agitated state of mind that often accompanies a misplacement. Go back and look again. Return to your armchair and get calm."

It is possible to look right at a problem in code and not see it. This happens because you confuse what you know the code is supposed to do with what it is actually doing. One way to overcome this blindness is to explain what you think the code is doing to someone else. This method has been discussed previously.

A second way to break out of your mental model is to hand-execute the code you suspect to determine whether it does what you think it does. We form mental models when we read code, and these mental models aren't always correct. Write down the line number of each statement as it is encountered and the value of each variable as it is assigned. This method has been recommended in the past as a way to check code and is called desk checking. Here we're using it not to determine the correctness of a program, but to understand the behavior of a code segment we know to be incorrect.

Another way to break out of the mental model you have formed is to run a detailed trace of the code in question. In such a trace, the line number of each executable statement is printed as it's encountered. For each executable statement, the values stored to memory and the names of the variables assigned are also printed. Such traces can generate a lot of output. They can show you that statements aren't being executed in the order you thought or that the values being generated aren't the values you thought.

If you know that a given piece of code must be the source of a problem, but after a thorough investigation, you're unable to identify the source, perhaps you should just write the code over again. There is a point at which it's more cost effective to rewrite a piece of code than it's to stare at it. The smaller the code segment in question, the quicker you come to that point.

4.2.9 **The camouflage effect**

"Your object may be right where you thought it was—but it has become hidden from view. Be sure to check under anything that could be covering your object, having inadvertently been placed on top of it."

You may have identified a particular code segment as the cause of a problem, yet been unable to see the problem source. There are a number of programming constructs that can place a problem out of view:

- Preprocessor macros
- Procedure calls
- Exception handling
- Complex language constructs (C++, Ada, PL/I)

Some languages, such as C, C++, and PL/I, are normally used with a preprocessing phase. Preprocessor macros can obscure the source of a problem. If you're sure a given source file contains a problem, consider reading the output of the preprocessor. Most compilers that apply preprocessors provide a command-line option to generate this output, even if the preprocessor has been integrated into the compiler. There are publicly available tools that will selectively preprocess a file, which will reduce the amount of code you will have to review. When you apply preprocessing selectively, you can control which files will be included and which macro definitions will be expanded.

All high-level languages have procedures that can be invoked, no matter whether they're called subroutines, functions, or methods. Most modern languages have exception-handling facilities, and even C has the primitive **setjmp/longjmp** facility, both very powerful programming facilities, but they can obscure the cause of a problem because they introduce nonlocal flow of control.

If a code segment you suspect has procedure invocations, you have two choices. You can turn off the calls, perhaps by commenting them out or using a preprocessor command, and determine whether the problem exists.

Or, you can go through the process of determining that all of the code executed by the called procedure isn't the problem. You can take a similar approach to code invoked by exception handlers. These can involve quite a bit of effort to verify, since the handler may not even be visible in the code you suspect.

As a last resort, you can look at the assembly code or bytecode generated by the compiler you're using. While this is very tedious, it's sometimes necessary to see what is really going on in a code segment you know is the source of a problem.

4.2.10　Think back

"You were there when the object was put down—was left in an obscure location—was consigned to oblivion. You were there—because you did it! So you must have a memory—however faint—of where this happened."

These comments obviously only apply to code for which you're solely responsible. You can think back much more easily if you have made a record of your actions.

There are several automatic ways you can keep track of what you did. There are also at least three levels of history you may want to track.

Changes to a single file during an editing session occur with high frequency. Source files can remain open across compilations in both command-line environments and integrated development environments (IDEs).

Some commercial editing tools and IDEs keep an "undo" history in a separate file, which you may want to archive. You can get the source code to the most popular command-line editors, *vi* and *EMACS*, which are freely available from the GNU project. If you want to track changes at this level, one way to do so is to use a modified version of your editor. This special version writes the "undo" history to a file, either by a special command or at regular intervals.

Changes that you save when you complete editing of a given source file occur with medium frequency. If you develop in a command-line environment, make good use of the history features of the shell you're using. Keep the maximum history that the shell allows. Memory is cheap compared with the cost of redoing work. This history tells you which files you edited last, therefore which is the most logical place to look for a newly introduced bug.

You can extend the benefit of this history even further. Change your logout procedure so it appends your history to a separate file. This will make it possible to recall actions taken in previous logon sessions. This history will contain, among other things, both editor invocations and execution of whatever source control system you're using. There should be a correlation between edits and checkins, which can be verified automatically with a tool that processes your long-term history.

If you're developing with an IDE, use the feature that lists recently opened files on the File menu. Some systems provide you with the ability to set the number of files listed there. Set this value to the maximum allowed.

The least frequently changed level of history is source-code checkins. You should be using a source control system of some sort. The use of source control systems is discussed later in this chapter.

4.2.11 Look once, look well

"Once you've checked a site, do not go back and check again. No matter how promising a site—if the object wasn't there the first time, it won't be there the second. Assuming, of course, that your first check was thorough."

At each potential problem location, use all relevant tools to identify the source of the problem. See Chapter 14 for some suggestions for tools you might not be using.

If you're going to ensure that you don't visit a code segment more than once, it's important to keep a record of where you have looked so far. This might seem trivial when you're tracking down bugs that take only ten or fifteen minutes to resolve. It is much more important when you are working on a bug that takes ten or fifteen days to diagnose.

There are several ways to keep a record of your search. You can put a comment in each procedure as you investigate it. You can make a handwritten list or type your list into an editor screen or a hand-held computer.

You can even use a voice-activated recorder. This has the advantage of not requiring you to remove your hands from the keyboard. Of course, if you work in an office with cubicles, your coworkers might not appreciate your new technique.

If you don't know how to describe an investigation verbally, watch a television program that shows physicians handling medical emergencies. They have an excellent protocol for describing what they see as they encounter it.

4.2.12   The eureka zone

"The majority of lost objects are right where you figure. Others, however, are in the immediate vicinity of that place. They have undergone a displacement."

Physical locality isn't a primary concern when debugging software. Displacements of problems are more likely to occur temporally rather than spatially. Here is a list of items that are likely to be temporally displaced from the source of a problem:

- Suspect those variables that were most recently modified before the problem became visible.

- Suspect those statements that were most recently executed in the current procedure before the problem became visible.

- Suspect those procedures that are closest on the call stack to the procedure where the problem became visible.

Physical displacement of problems is mostly a concern when using languages that provide arbitrary pointer manipulation, such as C and C++. Here is a list of items that are likely to be spatially displaced from the source of a problem:

- Suspect references to variables in the same heterogeneous storage construct as the variable in which the problem became visible. This applies to constructs such as **struct** in C, **class** in C++, or **COMMON** in Fortran.

- Suspect references to variables that are on the stack at the same time, as the variable that manifests an incorrect value. These variables are chiefly the local variables in the same procedure but can also include the arguments.

- Suspect references to storage allocated on the heap at about the same time as the variable in which the problem became visible.

4.2.13   Tail thyself

"If you still haven't found your object, it may be time to Recreate the Crime. Remove your thinking cap and don your detective's cap. You are about to follow your own trail."

Earlier in this chapter, we recommended keeping the history of your work on several levels. If you want to be able to "tail yourself," you need the information provided by a revision control system.

If you want to be a productive debugger, be a revision control fanatic. Check in everything you work on, and do so on a daily or even hourly basis.

If you are a part of a group programming project that uses a heavy-duty commercial source control system, you may want to use a lightweight source control system to keep track of your own work. Group projects generally want you to check things in only when they're in a stable state. This is laudable but contradictory to the philosophy of using a source control system to enable you to "tail yourself." You want to be able to compare source files that you know don't work, not just the ones that you have determined are stable.

The simplest source control methodology is to make a separate directory at regular intervals, and copy your source files into that directory.

To go beyond this, you should use one of the good source control systems that are publicly available.

The Revision Control System (RCS) [Ti85] has been used on UNIX™ systems for nearly two decades, and it's perfectly adequate for projects with a small number of programmers. It doesn't handle multisite projects, nor does it have a concept of multifile modules.

The Concurrent Versions System (CVS) [Be90] supports multiple programmers working on a single source base, multiple directories of source, and distributed development across a wide-area network. Both RCS and CVS are open-source systems available from the GNU project.

While debugging, each time you make a change to test a hypothesis, mark the changed code with comments. This also means that you won't delete code, just render it nonoperational. You can do this by commenting it out, put it under the control of a conditional compilation directive, or under the control of a control-flow statement that never is executed.

You can't see changes that cause a problem if you can't track the deltas. Here are some tags you can use to indicate tentative changes:

```
// comment out deleted code // D
// A: added code
// C: changed code
```

4.2.14   **It wasn't you**

"When all else has failed, explore the possibility that your object hasn't been misplaced. Rather, it is been misappropriated. Perhaps someone you know has borrowed or moved the object you are looking for."

After you have made a heroic effort to diagnose your problem, it's reasonable to consider whether your code may not be the culprit. Problems that show up in applications can be caused by libraries and middleware, compilers, and operating systems. The developers of these systems are mere mortals too, and they have their share of bugs. On the other hand, they also typically have the benefit of large numbers of users to exercise their code and work out the bugs. This is why you should suspect your code first.

If you want to get help with a problem in other people's software, it's important to create a minimal test case that demonstrates the problem. The downside to having all those users is that software vendors receive many bogus defect reports from those same users. The natural human tendency is to look at the problems that are easiest to diagnose, and those are the ones with the shortest test cases. You are far more likely to get a rapid response from a responsible software vendor with a well-structured test case than by pressure tactics.

A well-designed test case is self-contained, prints a simple pass/fail message, and takes up less than a page of code. When we submit such defect reports, we take great care to double- and triple-check the behavior with which we're unhappy. There are few things more embarrassing than submitting a bogus bug report and displaying your ignorance in public.

4.3   **Review**

Don't begin debugging by looking at source code or running the application in question. Begin by making a list of criteria to evaluate possible causes and a list of similar defects you have seen before.

A bug is a behavior that is as yet unexplained. It isn't impossible to explain it; it has merely not yet been explained. A systematic searcher can tell you what he or she has already searched, what he or she is currently searching, and what remains to be searched.

The physical tension caused by squinting, sitting in unnatural positions, and other uncomfortable practices translates into mental tension. This tension isn't conducive to thinking. If you use the methods in this book, you can have confidence that you will find the bug you're analyzing.

Work backward from the code that evidences a defective value, through the computations that generate it, to the code that reads in the input values used in the computation, to the input values themselves.

The customary place for a bug to occur is the last place that was modified. To find the source of a defective value that has drifted down the dataflow graph, work backward from the manifestation to the definition.

It is possible to look right at a problem in code and not see it, because you confuse what you know the code is supposed to do with what it is actually doing. If you know that a given piece of code must be the source of a problem, but after a thorough investigation, you are unable to identify the source, you should just write the code over again.

You may have identified a particular code segment as the cause of a problem, yet be unable to see the problem source. There are a number of programming constructs that can place a problem out of view.

Thinking back is greatly aided by a record of your actions. Use one of several possible automatic ways you can keep track of what you did.

If you are going to ensure that you don't visit a code segment more than once, it is important to keep a record of where you have looked so far.

Physical locality isn't a primary concern when debugging software. Displacements of problems are more likely to occur temporally rather than spatially.

If you want to be a productive debugger, be a revision control fanatic. There are good source control systems publicly available. You can't see changes that caused a problem if you can't track the deltas.

After you have made a heroic effort to diagnose your problem, it is reasonable to consider whether your code may not be the culprit. If you want to get help with a problem in other people's software, it is important to create a minimal test case that demonstrates the problem.

Case Studies I

5.1   Case Study I

5.1.1   The program

The purpose of the case studies in this book is to demonstrate the use of some of the concepts presented in the preceding chapters. The defects analyzed are the actual mistakes made by the author when developing this software. Different people are prone to make different mistakes. Focus on the method used in debugging, rather than the particular error in question.

The algorithms implemented in the case studies for this book were chosen based on the following criteria:

- There is a published design in pseudocode for the algorithm accessible in the computer science literature.

- The implementation should follow the original design relatively closely so that it is easy to compare it with the design.

- The algorithm computes a useful result. Toy programs do not make interesting examples.

- The algorithm has excellent computational complexity. Toy programs do not make convincing examples.

- The algorithm is complicated enough that some bugs would likely occur in implementing it.

The program we debug in this section is a heap sort that works on linked list structures. Heap sorts are usually explained in an undergraduate course in data structures. The data-structure books we reviewed for this example present heap sorts of integer data stored in arrays. See *Algorithms in C++* (3rd ed.) [Se98] for an excellent analysis of array-based heap sorts. This example presents a heap sort that works on linked lists, written in C++.

The data-structure books present array-based heap sorts because they can be coded very concisely. The linked-list heap sort requires a great deal more code. Some people say that if you want to sort a linked list, you should copy it into an array, sort the array, and then copy it back into another linked list. This approach works fine for small linked lists. The cost of copying data and allocating storage, as well as the extra memory required, make this approach prohibitive for large lists or small memory systems.

The first step in a heap sort is to insert all of the elements to be sorted into a heap structure. A common way to represent a heap is with a **complete binary tree**. A complete binary tree is created by appending nodes to the tree from left to right on a given level of the tree and starting a new level only when the current level is full.

If we create a binary tree such that the keys of the nodes satisfy the heap condition, we have represented a heap with a binary tree. The heap condition is the following: The key in each node is greater than or equal to the keys in any of its children. The largest key is stored in the root node of the tree.

After the heap is constructed, the sort loops as many times as there are elements. Each iteration of the loop removes the largest element from the heap and restructures the heap so that it retains the heap property.

The code for the original program is listed as follows:

```
#ifndef _Heap_h_
#define _Heap_h_

class Heap {
public:
    // constructors and destructors
    Heap(int, int);
    Heap(int, int *);

    // accessors
    inline int getKey() { return _key; }
    inline int getID() { return _id; }
    inline Heap * getLeft() { return _left; }
    inline Heap * getRight() { return _right; }
    inline Heap * getParent() { return _parent; }
```

```
                inline Heap * getPred() { return _pred; }
                inline Heap * getSucc() { return _succ; }

                inline Heap * getRoot() { return _root; }
                inline Heap * getActive() { return _active; }
                inline Heap * getLast() { return _last; }
                inline Heap * getFrontier() { return _frontier; }
                inline int get ower() { return _power; }

                // mutators
                inline void setKey(int x) { _key= x; }
                inline void setID(int x) { _id= x; }
                inline void setLeft(Heap * x) { _left= x; }
                inline void setRight(Heap * x) { _right= x; }
                inline void setParent(Heap * x) { _parent= x; }
                inline void setPred(Heap * x) { _pred= x; }
                inline void setSucc(Heap * x) { _succ= x; }

                inline void setRoot(Heap *x) { _root= x; }
                inline void setActive(Heap *x) { _active= x; }
                inline void setLast(Heap *x) { _last= x; }
                inline void setFrontier(Heap *x) { _frontier= x; }
                inline void setPower(int x) { _power= x; }

                // workers
                void insert();
                void movedown();
                void moveup();
                Heap * remove();
                void replace(Heap *);
                Heap * sort();
                void print();

            private:
                static Heap * _root;
                static Heap * _active;
                static Heap * _last;
                static Heap * _frontier;
                static int _power;

                int _key;
```

```
        int _id;
        Heap * _left;
        Heap * _right;
        Heap * _parent;
        Heap * _pred;
        Heap * _succ;
};

void list(Heap *);
void draw(Heap *);

#endif
```

```
#include <stdio.h>
#include <stdlib.h>
#include <assert.h>

#include "Heap.h"

//-----------------------------------------------------
// static variables
//-----------------------------------------------------

Heap * Heap::_root;
Heap * Heap::_active;
Heap * Heap::_last;
Heap * Heap::_frontier;
int Heap::_power;

//-----------------------------------------------------
// construct an individual heap node
//-----------------------------------------------------

Heap::Heap(int x, int y) {
        _key= x;
        _id= y;
        _left= 0;
        _right= 0;
```

```
        _parent= 0;
        _pred= 0;
        _succ= 0;
    }


    //----------------------------------------------------
    // construct a heap from the provided data
    // the node returned is located somewhere on the heap
    // to get the root:
    // Heap *n= new Heap(count,values);
    // Heap *root= n->getRoot();
    //----------------------------------------------------

    Heap::Heap(int n, int *x ) {
        _key= x[0];
        _id= 1;
        _left= 0;
        _right= 0;
        _parent= 0;
        _pred= 0;
        _succ= 0;

        _root= this;
        _active= this;
        _last= 0;
        _frontier= 0;
        _power= 2;

        for( int i= 1; i < n; ++i ) {
            Heap *node= new Heap(x[i], i+1);
            node->insert();
            node->moveup();
        }
    }


    //----------------------------------------------------
    // insert a Heap node at the end of the heap
    //----------------------------------------------------

    void Heap::insert() {
```

```
        this->setPred(0);
        this->setSucc(0);
        if( _active->getLeft() == 0 ) {
            _active->setLeft(this);
            this->setParent(_active);
            if ( this->getID() == _power ) {
                _frontier= this;
                _power *= 2;
            }
            _last= this;
        } else if( _active->getRight() == 0 ) {
            _active->setRight(this);
            this->setParent(_active);
            _last->setSucc(this);
            this->setPred(_last);
            if ( this->getID() == _power-1 ) {
                _active= _frontier;
            }
            _last= this;
        } else {
            _active= _last->getParent()->getSucc();
            if( _active == 0 ) {
                _active= _frontier;
            } else {
                _active->setLeft(this);
                this->setParent(_active);
            }
            _last->setSucc(this);
            this->setPred(_last);
            _last= this;
        }
    }


//----------------------------------------------------
// re-arrange the heap after appending a node at the
// end of the binary tree so that the heap property
// is preserved
//----------------------------------------------------


void Heap::moveup() {
```

```
                    Heap *temp;

              while( true  ) {
                  Heap * parent= this->getParent();
                  if( !parent || parent->getKey() >=
                                  this->getKey() ) {
                      break;
                  }

                  // swap ID numbers
                  int swap= parent->getID();
                  parent->setID(this->getID());
                  this->setID(swap);

                  // swap incoming vertical pointers
                  Heap * grand= parent->getParent();
                  if( grand != 0 ) {
                      if( parent == grand->getLeft() ) {
                          grand->setLeft(this);
                      } else if( parent == grand->getRight() ) {
                          grand->setRight(this);
                      }
                  }

                  // swap outgoing vertical pointers
                  parent->setParent(this);
                  this->setParent(grand);

                  if( this == parent->getLeft() ) {
                      if( this->getLeft() != 0 ) {
                          this->getLeft()->setParent(parent);
                      }
                      parent->setLeft(this->getLeft());
                      this->setLeft(parent);

                      if( this->getRight() != 0 ) {
                          if( parent->getRight() != 0 ) {
                              temp= parent->getRight()
                                          ->getParent();
                          parent->getRight()->setParent(this->
                                  getRight()->getParent());
```

```
                        this->getRight()->setParent(temp);
            } else {
                this->getRight()->setParent(0);
            }
        } else {
            if( parent->getRight() != 0 ) {
                parent->getRight()->setParent(0);
            }
        }

        temp= this->getRight();
        this->setRight(parent->getRight());
        parent->setRight(temp);
    } else if( this == parent->getRight() ) {
        if( this->getRight() != 0 ) {
            this->getRight()->setParent(parent);
        }
        parent->setRight(this->getRight());
        this->setRight(parent);

        if( this->getLeft() != 0 ) {
            if( parent->getLeft() != 0 ) {
                temp= parent->getLeft()->getParent();
                parent->getLeft()->setParent(this->
                        getLeft()->getParent());
                this->getLeft()->setParent(temp);
            } else {
                this->getLeft()->setParent(0);
            }
        } else {
            if( parent->getLeft() != 0 ) {
                parent->getLeft()->setParent(0);
            }
        }

        temp= this->getLeft();
        this->setLeft(parent->getLeft());
        parent->setLeft(temp);
    } else {
        assert(0);
    }
```

```
// swap incoming horizontal pointers
if( this->getPred() != 0 ) {
    if( parent->getPred() != 0 ) {
        temp= parent->getPred()->getSucc();
        parent->getPred()->setSucc(
                            this->getPred()
            ->getSucc());
        this->getPred()->setSucc(temp);
    } else {
        this->getPred()->setSucc(0);
    }
} else {
    if( parent->getPred() != 0 ) {
        parent->getPred()->setSucc(0);
    }
}
if( this->getSucc() != 0 ) {
    if( parent->getSucc() != 0 ) {
        temp= parent->getSucc()->getPred();
        parent->getSucc()->setPred(
                            this->getSucc()
            ->getPred());
        this->getSucc()->setPred(temp);
    } else {
        this->getSucc()->setPred(0);
    }
} else {
    if( parent->getSucc() != 0 ) {
        parent->getSucc()->setPred(0);
    }
}

// swap outgoing horizontal pointers
temp= parent->getPred();
parent->setPred(this->getPred());
this->setPred(temp);

temp= parent->getSucc();
parent->setSucc(this->getSucc());
this->setSucc(temp);
```

```
        // update variables
        _active= _last->getParent();
        if( _root == parent ) {
            _root= this;
        }
        _last= parent;
        _active= this;
        if ( _root == parent ) {
            _root= this;
        }
    }
}


//----------------------------------------------------
// re-arrange the heap after inserting a new root node
// in the binary tree so that the heap property
// is preserved
//----------------------------------------------------

void Heap::movedown() {

    Heap *temp, *child;

    while( true  ) {
        Heap * left= this->getLeft();
        Heap * right= this->getRight();
        if( left != 0 && right != 0  ) {
            if( left->getKey() <= this->getKey() &&
                right->getKey() <= this->getKey() ) {
                break;
            } else {
                child= (left->getKey() >=
                        right->getKey()) ?
                       left : right;
            }
        } else if ( left != 0 ) {
            if( left->getKey() <= this->getKey() ) {
                break;
            } else {
                child= left;
```

```
            }
    } else {
        break;
    }

    // swap ID numbers
    int swap= this->getID();
    this->setID(child->getID());
    child->setID(swap);

    // swap incoming vertical pointers
    Heap * grand= this->getParent();
    if( grand != 0 ) {
        if( this == grand->getLeft() ) {
            grand->setLeft(child);
        } else if( this == grand->getRight() ) {
            grand->setRight(child);
        }
    }

    // swap outgoing vertical pointers
    this->setParent(child);
    child->setParent(grand);

    if( child == this->getLeft() ) {
        if( child->getLeft() != 0 ) {
            child->getLeft()->setParent(this);
        }
        this->setLeft(child->getLeft());
        child->setLeft(this);

        if( child->getRight() != 0 ) {
            if( this->getRight() != 0 ) {
                temp= this->getRight()->getParent();
                this->getRight()->setParent(child->
                    getRight()->getParent());
                child->getRight()->setParent(temp);
            } else {
                child->getRight()->setParent(0);
            }
        } else {
```

```
                        if( this->getRight() != 0 ) {
                            this->getRight()->setParent(child);
                        }
                    }

                    temp= child->getRight();
                    child->setRight(this->getRight());
                    this->setRight(temp);
                } else if( child == this->getRight() ) {
                    if( child->getRight() != 0 ) {
                        child->getRight()->setParent(this);
                    }
                    this->setRight(child->getRight());
                    child->setRight(this);

                    if( child->getLeft() != 0 ) {
                        if( this->getLeft() != 0 ) {
                            temp= this->getLeft()->getParent();
                            this->getLeft()->setParent(child->
                                getLeft()->getParent());
                            child->getLeft()->setParent(temp);
                        } else {
                            child->getLeft()->setParent(0);
                        }
                    } else {
                        if( this->getLeft() != 0 ) {
                            this->getLeft()->setParent(child);
                        }
                    }

                    temp= child->getLeft();
                    child->setLeft(this->getLeft());
                    this->setLeft(temp);
                } else {
                    assert(0);
                }

                // swap incoming horizontal pointers
                if( child->getPred() != 0 ) {
                    if( this->getPred() != 0 ) {
                        temp= this->getPred()->getSucc();
```

```
                    this->getPred()->setSucc(
                                    child->getPred()
                       ->getSucc());
                child->getPred()->setSucc(temp);
            } else {
                child->getPred()->setSucc(this);
            }
        } else {
            if( this->getPred() != 0 ) {
                this->getPred()->setSucc(child);
            }
        }
        if( child->getSucc() != 0 ) {
            if( this->getSucc() != 0 ) {
                temp= this->getSucc()->getPred();
                this->getSucc()->setPred(
                                    child->getSucc()
                       ->getPred());
                child->getSucc()->setPred(temp);
            } else {
                child->getSucc()->setPred(this);
            }
        } else {
            if( this->getSucc() != 0 ) {
                this->getSucc()->setPred(child);
            }
        }

        // swap outgoing horizontal pointers
        temp= this->getPred();
        this->setPred(child->getPred());
        child->setPred(temp);

        temp= this->getSucc();
        this->setSucc(child->getSucc());
        child->setSucc(temp);

        // update variables
        _active= _last->getParent();
        if( _root == this ) {
            _root= child;
```

```
            }
        }
    }

    //----------------------------------------------------
    // display the contents of one Heap node
    //----------------------------------------------------

    void Heap::print() {

        fprintf(stderr,"%2d(%x) L %x R %x P %x S %x ^ %x\n",
            this->getKey(), this, this->getLeft(),
            this->getRight(), this->getPred(),
            this->getSucc(), this->getParent());
    }

    //----------------------------------------------------
    // remove the root node
    //----------------------------------------------------

    Heap * Heap::remove() {

        // unlink last node
        _last->getPred()->setSucc(0);
        if( _last == _last->getParent()->getLeft() ) {
            _last->getParent()->setLeft(0);
        } else {
            _last->getParent()->setRight(0);
        }

        // link last node in as root
        _last->setLeft(_root->getLeft());
        _last->setRight(_root->getRight());
        _last->setParent(_root->getParent());
        _last->setSucc(_root->getSucc());
        _last->setPred(_root->getPred());
        _last->setID(_root->getID());

        Heap * node= _root;
        _root= _last;
```

```
        // unlink root
        node->setLeft(0);
        node->setRight(0);
        node->setParent(0);
        node->setSucc(0);
        node->setPred(0);
        node->setID(0);

        movedown();

        return node;
    }


//----------------------------------------------------
// Heap sort integer array
//----------------------------------------------------

Heap * Heap::sort() {

    Heap *head;
    Heap *last= 0;
    do {
        Heap * next= this->remove();
        if( last == 0 ) {
            head= next;
            next->setPred(0);
            last->setSucc(next);
        } else {
            next->setPred(last);
            last->setSucc(next);
        }
        last= next;
    } while ( _root != 0 );
    _root= head;
    _last= last;
    _active= 0;
    _frontier= 0;
    return head;
}
```

5.1.2   Bug I

5.1.2.1   The evidence

The first debugging session began by running the application standalone.
The test input and test driver are shown as follows:

```
// sorted up, power of 2 length
int t01[8]= { 1,2,3,4,5,6,7,8 };

// sorted up, non-power of 2 length
int t02[9]= { 2,3,5,7,11,13,17,19,23 };

int main() {

    fprintf(stderr,"test 1:8\n");
    testBuild(new Heap(8, t01));
    fprintf(stderr,"test 2:9\n");
    testBuild(new Heap(9, t02));
}

void testBuild(Heap *node) {
    draw(node->getRoot());
    fprintf(stderr,"\n");
}

int indent= 0;
void draw(Heap * n) {
    int i;
    indent += 4;
    if( n != 0 ) {
        for( i=0; i<indent; ++i ) {
            fputc(' ',stderr);
        }
        fprintf(stderr,"%d\n",n->getKey());
        draw(n->getRight());
        draw(n->getLeft());
    }
    indent -= 4;
}
```

The results of executing this test are shown below.

```
test 1:8
    5
        3
            2
        1

test 2:9
    11
        5
            3
        2
```

5.1.2.2   The investigation

It is obvious that this output is faulty—over half of the key values are not even represented. The first thing we would like to do is generate a standard with which to compare the actual output. There many potential valid heap representations of the inputs of these test cases. We will construct one that is representative.

```
test 1:8
    8
        6
            5
            2
        7
            3
            4
                1

test 2:9
    23
        13
            11
```

                                  3
                      19
                                  5
                      17
                                        7
                                        2

We observe that at least half of the key values are missing, and that those
missing do not come from consecutive positions in the original input stream.
We need more data to work with. We decide to insert a call to a function that
will list the details of the data structure. We insert this call at the end of each
execution of the *insert* function. We also insert an output statement at the
beginning of the *insert* function that tells us the key value of the node being
inserted. This is what the output looks like. We have decided that since the
first two test cases fail similarly, we will focus on the first for now.

```
test 1:8
insert 2
    1(804b9f0) L 804ba10 R 0 P 0 S 0 ^ 0
        2(804ba10) L 0 R 0 P 0 S 0 ^ 804b9f0

insert 3
    2(804ba10) L 804b9f0 R 804ba30 P 0 S 0 ^ 0
        3(804ba30) L 0 R 0 P 804b9f0 S 0 ^ 804ba10
        1(804b9f0) L 0 R 0 P 0 S 804ba30 ^ 804ba10

insert 4
    3(804ba30) L 804b9f0 R 804ba10 P 0 S 0 ^ 0
        2(804ba10) L 0 R 0 P 804b9f0 S 804ba50 ^ 804ba30
        1(804b9f0) L 0 R 0 P 0 S 0 ^ 0

insert 5
    3(804ba30) L 804b9f0 R 804ba10 P 0 S 0 ^ 0
        2(804ba10) L 804ba70 R 0 P 804b9f0 S 804ba50 ^ 804ba30
            5(804ba70) L 0 R 0 P 0 S 0 ^ 804ba10
        1(804b9f0) L 0 R 0 P 0 S 0 ^ 0

insert 6
    5(804ba70) L 804b9f0 R 804ba30 P 0 S 0 ^ 0
        3(804ba30) L 804ba10 R 0 P 804b9f0 S 804ba90 ^ 804ba70
            2(804ba10) L 0 R 0 P 0 S 0 ^ 0
        1(804b9f0) L 0 R 0 P 0 S 0 ^ 804ba70

insert 7
    5(804ba70) L 804b9f0 R 804ba30 P 0 S 0 ^ 0
```

```
            3(804ba30) L 804ba10 R 0 P 804b9f0 S 804ba90 ^ 804ba70
              2(804ba10) L 804bab0 R 0 P 0 S 0 ^ 0
                7(804bab0) L 0 R 0 P 0 S 0 ^ 804ba10
            1(804b9f0) L 0 R 0 P 0 S 0 ^ 804ba70

insert 8
      5(804ba70) L 804b9f0 R 804ba30 P 0 S 0 ^ 0
            3(804ba30) L 804ba10 R 0 P 804b9f0 S 804ba90 ^ 804ba70
              2(804ba10) L 0 R 0 P 0 S 804bad0 ^ 804bab0
            1(804b9f0) L 0 R 0 P 0 S 0 ^ 804ba70


      5
          3
              2
          1
```

Each row of the display shows

- The node key

- The node address

- The left child pointer ("L")

- The right child pointer ("R")

- The predecessor pointer ("P")

- The successor pointer ("S")

- The parent pointer ("^")

Indentation shows the parental relationship between nodes graphically as well.

We can see that the data structure is invalid by the time the call to insert the node with key "4" has completed. We need more data to work with. We decide to step through the execution of the *insert* function in the debugger. We set a breakpoint at the beginning of the function and continue execution when the breakpoint is reached, until the call that inserts the node with key "4" is reached.

We observe that there are three cases in this function and that the third case is the one selected for processing this node. We step through this case one statement at a time. Control flows through the true branch of an *if-then-else.* It becomes clear that no statement is executed that sets the left child of some node to point to the current node, nor does any statement set

the parent pointer of the current node to anything. Since this is the fundamental operation of inserting a node in a tree, it is not surprising that the
node with key "4" fails to show up when we list the contents of the tree.

5.1.2.3   **The fault and correction**

We make three changes to correct the problems we have observed.

First, we attach the node being processed to the data structure by inserting the following statements:

```
_active->setLeft(this);
this->setParent(_active);
```

Second, we move statements that were being unconditionally executed
in the case we observed to be executed only under the *else* clause. It makes
no sense to try to set the predecessor pointer when a node is at the left edge
of a row and has no predecessors.

```
_last->setSucc(this);
this->setPred(_last);
```

Finally, we observe that since the case being handled is the left edge, we
should be updating the variable that is supposed to be tracking that same
left edge. We insert the following statement to cover this:

```
_frontier= this;
```

In this round of debugging, we applied the following methods from
Chapter 2:

- Pay attention to unusual details.

- Gather facts before hypothesizing.

We found two defects that had the following root causes, explained in
Chapter 11:

- Missing operations—missing statements

> ■ Control-flow problems—statements controlled by the wrong control
> condition

5.1.3   **Bug 2**

5.1.3.1   **The evidence**

The second debugging session began by running the application standalone.
We use the same test input and test driver as in the previous test. The results
of executing this test are shown below.

```
test 1:8
    8
        3
            2
        7
```

We definitely fixed problems in the previous session. Unfortunately,
while the output of this run is different, it still is not correct.

5.1.3.2   **The investigation**

We turn on the same diagnostic output that we used before. This is what
the output looks like:

```
test 1:8
insert 2
    1(804bad0) L 804baf0 R 0 P 0 S 0 ^ 0
        2(804baf0) L 0 R 0 P 0 S 0 ^ 804bad0

insert 3
    2(804baf0) L 804bad0 R 804bb10 P 0 S 0 ^ 0
        3(804bb10) L 0 R 0 P 804bad0 S 0 ^ 804baf0
        1(804bad0) L 0 R 0 P 0 S 804bb10 ^ 804baf0

insert 4
    3(804bb10) L 804bad0 R 804baf0 P 0 S 0 ^ 0
        2(804baf0) L 804bb30 R 0 P 804bad0 S 0 ^ 804bb10
            4(804bb30) L 0 R 0 P 0 S 0 ^ 804baf0
        1(804bad0) L 0 R 0 P 0 S 0 ^ 0

insert 5
    4(804bb30) L 804bb50 R 804bb10 P 0 S 0 ^ 0
```

```
        3(804bb10) L 804baf0 R 0 P 804bad0 S 0 ^ 804bb30
           2(804baf0) L 0 R 0 P 0 S 0 ^ 0
        5(804bb50) L 0 R 0 P 0 S 0 ^ 804bb30

 insert 6
     5(804bb50) L 804bb70 R 804bb10 P 0 S 0 ^ 0
        3(804bb10) L 804baf0 R 0 P 804bad0 S 0 ^ 0
           2(804baf0) L 0 R 0 P 0 S 0 ^ 0
        6(804bb70) L 0 R 0 P 0 S 0 ^ 804bb50

 insert 7
     6(804bb70) L 804bb90 R 804bb10 P 0 S 0 ^ 0
        3(804bb10) L 804baf0 R 0 P 804bad0 S 0 ^ 0
           2(804baf0) L 0 R 0 P 0 S 0 ^ 0
        7(804bb90) L 0 R 0 P 0 S 0 ^ 804bb70

 insert 8
     7(804bb90) L 804bbb0 R 804bb10 P 0 S 0 ^ 0
        3(804bb10) L 804baf0 R 0 P 804bad0 S 0 ^ 0
           2(804baf0) L 0 R 0 P 0 S 0 ^ 0
        8(804bbb0) L 0 R 0 P 0 S 0 ^ 804bb90


    8
      3
        2
      7
```

All of the nodes that are missing from the output appear briefly in the data structure after they are inserted, but then disappear after other nodes are inserted. We decide that the actions of the *moveup* function may be masking a problem in the *insert* function. We modify the test case by commenting out the call to *moveup* and try the same case again. We have elided all but the last listing of the data-structure details in the interest of saving space.

```
 test 1:8
 insert 2
 insert 3
 insert 4
 insert 5
 insert 6
 insert 7
 insert 8
     1(804ba10) L ba30 R 804ba50 P 0 S 0 ^ 0
        3(804ba50) L 804bab0 R 804bad0 P 804ba30 S 0 ^ 804ba10
           7(804bad0) L 0 R 0 P 804bab0 S 0 ^ 804ba50
           6(804bab0) L 0 R 0 P 804ba90 S 804bad0 ^ 804ba50
```

```
  2(804ba30) L 804ba70 R 804ba90 P 0 S 804ba50 ^ 804ba10
    5(804ba90) L 0 R 0 P 804ba70 S 804bab0 ^ 804ba30
    4(804ba70) L 804baf0 R 0 P 0 S 804ba90 ^ 804ba30
      8(804baf0) L 0 R 0 P 0 S 0 ^ 804ba70
```

```
 1
   3
     7
     6
   2
     5
     4
       8
```

We are quite pleased with the results, but cautiously optimistic, since the test case has keys in strict ascending order. We check over all the pointers in the data structure, and they are all correct. Just to make sure, we reverse the order of the keys in the input and try again. Here is the result:

```
test 1:8
insert 7
insert 6
insert 5
insert 4
insert 3
insert 2
insert 1
      8(804ba30) L 804ba50 R 804ba70 P 0 S 0 ^ 0
        6(804ba70) L 804bad0 R 804baf0 P 804ba50 S 0 ^ 804ba30
          2(804baf0) L 0 R 0 P 804bad0 S 0 ^ 804ba70
          3(804bad0) L 0 R 0 P 804bab0 S 804baf0 ^ 804ba70
        7(804ba50) L 804ba90 R 804bab0 P 0 S 804ba70 ^ 804ba30
          4(804bab0) L 0 R 0 P 804ba90 S 804bad0 ^ 804ba50
          5(804ba90) L 804bb10 R 0 P 0 S 804bab0 ^ 804ba50
            1(804bb10) L 0 R 0 P 0 S 0 ^ 804ba90
```

```
 8
   6
     2
     3
   7
     4
     5
       1
```

Now we have greater confidence in the *insert* function, so we focus our attention on the *moveup* function. After staring at the output for a while, we remember that the input of the *moveup* function includes not only the data structure as displayed, but also a small set of static variables that capture key values used during the process.

We plan our investigation as follows:

- *Problem:* Nodes are disappearing from the data structure at random after they are inserted when *moveup* is used.

- *Hypothesis:* Static variables are not getting set properly on input to *moveup.*

- *Experiment:* Run test case 1 with detailed debugging output of the data structure displayed after each execution of the *moveup* function. Also display the static variables used by both functions.

When we run the experiment, we get the following results, with some of the detailed output omitted in the interest of saving space:

```
test 1:8
insert 2
*** moveup ***
_last= 804bb40, _active= 804bb20, _frontier= 804bb40
    1(804bb20) L 804bb40 R 0 P 0 S 0 ^ 0
        2(804bb40) L 0 R 0 P 0 S 0 ^ 804bb20

### moveup ###
_last= 804bb20, _active= 804bb40, _frontier= 804bb40
    2(804bb40) L 804bb20 R 0 P 0 S 0 ^ 0
        1(804bb20) L 0 R 0 P 0 S 0 ^ 804bb40

insert 3
*** moveup ***
_last= 804bb60, _active= 804bb40, _frontier= 804bb40
    2(804bb40) L 804bb20 R 804bb60 P 0 S 0 ^ 0
        3(804bb60) L 0 R 0 P 804bb20 S 0 ^ 804bb40
        1(804bb20) L 0 R 0 P 0 S 804bb60 ^ 804bb40

### moveup ###
_last= 804bb40, _active= 804bb60, _frontier= 804bb40
    3(804bb60) L 804bb20 R 804bb40 P 0 S 0 ^ 0
```

```
    2(804bb40) L 0 R 0 P 804bb20 S 0 ^ 804bb60
    1(804bb20) L 0 R 0 P 0 S 0 ^ 0
```

insert 4
*** moveup ***
_last= 804bb80, _active= 804bb40, _frontier= 804bb80
```
    3(804bb60) L 804bb20 R 804bb40 P 0 S 0 ^ 0
        2(804bb40) L 804bb80 R 0 P 804bb20 S 0 ^ 804bb60
            4(804bb80) L 0 R 0 P 0 S 0 ^ 804bb40
    1(804bb20) L 0 R 0 P 0 S 0 ^ 0
```

moveup
_last= 804bb60, _active= 804bb80, _frontier= 804bb80
```
    4(804bb80) L 804bb20 R 804bb60 P 0 S 0 ^ 0
        3(804bb60) L 804bb40 R 0 P 804bb20 S 0 ^ 804bb80
            2(804bb40) L 0 R 0 P 0 S 0 ^ 0
    1(804bb20) L 0 R 0 P 0 S 0 ^ 804bb80
```

insert 5
*** moveup ***
_last= 804bba0, _active= 804bb80, _frontier= 804bba0
```
    4(804bb80) L 804bba0 R 804bb60 P 0 S 0 ^ 0
        3(804bb60) L 804bb40 R 0 P 804bb20 S 0 ^ 804bb80
            2(804bb40) L 0 R 0 P 0 S 0 ^ 0
    5(804bba0) L 0 R 0 P 0 S 0 ^ 804bb80
```

moveup
_last= 804bb80, _active= 804bba0, _frontier= 804bba0
```
    5(804bba0) L 804bb80 R 804bb60 P 0 S 0 ^ 0
        3(804bb60) L 804bb40 R 0 P 804bb20 S 0 ^ 0
            2(804bb40) L 0 R 0 P 0 S 0 ^ 0
    4(804bb80) L 0 R 0 P 0 S 0 ^ 804bba0
```

insert 6
*** moveup ***
_last= 804bbc0, _active= 804bba0, _frontier= 804bbc0
```
    5(804bba0) L 804bbc0 R 804bb60 P 0 S 0 ^ 0
        3(804bb60) L 804bb40 R 0 P 804bb20 S 0 ^ 0
            2(804bb40) L 0 R 0 P 0 S 0 ^ 0
    6(804bbc0) L 0 R 0 P 0 S 0 ^ 804bba0
```

```
### moveup ###
_last= 804bba0, _active= 804bbc0, _frontier= 804bbc0
    6(804bbc0) L 804bba0 R 804bb60 P 0 S 0 ^ 0
        3(804bb60) L 804bb40 R 0 P 804bb20 S 0 ^ 0
            2(804bb40) L 0 R 0 P 0 S 0 ^ 0
        5(804bba0) L 0 R 0 P 0 S 0 ^ 804bbc0

insert 7
*** moveup ***
### moveup ###
insert 8
*** moveup ***
### moveup ###
    8
        3
            2
        7
```

The values of these static variables are not what they should be.

5.1.3.3   **The fault and correction**

We insert the following code and rerun the test:

```
Heap * parent= this->getParent();
if( this->getKey() > parent->getKey() ) {
    // update variables
    if ( _frontier == this ) {
        _frontier= parent;
    }
    _last= parent;
    _active= this;
}
```

The values of the static variables are correct on input to the *movedown* function. The values are incorrect on exit from the *movedown* function, and nodes are still disappearing. Still, we are making progress.

In this round of debugging, we applied the following methods from Chapter 2:

- Pay attention to unusual details.

- Gather facts before hypothesizing.

We found two defects that had the following root causes, explained in Chapter 11:

- Missing operations—missing statements

- Reference errors—variable not assigned

5.1.4   Bug 3

5.1.4.1   The evidence

The third debugging session began by running the application standalone again. The test input and test driver are still the same. The results of executing this test are shown as follows:

```
test 1:8

insert 2

*** moveup ***
_last= 804bb60, _active= 804bb80, _frontier= 804bb60
    1(804bb60) L 804bb80 R 0 P 0 S 0 ^ 0
        2(804bb80) L 0 R 0 P 0 S 0 ^ 804bb60

### moveup ###
_last= 804bb60, _active= 804bb80, _frontier= 804bb60
    2(804bb80) L 804bb60 R 0 P 0 S 0 ^ 0
        1(804bb60) L 0 R 0 P 0 S 0 ^ 804bb80

insert 3

*** moveup ***
_last= 804bb80, _active= 804bba0, _frontier= 804bb60
    2(804bb80) L 804bb60 R 804bba0 P 0 S 0 ^ 0
        3(804bba0) L 0 R 0 P 804bb60 S 0 ^ 804bb80
        1(804bb60) L 0 R 0 P 0 S 804bba0 ^ 804bb80
```

```
### moveup ###
_last= 804bb80, _active= 804bba0, _frontier= 804bb60
    3(804bba0) L 804bb60 R 804bb80 P 0 S 0 ^ 0
        2(804bb80) L 0 R 0 P 804bb60 S 0 ^ 804bba0
        1(804bb60) L 0 R 0 P 0 S 0 ^ 0


insert 4


*** moveup ***
_last= 804bb60, _active= 804bbc0, _frontier= 804bb60
    3(804bba0) L 804bb60 R 804bb80 P 0 S 0 ^ 0
        2(804bb80) L 0 R 0 P 804bb60 S 0 ^ 804bba0
        1(804bb60) L 804bbc0 R 0 P 0 S 0 ^ 0
            4(804bbc0) L 0 R 0 P 0 S 0 ^ 804bb60


### moveup ###
_last= 804bb60, _active= 804bbc0, _frontier= 804bb60
    3(804bba0) L 804bb60 R 804bb80 P 0 S 0 ^ 0
        2(804bb80) L 0 R 0 P 804bb60 S 0 ^ 804bba0
        1(804bb60) L 0 R 0 P 0 S 0 ^ 804bbc0


insert 5


*** moveup ***
_last= 804bbc0, _active= 804bbe0, _frontier= 804bb60
    3(804bba0) L 804bb60 R 804bb80 P 0 S 0 ^ 0
        2(804bb80) L 0 R 0 P 804bb60 S 0 ^ 804bba0
        1(804bb60) L 0 R 0 P 0 S 804bbe0 ^ 804bbc0


### moveup ###
_last= 804bbc0, _active= 804bbe0, _frontier= 804bb60
    3(804bba0) L 804bb60 R 804bb80 P 0 S 0 ^ 0
        2(804bb80) L 0 R 0 P 804bb60 S 0 ^ 804bba0
        1(804bb60) L 0 R 0 P 0 S 0 ^ 0


insert 6


*** moveup ***
_last= 804bb60, _active= 804bc00, _frontier= 804bb60
    3(804bba0) L 804bb60 R 804bb80 P 0 S 0 ^ 0
        2(804bb80) L 0 R 0 P 804bb60 S 0 ^ 804bba0
```

```
                    1(804bb60) L 804bc00 R 0 P 0 S 0 ^ 0
                        6(804bc00) L 0 R 0 P 0 S 0 ^ 804bb60


### moveup ###
_last= 804bb60, _active= 804bc00, _frontier= 804bb60
    3(804bba0) L 804bb60 R 804bb80 P 0 S 0 ^ 0
        2(804bb80) L 0 R 0 P 804bb60 S 0 ^ 804bba0
        1(804bb60) L 0 R 0 P 0 S 0 ^ 804bc00


insert 7


*** moveup ***
_last= 804bc00, _active= 804bc20, _frontier= 804bb60
    3(804bba0) L 804bb60 R 804bb80 P 0 S 0 ^ 0
        2(804bb80) L 0 R 0 P 804bb60 S 0 ^ 804bba0
        1(804bb60) L 0 R 0 P 0 S 804bc20 ^ 804bc00


### moveup ###
_last= 804bc00, _active= 804bc20, _frontier= 804bb60
    3(804bba0) L 804bb60 R 804bb80 P 0 S 0 ^ 0
        2(804bb80) L 0 R 0 P 804bb60 S 0 ^ 804bba0
        1(804bb60) L 0 R 0 P 0 S 0 ^ 0


insert 8


*** moveup ***
_last= 804bb60, _active= 804bc40, _frontier= 804bb60
    3(804bba0) L 804bb60 R 804bb80 P 0 S 0 ^ 0
        2(804bb80) L 0 R 0 P 804bb60 S 0 ^ 804bba0
        1(804bb60) L 804bc40 R 0 P 0 S 0 ^ 0
            8(804bc40) L 0 R 0 P 0 S 0 ^ 804bb60


### moveup ###
_last= 804bb60, _active= 804bc40, _frontier= 804bb60
    3(804bba0) L 804bb60 R 804bb80 P 0 S 0 ^ 0
        2(804bb80) L 0 R 0 P 804bb60 S 0 ^ 804bba0
        1(804bb60) L 0 R 0 P 0 S 0 ^ 804bc40



      3

        2

        1
```

5.1.4.2   The investigation

The data structure has become defective by the end of the *moveup* function processing for the node with key "4." That node has disappeared, and the node with key "1" has a pointer to a parent that does not exist, which happens to be the address of the missing node.

We decide that we should run the application under the debugger, set breakpoints at key sections of the code, and dump the data structure at those points. The results of this experiment are listed as follows:

```
(gdb)
Breakpoint 1 at 0x8048bc8: file Heap.c, line 144.
Breakpoint 2 at 0x8048d78: file Heap.c, line 168.
Breakpoint 3 at 0x8048f40: file Heap.c, line 197.
Breakpoint 4 at 0x804911b: file Heap.c, line 225.

(gdb) run
test 1:8

insert 2

*** moveup ***
_last= 804bb60, _active= 804bb80, _frontier= 804bb60
    1(804bb60) L 804bb80 R 0 P 0 S 0 ^ 0
        2(804bb80) L 0 R 0 P 0 S 0 ^ 804bb60


...


### moveup ###
_last= 804bb60, _active= 804bb80, _frontier= 804bb60
    2(804bb80) L 804bb60 R 0 P 0 S 0 ^ 0
        1(804bb60) L 0 R 0 P 0 S 0 ^ 804bb80

insert 3

*** moveup ***
_last= 804bb80, _active= 804bba0, _frontier= 804bb60
    2(804bb80) L 804bb60 R 804bba0 P 0 S 0 ^ 0
        3(804bba0) L 0 R 0 P 804bb60 S 0 ^ 804bb80
        1(804bb60) L 0 R 0 P 0 S 804bba0 ^ 804bb80


...


### moveup ###
_last= 804bb80, _active= 804bba0, _frontier= 804bb60
```

```
    3(804bba0) L 804bb60 R 804bb80 P 0 S 0 ^ 0
      2(804bb80) L 0 R 0 P 804bb60 S 0 ^ 804bba0
      1(804bb60) L 0 R 0 P 0 S 0 ^ 0

insert 4

*** moveup ***
_last= 804bb60, _active= 804bbc0, _frontier= 804bb60
    3(804bba0) L 804bb60 R 804bb80 P 0 S 0 ^ 0
      2(804bb80) L 0 R 0 P 804bb60 S 0 ^ 804bba0
      1(804bb60) L 804bbc0 R 0 P 0 S 0 ^ 0
        4(804bbc0) L 0 R 0 P 0 S 0 ^ 804bb60


Breakpoint 1, moveup__4Heap (this=0x804bbc0) at Heap.c:144
144        if( this == parent->getLeft() ) {
    3(804bba0) L 804bb60 R 804bb80 P 0 S 0 ^ 0
      2(804bb80) L 0 R 0 P 804bb60 S 0 ^ 804bba0
      1(804bb60) L 804bbc0 R 0 P 0 S 0 ^ 804bbc0
        4(804bbc0) L 0 R 0 P 0 S 0 ^ 0

Breakpoint 3, moveup__4Heap (this=0x804bbc0) at Heap.c:197
197        if( this->getPred() != 0 ) {
    3(804bba0) L 804bb60 R 804bb80 P 0 S 0 ^ 0
      2(804bb80) L 0 R 0 P 804bb60 S 0 ^ 804bba0
      1(804bb60) L 0 R 0 P 0 S 0 ^ 804bbc0
```

The results from the first set of breakpoints show us that the data structure is valid at line 144 and invalid at line 197. This eliminates the code outside of these bounds. The node with key "4" has disappeared by the end-point of this segment.

Having eliminated a large part of the code as a source of possible causes, we move on to a manual inspection of these lines. We are looking for code that would cause an existing node to become unlinked from the data structure. To unlink something is to make its pointer null.

5.1.4.3   **The fault and correction**

As we review the code, we find two statements in our zone of suspicion that are setting pointers to null when they should be setting them to *this,* and two that should be setting them to the parent of the node, and yet two more that should be setting pointers to *this.*

```
parent->getRight()->setParent(0);
```

```
parent->getLeft()->setParent(0);

this->getPred()->setSucc(0);

this->getSucc()->setPred(0);

parent->getPred()->setSucc(0);

parent->getSucc()->setPred(0);
```

We change the arguments to *this* and *parent* as appropriate.

In this round of debugging, we applied the following methods from Chapter 2:

■ Start by observing.

■ Eliminate impossible causes.

We found two defects that had the following root causes, explained in Chapter 11:

■ Reference errors—wrong variable referenced

■ Reference errors—wrong constant referenced

5.1.5   **Bug 4**

5.1.5.1   **The evidence**

The next debugging session began by running the application as before. The test input and test driver are still the same. The results of executing this test are shown as follows:

```
test 1:8

     8
         2
         7
             6
                 5
```

$$4$$
$$3$$
$$1$$

We are making some progress. We are now getting all of the nodes inserted into the data structure. Unfortunately, the structure is still invalid.

5.1.5.2   The investigation

We start our investigation by turning on the detailed display of the data structure and rerunning the application. We get the following results:

```
test 1:8
insert 2
*** moveup ***
_last= 804bc20, _active= 804bc40, _frontier= 804bc20
    1(804bc20) L 804bc40 R 0 P 0 S 0 ^ 0
        2(804bc40) L 0 R 0 P 0 S 0 ^ 804bc20

### moveup ###
_last= 804bc20, _active= 804bc40, _frontier= 804bc20
    2(804bc40) L 804bc20 R 0 P 0 S 0 ^ 0
        1(804bc20) L 0 R 0 P 0 S 0 ^ 804bc40

insert 3
*** moveup ***
_last= 804bc40, _active= 804bc60, _frontier= 804bc20
    2(804bc40) L 804bc20 R 804bc60 P 0 S 0 ^ 0
        3(804bc60) L 0 R 0 P 804bc20 S 0 ^ 804bc40
        1(804bc20) L 0 R 0 P 0 S 804bc60 ^ 804bc40

### moveup ###
_last= 804bc40, _active= 804bc60, _frontier= 804bc20
    3(804bc60) L 804bc20 R 804bc40 P 0 S 0 ^ 0
        2(804bc40) L 0 R 0 P 804bc20 S 0 ^ 804bc60
        1(804bc20) L 0 R 0 P 0 S 804bc40 ^ 804bc60

insert 4
*** moveup ***
_last= 804bc20, _active= 804bc80, _frontier= 804bc20
    3(804bc60) L 804bc20 R 804bc40 P 0 S 0 ^ 0
        2(804bc40) L 0 R 0 P 804bc20 S 0 ^ 804bc60
        1(804bc20) L 804bc80 R 0 P 0 S 804bc40 ^ 804bc60
            4(804bc80) L 0 R 0 P 0 S 0 ^ 804bc20
```

```
### moveup ###
_last= 804bc60, _active= 804bc80, _frontier= 804bc20
    4(804bc80) L 804bc60 R 804bc40 P 0 S 0 ^ 0
        2(804bc40) L 0 R 0 P 804bc60 S 0 ^ 804bc80
        3(804bc60) L 804bc20 R 0 P 0 S 804bc40 ^ 804bc80
            1(804bc20) L 0 R 0 P 0 S 0 ^ 804bc60

insert 5
*** moveup ***
_last= 804bc20, _active= 804bca0, _frontier= 804bc20
    4(804bc80) L 804bc60 R 804bc40 P 0 S 0 ^ 0
        2(804bc40) L 0 R 0 P 804bc60 S 0 ^ 804bc80
        3(804bc60) L 804bc20 R 0 P 0 S 804bc40 ^ 804bc80
            1(804bc20) L 804bca0 R 0 P 0 S 0 ^ 804bc60
                5(804bca0) L 0 R 0 P 0 S 0 ^ 804bc20


### moveup ###
_last= 804bc80, _active= 804bca0, _frontier= 804bc20
    5(804bca0) L 804bc80 R 804bc40 P 0 S 0 ^ 0
        2(804bc40) L 0 R 0 P 804bc80 S 0 ^ 804bca0
        4(804bc80) L 804bc60 R 0 P 0 S 804bc40 ^ 804bca0
            3(804bc60) L 804bc20 R 0 P 0 S 0 ^ 804bc80
                1(804bc20) L 0 R 0 P 0 S 0 ^ 804bc60

insert 6
*** moveup ***
_last= 804bc20, _active= 804bcc0, _frontier= 804bc20
    5(804bca0) L 804bc80 R 804bc40 P 0 S 0 ^ 0
        2(804bc40) L 0 R 0 P 804bc80 S 0 ^ 804bca0
        4(804bc80) L 804bc60 R 0 P 0 S 804bc40 ^ 804bca0
            3(804bc60) L 804bc20 R 0 P 0 S 0 ^ 804bc80
                1(804bc20) L 804bcc0 R 0 P 0 S 0 ^ 804bc60
                    6(804bcc0) L 0 R 0 P 0 S 0 ^ 804bc20


### moveup ###
_last= 804bca0, _active= 804bcc0, _frontier= 804bc20
    6(804bcc0) L 804bca0 R 804bc40 P 0 S 0 ^ 0
        2(804bc40) L 0 R 0 P 804bca0 S 0 ^ 804bcc0
        5(804bca0) L 804bc80 R 0 P 0 S 804bc40 ^ 804bcc0
            4(804bc80) L 804bc60 R 0 P 0 S 0 ^ 804bca0
                3(804bc60) L 804bc20 R 0 P 0 S 0 ^ 804bc80
                    1(804bc20) L 0 R 0 P 0 S 0 ^ 804bc60

insert 7
*** moveup ***
_last= 804bc20, _active= 804bce0, _frontier= 804bc20
    6(804bcc0) L 804bca0 R 804bc40 P 0 S 0 ^ 0
```

```
                    2(804bc40) L 0 R 0 P 804bca0 S 0 ^ 804bcc0
                  5(804bca0) L 804bc80 R 0 P 0 S 804bc40 ^ 804bcc0
                4(804bc80) L 804bc60 R 0 P 0 S 0 ^ 804bca0
              3(804bc60) L 804bc20 R 0 P 0 S 0 ^ 804bc80
            1(804bc20) L 804bce0 R 0 P 0 S 0 ^ 804bc60
          7(804bce0) L 0 R 0 P 0 S 0 ^ 804bc20


### moveup ###
_last= 804bcc0, _active= 804bce0, _frontier= 804bc20
    7(804bce0) L 804bcc0 R 804bc40 P 0 S 0 ^ 0
      2(804bc40) L 0 R 0 P 804bcc0 S 0 ^ 804bce0
      6(804bcc0) L 804bca0 R 0 P 0 S 804bc40 ^ 804bce0
        5(804bca0) L 804bc80 R 0 P 0 S 0 ^ 804bcc0
          4(804bc80) L 804bc60 R 0 P 0 S 0 ^ 804bca0
            3(804bc60) L 804bc20 R 0 P 0 S 0 ^ 804bc80
              1(804bc20) L 0 R 0 P 0 S 0 ^ 804bc60


insert 8
*** moveup ***
_last= 804bc20, _active= 804bd00, _frontier= 804bc20
    7(804bce0) L 804bcc0 R 804bc40 P 0 S 0 ^ 0
      2(804bc40) L 0 R 0 P 804bcc0 S 0 ^ 804bce0
      6(804bcc0) L 804bca0 R 0 P 0 S 804bc40 ^ 804bce0
        5(804bca0) L 804bc80 R 0 P 0 S 0 ^ 804bcc0
          4(804bc80) L 804bc60 R 0 P 0 S 0 ^ 804bca0
            3(804bc60) L 804bc20 R 0 P 0 S 0 ^ 804bc80
              1(804bc20) L 804bd00 R 0 P 0 S 0
                                        ^ 804bc60
                8(804bd00) L 0 R 0 P 0 S 0
                                        ^ 804bc20


### moveup ###
_last= 804bce0, _active= 804bd00, _frontier= 804bc20
    8(804bd00) L 804bce0 R 804bc40 P 0 S 0 ^ 0
      2(804bc40) L 0 R 0 P 804bce0 S 0 ^ 804bd00
      7(804bce0) L 804bcc0 R 0 P 0 S 804bc40 ^ 804bd00
        6(804bcc0) L 804bca0 R 0 P 0 S 0 ^ 804bce0
          5(804bca0) L 804bc80 R 0 P 0 S 0 ^ 804bcc0
            4(804bc80) L 804bc60 R 0 P 0 S 0 ^ 804bca0
              3(804bc60) L 804bc20 R 0 P 0 S 0
                                        ^ 804bc80
                1(804bc20) L 0 R 0 P 0 S 0
                                        ^ 804bc60


          8
            2
            7
```

```
        6
      5
        4
          3
            1
```

We notice that the data structure goes bad after the node with key "5" is inserted. It is no longer a complete binary tree. The node with key "3" should have two children, "1" and "5," not one child with key "1" and one grandchild with key "5." Unlike the previous error, this one manifests itself at the beginning of the *moveup* function.

Three possibilities would lead to problems coming out of the *insert* function:

1. The code is incorrect, and the data being passed from *moveup* is incorrect.

2. The code is incorrect, even though the data being passed from *moveup* is correct.

3. The code is correct, but the data being passed from *moveup* is incorrect.

We need to determine which data might be at fault. We reason backward as follows: The symptom of the problem is that a node is being inserted as the left child of another node, instead of as its sibling (the right child of the parent). Three places in the *insert* function have the following sequence:

```
X->setLeft(Y)
Y->setParent(X)
```

If the data that controls the execution of one of these statements allows it to execute at the wrong time, the manifest problem would result.

The next step is to execute the application in the debugger and find out which of these sets of statements is performing the invalid insertion. This will enable us to determine whether the variables that control them are incorrect.

We find that the statements that are making the bad insertion are controlled by the following statements:

```
_active= _last->getParent()->getSucc();
if( _active == 0 ) {
...
}
```

The value of the *_last* variable is clearly wrong. We must identify the statement that assigned the value to it. This is easy, since the function previously executed was *moveup* and at the very end of that function, there are assignments to both *_last* and *_active*.

We consider the values being assigned and cannot come up with a good reason why these statements are in this function. We decide to comment them out, so that we can observe the values they are masking. We rebuild and restart the debugger. After setting a breakpoint on the statement we know is causing the problem, we rerun the program.

It stops once before the problem and then not again until several more nodes are inserted. Once we regain control, we display the data structure and are delighted to find that everything has been built correctly.

5.1.5.3   **The fault and correction**

To correct the problem, we delete the following code at the end of the *moveup* function:

```
_last= parent;
_active= this;
```

In this round of debugging, we applied the following methods from Chapter 2:

- Eliminate impossible causes.
- Gather facts before hypothesizing.
- Pay attention to unusual details.

We found two defects that had the following root cause, explained in Chapter 11:

- Extra operations—extra statements

Since we believe that we have the *insert* and *moveup* functions working properly, we subject them to a larger set of tests.

```
// sorted up, power of 2 length
int t01[8]= { 1,2,3,4,5,6,7,8 };

// sorted up, non-power of 2 length
int t02[9]= { 2,3,5,7,11,13,17,19,23 };

// sorted down, power of 2 length
int t03[16]= { 32,30,28,26,24,22,20,18,16,14,12,10,8,6,4,2 };

// sorted down, non-power of 2 length
int t04[14]= { 27,25,23,21,19,17,15,13,11,9,7,5,3,1 };

// "V" pattern, power of 2 length
int t05[16]= { 2, 5, 11, 17, 29, 37, 47, 57,
               61, 53, 41, 31, 23, 13, 7, 3 };

// "V" pattern, non-power of 2 length
int t06[11]= {  2, 4, 6, 8, 10, 12, 11, 9, 7, 5, 3 };

// inverse "V" pattern, power of 2 length
int t07[32]= { 109, 103, 97, 87, 79, 71, 61, 57,
               47, 41, 31, 23, 17, 11, 5, 2,
               3, 7, 13, 19, 29, 37, 43, 53,
               59, 67, 73, 83, 89, 101, 107, 111 };

// inverse "V" pattern, non-power of 2 length
int t08[31]= { 32, 30, 28, 26, 24, 22, 20, 18,
               16, 14, 12, 10, 8, 4, 2,
               1, 3, 5, 7, 9, 11, 13, 15,
               17, 19, 21, 23, 25, 27, 29, 31 };

// random values, power of 2 length
int t09[16]= { 2, 3, 43, 47, 5, 7, 37,
               41, 11, 13, 29, 31, 17, 23, 53, 57 };

// random values, non-power of 2 length
int t10[20]= { 2, 71, 3, 67, 5, 61,
```

```
                              7, 59, 11, 57, 13, 53, 17,
                              47, 23, 43, 29, 41, 31, 37 };

    int main() {

        fprintf(stderr,"test 1:8\n");
        testBuild(new Heap(8, t01));
        fprintf(stderr,"test 2:9\n");
        testBuild(new Heap(9, t02));
        fprintf(stderr,"test 3:16\n");
        testBuild(new Heap(16, t03));
        fprintf(stderr,"test 4:14\n");
        testBuild(new Heap(14, t04));
        fprintf(stderr,"test 5:16\n");
        testBuild(new Heap(16, t05));
        fprintf(stderr,"test 6:11\n");
        testBuild(new Heap(11, t06));
        fprintf(stderr,"test 7:32\n");
        testBuild(new Heap(32, t07));
        fprintf(stderr,"test 8:31\n");
        testBuild(new Heap(31, t08));
        fprintf(stderr,"test 9:16\n");
        testBuild(new Heap(16, t09));
        fprintf(stderr,"test 10:20\n");
        testBuild(new Heap(20, t10));
    }

    void testBuild(Heap *node) {
        draw(node->getRoot());
        fprintf(stderr,"\n");
    }

    //----------------------------------------------------

    int indent= 0;
    void draw(Heap * n) {
        int i;
        indent += 4;
        if( n != 0 ) {
            for( i=0; i<indent; ++i ) {
                fputc(' ',stderr);
```

```
        }
        fprintf(stderr,"%d\n",n->getKey());
        draw(n->getRight());
        draw(n->getLeft());
    }
    indent -= 4;
}
```

The results of running these tests are listed as follows:

```
test 1:8
    8
        6
            5
            2
        7
            3
            4
                1


test 2:9
    23
        13
            11
            3
        19
            5
            17
                7
                2


test 3:16
    32
        28
            20
                4
                6
            22
                8
                10
        30
```

```
                              24
                                 12
                                 14
                              26
                                 16
                                 18
                                    2

                  test 4:14
                     27
                        23
                           15
                              1
                           17
                              3
                              5
                        25
                           19
                              7
                              9
                           21
                              11
                              13

                  test 5:16
                     61
                        37
                           29
                              7
                              13
                           31
                              23
                              5
                        57
                        53
                           41
                           11
                           47
                              17
                              3
                                 2
```

```
test 6:11
    12
        11
            10
            4
        9
            6
                3
                5
            8
                7
                2

test 7:32
    111
        107
            101
                97
                    89
                    5
                83
                    61
                    11
            73
                71
                    67
                    17
                59
                    53
                    23
        109
            79
                43
                    37
                    31
                41
                    29
                    19
            103
                47
```

```
                                                13
                                                7
                                        87
                                                3
                                                57
                                                   2


            test 8:31
                32
                    31
                        29
                            28
                                27
                                2
                            25
                                20
                                4
                        23
                            22
                                21
                                8
                            19
                                17
                                10
                    30
                        24
                            15
                                13
                                12
                            14
                                11
                                9
                        26
                            16
                                7
                                5
                            18
                                3
                                1


            test 9:16
```

```
57
    47
        37
            23
            7
        31
            17
            3
    53
        29
            13
            5
        43
            11
            41
                2

    test 10:20
    71
        61
            47
                23
                7
            53
                17
                3
        67
            57
                13
                37
                    5
            59
                41
                    31
                    11
                43
                    29
                    2
```

At this point, the functions *insert* and *moveup* have undergone quite a bit of revision, but they seem to be working, so we list their sources as follows:

```
//----------------------------------------------------
// insert a Heap node at the end of the heap
//----------------------------------------------------

void Heap::insert() {

    this->setPred(0);
    this->setSucc(0);
    if( _active->getLeft() == 0 ) {
        _active->setLeft(this);
        this->setParent(_active);
        if ( this->getID() == _power ) {
            _frontier= this;
            _power *= 2;
        }
        _last= this;
    } else if( _active->getRight() == 0 ) {
        _active->setRight(this);
        this->setParent(_active);
        _last->setSucc(this);
        this->setPred(_last);
        if ( this->getID() == _power-1 ) {
            _active= _frontier;
        }
        _last= this;
    } else {
        _active= _last->getParent()->getSucc();
        if( _active == 0 ) {
            _active= _frontier;
            _active->setLeft(this);
            this->setParent(_active);
            _frontier= this;
        } else {
            _active->setLeft(this);
            this->setParent(_active);
            _last->setSucc(this);
            this->setPred(_last);
        }
        _last= this;
    }
```

```
        Heap * parent= this->getParent();
        if( this->getKey() > parent->getKey() ) {
            // update variables
            if ( _frontier == this ) {
                _frontier= parent;
            }
            _last= parent;
            _active= this;
        }
    }


    //----------------------------------------------------
    // re-arrange the heap after appending a node at the
    // end of the binary tree so that the heap property
    // is preserved
    //----------------------------------------------------

    void Heap::moveup() {

        Heap *temp;

        while( true  ) {
            Heap * parent= this->getParent();
            if( !parent || parent->getKey() >=
                            this->getKey() ) {
                break;
            }

            // swap ID numbers
            int swap= parent->getID();
            parent->setID(this->getID());
            this->setID(swap);

            // swap incoming vertical pointers
            Heap * grand= parent->getParent();
            if( grand != 0 ) {
                if( parent == grand->getLeft() ) {
                    grand->setLeft(this);
                } else if( parent == grand->getRight() ) {
                    grand->setRight(this);
                }
```

```
                    }

                    // swap outgoing vertical pointers
                    parent->setParent(this);
                    this->setParent(grand);

                    if( this == parent->getLeft() ) {
                        if( this->getLeft() != 0 ) {
                            this->getLeft()->setParent(parent);
                        }
                        parent->setLeft(this->getLeft());
                        this->setLeft(parent);

                        if( this->getRight() != 0 ) {
                            if( parent->getRight() != 0 ) {
                                temp= parent->getRight()
                                          ->getParent();
                                parent->getRight()->setParent(this->
                                        getRight()->getParent());
                                this->getRight()->setParent(temp);
                            } else {
                                this->getRight()->setParent(0);
                            }
                        } else {
                            if( parent->getRight() != 0 ) {
                                parent->getRight()->setParent(this);
                            }
                        }

                        temp= this->getRight();
                        this->setRight(parent->getRight());
                        parent->setRight(temp);
                    } else if( this == parent->getRight() ) {
                        if( this->getRight() != 0 ) {
                            this->getRight()->setParent(parent);
                        }
                        parent->setRight(this->getRight());
                        this->setRight(parent);

                        if( this->getLeft() != 0 ) {
                            if( parent->getLeft() != 0 ) {
```

```
                        temp= parent->getLeft()->getParent();
                        parent->getLeft()->setParent(this->
                                getLeft()->getParent());
                        this->getLeft()->setParent(temp);
                    } else {
                        this->getLeft()->setParent(0);
                    }
                } else {
                    if( parent->getLeft() != 0 ) {
                        parent->getLeft()->setParent(this);
                    }
                }

                temp= this->getLeft();
                this->setLeft(parent->getLeft());
                parent->setLeft(temp);
            } else {
                assert(0);
            }

            // swap incoming horizontal pointers
            if( this->getPred() != 0 ) {
                if( parent->getPred() != 0 ) {
                    temp= parent->getPred()->getSucc();
                    parent->getPred()->setSucc(this->
                            getPred()->getSucc());
                    this->getPred()->setSucc(temp);
                } else {
                    this->getPred()->setSucc(parent);
                }
            } else {
                if( parent->getPred() != 0 ) {
                    parent->getPred()->setSucc(this);
                }
            }
            if( this->getSucc() != 0 ) {
                if( parent->getSucc() != 0 ) {
                    temp= parent->getSucc()->getPred();
                    parent->getSucc()->setPred(this->
                            getSucc()->getPred());
                    this->getSucc()->setPred(temp);
```

```
                    } else {
                        this->getSucc()->setPred(parent);
                    }
                } else {
                    if( parent->getSucc() != 0 ) {
                        parent->getSucc()->setPred(this);
                    }
                }

                // swap outgoing horizontal pointers
                temp= parent->getPred();
                parent->setPred(this->getPred());
                this->setPred(temp);

                temp= parent->getSucc();
                parent->setSucc(this->getSucc());
                this->setSucc(temp);

                // update variables
                _active= _last->getParent();
                if( _root == parent ) {
                    _root= this;
                }
            }
        }
```

5.1.6   Bug 5

5.1.6.1   The evidence

The next debugging session began by running the application under the GNU debugger (*gdb*). The test input and test driver are listed as follows:

```
void testSort(Heap *);

// sorted up, power of 2 length
int t01[8]= { 1,2,3,4,5,6,7,8 };

int main() {
```

```
        Heap *node, *first;

        fprintf(stderr,"test 1:8\n");
        testSort(new Heap(8, t01));
    }

void testSort(Heap *in) {
    Heap * node=  in->sort();
    for( ; node != 0; node= node->getSucc() ) {
        fprintf(stderr,"%d ", node->getKey());
    }
    fprintf(stderr,"\n");
}
```

The results of running this test are shown as follows:

```
(gdb) run
Starting program: /home/metzger/h.exe
test 1:8

Program received signal SIGSEGV, Segmentation fault.
0x0804a585 in setSucc__4HeapP4Heap (this=0x0, x=0x0) at
Heap.h:34
34      inline void setSucc(Heap * x) { _succ= x; }
(gdb) bt
#0  0x0804a585 in setSucc__4HeapP4Heap (this=0x0, x=0x0) at
Heap.h:34
#1  0x080499f1 in remove__4Heap (this=0x804c038) at
Heap.c:396
#2  0x08049be3 in sort__4Heap (this=0x804c038) at Heap.c:441
#3  0x0804a25d in testSort__FP4Heap (in=0x804c038) at
HeapTest.c:110
...
```

5.1.6.2   The investigation

We observe that the immediate cause of the failure is that *this* does not point to a valid heap object, but rather has the null pointer value. We use one of our most basic tools, enumerating and eliminating possibilities.

1.   The variable should always have a null value.

2.   The variable should never have a null value.

3.   The variable should sometimes have a null value.

      a.   The statement should never be executed.

      b.   The statement should sometimes be executed.

      c.   The statement should always be executed.

Possibility 1 means that the pointer is useless, so we immediately eliminate it. The pointer in question is a predecessor. It is correct for the predecessor pointer to be null when the node is the leftmost node on a row. This eliminates possibility 2.

The problem was a result of the variable sometimes having a null value, and the statement always being executed, so we can reject possibility 3c. Possibility 3a means the code is meaningless, which we know isn't true, so we reject it. We reconsider the purpose of the original statement. When a node is removed from the data structure, all pointers to it should be removed. Since the statement is removing one of those pointers, the only logical possibility is that the statement should be executed only when the intermediate pointer has a nonnull value.

While we are eliminating logical impossibilities, we exercise some curiosity and review the code that will be executed later. In the *sort* function, we find a problem that is the converse of the one we just analyzed. We have a conditional statement guarding some pointer references that guarantees that one of the pointers is null. This statement can never be correctly executed under this condition.

In this round of debugging, we applied the following methods from Chapter 3:

- Enumerate possibilities.
- Exercise curiosity.

We found two defects that both had the following root cause, explained in Chapter 11:

- Control-flow problem—statement controlled by wrong control-flow condition.

5.1.6.3   The fault and correction

In this round of debugging, we found two problems. The *remove* function makes an unguarded reference thus:

```
_last->getPred()->setSucc(0);
```

We must guard it with a test for the value of the intermediate

pointer:

```
if ( _last->getPred() != 0 ) {
    _last->getPred()->setSucc(0);
}
```

The *sort* function makes a reference through a pointer that is known to be null, as a result of a careless symmetrical coding of cases that were not actually symmetric. The original code looked like the following:

```
if ( last == 0 ) {
    head= next;
    next->setPred(0);
    last->setSucc(next);
} else {
    next->setPred(last);
    last->setSucc(next);
}
```

The modified code removed the unnecessary operation.

```
if ( last == 0 ) {
    head= next;
    next->setPred(0);
} else {
    next->setPred(last);
    last->setSucc(next);
}
```

5.1.7 Bug 6

5.1.7.1 The evidence

The next debugging session began by running the application under the GNU debugger (*gdb*). We use the same test data and driver as in the previous session. We inserted the following line of code into the *sort* function, after the call to remove, to observe the progress of the sort:

```
fprintf(stderr,"remove %d\n",next->getKey());
```

The results of running this test are shown as follows:

```
(gdb) run
Starting program: /home/metzger/h.exe
test 1:8
remove 8
remove 7
remove 6
remove 5
remove 4

Program received signal SIGSEGV, Segmentation fault.
0x0804a512 in getLeft__4Heap (this=0x0) at Heap.h:15
15    inline Heap * getLeft() { return _left; }
(gdb) bt
#0  0x0804a512 in getLeft__4Heap (this=0x0) at Heap.h:15
#1  0x08049a24 in remove__4Heap (this=0x804c080) at
Heap.c:399
#2  0x08049bfb in sort__4Heap (this=0x804c080) at Heap.c:443
#3  0x0804a28d in testSort__FP4Heap (in=0x804c080) at
HeapTest.c:110
...
```

5.1.7.2 The investigation

We start the program under the debugger and set a breakpoint at the statement that is failing. Each time the statement is encountered, we print the value of the pointer variable in question. The statement executes four times before we encounter the problem.

We notice that the offending statement is another that contains multiple pointer dereferences. The question comes to mind, are there nodes that legitimately have a null pointer for a parent? The answer is yes, just one—the root. We print the value of the _root and _last variables and see that they are identical.

After correcting the problem, we run the code again under the debugger. It immediately goes into an endless loop. We start reading the code looking for a faulty termination condition. We do not find any termination condition at all.

In this round of debugging, we applied the following methods from Chapter 3:

- Show how something could be done.
- Exercise curiosity.

We found two defects that had the following root causes, explained in Chapter 11:

- Control-flow problem—statement controlled by wrong control-flow condition
- Control-flow problem—loop never terminates

5.1.7.3   The fault and correction

In this round of debugging, we found two problems. The *remove* function makes an unguarded reference thus:

```
if ( _last == _last->getParent()->getLeft() ) {
        _last->getParent()->setLeft(0);
} else {
        _last->getParent()->setRight(0);
}
```

The node pointed at by the _last variable has a null pointer for its parent. Thus, we must guard it with a test for the value of the intermediate pointer:

```
if( _last->getParent() != 0 ) {
    if ( _last == _last->getParent()->getLeft() ) {
        _last->getParent()->setLeft(0);
    } else {
        _last->getParent()->setRight(0);
    }
}
```

The *remove* function has a more serious flaw. It does not check for a termination condition. The removal process is finished when the node pointed at by the *_last* variable is the same node pointed at by the *_root* variable. We capture the value of the pointer in a local variable *_root* to perform the removal of links in the proper order. When the termination condition is detected, both the *_root* and *_last* variables are set to null to ensure that no further processing will occur.

```
Heap * node= _root;

if( _last != _root ) {
    // original function body inserted here
    _root= _last;
    movedown();
} else {
    _last= 0;
    _root= 0;
}
```

5.1.8   Bug 7

5.1.8.1   The evidence

The next debugging session began by running the application under the GNU debugger (*gdb*). We use the same test data and driver as in the first and second sessions. The results of running this test are shown as follows:

```
(gdb) run
Starting program: /home/metzger/h.exe
test 1:8
remove 8
```

```
remove 7
remove 6
remove 5
remove 4
remove 1
8 7 6 5 4 1
```

```
Program exited normally.
```

5.1.8.2   The investigation

We begin by listing the facts that we can observe:

- The program terminated normally.
- The items that were removed were processed in the correct order.
- Not all of the items were processed.
- The items that were not processed were both of the immediate children of the root.

These observations are suggestive, but we need more data. We add a function to list all of the fields of each node in the data structure.

```
int indent= 0;
void list(Heap * n) {
    indent += 4;
    if( n != 0 ) {
        for( int i=0; i<indent; ++i ) {
            fputc(' ',stderr);
        }
        fprintf(stderr,"%2d(%x)[%d] L %x R %x P
                       %x S %x ^ %x\n",
            n->getKey(), n, n->getID(),
            n->getLeft(), n->getRight(),
            n->getPred(), n->getSucc(),
            n->getParent());
        list(n->getRight());
        list(n->getLeft());
    }
```

```
        indent -= 4;
    }
```

We set a breakpoint at the entry of the *remove* function and display the details of the data structure each time the breakpoint is hit.

The output is shown as follows. The first time the function is entered, all the pointers point to the right node. The second time is also okay. The third time, we notice that the tree is no longer a complete binary tree. The correct node was removed, but the structure was not restored properly afterward.

```
(gdb) run
Starting program: /home/metzger/h.exe
Breakpoint 1 at 0x80499d6: file Heap.c, line 395.
test 1:8

Breakpoint 1, remove__4Heap (this=0x804ba80) at Heap.c:395
395     Heap * node= _root;
    8(804bb60) L 804bb40 R 804bb20 P 0 S 0 ^ 0
        6(804bb20) L 804baa0 R 804bb00 P 804bb40 S 0 ^ 804bb60
            5(804bb00) L 0 R 0 P 804baa0 S 0 ^ 804bb20
            2(804baa0) L 0 R 0 P 804bac0 S 804bb00 ^ 804bb20
        7(804bb40) L 804bae0 R 804bac0 P 0 S 804bb20 ^ 804bb60
            3(804bac0) L 0 R 0 P 804bae0 S 804baa0 ^ 804bb40
            4(804bae0) L 804ba80 R 0 P 0 S 804bac0 ^ 804bb40
                1(804ba80) L 0 R 0 P 0 S 0 ^ 804bae0
$1 = void
remove 8

Breakpoint 1, remove__4Heap (this=0x804ba80) at Heap.c:395
395     Heap * node= _root;
    7(804bb40) L 804bae0 R 804bb20 P 0 S 0 ^ 0
        6(804bb20) L 804baa0 R 804bb00 P 804bae0 S 0 ^ 804bb40
            5(804bb00) L 0 R 0 P 804baa0 S 0 ^ 804bb20
            2(804baa0) L 0 R 0 P 804bac0 S 804bb00 ^ 804bb20
        4(804bae0) L 804ba80 R 804bac0 P 0 S 804bb20 ^ 804bb40
            3(804bac0) L 0 R 0 P 804ba80 S 804baa0 ^ 804bae0
            1(804ba80) L 0 R 0 P 0 S 804bac0 ^ 804bae0
$2 = void
remove 7
```

```
Breakpoint 1, remove__4Heap (this=0x804ba80) at Heap.c:395
395     Heap * node= _root;
    6(804bb20) L 804bae0 R 804bb00 P 0 S 0 ^ 0
        5(804bb00) L 804baa0 R 804ba80 P 804bae0 S 0 ^ 804bb20
            1(804ba80) L 0 R 0 P 804baa0 S 0 ^ 804bb00
            2(804baa0) L 0 R 0 P 804bac0 S 804ba80 ^ 804bb00
        4(804bae0) L 0 R 804bac0 P 0 S 804bb00 ^ 804bb20
            3(804bac0) L 0 R 0 P 804ba80 S 804baa0 ^ 804bae0
$3 = void
remove 6
```

We carefully inspect the pointers in the output. The first and second displays are correct. In the third display, the node with key value of "3" has a predecessor pointer of "804ba80," even though it is the leftmost node at that level and has no logical predecessor.

We reason backward from effect to cause to find the source of the problem. When the root node is removed, the rightmost node on the lowest level is supposed to be inserted as the new root node and then moved down the tree until the data structure meets the heap criteria. The first time a node was removed, the rightmost node (with key "1") was inserted as the root and moved to an appropriate location. The next time a node was removed, the leftmost node (with key "1") was inserted as the root and moved down. This left the tree in an invalid state.

The variable _last_ identifies the variable that will be moved up. We look for the relevant assignment to this variable to determine why it is getting the wrong value. We find none and determine that the lack of an update is the problem.

In this round of debugging, we applied the following methods from Chapter 3:

- Reason based on facts.

- Use the power of logic.

We found a defect that had the following root cause, explained in Chapter 11:

- Reference error—variable was not assigned

5.1.8.3   The fault and correction

The problem is that the *remove* function is not updating the *_last* variable. We determine that the right thing to do is save the back pointer that the last node has to the penultimate node, move the last node, and then record the address of the penultimate node for future processing. This results in the following significant rewrite of this function:

```
Heap * Heap::remove() {

    Heap * node= _root;

    if( _last != _root ) {

        // unlink last node
        Heap * penult= _last->getPred();
        if( penult != 0 ) {
            penult->setSucc(0);
        }
        Heap * parent= _last->getParent();
        if( _last == parent->getLeft() ) {
            parent->setLeft(0);
        } else {
            parent->setRight(0);
        }

        // link last node in as root

        if( _root->getLeft() != 0 ) {
            _root->getLeft()->setParent(_last);
        }
        if( _root->getRight() != 0 ) {
            _root->getRight()->setParent(_last);
        }

        _last->setLeft(_root->getLeft());
        _last->setRight(_root->getRight());
        _last->setParent(_root->getParent());
        _last->setSucc(_root->getSucc());
        _last->setPred(_root->getPred());
        _last->setID(_root->getID());
```

```
            _root= _last;
            _last= penult;
            movedown();
        } else {
            _last= 0;
            _root= 0;
        }

        // unlink removed node
        node->setLeft(0);
        node->setRight(0);
        node->setParent(0);
        node->setSucc(0);
        node->setPred(0);
        node->setID(0);

        return node;
    }
```

5.1.9 Bug 8

5.1.9.1   The evidence

The next debugging session began by running the application under the GNU debugger (*gdb*). To have confidence in the input to the sorting process, we inserted a function to draw the tree using ASCII characters and indentation to show the structure. We also inserted calls at the start and end of the *movedown* function to show the tree data structure after each move. The test input and test driver are listed as follows:

```
void draw(Heap *);
void testBuild(Heap *);
void testSort(Heap *);

// sorted up, power of 2 length
int t01[8]= { 1,2,3,4,5,6,7,8 };

int main() {
```

```
        Heap *node, *first;

        fprintf(stderr,"test 1:8\n");
        node= new Heap(8, t01);
        testBuild(node);
        testSort(node);
    }

    void testBuild(Heap *node) {
        draw(node->getRoot());
        fprintf(stderr,"\n");
    }

    void testSort(Heap *in) {
        Heap * node=  in->sort();
        for( ; node != 0; node= node->getSucc() ) {
            fprintf(stderr,"%d ", node->getKey());
        }
        fprintf(stderr,"\n");
    }

    int indent= 0;
    void draw(Heap * n) {
        int i;
        indent += 4;
        if( n != 0 ) {
            for( i=0; i<indent; ++i ) {
                fputc(' ',stderr);
            }
            fprintf(stderr,"%d\n",n->getKey());
            draw(n->getRight());
            draw(n->getLeft());
        }
        indent -= 4;
    }
```

The results of running this test are shown as follows:

```
(gdb) run
Starting program: /home/metzger/h.exe
test 1:8
```

```
            8
        6
            5
            2
        7
            3
            4
                1


*** movedown ***
    1(804bb00) L 804bbc0 R 804bba0 P 0 S 0 ^ 0
        6(804bba0) L 804bb20 R 804bb80 P 804bbc0 S 0 ^ 804bb00
            5(804bb80) L 0 R 0 P 804bb20 S 0 ^ 804bba0
            2(804bb20) L 0 R 0 P 804bb40 S 804bb80 ^ 804bba0
        7(804bbc0) L 804bb60 R 804bb40 P 0 S 804bba0 ^ 804bb00
            3(804bb40) L 0 R 0 P 804bb60 S 804bb20 ^ 804bbc0
            4(804bb60) L 0 R 0 P 0 S 804bb40 ^ 804bbc0

Program received signal SIGSEGV, Segmentation fault.
0x0804a0f2 in getParent__4Heap (this=0x0) at Heap.h:17
17     inline Heap * getParent() { return _parent; }
(gdb) bt
#0  0x0804a0f2 in getParent__4Heap (this=0x0) at Heap.h:17
#1  0x0804994c in movedown__4Heap (this=0x804bb00) at Heap.c:375
#2  0x08049ba9 in remove__4Heap (this=0x804bb00) at Heap.c:426
#3  0x08049c4f in sort__4Heap (this=0x804bb00) at Heap.c:457
#4  0x08049e51 in testSort__FP4Heap (in=0x804bb00) at HeapTest.c:114
...
```

5.1.9.2   **The investigation**

After displaying the stack trace, we display the value of the pointer being referenced in the *movedown* function. The statement is

```
_active= _last->getParent();
```

and the _last_ variable has a null pointer. Since we just finished changing the statements that modify this variable, the logical thing to do is to review them for possible problems. We have been making a copy of the source for this program each time we make a significant change.

We use the UNIX™ *diff* program to compare the current source to the previous source. We quickly find the lines we recently modified.

There are only two interesting places where this variable is assigned, so we set a breakpoint at each of them. On the first try, we find that this variable is being assigned a null pointer from the penultimate pointer we had saved earlier.

Is there ever a condition under which the penultimate pointer will be null? The answer is yes: When the node is the leftmost node on a level, the predecessor pointer will be null, and this will be stored for this assignment.

In this round of debugging, we applied the following methods from Chapter 4:

■ Look for domestic drift.

■ Tail thyself.

We found defects that had the following root causes, explained in Chapter 11:

■ Reference error—variable not assigned

■ Control-flow problem—statement controlled by wrong control-flow condition

5.1.9.3   The fault and correction

It is clear that we need a more sophisticated way of backing up through the tree than just using the predecessor pointers. The natural solution is to use the same mechanism that we used in building the tree. When we built the tree, we relied on the fact that if we number the nodes in a complete binary tree successively from 1 as they are inserted, the number of nodes on the right-hand edge of each level will be a power of 2. This means that the numbers of the nodes on the right-hand side will be 1 less than a power of 2.

When we hop levels as we remove nodes, we must remember the parent as the frontier of the next level up. When we are about to save a null pointer into the variable that caused the original problem, we must instead save this pointer to the upper frontier.

After we get the parent of the node that we are going to move down the tree, we check its ID number. If it indicates that we are on the edge, we retain the parent for later use. The code looks like this:

```
if( _last->getID() == _power-1 ) {
    _frontier= parent;
}
```

Later in the function, we test the penultimate pointer to determine what to assign to the _last_ variable. The code looks as follows:

```
if ( penult != 0 ) {
    _last= penult;
} else {
    _last= _frontier;
}
```

5.1.10   Bug 9

5.1.10.1   The evidence

The next debugging session began by running the application under the GNU debugger (*gdb*). We ran the same test case with the same test driver. We modified the *movedown* function to display the data structure at the beginning and end of the execution of the function. These displays are marked with

```
*** movedown ***
```

and

```
### movedown ###
```

respectively.

The results of running this test are shown as follows:

```
(gdb) run
Starting program: /home/metzger/h.exe
test 1:8
    8
        6
            5
            2
        7
            3
            4
```

```
                          1

remove 8
*** movedown ***
      1(804bb38) L 804bbf8 R 804bbd8 P 0 S 0 ^ 0
         6(804bbd8) L 804bb58 R 804bbb8 P 804bbf8 S 0 ^ 804bb38
            5(804bbb8) L 0 R 0 P 804bb58 S 0 ^ 804bbd8
            2(804bb58) L 0 R 0 P 804bb78 S 804bbb8 ^ 804bbd8
         7(804bbf8) L 804bb98 R 804bb78 P 0 S 804bbd8 ^ 804bb38
            3(804bb78) L 0 R 0 P 804bb98 S 804bb58 ^ 804bbf8
            4(804bb98) L 0 R 0 P 0 S 804bb78 ^ 804bbf8
### movedown ###
      7(804bbf8) L 804bb98 R 804bbd8 P 0 S 0 ^ 0
         6(804bbd8) L 804bb58 R 804bbb8 P 804bb98 S 0 ^ 804bbf8
            5(804bbb8) L 0 R 0 P 804bb58 S 0 ^ 804bbd8
            2(804bb58) L 0 R 0 P 804bb78 S 804bbb8 ^ 804bbd8
         4(804bb98) L 804bb38 R 804bb78 P 0 S 804bbd8 ^ 804bbf8
            3(804bb78) L 0 R 0 P 804bb38 S 804bb58 ^ 804bb98
            1(804bb38) L 0 R 0 P 0 S 804bb78 ^ 804bb98
remove 7
*** movedown ***
      1(804bb38) L 804bb98 R 804bbd8 P 0 S 0 ^ 0
         6(804bbd8) L 804bb58 R 804bbb8 P 804bb98 S 0 ^ 804bb38
            5(804bbb8) L 0 R 0 P 804bb58 S 0 ^ 804bbd8
            2(804bb58) L 0 R 0 P 804bb78 S 804bbb8 ^ 804bbd8
         4(804bb98) L 0 R 804bb78 P 0 S 804bbd8 ^ 804bb38
            3(804bb78) L 0 R 0 P 804bb38 S 804bb58 ^ 804bb98
### movedown ###
      6(804bbd8) L 804bb98 R 804bbb8 P 0 S 0 ^ 0
         5(804bbb8) L 804bb58 R 804bb38 P 804bb98 S 0 ^ 804bbd8
            1(804bb38) L 0 R 0 P 804bb58 S 0 ^ 804bbb8
            2(804bb58) L 0 R 0 P 804bb78 S 804bb38 ^ 804bbb8
         4(804bb98) L 0 R 804bb78 P 0 S 804bbb8 ^ 804bbd8
            3(804bb78) L 0 R 0 P 804bb38 S 804bb58 ^ 804bb98
remove 6
*** movedown ***
      1(804bb38) L 804bb98 R 804bbb8 P 0 S 0 ^ 0
         5(804bbb8) L 804bb58 R 0 P 804bb98 S 0 ^ 804bb38
            2(804bb58) L 0 R 0 P 804bb78 S 0 ^ 804bbb8
         4(804bb98) L 0 R 804bb78 P 0 S 804bbb8 ^ 804bb38
            3(804bb78) L 0 R 0 P 804bb38 S 804bb58 ^ 804bb98
```

```
### movedown ###
     5(804bbb8) L 804bb98 R 804bb58 P 0 S 0 ^ 0
        2(804bb58) L 804bb38 R 0 P 804bb98 S 0 ^ 804bbb8
           1(804bb38) L 0 R 0 P 804bb78 S 0 ^ 804bb58
        4(804bb98) L 0 R 804bb78 P 0 S 804bb58 ^ 804bbb8
           3(804bb78) L 0 R 0 P 804bb38 S 804bb38 ^ 804bb98
remove 5
*** movedown ***
     2(804bb58) L 804bb98 R 0 P 0 S 0 ^ 0
        4(804bb98) L 0 R 804bb78 P 0 S 0 ^ 804bb58
           3(804bb78) L 0 R 0 P 804bb38 S 804bb38 ^ 804bb98
### movedown ###
     2(804bb58) L 804bb98 R 0 P 0 S 0 ^ 0
        4(804bb98) L 0 R 804bb78 P 0 S 0 ^ 804bb58
           3(804bb78) L 0 R 0 P 804bb38 S 804bb38 ^ 804bb98
remove 2
*** movedown ***
     4(804bb98) L 0 R 0 P 0 S 0 ^ 0
### movedown ###
     4(804bb98) L 0 R 0 P 0 S 0 ^ 0
remove 4

Program received signal SIGSEGV, Segmentation fault.
0x0804a102 in getLeft__4Heap (this=0x0) at Heap.h:15
15    inline Heap * getLeft() { return _left; }
(gdb) bt
#0  0x0804a102 in getLeft__4Heap (this=0x0) at Heap.h:15
#1  0x08049a5b in remove__4Heap (this=0x804bb38) at Heap.c:405
#2  0x08049c7b in sort__4Heap (this=0x804bb38) at Heap.c:464
#3  0x08049e7d in testSort__FP4Heap (in=0x804bb38) at HeapTest.c:114
```

5.1.10.2   The investigation

We have encountered another null pointer. We review the output and
notice that the data structure has lost the character of a complete binary tree
by the time the *movedown* function enters the second time. Since the structure is valid at the first exit and invalid on the second entry, the problem is
likely with the processing that occurred in between.

What occurs between these calls is the execution of the *remove* function, so we focus our attention here. We saw the same symptom in the previous session, so it appears that our change may not have been sufficient.

Since we have had several instances of statements being executed under the wrong control-flow conditions, we decide to watch the execution of the statements that assign the *_frontier* variable. There is only one such statement in the *remove* function, so we add a command list that prints the values used to control the expression each time the breakpoint is encountered. The results of running this test are shown as follows:

```
(gdb) b Heap.c:402
(gdb) commands
p Heap::_last->getID()
p Heap::_power-1
end

(gdb) run
Starting program: /home/metzger/h.exe
Breakpoint 1 at 0x8049a2b: file Heap.c, line 402.
test 1:8
    8
        6
            5
            2
        7
            3
            4
                1


remove 8

Breakpoint 1, remove__4Heap (this=0x804bb38) at Heap.c:402
402          if ( _last->getID() == _power-1 ) {
$1 = 8
$2 = 3

remove 7

Breakpoint 1, remove__4Heap (this=0x804bb38) at Heap.c:402
402          if ( _last->getID() == _power-1 ) {
$3 = 4
```

```
$4 = 3
(gdb) c

remove 6

Breakpoint 1, remove__4Heap (this=0x804bb38) at Heap.c:402
402            if ( _last->getID() == _power-1 ) {
$5 = 7
$6 = 3
(gdb) c

remove 5

Breakpoint 1, remove__4Heap (this=0x804bb38) at Heap.c:402
402            if ( _last->getID() == _power-1 ) {
$7 = 3
$8 = 3
(gdb) c

Breakpoint 1, remove__4Heap (this=0x804bb38) at Heap.c:402
402            if ( _last->getID() == _power-1 ) {
$9 = 2
$10 = 3
(gdb) c
Continuing.

remove 4

Breakpoint 1, remove__4Heap (this=0x804bb38) at Heap.c:402
402            if ( _last->getID() == _power-1 ) {
$11 = 0
$12 = 3
(gdb) c

Program received signal SIGSEGV, Segmentation fault.
0x0804a102 in getLeft__4Heap (this=0x0) at Heap.h:15
```

We decide that we need to use a system for organizing our investigation. We choose the observation-hypothesis-experiment method.

Observation 1: The *_power* variable starts with the value 4 when it should be 8.

Hypothesis 1: The process of building the data structure is not correctly updating the variable.

Experiment 1: Watch the variable during the construction process.

Observation 2: The value of the _power variable never changes.

Hypothesis 2: There is a missing statement in the *remove* function.

Experiment 2: Search the text for a statement that reduces the variable's value.

The results of running our first experiment are listed as follows:

```
Hardware watchpoint 1: Heap::_power
test 1:8
Hardware watchpoint 1: Heap::_power
Hardware watchpoint 1: Heap::_power
Hardware watchpoint 1: Heap::_power
Hardware watchpoint 1: Heap::_power
Hardware watchpoint 1: Heap::_power

Old value = 0
New value = 2
__4HeapiPi (this=0x804bb38, n=8, x=0x804b340) at Heap.c:44
Hardware watchpoint 1: Heap::_power

Old value = 2
New value = 4
insert__4Heap (this=0x804bb58) at Heap.c:66
(gdb) c

remove 8
remove 7
remove 6
remove 5
remove 2
remove 4

Program received signal SIGSEGV, Segmentation fault.
0x0804a102 in getLeft__4Heap (this=0x0) at Heap.h:15
15     inline Heap * getLeft() { return _left; }
```

Observation 3: The variable *_power* is assigned twice during the construction of the binary tree. It is initialized to 2. Later it is multiplied by 2 in the code that handles insertion of the initial left branch. It is never modified by the sections of code that handle insertion of left and right children after the initial special case.

Hypothesis 3: The variable should be multiplied by 2 in the code that handles insertion of left branches after the first one.

Experiment 3: Add the code and run the test case again.

In this round of debugging, we applied the following methods from Chapter 3:

- Eliminate impossible causes.
- Use a system for organizing facts.

We found defects that had the following root causes, which are explained in Chapter 11:

- Missing operation—missing statement
- Invalid expression—extra term

5.1.10.3   The fault and correction

After a great deal of work, we decide that the following changes are necessary. We insert the following statement into the *insert* function in the code that handles inserting left children when the child starts a new level:

```
_power *= 2;
```

We change the code that detects the edge of a level to the following:

```
if( _last->getID() == _power ) {
```

We insert a statement under the control of this statement, which reduces the *_power* variable when a level is detected:

```
_power /= 2;
```

5.1.11 Bug 10

5.1.11.1 The evidence

The next debugging session began by running the application under the GNU debugger (*gdb*). We tested using the same test input and test driver as the previous case. The results of running this test are shown as follows:

```
(gdb) run
Starting program: /home/metzger/h.exe
test 1:8
    8
        6
            5
            2
        7
            3
            4
                1

remove 8
last: 4
*** movedown ***
    1(804bbc0) L 804bc80 R 804bc60 P 0 S 0 ^ 0
        6(804bc60) L 804bbe0 R 804bc40 P 804bc80 S 0 ^ 804bbc0
            5(804bc40) L 0 R 0 P 804bbe0 S 0 ^ 804bc60
            2(804bbe0) L 0 R 0 P 804bc00 S 804bc40 ^ 804bc60
        7(804bc80) L 804bc20 R 804bc00 P 0 S 804bc60 ^ 804bbc0
            3(804bc00) L 0 R 0 P 804bc20 S 804bbe0 ^ 804bc80
            4(804bc20) L 0 R 0 P 0 S 804bc00 ^ 804bc80
### movedown ###
    7(804bc80) L 804bc20 R 804bc60 P 0 S 0 ^ 0
        6(804bc60) L 804bbe0 R 804bc40 P 804bc20 S 0 ^ 804bc80
            5(804bc40) L 0 R 0 P 804bbe0 S 0 ^ 804bc60
            2(804bbe0) L 0 R 0 P 804bc00 S 804bc40 ^ 804bc60
        4(804bc20) L 804bbc0 R 804bc00 P 0 S 804bc60 ^ 804bc80
            3(804bc00) L 0 R 0 P 804bbc0 S 804bbe0 ^ 804bc20
            1(804bbc0) L 0 R 0 P 0 S 804bc00 ^ 804bc20
remove 7
last: 4
*** movedown ***
```

```
    4(804bc20) L 0 R 804bc60 P 0 S 0 ^ 0
        6(804bc60) L 804bbe0 R 804bc40 P 804bc20 S 0 ^ 804bc20
            5(804bc40) L 0 R 0 P 804bbe0 S 0 ^ 804bc60
            2(804bbe0) L 0 R 0 P 804bc00 S 804bc40 ^ 804bc60
### movedown ###
    4(804bc20) L 0 R 804bc60 P 0 S 0 ^ 0
        6(804bc60) L 804bbe0 R 804bc40 P 804bc20 S 0 ^ 804bc20
            5(804bc40) L 0 R 0 P 804bbe0 S 0 ^ 804bc60
            2(804bbe0) L 0 R 0 P 804bc00 S 804bc40 ^ 804bc60
remove 4
8 7 4


Program exited normally.
```

5.1.11.2   The investigation

Our initial observation is that the data structure has lost the complete binary tree property after the item with key "7" has been removed. The tree display at the second entry to the *movedown* function has a null left child pointer. This can only occur when the root is the only node in the tree.

We also observe that the wrong node was inserted as the new root when the node with the key "7" was removed. The rightmost node on the lowest level should have been used. This was the item with key "5." Instead the leftmost node on the level above was used. This was the item with the key "4."

The candidate for next removal is identified by the variable *_last*.

The first course of action is to observe the values assigned to this variable. There are three places in the *remove* function where it is assigned. One of them always assigns a null pointer, and since this is not our problem, we can exclude it. We set a breakpoint at the remaining two assignments to watch the flow of values into this variable. On the first execution of the statement that assigns the value of the *_frontier* variable to the *_last* variable, the value is incorrect. The node with the key "4" is assigned, when it should be the node with key "5." Suspicion now falls on the *_frontier* variable. We delete our breakpoints and set a new one to observe the flow of values into this variable. It is only assigned once, and the value it receives is the address of the node with the key "4." We have found the culprit, but why is it getting this value?

After some consideration, we realize that we have overloaded the meaning of the variable. During both insertion and removal of nodes, this variable is intended to track the edge where nodes will next be inserted or removed. In the case of insertion, we track the left edge. In the case of removal, we track the right edge.

We have created the converse of an alibi. Instead of having multiple names for one value, we have one name for multiple values. Since the name covers both cases, and the phases are independent, perhaps this is not so bad. We must, however, use different means to identify the values that are assigned to this variable during these two phases.

In this round of debugging, we applied the following methods from Chapter 3:

- Use alibis as clues.
- Eliminate impossible causes.

We also applied the following method from Chapter 4:

- The eureka zone

We found a defect that had the following root causes, explained in Chapter 11:

- Missing operations—statements are missing
- Reference errors—variable not assigned

5.1.11.3   **The fault and correction**

The original code that assigned the *_frontier* variable looked like the following. It is invoked when an edge is detected.

```
if ( _last->getID() == _power ) {
    _frontier= parent;
    _power /= 2;
}
```

To get the rightmost edge, we must walk the list of successors until we find a node that does not have a successor. This is the right edge.

```
if ( _last->getID() == _power ) {
    for ( curr= parent; curr != 0 ; curr= curr->getSucc() ) {
        prev= curr;
    }
    _frontier= prev;
    _power /= 2;
}
```

5.1.12 Bug 11

5.1.12.1   The evidence

The next debugging session began by running the application under the GNU debugger (*gdb*). We use the same test driver and input as the previous session. The results of running this test are shown as follows:

```
(gdb) run
Starting program: /home/metzger/h.exe
test 1:8
    8
        6
            5
            2
        7
            3
            4
                1

remove 8
*** movedown ***
    1(804bb78) L 804bc38 R 804bc18 P 0 S 0 ^ 0
        6(804bc18) L 804bb98 R 804bbf8 P 804bc38 S 0 ^ 804bb78
            5(804bbf8) L 0 R 0 P 804bb98 S 0 ^ 804bc18
            2(804bb98) L 0 R 0 P 804bbb8 S 804bbf8 ^ 804bc18
        7(804bc38) L 804bbd8 R 804bbb8 P 0 S 804bc18 ^ 804bb78
            3(804bbb8) L 0 R 0 P 804bbd8 S 804bb98 ^ 804bc38
            4(804bbd8) L 0 R 0 P 0 S 804bbb8 ^ 804bc38
### movedown ###
    7(804bc38) L 804bbd8 R 804bc18 P 0 S 0 ^ 0
        6(804bc18) L 804bb98 R 804bbf8 P 804bbd8 S 0 ^ 804bc38
```

```
                   5(804bbf8) L 0 R 0 P 804bb98 S 0 ^ 804bc18
                   2(804bb98) L 0 R 0 P 804bbb8 S 804bbf8 ^ 804bc18
               4(804bbd8) L 804bb78 R 804bbb8 P 0 S 804bc18 ^ 804bc38
                   3(804bbb8) L 0 R 0 P 804bb78 S 804bb98 ^ 804bbd8
                   1(804bb78) L 0 R 0 P 0 S 804bbb8 ^ 804bbd8
remove 7
*** movedown ***
       5(804bbf8) L 804bbd8 R 804bc18 P 0 S 0 ^ 0
           6(804bc18) L 804bb98 R 0 P 804bbd8 S 0 ^ 804bbf8
               2(804bb98) L 0 R 0 P 804bbb8 S 0 ^ 804bc18
           4(804bbd8) L 804bb78 R 804bbb8 P 0 S 804bc18 ^ 804bbf8
               3(804bbb8) L 0 R 0 P 804bb78 S 804bb98 ^ 804bbd8
               1(804bb78) L 0 R 0 P 0 S 804bbb8 ^ 804bbd8
### movedown ###
       5(804bbf8) L 804bbd8 R 804bc18 P 0 S 0 ^ 0
           6(804bc18) L 804bb98 R 0 P 804bbd8 S 0 ^ 804bbf8
               2(804bb98) L 0 R 0 P 804bbb8 S 0 ^ 804bc18
           4(804bbd8) L 804bb78 R 804bbb8 P 0 S 804bc18 ^ 804bbf8
               3(804bbb8) L 0 R 0 P 804bb78 S 804bb98 ^ 804bbd8
               1(804bb78) L 0 R 0 P 0 S 804bbb8 ^ 804bbd8
remove 5
*** movedown ***
       2(804bb98) L 804bbd8 R 804bc18 P 0 S 0 ^ 0
           6(804bc18) L 0 R 0 P 804bbd8 S 0 ^ 804bb98
           4(804bbd8) L 804bb78 R 804bbb8 P 0 S 804bc18 ^ 804bb98
               3(804bbb8) L 0 R 0 P 804bb78 S 0 ^ 804bbd8
               1(804bb78) L 0 R 0 P 0 S 804bbb8 ^ 804bbd8
### movedown ###
       2(804bb98) L 804bbd8 R 804bc18 P 0 S 0 ^ 0
           6(804bc18) L 0 R 0 P 804bbd8 S 0 ^ 804bb98
           4(804bbd8) L 804bb78 R 804bbb8 P 0 S 804bc18 ^ 804bb98
               3(804bbb8) L 0 R 0 P 804bb78 S 0 ^ 804bbd8
               1(804bb78) L 0 R 0 P 0 S 804bbb8 ^ 804bbd8
remove 2
*** movedown ***
       3(804bbb8) L 804bbd8 R 804bc18 P 0 S 0 ^ 0
           6(804bc18) L 0 R 0 P 804bbd8 S 0 ^ 804bbb8
           4(804bbd8) L 804bb78 R 0 P 0 S 804bc18 ^ 804bbb8
               1(804bb78) L 0 R 0 P 0 S 0 ^ 804bbd8
### movedown ###
       3(804bbb8) L 804bbd8 R 804bc18 P 0 S 0 ^ 0
```

```
        6(804bc18) L 0 R 0 P 804bbd8 S 0 ^ 804bbb8
        4(804bbd8) L 804bb78 R 0 P 0 S 804bc18 ^ 804bbb8
            1(804bb78) L 0 R 0 P 0 S 0 ^ 804bbd8
remove 3
*** movedown ***
        1(804bb78) L 804bbd8 R 804bc18 P 0 S 0 ^ 0
            6(804bc18) L 0 R 0 P 804bbd8 S 0 ^ 804bb78
            4(804bbd8) L 0 R 0 P 0 S 804bc18 ^ 804bb78
### movedown ###
        6(804bc18) L 804bbd8 R 804bb78 P 0 S 0 ^ 0
            1(804bb78) L 0 R 0 P 804bbd8 S 0 ^ 804bc18
            4(804bbd8) L 0 R 0 P 0 S 804bb78 ^ 804bc18
remove 6
8 7 5 2 3 6

Program exited normally.
```

5.1.12.2   The investigation

Our initial observation is that the data structure has lost the heap property
after the node with key "7" is removed and the corresponding call to *movedown* has been completed. The node with key "5" is the parent of the node
with key "6," and that is not permissible. We will focus our attention on the
movedown function.

Since the body of this function iterates until it determines that a node
has moved into the right place, we decide to insert a statement at the top of
the loop that prints the node being processed. This will enable us to trace
the behavior of the loop. We also turn off the printing of the entire data
structure, since we already know where it goes bad.

```
test 1:8
remove 8
this 1, left 804bc20, right 804bc00
this 1, left 804bbc0, right 804bba0
this 1, left 0, right 0
remove 7
this 1, left 0, right 0
remove 5
this 1, left 0, right 0
remove 2
```

```
this 1, left 0, right 0
remove 3
this 1, left 804bbc0, right 804bc00
this 1, left 0, right 0
remove 6
8 7 5 2 3 6
```

As we stare at the output, looking for a pattern, it hits us all at once—we have been using the *this* variable to refer both to the structure as a whole and to one node being moved in particular. The reason the process seemed to work is that for this particular data set, the node pointed to by *this* was the correct one to move, at least initially.

In this round of debugging, we applied the following method from Chapter 3:

- Use gestalt understanding.

In this round of debugging, we also applied the following method from Chapter 4:

- You are looking right at it.

We found a defect that had the following root cause, explained in Chapter 11:

- Reference errors—wrong variable referenced

5.1.12.3   The fault and correction

The changes required for this correction are pervasive. Every reference to *this* in the function *movedown* has to be changed to a new variable *move*. This variable is initialized with the current root, which is the place where we always start moving a node. Since this function has changed so drastically, we have reproduced the new version here to facilitate discussion of the remaining bugs.

```
void Heap::movedown() {
```

```
Heap *temp, *child, *move;

move= _root;
while ( true  ) {
    Heap * left= move->getLeft();
    Heap * right= move->getRight();
    if ( left != 0 && right != 0  ) {
        if ( left->getKey() <= move->getKey() &&
            right->getKey() <= move->getKey() ) {
            break;
        } else {
            child= (left->getKey() >=
                    right->getKey()) ? left : right;
        }
    } else if ( left != 0 ) {
        if ( left->getKey() <= move->getKey() ) {
            break;
        } else {
            child= left;
        }
    } else {
        break;
    }

    // swap ID numbers
    int swap= move->getID();
    move->setID(child->getID());
    child->setID(swap);

    // swap incoming vertical pointers
    Heap * grand= move->getParent();
    if ( grand != 0 ) {
        if ( move == grand->getLeft() ) {
            grand->setLeft(child);
        } else if ( move == grand->getRight() ) {
            grand->setRight(child);
        }
    }

    // swap outgoing vertical pointers
    move->setParent(child);
```

```
                    child->setParent(grand);

        if ( child == move->getLeft() ) {
            if ( child->getLeft() != 0 ) {
                child->getLeft()->setParent(move);
            }
            move->setLeft(child->getLeft());
            child->setLeft(move);

            if ( child->getRight() != 0 ) {
                if ( move->getRight() != 0 ) {
                    temp= move->getRight()->getParent();
                    move->getRight()->setParent(child->
                        getRight()->getParent());
                    child->getRight()->setParent(temp);
                } else {
                    child->getRight()->setParent(0);
                }
            } else {
                if ( move->getRight() != 0 ) {
                    move->getRight()->setParent(child);
                }
            }

            temp= child->getRight();
            child->setRight(move->getRight());
            move->setRight(temp);
        } else if ( child == move->getRight() ) {
            if ( child->getRight() != 0 ) {
                child->getRight()->setParent(move);
            }
            move->setRight(child->getRight());
            child->setRight(move);

            if ( child->getLeft() != 0 ) {
                if ( move->getLeft() != 0 ) {
                    temp= move->getLeft()->getParent();
                    move->getLeft()->setParent(child->
                        getLeft()->getParent());
                    child->getLeft()->setParent(temp);
                } else {
```

```
                    child->getLeft()->setParent(0);
           }
        } else {
           if ( move->getLeft() != 0 ) {
              move->getLeft()->setParent(child);
           }
        }

        temp= child->getLeft();
        child->setLeft(move->getLeft());
        move->setLeft(temp);
     } else {
        assert(0);
     }

     // swap incoming horizontal pointers
     if ( child->getPred() != 0 ) {
        if ( move->getPred() != 0 ) {
           temp= move->getPred()->getSucc();
           move->getPred()->setSucc(child->
                getPred()->getSucc());
           child->getPred()->setSucc(temp);
        } else {
           child->getPred()->setSucc(move);
        }
     } else {
        if ( move->getPred() != 0 ) {
           move->getPred()->setSucc(child);
        }
     }
     if ( child->getSucc() != 0 ) {
        if ( move->getSucc() != 0 ) {
           temp= move->getSucc()->getPred();
           move->getSucc()->setPred(child->
                getSucc()->getPred());
           child->getSucc()->setPred(temp);
        } else {
           child->getSucc()->setPred(move);
        }
     } else {
        if ( move->getSucc() != 0 ) {
```

```
                              move->getSucc()->setPred(child);
                  }
          }

          // swap outgoing horizontal pointers
          temp= move->getPred();
          move->setPred(child->getPred());
          child->setPred(temp);

          temp= move->getSucc();
          move->setSucc(child->getSucc());
          child->setSucc(temp);

          // update variables
          _active= _last->getParent();
          if ( _root == move ) {
              _root= child;
          }
      }
  }
```

5.1.13   Bug 12

5.1.13.1   The evidence

The next debugging session began by running the application under the
GNU debugger (*gdb*). We are still using the same test input and test driver.
The results of running this test are shown as follows:

```
(gdb) run
Starting program: /home/metzger/src/sort/save11/h.exe
test 1:8
    8
        6
            5
            2
        7
            3
            4
                1
```

```
remove 8
remove 7
remove 6
remove 5
remove 4
remove 3
remove 2
remove 1

Program received signal SIGSEGV, Segmentation fault.
0x0804a772 in getLeft__4Heap (this=0x0) at Heap.h:15
15    inline Heap * getLeft() { return _left; }
(gdb) bt
#0  0x0804a772 in getLeft__4Heap (this=0x0) at Heap.h:15
#1  0x08049a87 in remove__4Heap (this=0x804c290) at Heap.c:414
#2  0x08049cb7 in sort__4Heap (this=0x804c290) at Heap.c:474
#3  0x0804a4f5 in testSort__FP4Heap (in=0x804c290) at HeapTest.c:131
...
```

5.1.13.2   The investigation

Once again, we find a null pointer being dereferenced. At least we have the satisfaction of seeing all items being removed from the heap in the correct order. The exception occurs as we try to remove the final element. Perhaps we are getting close to the end.

We do not have a good idea to start, so we look over our records of what we have done. Back in the discussion of Bug 4, we said that we were going to add a statement into the *insert* function in the code that handles inserting left children when the child starts a new level. When we look in this code, we do not see an assignment to the *_power* variable, as we expected.

In this round of debugging, we applied the following methods from Chapter 4:

- Tail thyself.

- Look once, look well.

We found a defect that had the following root cause, explained in Chapter 11:

- Missing operations—statements missing

5.1.13.3   The fault and correction

The change required to fix this problem is rather small. The following code is inserted as we had previously promised:

```
if ( this->getID() == _power ) {
    _power *= 2;
}
```

5.1.14   Bug 13

5.1.14.1   The evidence

The next debugging session began by running the application under the GNU debugger (*gdb*). Since our code seems to be getting more reliable, we decide to add some more tests. The test input and test driver are listed as follows:

```
// sorted up, power of 2 length
int t01[8]= { 1,2,3,4,5,6,7,8 };

// sorted up, non-power of 2 length
int t02[9]= { 2,3,5,7,11,13,17,19,23 };

// sorted down, power of 2 length
int t03[16]= { 32,30,28,26,24,22,20,18,16,14,12,10,8,6,4,2 };

// sorted down, non-power of 2 length
int t04[14]= { 27,25,23,21,19,17,15,13,11,9,7,5,3,1 };

// "V" pattern, power of 2 length
int t05[16]= { 2, 5, 11, 17, 29, 37, 47, 57,
               61, 53, 41, 31, 23, 13, 7, 3 };

// "V" pattern, non-power of 2 length
int t06[11]= {  2, 4, 6, 8, 10, 12, 11, 9, 7, 5, 3 };

// inverse "V" pattern, power of 2 length
int t07[32]= { 109, 103, 97, 87, 79, 71, 61, 57,
```

```
                        47, 41, 31, 23, 17, 11, 5, 2,
                        3, 7, 13, 19, 29, 37, 43, 53,
                        59, 67, 73, 83, 89, 101, 107, 111 };

// inverse "V" pattern, non-power of 2 length
int t08[31]= { 32, 30, 28, 26, 24, 22, 20, 18,
               16, 14, 12, 10, 8,  4,  2,
               1, 3, 5, 7, 9, 11, 13, 15,
               17, 19, 21, 23, 25, 27, 29, 31 };

// random values, power of 2 length
int t09[16]= { 2, 3, 43, 47, 5, 7, 37,
                41, 11, 13, 29, 31, 17, 23, 53, 57 };

// random values, non-power of 2 length
int t10[20]= { 2, 71, 3, 67, 5, 61,
                7, 59, 11, 57, 13, 53, 17,
                47, 23, 43, 29, 41, 31, 37 };


//---------------------------------------------------

int main() {

    Heap *node, *first;

    fprintf(stderr,"test 1:8\n");
    node= new Heap(8, t01);
    testBuild(node);
    testSort(node);
    fprintf(stderr,"test 2:9\n");
    node= new Heap(9, t02);
    testBuild(node);
    testSort(node);
    fprintf(stderr,"test 3:16\n");
    node= new Heap(16, t03);
    testBuild(node);
    testSort(node);
    fprintf(stderr,"test 4:14\n");
    node= new Heap(14, t04);
    testBuild(node);
    testSort(node);
```

```
        fprintf(stderr,"test 5:16\n");
        node= new Heap(16, t05);
        testBuild(node);
        testSort(node);
        fprintf(stderr,"test 6:11\n");
        node= new Heap(11, t06);
        testBuild(node);
        testSort(node);
        fprintf(stderr,"test 7:32\n");
        node= new Heap(32, t07);
        testBuild(node);
        testSort(node);
        fprintf(stderr,"test 8:31\n");
        node= new Heap(31, t08);
        testBuild(node);
        testSort(node);
    }

    void testBuild(Heap *node) {
        draw(node->getRoot());
        fprintf(stderr,"\n");
    }

    void testSort(Heap *in) {
        Heap * node=  in->sort();
        for( ; node != 0; node= node->getSucc() ) {
            fprintf(stderr,"%d ", node->getKey());
        }
        fprintf(stderr,"\n");
    }
```

The results of running this test are shown as follows. In the interest of conserving space, we show only the results from the first six tests.

```
    test 1:8
        8
            6
                5
                2
            7
                3
```

```
                                    4
                                      1

remove 8
remove 7
remove 6
remove 5
remove 4
8  7  6  5  4

test 2:9
       23
             13
                   11
                   3
             19
                  5
                  17
                        7
                        2

remove 23
remove 19
remove 17
remove 13
remove 11
remove 7
23  19  17  13  11  7

test 3:16
         32
               28
                    20
                          4
                          6
                    22
                          8
                          10
               30
                    24
                          12
```

```
                              14
                    26
                              16
                              18
                                   2

remove 32
remove 30
remove 28
remove 26
remove 24
remove 22
remove 20
remove 18
remove 16
remove 14
remove 12
remove 2
32 30 28 26 24 22 20 18 16 14 12 2

test 4:14
       27
           23
               15
                     1
               17
                     3
                     5
           25
               19
                     7
                     9
           21
               11
               13

remove 27
remove 25
remove 23
remove 21
remove 19
```

```
remove 13
27 25 23 21 19 13

test 5:16
    61
        37
            29
                7
                13
            31
                23
                5
        57
            53
                41
                11
            47
                17
                3
                    2

remove 61
remove 57
remove 53
remove 47
remove 41
remove 37
remove 31
remove 29
remove 23
remove 17
remove 13
remove 11
remove 2
61 57 53 47 41 37 31 29 23 17 13 11 2
test 6:11
    12
        11
            10
            4
        9
```

```
                                   6
                                    3
                                    5
                                  8
                                    7
                                    2

        remove 12
        remove 11
        remove 10
        remove 9
        remove 8
        remove 7
        remove 2
        12 11 10 9 8 7 2
```

5.1.14.2   The investigation

In each case, all of the items removed are in the proper order. Anywhere from two to six items are missing. Sometimes the node with the smallest key is removed, but sometimes it is not.

We are getting a little tired, so we decide to go after "the usual suspects" and look a little closer at the changes we just made. In this case, we insert some statements to generate a trace of important values in the *insert* function.

To make our life simpler, we go back to running just the first test case. We put four separate statements into the *insert* statement to print an identification, together with the key and sequential ID number of the node being sorted. We suspect that something is wrong with the variable that tracks the power of 2 that corresponds to the ID number of the complete binary tree nodes, so we print it as well. The results of the trace are listed as follows:

```
        test 1:8
        insert 1 key= 2, ID= 2
        insert 2 key= 3, ID= 3
        insert 3 key= 4, ID= 4
        insert 2 key= 5, ID= 5
        insert 4 key= 6, ID= 6
        insert 2 key= 7, ID= 7
        insert 3 key= 8, ID= 8
            8
```

```
                          6
                            5
                            2
                        7
                            3
                            4
                                1

        remove 8
        remove 7
        remove 6
        remove 5
        remove 4
        8  7  6  5  4
```

We observe that the value of the *_power* variable is given a final adjustment at the end of building the complete binary tree. Unfortunately, the
adjustment is in the wrong direction. While inserting nodes, the variable
tracks forward motion and leads the actual values referenced, except when
the threshold is reached. When removing nodes, the variable tracks backward motion and trails the actual values referenced, except when the threshold is reached. We were right to put a final adjustment of the variable, but
we adjusted it the wrong way.

In this round of debugging, we applied the following methods from
Chapter 4:

- You are looking right at it.

- Look for domestic drift.

We found a defect that had the following root cause, explained in
Chapter 11:

- Invalid expression—wrong arithmetic operator is used

5.1.14.3 The fault and correction

This correction is fairly easy. We change the final adjustment of the *_power*
variable from

```
_power *= 2;
```

to

```
_power /= 2;
```

5.1.15   Bug 14

5.1.15.1   The evidence

The next debugging session began by running the application under the GNU debugger (*gdb*). The test input and test driver are the same as the previous session. The results of running this test are listed as follows:

```
(gdb) run
Starting program: /home/metzger/src/sort/save14/h.exe
test 1:8
     8
        6
          5
          2
        7
          3
          4
            1
remove 8
remove 7
remove 6
remove 5
remove 4
remove 3
remove 2
remove 1

Program received signal SIGSEGV, Segmentation fault.
0x0804a152 in getLeft__4Heap (this=0x0) at Heap.h:15
15    inline Heap * getLeft() { return _left; }
(gdb) bt
#0  0x0804a152 in getLeft__4Heap (this=0x0) at Heap.h:15
#1  0x08049a9b in remove__4Heap (this=0x804bb58) at Heap.c:422
#2  0x08049ccb in sort__4Heap (this=0x804bb58) at Heap.c:482
#3  0x08049ed1 in testSort__FP4Heap (in=0x804bb58) at HeapTest.c:133
...
(gdb) q
```

5.1.15.2   The investigation

We are back to removing all the nodes in the correct order. This is the same result we had during session 8. We are once again dereferencing a null pointer. This pointer points to the parent of the node we are currently removing. Is there any case in which a node will have a null pointer for a parent? The answer is yes, when the node is the root of the tree. Either the node is the root, or it is not, and if it is, there is a great deal of processing in the *remove* function that is completely unnecessary. The *sort* function will terminate if the *_root* variable is a null pointer, so all we need to do when removing the final node is copy the value of the root pointer, set the root pointer to null, and return the copy. The calling function will see that it is done and terminate processing.

In this round of debugging, we applied the following method from Chapter 4:

■ Use the power of logic.

We found defects that had the following root causes, which are explained in Chapter 11:

■ Missing operations—statements are missing
■ Control-flow problems—statement controlled by wrong control-flow condition

5.1.15.3   The fault and correction

The correction is straightforward. We put the majority of the body of the *remove* function under the control of the following statement:

```
if ( parent != 0 ) {
```

This eliminates the exception.

5.1.16 Bug 15

5.1.16.1 The evidence

The next debugging session began by running the application under the GNU debugger (*gdb*). We are using the same test case and test input as in the previous session.

The results of running this test are shown as follows:

```
(gdb) run
Starting program: /home/metzger/src/sort/save15/h.exe
test 1:8
    8
        6
            5
            2
        7
            3
            4
                1

remove _root 8; _last 1
last: 5
### movedown ###
    7(804c3d8) L 804c378 R 804c3b8 P 0 S 0 ^ 0
        6(804c3b8) L 804c338 R 804c398 P 804c378 S 0 ^ 804c3d8
            5(804c398) L 0 R 0 P 804c338 S 0 ^ 804c3b8
            2(804c338) L 0 R 0 P 804c358 S 804c398 ^ 804c3b8
        4(804c378) L 804c318 R 804c358 P 0 S 804c3b8 ^ 804c3d8
            3(804c358) L 0 R 0 P 804c318 S 804c338 ^ 804c378
            1(804c318) L 0 R 0 P 0 S 804c358 ^ 804c378
remove _root 7; _last 5
last= 2
### movedown ###
    6(804c3b8) L 804c378 R 804c398 P 0 S 0 ^ 0
        5(804c398) L 804c338 R 0 P 804c378 S 0 ^ 804c3b8
            2(804c338) L 0 R 0 P 804c358 S 0 ^ 804c398
        4(804c378) L 804c318 R 804c358 P 0 S 804c398 ^ 804c3b8
            3(804c358) L 0 R 0 P 804c318 S 804c338 ^ 804c378
            1(804c318) L 0 R 0 P 0 S 804c358 ^ 804c378
remove _root 6; _last 2
```

```
last= 3
### movedown ###
    5(804c398) L 804c378 R 804c338 P 0 S 0 ^ 0
        2(804c338) L 0 R 0 P 804c378 S 0 ^ 804c398
        4(804c378) L 804c318 R 804c358 P 0 S 804c338 ^ 804c398
            3(804c358) L 0 R 0 P 804c318 S 0 ^ 804c378
            1(804c318) L 0 R 0 P 0 S 804c358 ^ 804c378
remove _root 5; _last 3
last= 1
### movedown ###
    4(804c378) L 804c358 R 804c338 P 0 S 0 ^ 0
        2(804c338) L 0 R 0 P 804c358 S 0 ^ 804c378
        3(804c358) L 804c318 R 0 P 0 S 804c338 ^ 804c378
            1(804c318) L 0 R 0 P 0 S 0 ^ 804c358
remove _root 4; _last 1
last: 2
### movedown ###
    3(804c358) L 804c318 R 804c338 P 0 S 0 ^ 0
        2(804c338) L 0 R 0 P 804c318 S 0 ^ 804c358
        1(804c318) L 0 R 0 P 0 S 804c338 ^ 804c358
remove _root 3; _last 2

last= 1
### movedown ###
    2(804c338) L 804c318 R 0 P 0 S 0 ^ 0
        1(804c318) L 0 R 0 P 0 S 0 ^ 804c338
remove _root 2; _last 1
last: 2
### movedown ###
    1(804c318) L 0 R 0 P 0 S 0 ^ 0
remove _root 1; _last 2
last= 3
### movedown ###
    1(804c318) L 0 R 0 P 0 S 0 ^ 0
remove _root 1; _last 3
last= 4
### movedown ###
    1(804c318) L 0 R 0 P 804c338 S 0 ^ 0
remove _root 1; _last 4
last= 5
### movedown ###
```

```
     1(804c318) L 0 R 0 P 804c318 S 804c318 ^ 0
remove _root 1; _last 5
last= 6
### movedown ###
     1(804c318) L 0 R 0 P 804c318 S 804c318 ^ 0
remove _root 1; _last 6
last= 7
### movedown ###
     1(804c318) L 0 R 0 P 804c318 S 804c318 ^ 0
remove _root 1; _last 7
last= 8
### movedown ###
     1(804c318) L 0 R 0 P 804c318 S 804c318 ^ 0
remove _root 1; _last 8

// infinite loop
```

5.1.16.2   The investigation

The obvious thing we notice is that while the _root_ variable converges to the node with the key of "1," as it should, the _last_ variable seems to cycle through nodes that have already been processed. It appears that it is referring to storage that is no longer connected to the tree. Is there somewhere that this variable should be updated? We look through the source for instances where _root_ is updated, but _last_ is not. We quickly find one at the end of the _movedown_ function, where after the pointers internal to the nodes are updated, several static variables are also updated.

This will fix the problem with the pattern of values in the _last_ variable, but does not address the infinite loop.

We look again at the condition controlling normal processing in the _remove_ function. What we want to detect is the situation where exactly one node exists in the tree, and that has no connections. The current test does not consider the connections, so we need an alternative.

In this round of debugging, we applied the following methods from Chapter 4:

- Exercise curiosity.

- Show how something could be done.

We found a defect that had the following root causes, explained in Chapter 11:

- Missing operations—statements are missing
- Control-flow problems—statement controlled by wrong control-flow condition

5.1.16.3   The fault and correction

We correct the lack of an update to the _last_ variable by including it in the swapping activity that is going on between the node pointed to by *move* and the one pointed to by *child*.

```
if( _last == child ) {
    _last= move;
}
```

We correct the condition guarding normal processing in the *remove* function by replacing it with the following test:

```
if( _root != 0 && _root->getLeft() != 0 ) {
```

This ensures that there is one node, no connections, and it tests the existence of the root pointer before dereferencing it.

To make sure that we have fixed the last problem, we run the program one more time with all test cases and minimal debugging output. The results are shown as follows:

```
test 1:8
8 7 6 5 4 3 2 1
test 2:9
23 19 17 13 11 7 5 3 2
test 3:16
32 30 28 26 24 22 20 18 16 14 12 10 8 6 4 2
test 4:14
27 25 23 21 19 17 15 13 11 9 7 5 3 1
test 5:16
61 57 53 47 41 37 31 29 23 17 13 11 7 5 3 2
test 6:11
12 11 10 9 8 7 6 5 4 3 2
```

```
test 7:32
111 109 107 103 101 97 89 87 83 79 73 71 67 61 59 57 53 47 43
41 37 31 29
      23 19 17 13 11 7 5 3 2
test 8:31
32 31 30 29 28 27 26 25 24 23 22 21 20 19 18 17 16 15 14 13 12
11 10 9 8
      7 5 4 3 2 1
test 9:16
57 53 47 43 41 37 31 29 23 17 13 11 7 5 3 2
test 10:20
71 67 61 59 57 53 47 43 41 37 31 29 23 17 13 11 7 5 3 2
```

The code for the final program is listed below.

```
#ifndef _Heap_h_
#define _Heap_h_

class Heap {
public:
    // constructors and destructors
    Heap(int, int);
    Heap(int, int *);

    // accessors
    inline int getKey() { return _key; }
    inline int getID() { return _id; }
    inline Heap * getLeft() { return _left; }
    inline Heap * getRight() { return _right; }
    inline Heap * getParent() { return _parent; }
    inline Heap * getPred() { return _pred; }
    inline Heap * getSucc() { return _succ; }

    inline Heap * getRoot() { return _root; }
    inline Heap * getActive() { return _active; }
    inline Heap * getLast() { return _last; }
    inline Heap * getFrontier() { return _frontier; }
    inline int getPower() { return _power; }

    // mutators
    inline void setKey(int x) { _key= x; }
```

```cpp
        inline void setID(int x) { _id= x; }
        inline void setLeft(Heap * x) { _left= x; }
        inline void setRight(Heap * x) { _right= x; }
        inline void setParent(Heap * x) { _parent= x; }
        inline void setPred(Heap * x) { _pred= x; }
        inline void setSucc(Heap * x) { _succ= x; }

        inline void setRoot(Heap *x) { _root= x; }
        inline void setActive(Heap *x) { _active= x; }
        inline void setLast(Heap *x) { _last= x; }
        inline void setFrontier(Heap *x) { _frontier= x; }
        inline void setPower(int x) { _power= x; }

        // workers
        void insert();
        void movedown();
        void moveup();
        Heap * remove();
        void replace(Heap *);
        Heap * sort();
        void print();
        void moveFrontier();

    private:
        static Heap * _root; // tree root
        static Heap * _active; // node currently
                               // receiving children
        static Heap * _last; // node with highest ID
                             // on current level
        static Heap * _frontier; // node on the edge of
                                 // the last full level
        static int _power; // ID value of leftmost node
                           // on each level

        int _key; // key value
        int _id; // successive integer assigned to nodes
        struct Heap * _left; // left child node
        struct Heap * _right; // right child node
        struct Heap * _parent; // parent node
        struct Heap * _pred; // predecessor node on this level
        struct Heap * _succ; // successor node on this level
```

```
};

void list(Heap *);
void draw(Heap *);

#endif
```

```
#include <stdio.h>
#include <stdlib.h>
#include <assert.h>

#include "Heap.h"

//----------------------------------------------------
// static variables
//----------------------------------------------------

Heap * Heap::_root;
Heap * Heap::_active;
Heap * Heap::_last;
Heap * Heap::_frontier;
int Heap::_power;

//----------------------------------------------------
// construct an individual heap node
//----------------------------------------------------

Heap::Heap(int x, int y) {
    _key= x;
    _id= y;
    _left= 0;
    _right= 0;
    _parent= 0;
    _pred= 0;
    _succ= 0;
}

//----------------------------------------------------
```

```
// construct a heap from the provided data
// the node returned is located somewhere on the heap
// to get the root:
// Heap *n= new Heap(count,values);
// Heap *root= n->getRoot();
//-----------------------------------------------------

Heap::Heap(int n, int *x ) {
    _key= x[0];
    _id= 1;
    _left= 0;
    _right= 0;
    _parent= 0;
    _pred= 0;
    _succ= 0;

    _root= this;
    _active= this;
    _last= 0;
    _frontier= 0;
    _power= 2;

    for ( int i= 1; i < n; ++i ) {
        Heap *node= new Heap(x[i], i+1);
        node->insert();
        node->moveup();
    }
    _power /= 2;
}


//-----------------------------------------------------
// insert a Heap node at the end of the heap
//-----------------------------------------------------

void Heap::insert() {

    this->setPred(0);
    this->setSucc(0);
    if ( _active->getLeft() == 0 ) {
        _active->setLeft(this);
        this->setParent(_active);
```

```
                 if ( this->getID() == _power ) {
                     _frontier= this;
                     _power *= 2;
                 }
                 _last= this;
             } else if ( _active->getRight() == 0 ) {
                 _active->setRight(this);
                 this->setParent(_active);
                 _last->setSucc(this);
                 this->setPred(_last);
                 if ( this->getID() == _power-1 ) {
                     _active= _frontier;
                 }
                 _last= this;
             } else {
                 _active= _last->getParent()->getSucc();
                 if ( _active == 0 ) {
                     _active= _frontier;
                     _active->setLeft(this);
                     this->setParent(_active);
                     _frontier= this;
                 } else {
                     _active->setLeft(this);
                     this->setParent(_active);
                     _last->setSucc(this);
                     this->setPred(_last);
                 }
                 if ( this->getID() == _power ) {
                     _power *= 2;
                 }
                 _last= this;
             }

             Heap * parent= this->getParent();
             if ( this->getKey() > parent->getKey() ) {
                 // update variables
                 if ( _frontier == this ) {
                     _frontier= parent;
                 }
                 _last= parent;
                 _active= this;
```

```
        }
    }

    //---------------------------------------------------
    // re-arrange the heap after appending a node at the
    // end of the binary tree so that the heap property
    // is preserved
    //---------------------------------------------------

    void Heap::moveup() {

        Heap *temp;

        while ( true  ) {
            Heap * parent= this->getParent();
            if ( !parent || parent->getKey() >=
                            this->getKey() ) {
                break;
            }

            // swap ID numbers
            int swap= parent->getID();
            parent->setID(this->getID());
            this->setID(swap);

            // swap incoming vertical pointers
            Heap * grand= parent->getParent();
            if ( grand != 0 ) {
                if ( parent == grand->getLeft() ) {
                    grand->setLeft(this);
                } else if ( parent == grand->getRight() ) {
                    grand->setRight(this);
                }
            }

            // swap outgoing vertical pointers
            parent->setParent(this);
            this->setParent(grand);

            if ( this == parent->getLeft() ) {
                if ( this->getLeft() != 0 ) {
```

```
                                this->getLeft()->setParent(parent);
                        }
                        parent->setLeft(this->getLeft());
                        this->setLeft(parent);

                        if ( this->getRight() != 0 ) {
                            if ( parent->getRight() != 0 ) {
                                temp= parent->getRight()
                                            ->getParent();
                                parent->getRight()->setParent(
                                        this->getRight()
                                        ->getParent());
                                this->getRight()->setParent(temp);
                            } else {
                                this->getRight()->setParent(0);
                            }
                        } else {
                            if ( parent->getRight() != 0 ) {
                                parent->getRight()->setParent(this);
                            }
                        }

                        temp= this->getRight();
                        this->setRight(parent->getRight());
                        parent->setRight(temp);
                } else if ( this == parent->getRight() ) {
                        if ( this->getRight() != 0 ) {
                            this->getRight()->setParent(parent);
                        }
                        parent->setRight(this->getRight());
                        this->setRight(parent);

                        if ( this->getLeft() != 0 ) {
                            if ( parent->getLeft() != 0 ) {
                                temp= parent->getLeft()->getParent();
                                parent->getLeft()->setParent(
                                                this->getLeft()
                                        ->getParent());
                                this->getLeft()->setParent(temp);
                            } else {
                                this->getLeft()->setParent(0);
```

```
        }
    } else {
        if ( parent->getLeft() != 0 ) {
            parent->getLeft()->setParent(this);
        }
    }

    temp= this->getLeft();
    this->setLeft(parent->getLeft());
    parent->setLeft(temp);
} else {
    assert(0);
}

// swap incoming horizontal pointers
if ( this->getPred() != 0 ) {
    if ( parent->getPred() != 0 ) {
        temp= parent->getPred()->getSucc();
        parent->getPred()->setSucc(
                            this->getPred()
                ->getSucc());
        this->getPred()->setSucc(temp);
    } else {
        this->getPred()->setSucc(parent);
    }
} else {
    if ( parent->getPred() != 0 ) {
        parent->getPred()->setSucc(this);
    }
}

if ( this->getSucc() != 0 ) {
    if ( parent->getSucc() != 0 ) {
        temp= parent->getSucc()->getPred();
        parent->getSucc()->setPred(
                            this->getSucc()
                ->getPred());
        this->getSucc()->setPred(temp);
    } else {
        this->getSucc()->setPred(parent);
    }
```

```
        } else {
            if ( parent->getSucc() != 0 ) {
                parent->getSucc()->setPred(this);
            }
        }

        // swap outgoing horizontal pointers
        temp= parent->getPred();
        parent->setPred(this->getPred());
        this->setPred(temp);

        temp= parent->getSucc();
        parent->setSucc(this->getSucc());
        this->setSucc(temp);

        // update variables
        _active= _last->getParent();
        if ( _root == parent ) {
            _root= this;
        }
    }
}


//----------------------------------------------------
// re-arrange the heap after inserting a new root node
// in the binary tree so that the heap property is
// preserved
//----------------------------------------------------

void Heap::movedown() {

    Heap *temp, *child, *move;

    move= _root;
    while ( true  ) {
        Heap * left= move->getLeft();
        Heap * right= move->getRight();
        if ( left != 0 && right != 0  ) {
            if ( left->getKey() <= move->getKey() &&
                 right->getKey() <= move->getKey() ) {
                break;
```

```
            } else {
                child= (left->getKey() >=
                        right->getKey()) ?
                        left : right;
            }
        } else if ( left != 0 ) {
            if ( left->getKey() <= move->getKey() ) {
                break;
            } else {
                child= left;
            }
        } else {
            break;
        }


        // swap ID numbers
        int swap= move->getID();
        move->setID(child->getID());
        child->setID(swap);


        // swap incoming vertical pointers
        Heap * grand= move->getParent();
        if ( grand != 0 ) {
            if ( move == grand->getLeft() ) {
                grand->setLeft(child);
            } else if ( move == grand->getRight() ) {
                grand->setRight(child);
            }
        }


        // swap outgoing vertical pointers
        move->setParent(child);
        child->setParent(grand);

        if ( child == move->getLeft() ) {
            if ( child->getLeft() != 0 ) {
                child->getLeft()->setParent(move);
            }
            move->setLeft(child->getLeft());
            child->setLeft(move);
```

```
                        if ( child->getRight() != 0 ) {
                            if ( move->getRight() != 0 ) {
                                temp= move->getRight()->getParent();
                                move->getRight()->setParent(
                                            child->getRight()
                                        ->getParent());
                                child->getRight()->setParent(temp);
                            } else {
                                child->getRight()->setParent(0);
                            }
                        } else {
                            if ( move->getRight() != 0 ) {
                                move->getRight()->setParent(child);
                            }
                        }

                        temp= child->getRight();
                        child->setRight(move->getRight());
                        move->setRight(temp);
                    } else if ( child == move->getRight() ) {
                        if ( child->getRight() != 0 ) {
                            child->getRight()->setParent(move);
                        }
                        move->setRight(child->getRight());
                        child->setRight(move);

                        if ( child->getLeft() != 0 ) {
                            if ( move->getLeft() != 0 ) {
                                temp= move->getLeft()->getParent();
                                move->getLeft()->setParent(
                                            child->getLeft()
                                        ->getParent());
                                child->getLeft()->setParent(temp);
                            } else {
                                child->getLeft()->setParent(0);
                            }
                        } else {
                            if ( move->getLeft() != 0 ) {
                                move->getLeft()->setParent(child);
                            }
                        }
```

```
            temp= child->getLeft();
            child->setLeft(move->getLeft());
            move->setLeft(temp);
        } else {
            assert(0);
        }

        // swap incoming horizontal pointers
        if ( child->getPred() != 0 ) {
            if ( move->getPred() != 0 ) {
                temp= move->getPred()->getSucc();
                move->getPred()->setSucc(
                        child->getPred()
                    ->getSucc());
                child->getPred()->setSucc(temp);
            } else {
                child->getPred()->setSucc(move);
            }
        } else {
            if ( move->getPred() != 0 ) {
                move->getPred()->setSucc(child);
            }
        }

        if ( child->getSucc() != 0 ) {
            if ( move->getSucc() != 0 ) {
                temp= move->getSucc()->getPred();
                move->getSucc()->setPred(
                        child->getSucc()
                    ->getPred());
                child->getSucc()->setPred(temp);
            } else {
                child->getSucc()->setPred(move);
            }
        } else {
            if ( move->getSucc() != 0 ) {
                move->getSucc()->setPred(child);
            }
        }
```

```
            // swap outgoing horizontal pointers
            temp= move->getPred();
            move->setPred(child->getPred());
            child->setPred(temp);

            temp= move->getSucc();
            move->setSucc(child->getSucc());
            child->setSucc(temp);

            // update variables
            _active= _last->getParent();
            if ( _root == move ) {
                _root= child;
            }
            if ( _last == child ) {
                _last= move;
            }
        }
}

//----------------------------------------------------
// remove the largest element from the heap and
// restore the structure to have the heap properties
//----------------------------------------------------

Heap * Heap::remove() {

    Heap * node= _root;
    Heap * curr, * prev;

    if ( _root == 0 ) {
        return 0;
    }

    if ( _root != 0 && _root->getLeft() != 0 ) {

        // unlink last node
        Heap * penult= _last->getPred();
        if ( penult != 0 ) {
            penult->setSucc(0);
        }
```

```
            Heap * parent= _last->getParent();

            if ( _last->getID() == _power ) {
               for ( curr= parent; curr != 0 ;
                       curr= curr->getSucc() ) {
                       prev= curr;
                  }
                  _frontier= prev;
                  _power /= 2;
            }

            if ( parent != 0 ) {
               if ( _last == parent->getLeft() ) {
                  parent->setLeft(0);
               } else {
                  parent->setRight(0);
               }

               // link last node in as root

               if ( _root->getLeft() != 0 ) {
                  _root->getLeft()->setParent(_last);
               }
               if ( _root->getRight() != 0 ) {
                  _root->getRight()->setParent(_last);
               }
               _last->setLeft(_root->getLeft());
               _last->setRight(_root->getRight());

               _last->setParent(0);
               _last->setSucc(0);
               _last->setPred(0);
               _last->setID(_root->getID());
               _root= _last;
            }

            if ( penult != 0 ) {
               _last= penult;
            } else {
               _last= _frontier;
            }
```

```
                          movedown();
               } else {
                   _last= 0;
                   _root= 0;
                   _frontier= 0;
               }

               // unlink removed node
               node->setLeft(0);
               node->setRight(0);
               node->setParent(0);
               node->setSucc(0);
               node->setPred(0);
               node->setID(0);

               return node;
     }


     //----------------------------------------------------
     // heap sort a linked list
     //----------------------------------------------------

     Heap * Heap::sort() {

         Heap * head;
         Heap * last= 0;
         Heap * next= 0;
         while( _root != 0 ) {
             next= this->remove();
             if ( next == 0 ) {
                 break;
             }
             if ( last == 0 ) {
                 head= next;
                 next->setPred(0);
             } else {
                 next->setPred(last);
                 last->setSucc(next);
             }
             last= next;
         }
```

```
        _root= head;
        _last= last;
        _active= 0;
        _frontier= 0;

        return head;
    }
```

Mathematical Problem Solving

Mathematics in the making appears as an experimental, inductive science.

—*George Polya*

6.1   Preview

This chapter draws an analogy between developing a proof for a mathematical theorem and developing the explanation for a software defect.

The first section of this chapter explains how concepts from the literature of instruction in mathematical proof techniques can be used in software debugging. It explains the worldview of the mathematician and presents a metaphor in which the software defect is considered a theorem to prove and the programmer is a mathematician.

The second section of this chapter describes and evaluates the Mathematical Heuristics movement begun by George Polya. The third section reviews the contributions of several popular texts about mathematical proof methods that have been published in the past two decades. It explains some of the contributions that each makes over Polya's original work.

The fourth section of this chapter describes Alan Schoenfeld's approach to teaching mathematical problem solving. It explains the hierarchy of "knowledge and behavior necessary for an adequate characterization of mathematical problem-solving performance" that he advocates.

The fourth section of this chapter applies Schoenfeld's approach to software debugging. It argues that Schoenfeld's categories can be transferred from the domain of mathematical problem solving to that of software debugging in a straightforward manner. It proposes that the three levels of the hierarchy in debugging are strategies, heuristics, and tactics.

6.2   Worldview of the mathematician

Devlin has defined mathematics as "the science of patterns" [De97]. The tools of that science are abstract notation, and the means of verifying the discoveries of that science are proofs based on logic.

When we follow the way of the mathematician, we use an analogy between developing a proof of a mathematical proposition and developing a diagnosis of a software defect in a program. In the past several centuries, mathematicians have developed numerous methods for constructing proofs. These methods, however, have only recently been organized and taught in a way that the average student can learn and apply as effectively as the mathematically gifted. This opens up a rich tradition of problem-solving methods that mathematicians have developed.

6.3   Polya and mathematical heuristics

The modern Mathematical Heuristics movement began with the publication of *How to Solve It* by George Polya in 1945 [Po45]. The book is popular in nature, and the content is accessible to high school students. Its popularity is demonstrated by the fact that it's still in print at the time this book goes to press, over half a century later.

Although his book pays special attention to the requirements of students and teachers of mathematics, it should interest anybody concerned with the ways and means of discovery. The book contains a list of questions that encapsulate his recommended methodology, followed by recommendations for use in the classroom and a short dictionary of heuristic concepts. He developed these ideas in a series of volumes over the following two decades. *Mathematics and Plausible Reasoning* was published in 1954 and *Mathematical Discovery* was published in two volumes in 1962 and 1965, respectively.

6.3.1   *How to Solve It*—G. Polya

Polya's "How to Solve It" list consists of four phases:

1. Understand the problem.

2. Find the connection between the data and the unknown. You may be obliged to consider auxiliary problems if an immediate connection can't be found. You should obtain eventually a plan of the solution.

3.   Carry out your plan.

4.   Examine the solution obtained.

Polya sought to provoke understanding of a problem by urging his readers to consider the following questions and suggestions:

- What is the unknown?
- What is the data?
- What is the condition?
- Is it possible to satisfy the condition?
- Is the condition sufficient to determine the unknown? Or is it insufficient? Or redundant? Or contradictory?
- Draw a figure. Introduce suitable notation.
- Separate the various parts of the condition. Can you write them down?

Polya sought to enable development of a plan by suggesting his readers should consider the following questions:

- Have you seen it before? Or have you seen the same problem in a slightly different form?
- Do you know of a related problem? Do you know of a theorem that could be useful?
- Look at the unknown! Can you think of a familiar problem having the same or a similar unknown?
- Here is a problem related to yours and solved before. Can you use it?
- Can you use its result? Can you use its method? Should you introduce some auxiliary element to make its use possible?
- Can you restate the problem? Can you restate it still differently?
- Go back to definitions.
- If you cannot solve the proposed problem try to solve first some related problem. Can you imagine a more accessible, related problem? A more

general problem? A more special problem? An analogous problem? Can you solve a part of the problem?

■ Keep only a part of the condition, drop the other part; how far is the unknown then determined, how can it vary? Can you derive something useful from the data?

■ Can you think of other data appropriate to determine the unknown?

■ Can you change the unknown or the data, or both if necessary, so that the new unknown and the new data are nearer to each other?

■ Have you used all the data? Have you used the whole condition? Have you taken into account all essential notions involved in the problem?

Polya encouraged the execution of a plan by advising his readers to consider the following questions and suggestions.

■ Carrying out your plan of the solution, check each step.

■ Can you see clearly that the step is correct?

■ Can you prove that it is correct?

Polya motivated the review of results by recommending that his readers ask the following questions:

■ Can you check the result?

■ Can you check the argument?

■ Can you derive the result differently?

■ Can you see it at a glance?

■ Can you use the result or the method for some other problem?

6.3.2   Evaluation

Alan Schoenfeld [Sc85] makes the following criticisms of the Mathematical Heuristic movement:

- "Faith in mathematical heuristics as useful problem-solving strategies has not been justified either by results from the empirical literature or by programming success in AI [artificial intelligence]."

- "Despite the fact that heuristics have received extensive attention in the mathematics education literature, heuristic strategies have not been characterized in nearly adequate detail."

- "The number of useful, adequately delineated techniques is not numbered in tens, but in hundreds. . . . The question of selecting which ones to use (and when) becomes a critical issue."

- "The literature of mathematics education is chock-full of heuristic studies. Most of these, while encouraging, have provided little concrete evidence that heuristics have the power that the experimenters hoped they would have."

It is fair to ask whether the use of heuristic methods as such have resulted in a meaningful, measurable improvement in student's mathematical competency. The second half of Schoenfeld's book contains empirical studies that support these criticisms, among others.

6.4 Mathematical proof texts

In the two decades prior to the writing of this book, numerous texts have been written to assist mathematics students in learning to do proofs. Many of them followed earlier texts in embedding short discussions of proof techniques in larger presentations on sets, functions, counting, and the like. These were aimed at the traditional course for mathematics majors who were moving from the calculus to upper division courses.

A few books, however, concentrated entirely on the methods of proof, without additional content. These books were suitable for use by high school students. In some cases they demonstrated the arguments of Schoenfeld, and in others they applied his results.

6.4.1 *The Nuts and Bolts of Proofs*—A. Cupillari

Antonella Cupillari published the first edition of *The Nuts and Bolts of Proofs* in 1989 and released a much enlarged second edition in 2001 [Cu01]. The work covers the following proof techniques:

- Direct proof

- Proof by contrapositive

- Equivalence theorems

- Use of counterexamples

- Mathematical induction

- Existence theorems

- Equality of sets

- Equality of numbers

The most innovative aspect of this work is the acknowledgment that students need a control structure to help them select the appropriate proof technique for a given problem. This structure is provided as a flowchart on the last page of the book. The flowchart has three binary decisions, one five-way decision, and eight possible procedures to execute based on the results of these decisions.

Unfortunately, in the second edition, this flowchart was photo reduced from the two-page version in the first edition, rendering it quite difficult to read. The concept, however, is still a good one. The significance of this work for debugging is that presentation of proof techniques has moved beyond a simple list of questions to a process of matching techniques to problems.

6.4.2 *Thinking Mathematically*—Mason, Burton, and Stacy

John Mason, with Leone Burton and Kaye Stacey, published the first edition of *Thinking Mathematically* in 1982, with a revised edition in 1985 [MBS85]. It differs from other works in that it tries to teach mathematical thinking in general, without addressing specific proof techniques.

This work divides the process of problem solving into three phases: entry, attack, and review. During each of these phases it encourages in the strongest terms that the problem solver keep a record of at least three things:

1.   The significant ideas that occur

2.   The goals you're trying to achieve

3.   The feelings you experience as you work

The book provides much explanation and many opportunities to employ what it promotes as four fundamental processes of mathematical thinking: specializing, generalizing, conjecturing, and justifying. While formal proof methods aren't taught, the material on justifying provides an intellectual foundation for using them.

There are several innovative aspects of this work. First, it addresses the emotions that people feel when they solve mathematical problems. It may be the first serious preventative to the "mathophobia" that so many students develop by the time they reach high school. In this respect, it applies some of the ideas that Schoenfeld developed on mathematical belief systems.

Second, it encourages the use of a log or set of discovery notes throughout the problem-solving process. Not only does it suggest that you write this information down, but it also tells how you can employ it during the process.

Third, it devotes an entire chapter to "Developing an Internal Monitor." In this respect, it applies some of the ideas Schoenfeld developed on the need for a control mechanism during problem solving. The internal monitor keeps the student on track, identifies when the student has become stuck, suggests alternatives when needed, and evaluates ideas for further consideration.

There are two reasons that this work is significant for debugging. First, it applies and extends Schoenfeld's ideas about belief systems and the need for control mechanisms. Second, it promotes the use of discovery diaries as a means for teaching and using problem-solving skills.

6.4.3 *How to Read and Do Proofs*—Daniel Solow

Daniel Solow published the first edition of *How to Read and Do Proofs* in 1982, delivered an enlarged second edition in 1990, and updated a third edition in 2002 [So02]. The work covers the following proof techniques:

- The forward-backward method
- The construction method
- The choose method
- Induction
- Specialization
- Nested quantifiers
- The contradiction method

- The contrapositive method

- The direct uniqueness method

- The indirect uniqueness method

- Proof by elimination

- Proof by cases

- Max/min methods

There are two innovative aspects of this work that go beyond the traditional approaches and litanies of heuristics. The first is the level of detail that the author provides in describing how to employ the method. To put these in perspective, his text summaries of how to use each method are all over 150 words long, and some are twice that length.

The second innovative aspect of this work is to provide a table that summarizes the thirteen methods described in the book. For each method, columns describe the name of the technique, the conditions under which it should be used, what should be assumed, what should be concluded, and how to employ the method.

The advantages of this work are twofold. First, it no longer makes the assumption that students will learn the steps of proof by osmosis if they're exposed to a sufficient quantify of those proofs. The level of detail in the method description makes explicit what other texts assume. Second, the summary table goes beyond Cupillari's flowchart by listing not only the usage conditions and names of methods, but also assumptions, conclusions, and a concise summary of how to apply the method.

The significance of this work for debugging is recognizing that some students won't learn procedures from practice alone, without those procedures being described explicitly. Students of computer programming have been held back by the same lack of explicit description of debugging procedures.

6.5   Schoenfeld and mathematical problem solving

Schoenfeld defines a hierarchy of four elements of "knowledge and behavior necessary for an adequate characterization of mathematical problem-solving performance":

1.   Resources

2.   Heuristics

3. Control

4. Belief systems

6.5.1 Resources per Schoenfeld

Schoenfeld defines resources as follows:

> Mathematical knowledge possessed by the individual that can be brought to bear on the problem at hand:
>
> - Intuitions and informal knowledge regarding the domain
> - Facts
> - Algorithmic procedures
> - Routine nonalgorithmic procedures
> - Propositional knowledge about the agreed-upon rules for working in the domain.

Schoenfeld draws an analogy between resources in other fields of intellectual endeavor and those of mathematical problem solving. He notes that chess masters develop a "vocabulary" of tens of thousands of complete game configurations and that they also have learned a stereotypical response to this configuration.

In artificial intelligence (AI), this type of knowledge is stored as condition-action pairs, also called "productions." Expert systems are often built using knowledge structured in this way.

His research showed that in mathematics, too, expert problem solvers are able to match stereotypical problem situations to stereotypical responses quickly. He also argues that resources of this type can be quite complex, even though they invoke automatic responses.

6.5.2 Heuristics per Schoenfeld

Schoenfeld defines heuristics as:

> Strategies and techniques for making progress on unfamiliar problems; rules of thumb for effective problem solving:
>
> - Drawing figures
> - Introducing notation

- Exploiting related problems
- Reformulating problems
- Working backwards
- Testing and verification procedures

Schoenfeld believes that the heuristics used in mathematics education are actually names for families of closely related heuristics. These heuristics have to be developed in detail before they can be used by students in problem solving. He also argues that while heuristics are useful, they're no substitute for subject-matter knowledge.

6.5.3 Control per Schoenfeld

Schoenfeld defines control as:

Global decisions regarding the selection and implementation of resources and strategies:

- Planning
- Monitoring and assessment
- Decision making
- Conscious metacognitive acts

Control decisions determine which way to go and which way to abandon. They determine the use of resources, particularly time. Schoenfeld asserts that an effective control mechanism must have "periodic monitoring and assessment of solutions."

He describes a control strategy that he used in teaching integration in a calculus. The three steps of this strategy successively apply more general, difficult, and time-consuming procedures to the problem. At each step, the form of the integrand was matched against forms to which a set of procedures was applicable.

Schoenfeld also describes a general strategy that he taught in a class on mathematical problem solving. It prescribes five phases: analysis, design, exploration, implementation, and verification. The strategy integrated many common heuristics, and the students were trained in monitoring their own progress and assessing their solutions. The evidence from his studies of these classes indicates that the students became much more adept at dealing with problems unlike those that were presented in class. He summarizes their development thus: "The most impressive result is that the students did quite well on a set of problems that had been placed on their exam precisely because I did not know how to solve them!"

6.5.4 Belief systems per Schoenfeld

Schoenfeld defines belief systems as:

> One's "mathematical world view," the set of (not necessarily conscious) determinants of an individual's behavior:
>
> - Self
> - The environment
> - The topic, and mathematics itself

6.6 Applying Schoenfeld to debugging

We believe that Schoenfeld's categories can be transferred from the domain of mathematical problem solving to that of software debugging in a straightforward manner.

6.6.1 Transferring the hierarchy

Debugging tactics are programming skills that produce information. Programmers who are competent in debugging have an inventory of tactics they can quickly match to situations. They can apply those tactics automatically without requiring contemplation.

Debugging heuristics are techniques for making progress on unfamiliar problems or rules of thumb for effective problem solving. Heuristics aren't guaranteed to produce a result. Programmers who are competent in debugging use a variety of means to generate ideas on the root cause of a bug.

Debugging strategies are global decisions regarding the selection and implementation of heuristics and tactics. Programmers who are competent in debugging plan their diagnosis activities and know when to give up on a line of analysis and try a different approach.

6.6.2 The military analogy

One way to look at these three levels is with a military analogy. Military analysts look at three levels of activity: strategic, operational, and tactical.

Strategic decisions are made at the top of the organizational hierarchy. Strictly speaking, only one strategy is being employed at a time, although in an extremely large undertaking, there may be a second level of strategy in independent areas of operation.

In World War II, the strategy of the United States and the United Kingdom was to force the Germans to surrender unconditionally first, and then do the same with the Japanese. Within the European Theater of Operations, the strategy was to liberate Western Europe by a cross-channel invasion from Britain. Within the Pacific Theater of Operations, the strategy was to bring the war ever closer to Japan through a series of "island-hopping" actions from the periphery of Japan's empire. Strategic decisions cover the largest scope geographically and often take months, or years, to implement.

Operational decisions are made at the mid-level of the organizational hierarchy. Operational decisions cover a smaller scope geographically than strategic decisions, but still can cover a large area. Operational decisions can involve large organizations, but unlike strategies, a number of operational decisions can be enacted independently and simultaneously. Operational decisions take days or weeks to implement.

Tactical decisions are made at the bottom of the organizational hierarchy. They cover only a small geographic scope and involve the actions of individual soldiers and pieces of equipment. Tactical decisions take only minutes or hours to implement.

6.6.3 Hypothesis generation and evaluation

Another way to look at these three levels is with respect to hypothesis generation and evaluation. Strategies tell you which hypothesis to explore. A good strategy will tell you how to choose a hypothesis, how to validate it, how to refine it, and when to discard it. Previous works on debugging don't recognize the concept of strategies as such.

Heuristics suggest new hypotheses or new tactics to employ. Heuristics are most useful when our current hypothesis has proven false or insufficiently precise. Rather than stare at a problem in the hopes that a new hypothesis will leap from the page, we get out our list of heuristics and employ one.

Since there is no guarantee that a heuristic will yield a result, there is no guarantee that employing a debugging heuristic will suggest a hypothesis to us. Experience has taught us, however, that the probability is high that if we employ several heuristics, one of them will help us to see the problem in a new light. Previous works on debugging don't distinguish heuristics from tactics as such.

Tactics tell you about the state of the program when it's running, so that you can validate or invalidate the current hypothesis. Tactics aren't helpful if you're working with a pseudohypothesis, that is, a statement that can't be completely proved or disproved. Previous works on debugging usually don't articulate the relationship between tactics and the current working hypothesis.

6.7 Review

The modern Mathematical Heuristics movement began with the publication of *How to Solve It* by George Polya in 1945. Polya's "How to Solve It" list consists of four phases: understanding the problem, developing a plan for a solution, executing the plan, and reviewing the results. While Polya's ideas on heuristics have been expanded upon and widely employed in teaching mathematics, they don't seem to have caused a meaningful change in student performance.

There have been numerous texts written to assist mathematics students in learning to do proofs. Cupillari's *The Nuts and Bolts of Proofs* is an advance over previous works because it provides students a control structure to help them select the appropriate proof technique for a given problem. Mason's *Thinking Mathematically* is an advance over previous works because it addresses the belief systems of students and provides a method for learning how to become self-aware during problem solving. Solow's *How to Read and Do Proofs* is an advance over previous works because it provides a greater level of detail describing how to employ each proof method and because it provides a tabular summary and comparison of the methods described in the book.

Schoenfeld defines a hierarchy of four elements of "knowledge and behavior necessary for an adequate characterization of mathematical problem-solving performance." These are resources, heuristics, control, and belief systems.

Schoenfeld's research shows that in mathematics, expert problem solvers are quickly able to match stereotypical problem situations to stereotypical responses, which he terms resources. He believes that the heuristics used in mathematics education are actually names for families of closely related heuristics. He defines control in terms of evaluating lines of inquiry and allocating resources, particularly time.

We believe that Schoenfeld's categories can be transferred from the domain of mathematical problem solving to that of software debugging in a straightforward manner. We suggest that there are three levels of activities in debugging: strategies, heuristics, and tactics.

One way to look at these three levels is a military analogy. Military analysts look at three levels of activity: strategic, operational, and tactical.

Another way to look at these three levels is with respect to hypothesis generation and evaluation. Strategies tell you which hypothesis to explore. Heuristics suggest new hypotheses or new tactics to employ. Tactics tell you about the state of the program when it's running, so that you can validate or invalidate the current hypothesis.

7

Debugging Strategies

Strategy is the art of making use of time and space. I am less chary of the latter than the former. Space we can recover, lost time never.

—Napoleon Bonaparte

7.1   Preview

This chapter presents the definitions of debugging strategies. These strategies are defined in terms of their assumptions and control structure. The first part explains the evaluation criteria that can be used to determine whether a given strategy is leading to progress in diagnosing a defect. The last part explains how to choose among the various strategies presented.

7.2   Evaluation mechanisms

Every debugging strategy consists of three parts: a set of assumptions, a control structure, and an evaluation mechanism. While the set of assumptions and the control structure are unique to each strategy, the evaluation mechanisms are independent and can be used interchangeably with different strategies.

The purpose of the evaluation mechanism is to tell you whether you're making progress. If you have been using a strategy for a while and the evaluation mechanism says that you aren't making progress, it's time to apply another strategy and, perhaps, try a different hypothesis.

There are several ways to evaluate whether a strategy is working.

- The number of plausible hypotheses disproved should be increasing.
- The effort required to reproduce the problem should be decreasing.

- The size of the input required to reproduce the problem should be decreasing.

- The amount of code excluded from consideration should be increasing.

These evaluation mechanisms are listed in increasing order of strength. The number of plausible hypotheses may be quite large, and more importantly, isn't known at the time you start looking for a bug. On the other hand, the size of the input that initially causes the bug report, and the size of the program that has the reported bug, are fixed and are known when the search begins.

7.3 Binary search strategy

7.3.1 Binary search assumptions

The binary search strategy is analogous to the binary search algorithm taught in introductory data structures or algorithms classes. It works quickly because when it's applicable, it converges on a solution in time proportional to the logarithm of the number of code segments under scrutiny.

This strategy assumes that the code segments under investigation have some linear ordering. The statements, code blocks, or loop nests in a procedure can be ordered according to the lexical order in which they appear in the program text. The procedures in a program can be ordered by topologically sorting the call graph of the program.

A **code block** is a group of sequentially executed statements with a single exit point. Literature on compilers often refers to these as **basic blocks.**

A graph consists of a set of nodes and a set of edges. A **topological sort** of a directed graph is a listing of the nodes such that if one node directly or indirectly precedes another node in the graph, the first node is listed before the second node in the listing.

7.3.2 Binary search control structure

The next code sample shows the control structure for the binary search strategy.

```
Set S to the set of all code segments in question
Do while S has more than one element
```

```
        Split the set S into two subsets, L and R,
            of the same size
        Determine in which of the two subsets the problem
            first occurs
        Set S to the offending subset
    End-do
    The remaining element is the code segment that
    contains the bug
```

7.4 Greedy search strategy

7.4.1 Greedy search assumptions

The greedy search strategy is analogous to the greedy method taught in introductory algorithms classes. The greedy method works in stages, considering one input element at a time. At each stage, the method decides whether an input is part of an optimal solution. The choice of the input element to examine at any stage is based on an optimization measure.

This strategy assumes that the program is divisible into segments that can be tested for responsibility for the defect. A procedure can be divided into its statements, code blocks, or loop nests. The procedures in a program can be divided into groups in which the procedures are all invoked by a common procedure.

7.4.2 Greedy search control structure

The next code sample shows the control structure for the greedy search strategy.

```
    Set P to the set of all code segments in question
    Set S to the empty set
    Do while P has elements remaining
        Pick an element E from P and remove it from P
        If E isn't responsible for the problem
        Then
            Set S = Union(S, {E})
         End-if
    End-do
    S is the set of code segments that causes the bug
```

The key to the greedy strategy is finding a selection method that maximizes the benefit and minimizes the cost for each iteration of the strategy.

The following are measures of the benefit:

- The number of lines of code validated
- The number of procedures validated
- The number of paths through the code validated

The following are measures of the cost:

- The CPU time it takes to execute the validated code
- The wall-clock time it takes to execute the validated code
- The labor required to set up the validation exercise

7.5   Breadth-first search strategy

7.5.1   Breadth-first search assumptions

The breadth-first search strategy is analogous to the breadth-first search method taught in introductory algorithm classes. The strategy assumes that the program being debugged has a single main procedure. If the problem system has multiple main procedures, because there are multiple executables in the system, wrap an outer loop around the control structure that visits each main procedure in turn. If the problem system has no main procedure, as in the case of libraries, treat the test case that is invoking the library as the main procedure.

This strategy is easier to use if you have a tool available that will generate a tree structure showing the calling hierarchy of the application. Failing that, a cross-reference listing of the application can also be useful.

7.5.2   Breadth-first control structure

The next code sample shows the control structure for the breadth-first strategy.

```
Set suspect list to empty
Invoke BFS with name of top level procedure
```

```
BFS ( ancestor )
    Set visited(ancestor) = true
    Set queue to the empty list
    Loop forever
        For each descendant procedure called by ancestor
            procedure
            If visited(descendant) is false
            Then
                Append descendant at end of queue
                Set visited(descendant) to true
            End-if
        End-for
        If queue is empty
        Then
            Return
        End-if
        Set candidate to the first element of queue
        Delete first element of queue
        Test the hypothesis that the errors occurs
            during the execution of the candidate
        If the hypothesis is true
        Then
            If the candidate has no descendants
                Set the suspect list to the candidate
                Return
            Else
                Prepend the candidate to the front of
                    the suspect list
            End-if
        End-if
    End-loop
End-BFS
The first element of the suspect list is the procedure
    in which the defect occurs
```

7.6   Depth-first search strategy

7.6.1   Depth-first search assumptions

The depth-first search strategy is analogous to the depth-first search method taught in introductory algorithms classes. The strategy assumes that the program being debugged has a single main procedure. If the problem system has multiple main procedures, because there are multiple executables in the system, wrap an outer loop around the control structure that visits each main procedure in turn. If the problem system has no main procedure, as in the case of libraries, treat the test case that is invoking the library as the main procedure.

This strategy is easier to use if you have a tool available that will generate a tree structure showing the calling hierarchy of the application. Failing that, a cross-reference listing of the application can also be useful.

7.6.2 Depth-first control structure

The next code sample shows the control structure for the depth-first strategy.

```
Set suspect list to empty
Invoke DFS with name of top level procedure
DFS ( ancestor )
    Set visited(ancestor) to true
    For each descendant procedure called by ancestor
        procedure
        If visited(descendant) is false
        Then
            Test the hypothesis that the errors occurs
                during the execution of descendant
            If the hypothesis is true
            Then
                Prepend the candidate to the front of
                    the suspect list
            End-if
            DFS(descendant)
        End-if
    End-for
End-DFS
The first element of the suspect list is the procedure
    in which the defect occurs
```

7.7   Program slice strategy

7.7.1   Program slice assumptions

The program slice strategy assumes that a tool is available that will perform control and data-flow analysis on the application and provide the slicing information. Doing this analysis by hand can be quite tedious. If the variable that has an incorrect value is a local variable, intraprocedural analysis may suffice. Otherwise, interprocedural analysis is needed.

A **program slice** of a program, with respect to a specific location in a program and a set of variables referenced at that location, is the set of statements and predicates in the program that may affect the value of the variables at that location.

Intraprocedural analysis is performed within the scope of an individual procedure (C++ function, Java method). **Interprocedural** analysis is performed across the boundaries of individual procedures (C++ functions, Java methods) and is performed on all of the procedures in an executable program. It can sometimes make sense to perform interprocedural analyses within an intermediate level, such as a library or a Java package.

7.7.2   Program slice control structure

The next code sample shows the control structure for the program slice strategy.

```
Identify a variable that has an incorrect value
Generate a slice of the application that shows all the
    calculations that contributed to the value of
    that variable, considering both control flow
    and data flow
Do while there are more unexamined contributing
    variables
    Observe the values taken on by one of the variables
    If any of the values of this variable are invalid,
    Then
        repeat the slicing process on this variable
    End-if
End-do
The code segments that have all valid input values but
which contribute invalid values are the cause of the bug
```

7.8 Deductive-analysis strategy

7.8.1 Deductive-analysis assumptions

Deduction is "the process of reasoning in which a conclusion follows necessarily from the stated premises" or "inference by reasoning from the general to the specific," according to the *American Heritage Dictionary of the English Language*.

The deductive-analysis strategy assumes that you have extensive experience in programming to draw on and a thorough understanding of the details of the application you're debugging. This body of general knowledge supplements the specific information you have about the bug, making it possible to work from this general knowledge to a specific hypothesis. We don't recommend this approach for people who are relative programming novices or who are attempting to debug a very large system.

7.8.2 Deductive-analysis control structure

The next code sample shows the control structure for the deductive-analysis strategy.

```
Generate an initial hypothesis
Do while there are more untested hypotheses
    Select a hypothesis according to one of the
        debugging heuristics
    If the hypothesis is false
    Then
        Generate more hypotheses
    Else
        Terminate search successfully
    End-if
End-do
Last hypothesis evaluated explains the cause of the bug
```

7.9 Inductive-analysis strategy

7.9.1 Inductive-analysis assumptions

Induction is "the process of deriving general principles from particular facts or instances," according to the *American Heritage Dictionary of the English Language*.

The inductive-analysis strategy makes the following assumptions:

- There exists a set of facts or observations that need to be explained.
- There exists a method for evaluating the quality of hypotheses generated.
- The default hypothesis-evaluation method is to judge simplicity.

7.9.2   Inductive-analysis control structure

The next code sample shows the control structure for the inductive-analysis strategy.

```
Do while no hypothesis explains all facts
    Generate a hypothesis
    Ensure that the hypothesis is compatible with other
        knowledge
    Ensure that the hypothesis explains as much as
        possible
    Count the facts accounted for
    Compare hypotheses, ensuring that this is a better
        explanation than its alternatives
    If the best hypothesis explains all the facts,
    Then
        Terminate search successfully
    End-if
End-do
Last hypothesis evaluated explains the cause of the bug
```

7.10   Choosing a strategy

How do you choose a strategy for a given debugging effort? The assumptions provide the key.

The binary search strategy is very powerful but requires a linear ordering of code segments. This means that it's applied to programs whose components act as a series of filters on the input, applied one after another. A program that is structured with lots of callbacks to event handlers won't work with this strategy.

The greedy search strategy requires that the programmer keep good records. He or she must be comfortable with a quantitative approach to decision making and consistent in collecting the metrics required for input to the strategy. A development environment in which it's easy to run test cases and collect statistics is highly desirable if you're going to use the greedy search strategy. If that environment includes scripting tools for processing the statistics, it will make using this strategy that much easier.

The breadth-first search strategy makes sense when you're working on a system that is unfamiliar to you. It works like peeling an onion. You explore each level of the control-flow hierarchy in turn. It allows you to determine whether a part of an application is causing the defect without actually knowing all about the part in question. The breadth-first strategy is more conservative than the depth-first search and tends to require less work when the depth of the leaves varies widely.

The depth-first search strategy makes sense if you have reason to believe that the problem is localized to a particular area of an application. If diagnosis will cause you to look at widely separate sections of the application, this strategy may result in analyzing many procedures that aren't relevant to the problem. The depth-first strategy is more aggressive than the breadth-first search and tends to evaluate fewer candidates when the depth of the leaves varies little.

The program slicing strategy assumes either that a slicing tool is available or that it's tractable to do the data-flow analysis by hand. If the problem shows up in a local variable whose values are only fed by arguments to a procedure, manual analysis may be possible. Otherwise, the tool is necessary to apply this strategy in a timely manner. There is a commercial tool for slicing that currently supports the C language, and there are academic projects that have support for C++ as well. See Chapter 14 for more information on slicing tools.

The concept of slicing has been known for over twenty years at the time this book goes to press. The growth in the research understanding of the problems in implementing a slicing system has grown considerably. We have reason to be optimistic about the future availability of slicing tools for other programming languages.

The deductive-analysis strategy works best for experienced programmers who are knowledgeable about all aspects of the system on which they're working. It requires a large body of knowledge about programming in general and the application in particular. The deductive-analysis strategy is most useful for small- to medium-sized systems that were designed by very small teams. A programmer who uses the deductive strategy should be one of the primary developers of the system.

The inductive-analysis strategy assumes that the programmer can generate lots of observations that will inform his hypotheses. If the programmer cannot have direct access to the application to run experiments for logistical or security reasons, don't choose this strategy. If turnaround time for experiments will take hours or even days, don't choose this strategy.

7.11 Review

Every debugging strategy consists of three parts: a set of assumptions, a control structure, and an evaluation mechanism. The purpose of the evaluation mechanism is to tell you whether you're making progress.

The binary search strategy is analogous to the binary search algorithm taught in every beginner's data structures or algorithms class. This strategy assumes that the code segments under investigation have some linear ordering.

The greedy search strategy is analogous to the greedy method taught in introductory algorithms classes. This strategy assumes that the program is divisible into segments that can be tested for responsibility for the defect. The key to the greedy search strategy is finding a selection method that maximizes the benefit and minimizes the cost for each iteration of the strategy.

A program slice gives the set of statements and predicates in a program that may affect the value of a set of variables at specific location in that program. The program slice strategy assumes that a tool is available that will perform control- and data-flow analysis on the application and provide the slicing information.

The deductive-analysis strategy reasons from a general body of knowledge to a specific conclusion about the problem at hand. This strategy assumes that you have extensive experience in programming to draw on and a thorough understanding of the details of the application you're debugging.

The inductive-analysis strategy reasons from a set of specific facts to an increasingly precise hypothesis that explains them. This strategy assumes that there exists a set of observations to start from and that there is a method for evaluating the quality of the hypotheses generated.

Choose a debugging strategy based on which set of assumptions fit the situation you're working on.

8

Debugging Heuristics

I have found it! (in Greek, "Heurisko!")

—*Archimedes*

8.1   Preview

This chapter presents the definitions of debugging heuristics, with examples of using each to find actual bugs. It explains that debugging heuristics don't lend themselves to easy categorization, as is the case with strategies and tactics. It notes that many debugging heuristics are similar to the mathematical heuristics described in Polya's book.

We have identified the following debugging heuristics:

- Modify the program so that you can repeat the problem at will.

- Create a test case that will demonstrate the problem when desired.

- Reduce the input required to reproduce the problem.

- Categorize the problem according to a standard set of questions.

- Describe the problem according to a standard methodology.

- Explain the problem to someone else.

- Recall a similar problem from the past.

- Draw a diagram.

- Choose a hypothesis from historical data.

8.2   Stabilize the program

Most works on debugging recommend a process often called *stabilizing the problem*. The goal of stabilization is reproducibility. Defects that can't be stabilized can't be fixed. Stabilizing a defect can be the hardest part of the debugging task.

The first step in stabilizing a bug is to run the defective program several times. If you don't always get an undesired behavior, you will need to modify the program or the environment in which you're running it. These types of defects will show a premature termination on one run, an infinite execution on another run, and so on.

Even getting an undesired behavior each time is no guarantee that you don't need to stabilize at this level. It can just mean that you haven't run the program enough times for a nondeterministic defect to show itself, or that you haven't run it in the right environment or on the right platform.

At this point, if you do get different behaviors on different runs, several hypotheses should suggest themselves. These types of bugs often involve memory corruption, data-structure violations, or problems with the environment or platform.

There is one circumstance in which it may not be possible to cause the undesirable behavior on each execution. This occurs when your application has multiple independent streams of control. Parallel execution can occur at the thread level or the process level. If you know that the application has parallel execution, then you may need to be satisfied with increasing the frequency of the problem occurrence. When a problem is caused by nondeterminism, it's often impossible to cause a problem to manifest on every run.

The second step in stabilizing a bug is to run the defective program several times again if you had to make changes to cause an undesired behavior to occur with each run. If the same undesired behavior occurs with each run, you can move on to the next step. If you don't always get the same undesired behavior, you will need to modify the program or the environment you're running it in again.

Once you have completed this task, the same group of hypotheses should suggest themselves. These types of bugs often involve memory corruption, data-structure violations, or problems with the environment or platform.

Now that you're getting the same undesired behavior with each execution of the program, you would be wise to try another level of stabilization. Try running the offending program in a different environment. By environment, we mean things like user account, environment variables, registry settings, system load, and so forth. A different environment still means on the same platform, by which we mean operating system and hardware architecture.

Under what circumstances is this type of stabilization helpful? If a problem occurs on the submitter's account, but not on the developer's account, a hypothesis of initialization errors, data-structure violations, or memory problems is a good place to start. The same hypotheses are also indicated if a program fails when running standalone but works correctly when running under a debugger.

Finally, it's sometimes useful to try running the offending program on a different platform. Of course, if the program relies on specific features of the operating system or hardware, this may not be possible. Even if a completely different platform is out of the question, you may be able to use related platforms, such as different versions of the same operating system. For example, you might not be able to take a program developed on a version of UNIX™ and run it on Windows™, but you might be able to run it on Linux™.

Under what circumstances is this type of stabilization helpful? If you run the program on a different platform and notice that discrepancies in floating-point output change, a hypothesis of value corruption due to different floating-point hardware or libraries is reasonable. If the application is dependent on vendor-provided versions of industry-standard libraries, and you see differences in behavior from one platform to another, a hypothesis of problems in other people's software is warranted.

Stabilization is one of the first things we do when diagnosing a bug. If done correctly, it can provide you with a number of qualified working hypotheses.

8.3   Create a test case

Almost all works on debugging recommend creating a standalone test case from the original defective program. There are several benefits to creating such a test case.

First, if done correctly, your test case should take significantly less time to manifest the problem than the original program. This means that you will be able to complete experiments much more quickly than if you run the original program.

Second, if the test case can execute standalone and indicate whether it passed or failed to a script that executes it, it can easily be incorporated into a suite of regression tests. This makes it more likely that the problem won't resurface in the future.

Third, if it turns out that the problem isn't in code that you're responsible for, you can turn the problem over to the people who are responsible. Having a good test case ready will enable the responsible party to turn a correction around more quickly.

A test case typically has two parts: the program and the input data. In this heuristic, we focus on the program. The next heuristic focuses on the input data to that program.

If you're working on platform like UNIX™, on which programs can return status codes that can be inspected by a shell script, your test case should return a 0 (for no problem) if the test passes and return a positive integer if the test fails. This makes it possible to easily include your test case in automated suites. In addition, the test case should print a pass/fail message, so that a simple search of the output will show you the outcome.

8.3.1   Cutting down a simple application problem

If you're diagnosing a problem with an application that works like a file-oriented filter, you can use the following procedure to cut down the program into a more manageable test case. A **filter** takes all of its input from the operating system standard input and sends all of its output to the operating system standard output.

1.   Create an input file that contains all of the keyboard entries up to, but not including, the step that causes the problem to manifest. On a UNIX™ system, you can use the *script* command to capture these entries in a file as you enter them.

2.   Create a driver that replays these actions to the application. This may be as simple as a shell script that redirects the standard input to the previously captured entries.

3.   Identify the procedure that responds to the input that manifests the problem. Just before the call to this procedure, insert a call to a new procedure that captures the state of the program at entry to this procedure. The program state includes the values of all global variables, actual arguments to the procedure, open files, and so forth. The new procedure should write all of these values to a text file.

4. Execute the driver and capture the state of the program at entry to the procedure that manifests the problem. Terminate the application at that point.

5. Create a new main procedure that sets all of the program state without having to execute that part of the application that normally creates it. The driver should do the following:

    ▪ Open all files and set them to the status that was captured.

    ▪ Set all global variables to the values captured.

    ▪ Call the procedure that manifests the problem with the argument values that were captured.

6. Remove all procedures from the application that were executed only before the procedure that manifests the problem. Use a call graph program to identify these if the application is large or you're unfamiliar with all of its parts.

7. Remove the normal main procedure and insert the new main procedure you have created. You should now be able to run the program and see the problem manifested almost immediately.

8.3.2 Cutting down a GUI application problem

Cutting down a problem with an application that uses a graphical user interface (GUI) is more involved. Capturing the sequence of inputs required to duplicate a problem means capturing the mouse movements, mouse clicks, and keyboard entries that result in a series of GUI objects being manipulated. Not only do these mouse actions and keyboard entries need to be captured they must also be replayed up to the point at which the problem occurred.

Different GUI environments provide varying levels of support for capturing mouse actions and keyboard entries. Java provides the *java.awt.robot* class for recording and playing back user actions. A number of software packages provide analogous functionality for X/Motif and the Windows™ environment. See our Website for software recommendations.

The first step in cutting down a GUI application problem is to create a log that contains all of the keyboard and mouse entries up to, but not including, the step that causes the problem to manifest. Use the appropriate system-dependent logging functionality as described previously.

Second, create a driver that replays these actions to the application. This means linking in additional libraries that will read the log file and short-circuit the normal entry of keyboard and mouse actions.

From this point, you can follow steps 3 through 7 for cutting down a command-line application problem.

8.3.3   **Cutting down a compiler problem**

If you're working on a compiler, you can use some special techniques to build a minimal test case.

1.   Identify the procedure in the user's application that was being processed when the compiler defect manifested itself. This evidence can be a premature termination of the compiler, an assertion message, generation of wrong code for that particular procedure, and so forth.

2.   Correlate internal compiler data structures back to the source position in the user's application. If the compiler you're working on doesn't annotate its representation of the user program with the source file name, line number, and column number of the corresponding lexical element of the user's program, you're working on a toy, not a real compiler. Fix this problem now; the payback will be nearly immediate.

3.   Remove as much of the user application code that hasn't been processed yet as possible. It is better to remove both the calls and the definitions of procedures that haven't been processed. If you can't remove the calls to procedures that haven't been compiled, at least replace the bodies with stubs.

4.   Perform a series of binary searches to remove irrelevant loop nests, code blocks, and statements from the offending procedure. In each search, you can effectively remove half of the items under question either by commenting them out or by using a preprocessor directive. If, after you remove them from the compilation, the problem still occurs, cut the remaining code in half and omit it from the compilation. Using this process recursively, remove all loop nests that aren't needed to manifest the problem. Then, remove all code blocks from those loop nests that aren't needed to manifest the problem. Finally, remove all statements from those code blocks that aren't needed to manifest the problem.

How does creating a test case suggest hypotheses? It focuses your attention on just those parts of the program that are actually causing problems. If a test program doesn't include a particular part feature of the application, there is no point in forming a hypothesis that the handling of that feature is the cause of the defect. By the time you have cut down a test case program to the minimum size required to manifest the defect, you will have eliminated a whole host of potential hypotheses from further consideration.

Creating a standalone test case is one of the first things we do when diagnosing a bug. If done correctly, it can provide you with additional hypotheses and refined hypotheses from stabilization activities.

8.4   Reduce the required input

The best test case is the one in which all input elements have been removed that have no bearing on whether the undesired behavior occurs. If the defective program fails when processing a large input data set, it's very important to reduce that data set before attempting to diagnose the problem.

If the input is a homogeneous aggregate of values, such as a matrix of floating-point numbers, you can try a matrix that just has the first and last rows of the matrix, or the first and last columns. If this doesn't cause the problem to manifest, keep adding rows (or columns) from the original input back in, until it does manifest itself. You can also start with the upper left corner of the array and simultaneously add a row and a column.

If the input is a collection of heterogeneous aggregates, the techniques required to cut down the input are a bit more complicated. If the input file is a collection of independent records, you can take a random selection of 10 percent of the records. If the problem still manifests itself, take a random selection of 10 percent of the remaining records, and repeat the process until the problem no longer manifests itself. As an alternative, you can try cutting the input set in half, and if the problem persists, continue cutting it in half until the problem no longer manifests itself.

If the reported problem was related to a particular key or combination of key values in the records, try selecting those records that have the problematic key or keys. If that selection still manifests the problem, use the random 10 percent method or the binary selection method to cut down the input set until the problem no longer manifests itself.

Another approach to cutting down a test input data set is warranted if the input has a complex structure, such as an application program that is being input to a faulty compiler. This approach considers the frequency of use and misuse of the elements of the structure. The following elements should be selected from the original input:

- The elements that are least frequently used

- The elements that are most frequently misused

- The combinations and sequences that are least frequently used

- The combinations and sequences that are most frequently misused

Opportunities for misusing input data elements arise out of complex input structures. A program in a high-level programming language is an input data set for a compiler. Examples of frequently misused input elements are **goto** statements, data overlays such C/C++ **union**, and Fortran **COMMON** statements.

Yet another approach to cutting down a test input data set is to try to reduce more than one aspect of the input at a time, keeping the others constant. The aspects of a test data set include size, sequence, and values. The size aspect includes both the number of items, as well as the number of dimensions, in the case of arrays. The sequence aspect includes repeating patterns and ascending or descending ordering. The values aspect includes magnitude and the set of unique values represented.

How does reducing the required input suggest hypotheses? It focuses your attention on just those parts of the input that are causing problems. If a test data set doesn't include a particular feature, there is no point in forming a hypothesis that the handling of that feature is the cause of the defect. By the time you have cut down your test case input to the minimum size required to manifest the defect, you will have eliminated a whole host of potential hypotheses from further consideration.

8.5   Categorize the problem

8.5.1   Correctness

Here is a list of questions useful in categorizing a problem with the correctness of the output of a program:

- Is there any output at all?

- Is any output missing (deletion)?

- Is there extra output (insertion)?

- Are the individual output values correct (substitution)?

- Are the individual output values in the correct order (transposition)?

- Are the individual output values close to correct, but not acceptable?

What hypotheses do these questions suggest? Are complete elements missing, or are individual elements (numbers, strings) only partially displayed? Are numerical values missing because they have been incorrectly aggregated with others? Is an entire sequence of values missing from either the beginning or the end of the output? Are individual random items missing, or are groups of items missing?

Are the extra values due to repetition of correct values? Is an entire sequence of values inserted at either the beginning or the end of the output? Are individual random items inserted, or are groups of adjacent items inserted?

Is the same value incorrectly substituted in many places, or are there different values substituted in each erroneous location? Are the values substituted a progression of related values?

Are the transposed values adjacent to their correct position, or are they some distance from where they belong? Is the distance from the correct position a constant for all values, or is it random? Are individual random items out of position, or are groups of adjacent items out of position, but in position with respect to each other?

Is the difference between the actual and expected values in the least significant digits? Are the actual values off from the expected values by a random or a constant amount? Are the actual values off from the expected values by a constant factor or a progression of factors?

Identifying one of these situations doesn't guarantee that it's the cause of correctness problems. If you find one, however, it's a good candidate for an initial hypothesis.

8.5.2   Completion

Here is a list of questions useful in categorizing a problem with the completion of a program:

- Did the program appear to be in an infinite loop?

- Did the program stop prematurely?

- Did the program shut itself down, or did it just abort?

- Which procedure did the program abort in?

- Which source statement did the program abort in?

- Which machine instruction caused the program to abort?

- Which type of exception was taken?

- What was the program return code?

What hypotheses do these questions suggest? How do you know that the program is in an infinite loop? Did it stop producing output, or did it produce the same output many, many times? Could it just be running very slowly?

While the symptom of the defect may be showing up in a particular loop running without stopping, you must be careful not to assume that the problem must be in the loop itself. Any statement executed prior to the loop might be the actual cause. In the same manner, for all the questions regarding the place where the program stopped, the initial hypothesis must be that some previously executed statement caused the problem.

Identifying one of these situations doesn't guarantee that it's the cause of completion problems. If you find one, however, it's a good candidate for an initial hypothesis.

8.5.3 **Robustness**

Here is a list of questions useful in categorizing a problem with the robustness of a program:

- Did the program reject valid inputs?

- Did the program give incorrect warnings about valid inputs?

- Did the program accept invalid inputs?

- Did the program fail to give warnings about invalid inputs?

What hypotheses do these questions suggest? Obviously, if a program isn't checking its input correctly, a logical hypothesis is that the input checking code is at fault.

Look at the Boolean logic inside each of the input checks. Are the senses of the comparison operators correct? Do they include the proper boundary conditions? Are the proper Boolean operators used to connect the comparisons?

Look at the values being used to check the input. Are they arbitrary choices based on the implementation, or do they reflect the application context? Are reasonable tolerances used when testing floating-point values?

Identifying one of these situations doesn't guarantee that it's the cause of a robustness problem. If you find one, however, it's a good candidate for an initial hypothesis.

8.5.4 **Efficiency**

Here is a list of questions useful in categorizing a problem with the efficiency of a program:

- Does the program take too long to process the inputs?
- Does the execution time grow linearly with the size of the input set?
- Are there inputs sets of different sizes, which cause the program to run too long?

What hypotheses do these questions suggest? If the execution time of a program doesn't grow linearly with the size of the input set, then the logical place to look for a problem is in those parts of the program that are most likely to have time complexity worse than linear time.

Look at all the places where data is being sorted in the program. Do any of the sorting algorithms have an average complexity worse than $O(n \log n)$? (This is the complexity of the most commonly used high-performance sorting algorithms.) Are sorting algorithms being used that have a worst-case complexity different from the average case?

Look at all the places where data is being searched in the program. Do any of the searching algorithms have an average complexity worse than $O(n)$?

Look at all nested loops, even if they aren't involved in sorting or searching. Is the number of iterations of each loop in the nest proportional to the size of the input?

Look at the input sets that cause unacceptable performance. Is the data ordered randomly? Is the data ordered differently than it's processed? Are there aggregate structures or elemental data items that only occur in the input sets with unacceptable performance? Are there aggregate structures or elemental data items that will cause excessive memory allocation?

Identifying one of these situations doesn't guarantee that it's the cause of unacceptable performance. If you find one, however, it's a good candidate for an initial hypothesis.

These questions aren't an exhaustive list of ways you can categorize a software defect. They do illustrate the kind of questions you should be asking to generate relevant hypotheses.

8.6   Describe the problem

Describing the problem according to a standard methodology is a helpful heuristic in the early stages of diagnosis. When you collect information to describe the problem, think of yourself as a reporter who will have to describe the problem to people who have no opportunity to observe the situation directly.

Table 8.1 shows a standard approach to describing a situation or problem. The focus is on those things that occurred, existed, or were observed versus those things that did not occur, did not exist, or weren't observed.

Table 8.1   *Questions about State*

	Is	Is Not
What (identity)		
When (timing)		
Where (location)		
How much, how many (extent)		

Table 8.2 shows another standard approach to describing a situation or problem. The focus here is on the difference between the normal or expected situation and what actually happened.

Table 8.2   *Questions about Differences*

	Difference/ Change	Effect
What (conditions, activities, components)		
When (status, schedule, process)		
Where (physical location)		
How (omitted, extra, or out-of-sequence action)		
Who (actors, observers, supervisors)		

8.7   Explain the problem to someone else

This heuristic is helpful when you have used up the hypotheses generated by the other heuristics. If you can't articulate the problem, you don't know enough about it yet. Thus, this heuristic isn't as valuable early on in the process of diagnosing a bug.

Communicating forces us to organize our thoughts so that the other person will understand. Don't tell the other person your conclusions or the hypotheses that you have already disproved. This will distract your listener and lead him or her down the same dead-ends you have already followed. Stick to your observations. After you have explained the facts, ask for the other person's hypotheses.

The other person won't necessarily share your internalized assumptions, and you will have to explain them to make sense of the problem. New hypotheses generated using this heuristic are often related to things you have been assuming that the other person doesn't assume.

As an alternative, have someone else explain your program to you. This is another way to get false assumptions out of the way. Try to create new hypotheses based on the reader's interpretation of your program.

8.8   **Recall a similar problem**

Recalling a similar problem is much easier if you keep a log of bugs you have worked on. Two problems can be similar along a number of dimensions. Similarity is a relative concept, and along each dimension are degrees of similarity.

Here is a list of dimensions of similarity:

- Symptom and symptom family

- Input type, volume, structure

- Output type, volume, structure

- Programming language used

- Data structures used

- Algorithms used

- Development environment

- Deployment platform

- Application architecture

- Auxiliary components

Symptoms and symptom families are described in Chapter 11. Symptoms are more similar if they belong to the same family.

Input and output type include file type, user actions, and so forth. A text file is more similar to a socket, with respect to access, than to a mouse action. Input and output volume are measured in bytes, records, and so forth. A relational database input is more similar with respect to structure to a spreadsheet than to an ASCII file containing embedded newlines.

The similarity of programming languages is measured by their level of abstraction and size of runtime library, rather than by syntax. C is more similar to assembly language than it is to Java, for example, even though C and Java have some similar syntax.

Data structures used include both those data structures that are built into the language as primitives, as well as those that are implemented using these built-ins. Data structures are similar both due to the features they provide and the methods used to implement them.

Algorithms used are similar in complexity and approach. Two algorithms are similar, for example, if they both use a divide-and-conquer approach.

Development environment includes compilers, debuggers, source control systems, and so forth. The development environment is more similar when it shares components that have common designs and shared components. Deployment platform is hardware and operating system. Linux™ is more similar to UNIX™, for example, than it's to Windows™.

Application architecture includes multiprocessing, multithreading, design patterns, and so forth. Two applications are similar in architecture if they use the same design patterns to address common problems.

Auxiliary components include statically and dynamically linked libraries, subordinate processes, and so forth. Two applications are similar, for example, if they use some of the same functionality from the same libraries.

The more dimensions along which two problems are similar, the more similar the problems are as a whole. Two problems aren't similar if they're similar along just a single dimension.

Once you have recalled a problem that has a good deal of similarity, the obvious hypothesis is that the current problem has the same root cause as the problem you have recalled.

8.9   Draw a diagram

Drawing the following diagrams can be a useful heuristic:

- A control-flow graph with decisions actually taken
- A data-flow graph that shows paths actually taken
- Complex data structures that use pointers

A **control-flow graph** is a directed graph in which executed statements (or procedures) are represented by the nodes, and control flow is represented by the arcs. For the purpose of hypothesis generation, limit your control-flow graph to statements or procedures that were actually executed. You can develop this information using a program trace or an execution profile.

A **data-flow graph** is a directed graph in which assignments and references to variables are represented by the nodes, and information flow is represented by the arcs. For the purpose of hypothesis generation, limit your data-flow graph to assignments and references that were actually executed.

Obviously, it's much easier to develop this graph if you have first developed a statement-level control-flow graph.

What kind of hypotheses do these diagrams suggest? If you see an unanticipated control-flow path, a reasonable hypothesis is that there is a problem with one of the predicates that controls the path. If you see a missing flow of information, a reasonable hypothesis is that there is a problem with the predicates controlling the statements that did not get executed, in between the assignment and reference of the variable in question.

Given a diagram of the static relationships of a complex structure built from pointers, and given that you know that this structure is being manipulated when the problem manifests itself, ask yourself how this structure could be violated. What assignments could be missed or performed in the wrong order, causing the structure to lose integrity? Each would give rise to a reasonable hypothesis.

Other useful diagrams you may want to draw are application specific. You can work either from a representation of the actual behavior of the program, such as the control-flow or data-flow graph, or from a representation of the ideal behavior of the program, such as the data-structure layout. In the former case, look for actual anomalies. In the latter case, look for potential anomalies.

8.10　Choose a hypothesis from historical data

The following heuristics can be used to select a hypothesis from historical records and general knowledge about the programming language being used:

- The error is the one the programmer makes most often.
- The error is one of the most common errors made when coding in this language.
- The error is one of the most common errors made regardless of programming language.
- The error is in the most recently changed code.
- The error is the easiest hypothesis to evaluate.

Choosing a hypothesis from historical data is appropriate when you have been working on a defect for some time and you're running out of hypotheses.

If you want to choose as a hypothesis that the problem is one that the programmer makes frequently, you need records on the root causes of previous defects diagnosed in the system in question. If you want to choose as a hypothesis that the problem is one of the most common errors made when using the particular programming language selected for this application, consult an error checklist from a programming text, or Appendix A.

If you want to choose as a hypothesis that the problem is one of the most common errors made by all programmers, you might find it useful to consult Chapter 11. If you want to choose as a hypothesis that the problem is in recently changed code, you need to have been using a source control system.

8.11 Review

Debugging heuristics don't lend themselves to easy categorization, as strategies and tactics do.

The first heuristic to apply is often called *stabilizing the problem*. The goal of stabilization is reproducibility. The first step in stabilizing a program is to obtain an undesired behavior each time the program executes. The next step is to obtain the same undesired behavior each time the program executes. The third step is to obtain the same undesired behavior in different environments. The fourth step is to obtain the same undesired behavior on different platforms.

The second heuristic to apply is to create a standalone test case. A test case typically has two parts: the program and the input data. We present heuristics for creating test case programs and test input data.

To cut down a file-oriented application into a standalone test, create a file that contains the inputs required to get the program just prior to the point where the problem occurs. Insert a call to record the program state just prior to the problem. Run the program with the log file, capture the program state, build a new driver that sets that state directly, and replace the old driver with the new one.

To cut down a GUI application into a standalone test, create a log that contains the mouse and keyboard actions required to get the program just prior to the point where the problem occurs. Insert a call to record the program state just prior to the problem. Run the program with the log file, capture the program state, build a new driver that sets that state directly, and replace the old driver with the new one.

To cut down a problem with a compiler into a standalone test, identify the part of the input program that caused the problem and correlate it with the compiler's internal data structures. Remove all parts of the input program that aren't required to reproduce the problem.

The best test case is the one in which all input elements have been removed that have no bearing on whether the undesired behavior occurs. One approach to cutting down a test input data set is to take a random selection of elements and either add or remove elements until you have just enough to cause the problem to manifest itself.

A second approach to cutting down a test input data set is to consider frequency of use and misuse of the elements of the structure. Another approach to cutting down a test input data set is to reduce several aspects of the input simultaneously. The aspects of a test data set include size, sequence, and values.

Categorizing the problem is a heuristic that can be used any time in the debugging process. Use a collection of general questions to categorize the behavior of the program with regard to correctness, completion, robustness, and efficiency.

Describing the problem according to a standard methodology is a heuristic that is normally used in the early stages of diagnosis. One approach is to answer standard questions that focus on those things that occurred or existed or were observed versus those things that did not occur or exist or weren't observed. Another approach is to answer standard questions that focus on the difference between the normal or expected situation and what actually happened.

Explaining the problem to someone else is helpful when you have used up the hypotheses generated by the other heuristics. Communicating forces us to organize our thoughts so that the other person will understand. The other person won't necessarily share our internalized assumptions, and we will have to explain them to make sense of the problem.

Recalling a similar problem is a heuristic that can be used at any time in the debugging process. It is much easier if you keep a log of bugs you have worked on. There are a number of dimensions along which two problems can be similar, and there are degrees of similarity along these dimensions. It is reasonable to hypothesize that two problems that are similar in a number of dimensions may have the same root problem.

Drawing a diagram is a heuristic that can be used any time in the debugging process. If you draw a representation of the actual behavior of the program, such as the control-flow or data-flow graph, look for actual anomalies. If you draw a representation of the ideal behavior of the program, such as the data-structure layout, look for potential anomalies.

Choosing a hypothesis from historical data is a heuristic to use when you have been working on a defect for some time, and you're running out of hypotheses.

Debugging Tactics

> *Experiments are like cross-questioning a witness who will tell the truth but not the whole truth.*
>
> *—Alan Gregg*

9.1 Preview

This chapter describes in detail basic and refined debugging tactics that every programmer should be able to use, given that they're supported in his or her development environment. It develops a standard methodology for defining tactics according to a list of questions. Each tactic is described using this methodology and is concluded by an example of finding an actual bug using it.

The following debugging tactics are described as follows:

- Read the source code looking for problems.

- Write and execute a unit test for a procedure.

- Insert a statement in the source to print the value of a variable.

- Insert a statement in the source to print a message when a code block is executed, listing the procedure name and some locality identifier.

- Insert statements in the source to print the values of arguments on entry to a procedure.

- Run the application under an interpreter or high-level debugger and generate a trace of all statements executed.

- Run the application under an interpreter or high-level debugger and generate a snapshot of all variable values each time a statement in a specified procedure is executed.

- Generate a memory map when the application is compiled and a memory dump when it completes execution.

- Generate a memory map when the application is compiled and a memory dump when it completes execution.

- Insert assertions into the program source that make the assumptions of the code explicit.

- Insert calls to procedures that check the validity of user data structures.

- Insert calls to procedures that display user data structures.

- Use compiler options to generate runtime subscript checking.

- Use compiler options to generate runtime checking of stack integrity.

- Use a memory allocator that performs runtime checking of heap integrity.

- Use compiler options to initialize statically with unusual or invalid values those global variables that aren't explicitly initialized.

- Use compiler options to initialize dynamically with unusual or invalid values those local (stack) variables that aren't explicitly initialized.

- Change local variable references to be global variables.

- Compile your source code with a compiler from a different vendor.

- Compile your source code to assembly code.

- Compile and run the application on a computer system with a different operating system or hardware architecture.

9.2   Read the source code

9.2.1   Basic tactic

Read each statement in a procedure and summarize the logical purpose of the statement, ignoring any comments.

9.2.2   Purpose

Determine what the program is actually doing, as opposed to what it was intended to do.

9.2.3 **Questions answered**

- What are the values computed by a procedure?

- What are the side effects caused by invoking a procedure?

9.2.4 **Potential problems**

- We tend to believe comments, even when they contradict our interpretation of the source code. It may be necessary to strip the comments before reading.

- We tend to believe the names given to procedures and variables. It may be necessary to rename them to arbitrary strings before reading.

9.2.5 **Refined tactics**

1. Read the text, while marking it to identify problems.

   - Mark (highlight or underline) definitions of variables with one color and mark uses of the same variables with another color.

   - Read with a specific input data set in mind, and mark statements the first time you determine they will be executed.

2. Read looking for unknown patterns. Underline or highlight common elements of repeated patterns that you identify. Go back over your listing and find candidate patterns that have some missing elements. Decide whether you have two different patterns, one pattern with elements missing from some instances, or one pattern with extraneous elements in some instances.

3. Read looking for an exception to a known pattern. Underline or highlight just the elements of the pattern in question. Review all the instances of the pattern, looking for omitted or extraneous elements.

9.2.6 **Related tactics**

- Use a syntax-directed editor or browser to do one of the following:

   - Read the control flow of a procedure or calling tree of the program in a breadth-first manner. Open all the control-flow constructs at the same nesting level, read them top to bottom, and proceed to the next level until done.

- Read the control flow of a procedure or calling tree of the program in a depth-first manner. Open a control-flow construct until it's completely unfolded, and read the entire nested construct. Repeat for each top-level nested construct, top to bottom, until done.

- Use a class-hierarchy browser to do one of the following:

  - Review the inheritance hierarchy of the program in a breadth-first manner. Open all the derived classes at the same nesting level, review them top to bottom, and proceed to the next level until done.

  - Read the inheritance hierarchy of the program in a depth-first manner. Open a base class until it's completely unfolded, and review the hierarchy. Repeat for each base class, top to bottom, until done.

- Use a word processor that supports underlining and multiple text colors to read the text and apply one of the refined tactics to the program text.

9.3   Write a unit test

9.3.1   Basic tactic

Write a test that invokes a procedure in question and compares its result or side effects with an expected result that is embedded in the test procedure.

9.3.2   Purpose

Determine whether a specific procedure is functioning as you expect it should.

9.3.3   Questions answered

- What inputs does a procedure accept?

- What results does a procedure compute?

- What side effects does a procedure cause?

- What exceptions does a procedure activate?

- What outputs does a procedure display?

9.3.4   Potential problems

Complex procedures may require many unit tests to test thoroughly. Knowing when you have a complete set can be difficult.

9.3.5   Refined tactics

1.   Copy code you have inserted into the procedure as debugging infrastructure into unit tests.

2.   Copy code you executed in a debugger to exercise the procedure into unit tests.

9.3.6   Related tactics

Use a unit testing framework such as JUnit. Unit testing frameworks for many other programming languages are also available. See our Website for further information.

9.4   Display variable values

9.4.1   Basic tactic

Insert a statement in the source to print the value of a variable.

9.4.2   Purpose

- Determine the sequence of the pattern of values assigned to a variable.

- Determine whether the variable ever had an incorrect value.

- Find the earliest point in the execution of the program when the variable had an incorrect value.

- Find the first location in the program source where the variable had an incorrect value.

9.4.3   Questions answered

- What was the value of the variable each time the code block that contains the output statement was executed?

- Was that same code block ever executed?

- How many times was that code block executed?

9.4.4 **Potential problems**

- If the problem is caused by stack or heap corruption, the presence of an output statement may cause the symptom to disappear. This is because the runtime library that generates the output will shift things on the stack and may allocate memory on the heap.

- If the problem is caused by optimizations performed by the compiler, the presence of an output statement may cause the optimizer not to perform the offending optimization or to perform it differently.

9.4.5 **Refined tactics**

1. Insert a statement in the source that tests a variable and prints the value if it's unexpected.

2. In addition to the inserted print statement, do the following:

   - Add an execution option to the program.

   - Insert a conditional statement that executes the print statement only if the execution option was used.

3. Insert print statements immediately before each reference to a variable of interest and after each assignment of that variable.

4. Print the value of the variable in several different formats: floating-point, decimal integer, hexadecimal, address.

9.4.6 **Related tactics**

- Use a high-level debugger or interpreter to do the following:
  - Set a breakpoint at the code block of interest.
  - Add a command list to the breakpoint to print the value of the variable and continue execution.

- Use a high-level debugger or interpreter to do the following:
  - Set a conditional breakpoint at the code block of interest that tests whether the value of the variable is unexpected.
  - Add a command list to the breakpoint to print the value of the variable and continue execution.
  - Add an execution option to the program.

- Use a high-level debugger or interpreter to do the following:

- Set a conditional breakpoint at the code block of interest that tests whether the execution option was used.
- Add a command list to the breakpoint to print the value of the variable and continue execution.

9.4.7 Choosing tactics

Use the basic tactic when one of the following conditions is true:

- No high-level debugger is available.

- You don't want to have to interact with a high-level debugger.

- It is quicker to recompile with a new statement inserted than to recompile, relink, and start up with a high-level debugger.

- You want a file containing all values the variable contains at that point in the program.

Use the refined tactic 1 when the variable takes on a range of values that is predictable. Examine the source code and input data to determine whether this condition is true and what the range is. The refined tactic is more important when an entire array is under question. Typically, you can reduce the amount of output by just printing the nonzero values. Or, you can just print the values in some particular section of the array, such as the main diagonal of a matrix.

Use refined tactic 2 when compile or link times are relatively long, or when you anticipate wanting to display this variable again in the future.

9.5 Display execution messages

9.5.1 Basic tactic

Insert a statement in the source to print a message when a code block is executed, which lists the procedure name and some locality identifier.

9.5.2 Purpose

Determine the control-flow path taken by the program when processing a given set of inputs.

9.5.3 Questions answered

- Was the code block ever executed?
- How many times was the block executed?

9.5.4 Potential problems

- If the problem is caused by stack or heap corruption, the presence of an output statement may cause the symptom to disappear. This is because the runtime library that generates the output will shift things on the stack and may allocate memory on the heap.

- If the problem is caused by optimizations performed by the compiler, the presence of an output statement may cause the optimizer not to perform the offending optimization or to perform it differently.

9.5.5 Refined tactics

1. Rather than trace code blocks, insert print statements right after entry to a procedure and right before exit from that procedure.

2. In addition to inserting the print statement, do the following:

   - Insert a statement to initialize a variable.

   - Insert a statement to increment the variable each time a block is executed.

   - Insert a statement that tests the variable and prints a message if it has been executed a specific number of times.

3. Insert statements in the source to print the values of all of the variables used to determine whether the block is executed.

4. In addition to the inserted print statement, do the following:

   - Add an execution option to the program.

   - Insert a conditional statement that executes the print statement only if the execution option was used.

9.5.6 Related tactics

- Use a high-level debugger or interpreter to do the following:
  - Set a breakpoint at the code block of interest.
  - Step through execution.

- Insert a statement to initialize a variable.
- Use a high-level debugger or interpreter to do the following:
  - Set a breakpoint at the code block of interest.
  - Add a command list to the breakpoint that increments the added variable.
  - Set a conditional breakpoint at that code block, which will execute when the added variable reaches a specific value.
  - Add a command list to the breakpoint that prints a message and continues execution.
- Use a high-level debugger or interpreter to do the following:
  - Set a breakpoint at the start of the code block of interest.
  - Add a command list to the breakpoint that prints the values of all of the variables used to determine whether the block is executed.
- Use a high-level debugger or interpreter to do the following:
  - Set a conditional breakpoint at that code block, which will execute if the execution option was used.
  - Add a command list to the breakpoint that prints a message and continues execution.

9.5.7   Choosing tactics

Use the basic tactic when one of the following conditions is true:

- No high-level debugger is available.
- You don't want to have to interact with a high-level debugger.
- It is quicker to recompile with a new statement inserted than to recompile, relink, and start up with a high-level debugger.
- You want a file containing a listing of every time certain code blocks are executed.

Use refined tactic 1 when the code block of interest will be executed many times.

Use refined tactic 2 when the code block of interest will be executed many times, and the statement controlling the block contains a complex Boolean statement.

Use refined tactic 3 when compile or link times are relatively long or when you anticipate wanting to display this variable again in the future.

9.6   Display procedure arguments

9.6.1   Basic tactic

Insert statements in the source to print the values of arguments on entry to a procedure.

9.6.2   Purpose

Determine the values that are inputs to each procedure.

9.6.3   Questions answered

- What were the values of all arguments each time the procedure was invoked?

- Was the procedure ever invoked?

- How many times was the procedure invoked?

9.6.4   Potential problems

- If the problem is caused by stack or heap corruption, the presence of an output statement may cause the symptom to disappear. This is because the runtime library that generates the output will shift things on the stack and may allocate memory on the heap.

- If the problem is caused by optimizations performed by the compiler, the presence of an output statement may cause the optimizer not to perform the offending optimization or to perform it differently.

- Some languages allow arguments to be omitted. Your output statement should be guarded so that it doesn't refer to a nonexistent argument.

9.6.5   Refined tactics

1.   Print relevant global variables as well as arguments.

2.   Print function results before returning. This is made much easier if the function is coded to have a single exit.

3.   In addition to the inserted print statements, do the following:

- Add an execution option to the program.
- Insert a guard statement that executes the print statement only if the execution option was used.

9.6.6 **Related tactics**

- Use a high-level debugger or interpreter to do the following:
  - Set a breakpoint at the entry to the procedure.
  - Print the values of the arguments if the breakpoint is taken.
- Use a high-level debugger or interpreter to do the following:
  - Set a breakpoint at the entry to the procedure.
  - Add a command list to the breakpoint that prints the values of the arguments if the breakpoint is taken and continues execution.
- Use a high-level debugger or interpreter to do the following:
  - Set a breakpoint at the exits from the procedure.
  - Add a command list to the breakpoint that prints the return value if the breakpoint is taken.
- Use a high-level debugger or interpreter to do the following:
  - Set a breakpoint at the entry to the procedure.
  - Add a command list to the breakpoint that prints the values of global variables if the breakpoint is taken.

9.6.7 **Choosing tactics**

Use the basic tactic when one of the following conditions is true:

- No high-level debugger is available.
- You don't want to have to interact with a high-level debugger.
- It is quicker to recompile with a new statement inserted than to recompile and relink for debugging with a high-level debugger.
- You want a file containing all values the arguments take on during the execution of the program.

9.6.8 **Language specifics**

- *C++:* Also include class data members.

- *Java:* For global variables, substitute class data members.
- *C:* Use the *varargs.h* header file to access the arguments of functions with varying numbers of arguments.
- *Fortran:* Create separate **PRINT** statements for each **ENTRY**.

9.7   Generate a flow trace

9.7.1   Basic tactic

Run the application under an interpreter or high-level debugger, and generate a trace of all statements executed.

9.7.2   Purpose

Determine whether the code was ever executed.

9.7.3   Questions answered

- What order were statements executed in?
- What statements were and weren't executed?

9.7.4   Potential problems

- You can generate so much data that it becomes overwhelming.
- If the problem is caused by stack or heap corruption, running under an interpreter or high-level debugger may cause the symptom to change or disappear because the stack and heap will be different.

9.7.5   Refined tactics

1.   Trace only selected statements.
2.   Trace only statements that control others—loop heads, conditional statements.

9.7.6   Related tactics

None.

9.7.7 Choosing tactics

Traces are only appropriate in a few situations:

- The application is legitimately **goto** oriented. It could be a finite state machine or the output of another program.

- The program is written in a very high-level language (VHLL) or in assembly language. In a VHLL, each statement has a high semantic content. In an assembly language, a simulator may be able to provide information not otherwise obtainable.

9.8   Generate a variable snapshot

9.8.1 Basic tactic

Run the application under an interpreter or high-level debugger. Generate a snapshot of a set of variable values each time a statement in a specified procedure is executed.

9.8.2 Purpose

Determine the values of a set of variables.

9.8.3 Questions answered

- Were any of these variables modified since the last time the dump was made?

- Do all of these variables have reasonable values?

9.8.4 Potential problems

- You can generate a lot of data if the statement is executed frequently.

- If the problem is caused by stack or heap corruption, running under an interpreter or high-level debugger may cause the symptom to change or disappear. This happens because the values on the stack and heap will be different.

9.8.5 Refined tactics

Dump only selected elements of arrays, such as the first and last element of each row or column, or the diagonal elements.

9.8.6 Related tactics

- Call a function that dumps a specific number of words starting at a base address. Call it with the address of the last local variable declared in the function. Print each word in several formats (character, numeric).

- For languages that keep most of their data in global variables, dump the entire global area.

9.8.7 Choosing tactics

Use the basic tactic when one of the following conditions is true:

- No high-level debugger is available.

- It isn't feasible to run the application interactively.

9.8.8 Language specifics

- *C++:* Dump the data members of the object currently referenced by *this,* and recursively dump all data members of objects pointed to or referenced by that object.

- *Java:* Dump the data members of the object currently referenced by *this,* and recursively dump all data members of objects referenced by that object. Use reflection to implement this facility.

- *C:* There is no way to get the names or addresses of all global variables without explicitly listing them.

- *Fortran:* Dump the contents of blank **COMMON**, or of all **COMMON** blocks.

9.9   Generate memory dump

9.9.1 Basic tactic

Generate a memory map when the application is compiled and a memory dump when it completes execution.

9.9.2 **Purpose**

Determine the state of all program variables.

9.9.3 **Questions answered**

- What were the values of all active variables when the program stopped?

9.9.4 **Potential problems**

- Memory dumps of virtual memory programs can use hundreds of megabytes of file storage.

- Identifying patterns in large dumps requires good tools or lots of time.

9.9.5 **Refined tactics**

1. Run the binary dump values through a program that has access to all the header files and dumps values in their natural container size and format.

2. Run the binary dump through a tool that extracts only certain ranges of addresses.

9.9.6 **Related tactics**

- Insert an event handler in the main procedure that will catch all unhandled events.

- Use a high-level debugger or interpreter to do the following:
  - Set a breakpoint at the entry to the event handler.
  - Add a command list to the breakpoint that prints a stack trace if the breakpoint is taken.

- If the application terminated abnormally, some operating systems will automatically produce an image of the executable when it quit. On UNIX™ systems, these are called core files. This is because they replicate the memory image of the program, and back in the bad old days when UNIX™ was invented, computers still used ferrite core rings to represent bits of information in memory. On Windows™ systems, these files are called Dr. Watson log files. Dr. Watson was Sherlock Holmes's assistant.

Regardless of the platform, these logs can be used to identify the source of a problem in a postmortem fashion. You must run a tool, either the normal interactive debugger or a special tool (the Dr. Watson program), which will generate the following information for you:

- Stack trace at the time the program stopped

- Event/exception/fault that caused the failure

- Assembly instruction that failed

- If the source code is available, the high-level language statement that failed

- Contents of hardware registers

- System status and other miscellaneous information

On some systems, you may have to start a monitoring program, or change the properties of the executable to have these log files generated for you.

9.9.7   Choosing tactics

Use basic or refined tactics when dealing with a program that must reside in memory for long periods of time. Two types of programs that have this characteristic are operating system kernels and database managers.

Use related tactic 2 when you don't have access to the system on which the failure occurred and the user is unable to provide enough useful information on how the program failed for you to diagnose the problem. Instruct the user to do what is necessary to cause a log file to be generated and send the log file to you.

9.10   Force variable value

9.10.1   Basic tactic

Insert code to force a variable to take on a specific value.

9.10.2   Purpose

Determine what happens when a variable takes on a known value.

9.10.3 Questions answered

- What are the side effects of executing a code segment at a particular point in time?

9.10.4 Potential problems

This tactic doesn't answer the question of why the variable did not have the value originally.

9.10.5 Refined tactics

1. Force a *while* loop to execute at least once.

2. Force a *counted* loop to execute a certain number of times.

9.10.6 Related tactics

- Use a high-level debugger or interpreter to do the following:
  - Set a breakpoint at the code block of interest.
  - Add a command list to the breakpoint to assign a variable a specific value and continue execution.
- Use a high-level debugger or interpreter to do the following:
  - Set a breakpoint at the code block of interest.
  - Add a command list to the breakpoint step over a loop control statement to cause the loop to execute at least once

9.10.7 Choosing tactics

If there is a control path that isn't being executed, and a variable that can take on a value that will exercise that path, use the basic or refined tactics. If you have a high level debugger, you can also use the related tactics.

9.11 Assert assumptions

9.11.1 Basic tactic

Insert assertions into the program source.

9.11.2   **Purpose**

Make the assumptions of the code explicit.

9.11.3   **Questions answered**

The questions answered depend on the assertion used. Common assertions answer these questions:

- Which procedures are getting unexpected input values?
- Which procedures are returning unexpected output values?
- Which local variables are getting assigned unexpected input values?

9.11.4   **Potential problems**

- Some assertions can be costly to test. Others that are made in frequently executed functions may be costly in the aggregate.
- Some programmers don't like having users see assertions print if a problem occurs. You must assess which of two options will cause more trouble for the user: Your program can continue execution in a known error state, or it can terminate the application and print a message that won't be of much help to the user.
- You must be careful not to include any code that has side effects inside of the assertion expression. If you have such code and you turn assertion checking off, you will change the behavior of the program.

9.11.5   **Refined tactics**

Make assertions preprocessor macros instead of procedures so they can be eliminated by redefining the macro.

9.11.6   **Related tactics**

Distinguish between fatal and nonfatal assumptions that are being violated. Report the nonfatal ones, but continue processing, possibly after remedying the problem.

9.11.7 **Choosing tactics**

Do a complete test run, with all assertions active, at least once before the program is put into production.

9.12 **Check data structures**

9.12.1 **Basic tactic**

Insert calls to procedures that check the validity of user data structures.

9.12.2 **Purpose**

Identify invalid data structures.

9.12.3 **Questions answered**

- Which data structures become invalid?
- When do those data structures become invalid?
- What element of the data structure becomes invalid?

9.12.4 **Potential problems**

- Checking complex data structures can be computationally expensive.
- If the problem is caused by stack or heap corruption, the presence of a call to a checking procedure may cause the symptom to disappear. This happens because the checking procedure will shift things on the stack and may allocate memory on the heap.
- If the problem is caused by optimizations performed by the compiler, the presence of a call to the checking procedure may cause the optimizer not to perform the offending optimization or to perform it differently.

9.12.5 **Refined tactics**

In addition to the inserted call statement, do the following:

- Add an execution option to the program.

- Insert a conditional statement that executes the validation only if the execution option was used.

9.12.6　Related tactics

Implement data structures that use pointer redundancy to enable error detection and correction.

9.12.7　Choosing tactics

Do a complete test run with all data-structure checking turned on at least once before the program is put into production.

9.12.8　Language specifics

- *C++:* Data structures that use pointer redundancy can be helpful.

- *Java:* Since memory can't be corrupted in Java, data structures that use pointer redundancy checking aren't necessary.

- *C:* Data structures that use pointer redundancy can be helpful.

- *Fortran:* Due to the nature of pointers in Fortran 95, it's harder to corrupt their values than in C or C++, but it can be done if array subscripts go past their bounds unchecked.

9.13　Display data structures

9.13.1　Basic tactic

- Insert calls to procedures that display user data structures.

- Print the name of an enumeration value, not the integer.

- Print bit data in hexadecimal or binary form, not integer.

- Print the names of all flags turned on in flag words, rather than just the value of the word.

- Rather than print the values of pointers and references, do the following:
  - Place the pointer/pointee or reference/referent adjacently.
  - Draw relationships with arrows.
  - Use indentation to show hierarchy.

- Print data in unions with the proper format, based on a variant record tag.

- Suppress default or zero data as appropriate.

- Provide self-identifying data.

- Provide multiple views for the same data—implement both a sketch and a full detail view.

9.13.2 Purpose

- Determine whether a data structure ever had an incorrect value.

- Find the earliest point in the execution of the program when the data structure contained an incorrect value.

- Find the first location in the program source where a data structure contained an incorrect value.

9.13.3 Questions answered

- What are the contents of major data structures as they're built and used?

9.13.4 Potential problems

- If these procedures are called frequently or display very large structures, the display can use up a lot of file space.

- If the problem is caused by stack or heap corruption, the presence of a call to a data-structure display procedure may cause the symptom to disappear. This happens because the display procedure will shift things on the stack and may allocate memory on the heap.

- If the problem is caused by optimizations performed by the compiler, the presence of a call to the display procedure may cause the optimizer not to perform the offending optimization or to perform it differently.

9.13.5 Refined tactics

Test values in other data structures, and only print the values when exceptional conditions occur.

9.13.6 Related tactics

- Use a high-level debugger or interpreter to do the following:

- Set a breakpoint at a place where you know that the data structure is completely built.
- Add a command list to the breakpoint that calls the data-structure display procedure and continues execution.
- Use a high-level debugger or interpreter to do the following:
  - Set a watch point to a variable that will contain a pointer or reference to the data structure.
  - Add a command list to the watch point that calls the data-structure display procedure and continues execution.

9.13.7 Choosing tactics

Use either the basic or refined tactics when your data structures are complicated hierarchical structures.

9.14 Use runtime subscript checking

9.14.1 Basic tactic

Use compiler options to generate runtime subscript checking.

9.14.2 Purpose

Determine whether there are any array subscripts that are invalid for the test data you have available.

9.14.3 Questions answered

- Where are invalid array references coming from?
- When are invalid array references occurring?

9.14.4 Potential problems

- If your program makes a lot of array references in tightly nested loops, you could slow down execution significantly.
- Some compilers don't offer this option.

9.14.5 Related tactics

- Put pad variables between arrays so that invalid references that haven't been found yet don't effect computation.

- Reorder array declarations so that invalid references that haven't been found yet don't effect computation.

- Use preprocessor macros to cover array accesses and check subscripts.

9.14.6 Choosing tactics

Use this tactic when one of the following conditions is true:

- The compiler doesn't do subscript checking by default.

- A bug occurs when the program is run standalone, but not when it's run under a debugger.

- A bug occurs when the program is run under one user account (and environment), but not when it's run under another.

Use this tactic at least once before the program is put into production, as an additional testing strategy.

9.14.7 Language specifics

- *C++:* Pointer arithmetic can be the equivalent of array indexing, so it's desirable to check pointer references as well.

- *Java:* The Java runtime always checks array references, so the tactic is unnecessary.

- *C:* Pointer arithmetic can be the equivalent of array indexing, so it's desirable to check pointer references as well.

- *Fortran:* This tactic isn't relevant to Fortran pointers.

9.15 Use runtime stack checking

9.15.1 Basic tactic

Use compiler options to generate runtime checking of stack integrity.

9.15.2 Purpose

Determine whether stack corruption is occurring.

9.15.3 Questions answered

- Which procedure's stack frame is being corrupted?
- When is the stack being corrupted?

9.15.4 Potential problems

- If your program makes a lot of procedure calls, checking the integrity of the stack on every call could slow down execution significantly.
- Some compilers may not support this option.

9.15.5 Refined tactics

None.

9.15.6 Related tactics

- Insert calls to user procedures to perform runtime checking of stack integrity.
- Use a high-level debugger or interpreter to do the following:
  - Set a breakpoint at a place where you would like to begin checking the integrity of the stack.
  - Add a command list to the breakpoint that calls a user procedure to perform checking of stack integrity, and then continue execution.

9.15.7 Choosing tactics

Use this tactic when one of the following conditions is true:

- The compiler doesn't generate runtime stack checking by default.
- A bug occurs when the program is run standalone, but not when it's run under a debugger.
- A bug occurs when the program is run under one user account and environment, but not when it's run under another.

Use this tactic at least once before the program is put into production, as an additional testing strategy.

9.15.8   Language specifics

- *C++:* The stack pointer can be corrupted by bad pointer references.
- *Java:* Java guarantees stack integrity, so the tactic is unnecessary.
- *C:* The stack pointer can be corrupted by bad pointer references.
- *Fortran:* Stack integrity can only be compromised by invalid array subscripts.

9.16   Use runtime heap checking

9.16.1   Basic tactic

Use a memory allocator that performs runtime checking of heap integrity.

9.16.2   Purpose

Identify corruption to the memory allocator data structures.

9.16.3   Questions answered

- Which block of memory is being corrupted?
- When is the corruption occurring?

9.16.4   Potential problems

- If heap integrity is checked every time memory is allocated or freed, the application may become much slower.
- If you only check the heap when memory is allocated and freed, many pointer references may occur in between. This tactic isn't as strong as checking every pointer reference.

9.16.5   Refined tactics

Make every pointer reference through one of two macros. One of them just resolves to the pointer reference. The other makes a function call, which calls the heap integrity checker before dereferencing the pointer. Change the first macro to the second, file by file, until you find the problem. This will cause a drastic slowdown in the program.

9.16.6   Related tactics

- Implement wrapper functions around the standard memory allocation and deallocation procedures. The functions should maintain and check their own list of allocated storage.

- Use a high-level debugger or interpreter to do the following:
  - Set a breakpoint at a place where you would like to begin checking the integrity of the heap.
  - Add a command list to the breakpoint that calls a user procedure to perform checking of heap integrity, and then continue execution.

9.16.7   Choosing tactics

Use this tactic when one of the following conditions is true:

- A bug occurs when the program is run standalone, but not when it's run under a debugger.

- A bug occurs when the program is run under one user account (and environment), but not when the program is run under another.

Use this tactic at least once before the program is put into production, as an additional testing strategy.

9.16.8   Language specifics

- *C++:* You can overload **new** and **delete**. You can also create special versions of **new** or **delete**, using the placement argument, that perform heap checking before using the normal form of these procedures to allocate storage.

- *Java:* Java guarantees heap integrity, so the tactic is unnecessary.

- *C:* Several publicly available versions of **malloc** and **free** perform heap integrity checking.

- *Fortran:* Heap integrity can only be compromised by invalid array subscripts.

9.17 Initialize global variables

9.17.1 Basic tactic

Use compiler options to initialize statically with unusual or invalid values those global variables that aren't explicitly initialized.

9.17.2 Purpose

Identify uninitialized variables that need to be initialized.

9.17.3 Questions answered

- Which global variables are getting random values that are being used in computation?
- Where is the first place that the random values are being used?

9.17.4 Potential problems

Computations may not fail with the values assigned.

9.17.5 Refined tactics

Initialize floating-point variables to IEEE Not a Number (NaN), pointer variables to an invalid address, and integer variables to the maximum representable integer.

9.17.6 Related tactics

- Add code that initializes all global variables.
- Run on a different system, where 0 isn't a valid address.

9.17.7 Choosing tactics

Use the refined tactic when your compiler doesn't support an option for the basic tactic.

Use basic or related tactics when any of the following is true:

- A bug occurs when the program is run standalone, but not when it's run under a debugger.

- A bug occurs when the program is run under one user account (and environment), but not when it's run under another.

Use this tactic at least once before the program is put into production, as an additional testing strategy.

9.17.8 Language specifics

- *C++:* Use constructors to ensure that all class members are properly initialized.

- *Java:* Java doesn't have global variables. Class members are always initialized, so the tactic is unnecessary.

- *C:* Some C implementations initialize all global variables to 0, while others do not. If you aren't using a compiler that conforms to the C99 standard, don't rely on this behavior.

- *Fortran:* Some Fortran implementations initialize all numeric variables in **COMMON** to 0. You shouldn't rely on this behavior if you aren't using a compiler that guarantees this behavior.

9.18 Initialize local variables

9.18.1 Basic tactic

Use compiler options to initialize dynamically with unusual or invalid values those local (stack) variables that aren't explicitly initialized.

9.18.2 Purpose

Reveal uninitialized variables that need to be initialized.

9.18.3 Questions answered

- Which local variables are getting random values that are being used in computation?

- Where is the first place that the random values are being used?

9.18.4 Potential problems

Computations may not fail with the values assigned.

9.18.5 Refined tactics

Initialize floating-point variables to IEEE NaN, pointer variables to an invalid address, and integer variables to the maximum representable integer.

9.18.6 Related tactics

- Add code to assign values to all local variables.
- Run the program on a different system, where 0 isn't a valid address.

9.18.7 Choosing tactics

Use the refined tactic when your compiler doesn't support an option for the basic tactic.

Use basic or related tactics when any of the following is true:

- A bug occurs when the program is run standalone, but not when it's run under a debugger.
- A bug occurs when the program is run under one user account and environment, but not when it's run under another.

Use this tactic at least once before the program is put into production, as an additional testing strategy.

9.18.8 Language specifics

- *C++:* Initializing all local pointer variables is cheap insurance.
- *Java:* Java requires the programmer to initialize local variables, so the tactic is unnecessary.
- *C:* Initializing all local pointer variables is cheap insurance.
- *Fortran:* Use initializers to ensure local variables have values.

9.19 Change storage class

9.19.1 Basic tactic

Change local variable references to be global variables.

9.19.2   Purpose

Determine whether stack corruption is causing the problem.

9.19.3   Questions answered

- Which stack variables were having their values overwritten?
- Was the stack frame itself being overwritten?

9.19.4   Potential problems

This approach won't work with algorithms that really need a stack.

9.19.5   Refined tactics

Put preprocessor conditional compile directives around all stack variable declarations so you can switch between locals and globals.

9.19.6   Related tactics

- Change local variable references to be heap variables pointed to by global variables.
- Change heap variables to be located on the stack with the use of **alloca** (nonportable).
- Put arrays of pad values between each true variable on the stack.

9.19.7   Choosing tactics

Use the basic or refined tactic when both of the following are true:

- Symptoms change radically between runs.
- Local variables are being overwritten, but their address isn't being taken.

9.19.8   Language specifics

- *C++:* This tactic can be useful for C++.
- *Java:* Java guarantees heap integrity, so this tactic is unnecessary.
- *C:* This tactic can be useful for C.

- *Fortran:* This tactic is awkward to implement in Fortran.

9.20 Use a different compiler

9.20.1 Basic tactic

Compile your source code with a compiler from a different vendor.

9.20.2 Purpose

Resolve problems using a new revision of same compiler or problems understanding what the current compiler is complaining about.

9.20.3 Questions answered

- What interpretations of the language standard are made by the compiler you're using that aren't made by all compilers?
- What potential problems in your code aren't being found by the compiler you're using?
- What implementation details of your current compiler are you relying on?

9.20.4 Potential problems

On a new or unique platform, there may be only one compiler available.

9.20.5 Refined tactics

None.

9.20.6 Related tactics

Try compiling and running the application on a computer system with a different operating system or hardware architecture.

9.20.7 Choosing tactics

Use this tactic when one of the following conditions is true:

- Your program uses features that are new or poorly defined in the language standard or the reference manual supplied by the vendor.

- You're using an optimizing compiler.

9.20.8   Language specifics

- *C++:* GNU *g++* is a good alternative to commercial compilers for this purpose.

- *Java:* Make sure the compiler is really different. Many vendors provide Sun's compiler as their own. The experimental Jikes compiler from IBM is a good alternative.

- *C:* GNU *gcc* is a good alternative to commercial compilers for this purpose.

- *Fortran:* There aren't a lot of alternative compilers on a given platform.

9.21   Compile to assembly code

9.21.1   Basic tactic

Compile your source code to assembly code.

9.21.2   Purpose

The machine language generated by a compiler from your source code is the ultimate definition of how the compiler interpreted your program. Some compilers provide options to generate assembly language output so that you can see this binary machine language in a human-readable form. Sometimes it's useful to generate such output when diagnosing a defect. Reading assembly code is tedious and error prone, and it should be among the last tactics you use to understand how the compiler interpreted your program.

9.21.3   Questions answered

- How did the language translator interpret the program I compiled?

- What hidden assumptions does my program make that the compiler must make specific?

9.21.4   Potential problems

Many people don't know the assembly language of the machine they work on.

9.21.5   Refined tactics

1. If the translator you're using applies a preprocessor to your code, it's sometimes necessary to look at the output of this preprocessing. This approach to getting translator feedback applies to C, C++, and PL/I, among other languages. To make this method effective, use selective preprocessing. This can reduce a huge quantity of code to a manageable size. There are several ways to apply selective preprocessing. You can expand only user macros, which can eliminate many definitions introduced by system header files. You can also just expand a single header file or a single definition.

2. Generate the intermediate representation of the compiler after performing semantic analysis, but before code generation. The intermediate representation is in effect another high-level language. This variation depends, of course, on having a compiler that will provide such output and having some knowledge of how compilers work internally.

9.21.6   Related tactics

- Some compilers translate into a lower-level language. These days, the most typical target for such compilers is C, since a C compiler is available for every processor that matters. The most likely choices for this implementation technique are VHLLs like APL, Lisp, ML, Scheme, SETL, and so forth. When you use this approach, you can see storage allocation, implicit conversions and copies, runtime routine dispatching, and the like. These are particularly important in VHLLs.

- Source-to-source translation is done by tools that make explicit all the defaults and shorthands that compilers may support. The obvious advantage to this approach is that you don't need to learn another language. It is most helpful for languages that allow the programmer to use shortcuts, such as C, Fortran, and PL/I.

When you do source-to-source translation, you can normally see the following:

- All attributes of every variable
- Scope of all control-flow statements
- Order of evaluation of expressions

A special form of this approach is to use a source-to-source translator that performs analysis for the purpose of introducing parallelism.

9.21.7   Choosing tactics

Use this tactic when one of the following conditions is true:

1.   If you're using a compiler that generates assembly code, use the basic tactic.

2.   If you're using a compiler that executes a preprocessor first, use refined tactic 1.

3.   If you have access to an open source or research compiler that will dump its intermediate representation for debugging purposes, use refined tactic 2.

4.   If you're using a very high level language, and you have access to a compiler for that language that generates a lower level language, used the related tactics.

9.21.8   Language specifics

- *C++:* This tactic is useful for exposing conversions and allocations.
- *Java:* Java compilers generate a platform-independent bytecode into *.class* files. There are numerous tools that will convert *.class* files into a readable form.
- *C:* This technique works best with C, because there is such a close relationship between C statements and generated assembly code.
- *Fortran:* Fortran 95 has an extensive runtime library, and many operations may be translated as calls to that library, rather than assembly code.

9.22 Execute on a different platform

9.22.1 Basic tactic

Compile and run the application on a computer system with a different operating system or hardware architecture.

9.22.2 Purpose

Resolve problems using a new or different version of the runtime environment.

9.22.3 Questions answered

- Was the program making invalid assumptions that are masked by the underlying operating system or hardware architecture?

- How portable is your code?

9.22.4 Potential problems

You may have only one platform available.

9.22.5 Refined tactics

None.

9.22.6 Related tactics

- Compile the application with a different compiler, but target it to the same operating system and hardware architecture.

- Compile the application with the same compiler, but target it to a different operating system or hardware architecture (cross-compilation).

9.22.7 Choosing tactics

Use this tactic when one of the following conditions is true:

- When the program is a numerical application whose results may depend on the floating-point representation used.

- The program uses pointers, you're having trouble stabilizing the problem, and either the operating system doesn't provide protection for memory locations that are outside of your static data, stack, and heap storage or the hardware permits you to address locations such as 0.

Use this tactic at least once before the program is put into production, as an additional testing strategy.

9.23   Review

We have summarized a comprehensive set of debugging tactics in terms of the following items:

- Definition of the basic tactic
- Purpose of the tactic
- Questions the tactics answers
- Potential problems in using the tactic
- Tactics that refine the basic approach
- Tactics that are related to the basic approach
- Language-specific issues in using the tactic
- Suggestions about how to choose from among the variants of the tactic

These tactics require only the basic software-development tools: an editor, compiler, operating system, and interactive debugger. Advanced tactics that require specialized tools will be discussed in Chapter 14.

10

Case Studies II

10.1 Case Study 2

10.1.1 The Program

The case studies in this book are intended to demonstrate the use of some of the concepts presented in the preceding chapters of this section of the book. The defects analyzed are the actual mistakes made by the author when developing this software. Different people are prone to make different mistakes. Focus on the method used in debugging, rather than the particular error in question.

This example presents a lexicographic sort that works on arrays of integers written in Java. The original design for this algorithm can be found in Aho, Hopcroft, and Ullman, *The Design and Analysis of Computer Algorithms* [AHU74]. A lexicographic sort orders a set of tuples or strings of values. Dictionaries for natural languages have entries sorted in lexicographic order. The tuples do not have to be the same length, and in general they are not the same length. Given the following set of integer tuples,

```
2 4
3 2 1
1 2 3 5
3 1 2 4
1 3 5
3 4 2
2 3 5
2 5
```

performing a lexicographic sort of this set produces the following output:

```
1 2 3 4 5
1 3 5
2 3 5
2 4
2 5
3 1 2 4
3 2 1
3 4 2
```

The algorithm works as follows:

1. Find the length of the longest tuple.

2. Make lists of value and location pairs that appear in the tuples.

3. Bucket sort the lists of value and location pairs.

4. Create lists of unique values at each location.

5. Make lists of all strings of the same length.

6. Process each group of tuples of the same length from longest to shortest.

7. Add to the queue the tuples of the same length.

8. Sort the tuples in the queue into buckets according to the value at the current position.

9. Read the tuples from buckets that contain partially sorted tuples and write them to the queue for more processing.

The code for the original program is listed as follows:

```java
import java.util.Vector;

//-------------------------------------------------------
// Input:
//   A sequence of string (tuples), A[1], A[2], ..
//    A[n-1],
//   whose components are integers in the range 0 to
//    m-1. Let l[i] be the
//   length of A[i] = (a[ill, a[i21, ., a[il,i]).
// Output:
```

```
//   A permutation B[1], B[2], ., B[n]
//   of the A[i]'s such that B[1] <= B[2] <= ... <= B[n]
//
//-----------------------------------------------------

public final class Sort {

    public static Vector lexSortTuples(
                        int [][] tupleList) {

        // find the length of the longest tuple

        int maxLen= -1;
        int tupleListLen= tupleList.length;
        for ( int j= 0; j<tupleListLen; ++j ) {
            int [] tuple= tupleList[j];
            maxLen= Math.max(maxLen, tuple.length);
        }

        // make list of value/location pairs that
        // appear in the tuples

        int maxVal= -1;
        Vector pairList= new Vector();
        for ( int j=0; j<tupleListLen; ++j ) {
            int [] tuple= tupleList[j];
            int tupleLen= tuple.length;
            for ( int k=0; k<tupleLen; ++k ) {
                int value= tuple[k];
                maxVal= Math.max(maxVal, value);
                int [] pair= new int[2];
                pair[0]= k+1;
                pair[1]= value;
                pairList.addElement(pair);
            }
        }

        // bucket sort lists of value/location pairs

        Vector bucket2= new Vector(1+maxVal);
        for ( int i=0; i<bucket2.size(); ++i ) {
```

```
        bucket2.setElementAt(new Vector(), i);
}
Vector bucket1= new Vector(1+maxLen);
for ( int i=0; i<bucket1.size(); ++i ) {
    bucket1.setElementAt(new Vector(), i);
}

for ( int j=0; j<pairList.size(); ++j) {
    int [] pair= (int [])pairList.
                    elementAt(j);
    Vector bucket= (Vector)bucket2.
                      elementAt(pair[1]);
    bucket.addElement(pair);
    bucket2.setElementAt(bucket, pair[1]);
}
for ( int j=0; j<bucket2.size(); ++j) {
    pairList= (Vector) bucket2.elementAt(j);
    for ( int k=0; k<pairList.size(); ++k) {
        int [] pair= (int [])pairList.
                        elementAt(k);
        Vector bucket= (Vector)bucket1.
                          elementAt(pair[0]);
        bucket.addElement(pair);
        bucket1.setElementAt(bucket, pair[0]);
    }
}

// create lists of unique values at
// each location

Vector unique= new Vector(1+maxLen);
for ( int i= 0; i<unique.size(); ++i ) {
    unique.setElementAt(new Vector(), i);
}
for ( int j= 0; j<bucket1.size(); ++j ) {
    pairList= (Vector)bucket1.elementAt(j);
    int [] prev= new int[2];
    prev[0]= -1;
    prev[1]= -1;
    for ( int k= 0; k < pairList.size(); ++k ) {
```

```
                    int [] curr= (int [])pairList.
                                elementAt(k);
                if ( prev[1] != curr[1] ) {
                    Vector update= (Vector)unique.
                                    elementAt(j);
                    update.addElement(new Integer(
                                    curr[1]));
                    unique.setElementAt(update, j);
                }
                prev= curr;
            }
        }


        // make lists of all strings of same length

        Vector sameLen= new Vector();
        for ( int i= 0; i<maxLen+1; ++i ) {
            sameLen.addElement(new Vector());
        }
        for ( int j=0; j<tupleListLen; ++j ) {
            int [] tuple= tupleList[j];
            int tupleLen= tuple.length;
            Vector update= (Vector)sameLen.
                            elementAt(tupleLen);
            update.addElement( tuple );
            sameLen.setElementAt(update, tupleLen);
        }


        Vector buckets= new Vector(maxVal);
        for ( int i=0; i<buckets.size(); ++i ) {
            buckets.addElement(new Vector());
        }


        Vector queue= new Vector();

        // process each group of tuples of the same
        // length from longest to shortest

        for ( int k=maxLen; k>=0; --k ) {

            // add to the queue tuples of length k
```

```
            queue.addElement( sameLen.elementAt(k) );

            // sort tuples in queue into buckets
            // according to value at this position

            while ( 0 != queue.size() ) {
                int [] tuple= (int []) queue.
                              elementAt(0);
                int index= tuple[k-1] - 1;
                queue.removeElementAt(0);
                Vector update= (Vector)buckets.
                              elementAt(index);
                update.addElement(tuple);
                buckets.setElementAt(update, index);
            }

            // read tuples from buckets that contain
            // partially sortedtuples and write them
            // to the queue for more processing

            Vector group= (Vector)unique.elementAt(k);
            for ( int j=0; j<group.size(); ++j ) {
                int index= ((Integer)group.
                          elementAt(j)).intValue() - 1;
                int [] tuple= (int []) buckets.
                              elementAt(index);
                queue.addElement(tuple);
                buckets.setElementAt(null, index);
            }
        }
        return queue;
    }
}
```

10.1.2 Bug 1

10.1.2.1 The evidence

The first debugging session began by running the application. The test input and test driver are shown as follows:

```
import java.util.Vector;

public final class AlgRec {

    static int [] [] tuples= {
        {2, 4}, {3, 2, 1}, {1, 2, 3, 5},
        {3, 1, 2, 4}, {1, 3, 5}, {3, 4, 2}, {2, 3, 5},
        {2, 5} };

    public static void main(String args[]) {
        Vector out= Sort.lexSortTuples(tuples);
        for( int i=0; i<out.size(); ++i ) {
            int [] tuple= (int [])out.elementAt(i);
            for( int j=0; j<tuple.length; ++j ) {
                System.err.print(tuple[j]+" ");
            }
            System.err.print("\n");
        }
    }
}
```

The results of executing this test are shown below.

```
Exception in thread "main" java.lang.ArrayIndexOutOfBounds
                                  Exception: 2 >= 0
        at java.util.Vector.elementAt(Vector.java:427)
        at Sort.lexSortTuples(Sort.java:57)
        at AlgRec.test(AlgRec.java:33)
        at AlgRec.main(AlgRec.java:7)
```

10.1.2.2   The investigation

We do not need to create a test case or cut down the input data set, since we already have a test case with a handful of data elements. We decide to use the observation-hypothesis-experiment method for investigating this problem.

Observation 1: Our initial observation is that we have an *ArrayIndexOutOf-BoundsException* event, in which index 2 is specified, but the length of the vector is 0. This occurs in method *LexSortTuples* at line 57.

Hypothesis 1: Our initial hypothesis is that the variable *maxVal* is not computed correctly. This variable is used in the construction of the vector that we are having problems accessing.

Experiment 1: Our first experiment is to print values of *maxVal* and *maxLen* after they are computed.

Observation 2: Our next observation is that *maxLen*=4 and *maxVal*=4. These are correct.

Hypothesis 2: Since our first hypothesis was not correct, we fall back on a more general assertion that *bucket2* is not constructed correctly.

Experiment 2: Our next experiment is to print the size of *bucket1* and *bucket2* after their construction.

Observation 3: The results of this experiment are that both vectors have a size of 0.

Hypothesis 3: Our next hypothesis is that we have used the method *Vector.setElement* when we should have used *Vector.addElement*.

Experiment 3: We change the source to use *addElement* instead.

Observation 4: The results of this experiment are that both vectors still have a size of 0. Clearly, elements are not getting added to the vectors.

Hypothesis 4: If the body of the loop is not the problem, then it must be the controls. We assert that the loop limits are incorrect.

Experiment 4: We look at the code and see that the loop is controlled by an upper limit based on the *size()* of the vector, instead of its *capacity()*. Since we have not added any elements to the vector, the *size()* will always be zero.

10.1.2.3   **The fault and the correction**

Since the loops in this code were cloned from an initial exemplar, we assume that we have made the same mistake elsewhere. This turns out to be true. The loops that initialize the variables *unique* and *sameLen* have the exact same problem.

We change three loops to use a different upper limit and a different method for adding elements, like the following:

```
for ( int i=0; i<bucket2.capacity(); ++i ) {
```

```
bucket2.addElement(new Vector());
```

We change one loop to use a different upper limit, per the following:

```
for ( int i=0; i<buckets.capacity(); ++i ) {
```

These errors are more characteristic of a novice than an expert. Unfortunately, when it comes to bugs, a moment of fatigue, illness, or distraction can turn any expert into an amateur.

In this round of debugging, we applied the following methods from Chapter 9:

- Use runtime subscript checking.
- Display variable values.

We found two defects that both had the same root causes, which are explained in Chapter 11:

- Initialization errors—aggregate variable always uninitialized
- Reference errors—wrong procedure called

10.1.3   Bug 2

10.1.3.1   The evidence

The next debugging session began by running the same test application. The results of executing this test are shown as follows:

```
Exception in thread "main" java.lang.ClassCastException:
                        java.util.Vector
        at Sort.lexSortTuples(Sort.java:130)
        at AlgRec.test(AlgRec.java:33)
        at AlgRec.main(AlgRec.java:7)
```

10.1.3.2 The investigation

Observation 1: Our initial observation is that we have a *ClassCastException: java.util.Vector* event, with a *java.util.Vector* object. This occurs in method *lexSortTuples* at line 130.

Hypothesis 1: The wrong object has been appended to the vector being referenced.

Experiment 1: There are two statements that append elements to the variable in question. We replace each with a call to a procedure that displays the type of the arguments before appending the value.

10.1.3.3 The fault and correction

The code is trying to convert a vector to an array of *int* because an entire vector was appended to another vector (the queue) as a single element. Instead, each *int* array tuple should have been appended separately to the queue.

We replace the following statement

```
queue.addElement( sameLen.elementAt(k) );
```

with a loop that does the appropriate initialization:

```
Vector tupleSet= (Vector)sameLen.elementAt(k);
for ( int i=0; i<tupleSet.size(); ++i) {
    queue.addElement( (int [])tupleSet.elementAt(i) );
}
```

We use almost identical code to replace the second statement that adds elements to the end of the *queue* variable.

In this round of debugging, we applied the following method from Chapter 9:

■ Display procedure arguments.

We found two defects that had the following root causes, explained in Chapter 11:

- Dynamic data-structure problems—invalid type conversion

- Initialization errors—aggregate variable initialized with wrong values

10.1.4 Bug 3

10.1.4.1 The evidence

The next debugging session began by running the same application. The results of executing this test are shown as follows:

```
Exception in thread "main" java.lang.NullPointerException
        at Sort.lexSortTuples(Sort.java:135)
        at AlgRec.test(AlgRec.java:33)
        at AlgRec.main(AlgRec.java:7)
```

10.1.4.2 The investigation

Observation 1: The variable that is a null reference, *update,* is created by extracting an element from the *buckets* vector. There is one statement that appends elements to this variable. It always appends a new vector, so it cannot be the cause of the problem. There are two places that set the elements of this vector. One of them always assigns a null pointer to the element it sets.

Hypothesis 1: The statement that sets elements of the variable in question to null pointers should instead be setting them to empty vectors.

Experiment 1: Change the statement and rerun the program.

10.1.4.3 The fault and correction

We change the assignment of the *buckets* variable to use empty vectors instead of null references.

```
buckets.setElementAt(new Vector(), index);
```

In this round of debugging, we applied the following methods from Chapters 2 and 3:

- Eliminate impossible causes

- Use a system for organizing facts

We found one defect that had the following root causes, which are explained in Chapter 11:

- Dynamic data-structure errors—uninitialized pointer dereferenced
- Initialization errors—aggregate variable initialized with wrong value

10.1.5   Bug 4

10.1.5.1   The evidence

The next debugging session began by running the application. The results of executing this test are shown as follows:

```
Exception in thread "main"
java.lang.ArrayIndexOutOfBoundsException
        at Sort.lexSortTuples(Sort.java:132)
        at AlgRec.test(AlgRec.java:33)
        at AlgRec.main(AlgRec.java:7)
```

10.1.5.2   The investigation

Observation 1: The variable that was used in the array index is k, which is a loop index running from *maxLen* to 0.

Hypothesis 1: There are invalid values in the tuples.

Experiment 1: We insert code to print tuple values as they are picked from queue.

```
for( int z=0; z<tuple.length; ++z) {
    System.err.print(tuple[z]+" ");
}
System.err.print("\n");
```

Observation 2: All tuple values are all valid.

Hypothesis 2: Since the arrays are valid, the array indices must be invalid. The loop counter k's last value should be 1, not 0, since the index variable is having 1 subtracted from it.

Experiment 2: We change the loop control accordingly. We also print the value of k before the array reference that caused a problem, just in case our hypothesis is not correct.

10.1.5.3   The fault and correction

We change the loop limit per the following:

```
for ( int k=maxLen; k>=1; --k ) {
```

In this round of debugging, we applied the following methods from Chapter 9:

- Use runtime subscript checking.
- Display data structures.

Of course, we did not actually have to do anything to get the runtime subscript checking, since Java does it automatically. Still, we should get credit for using it, since we chose the implementation language for this program.

We found one defect that had the following root cause, explained in Chapter 11:

- Control-flow problems—loop iterations off by one

10.1.5.4   Final test

The debugging process is not complete until the changes have been thoroughly tested. We present as follows a set of interesting tuples to exercise the sort program. While this set of test cases is far from exhaustive, it is suggestive of the kind of approach to take in unit testing. We have omitted the results of the tests from the book in the interest of brevity. The listing takes several pages, and all the tests passed.

```
import java.util.Vector;

public final class AlgRec {

    public static void main(String args[]) {

        test(tuples01);
        test(tuples02);
        test(tuples03);
```

```
                    test(tuples04);
                    test(tuples05);
                    test(tuples06);
                    test(tuples07);
                    test(tuples08);
                    test(tuples09);
                    test(tuples10);
                    test(tuples11);
                    test(tuples12);
                    test(tuples13);
                    test(tuples14);
                    test(tuples15);
                    test(tuples16);
                    test(tuples17);
                    test(tuples18);
                    test(tuples19);
                    test(tuples20);
                    test(tuples21);
                    test(tuples22);
                }

            private static void test(int [][] tuples) {
                Vector out= Sort.lexSortTuples(tuples);
                for( int i=0; i<out.size(); ++i ) {
                    int [] tuple= (int [])out.elementAt(i);
                    for( int j=0; j<tuple.length; ++j ) {
                        System.err.print(tuple[j]+" ");
                    }
                    System.err.print("\n");
                }
                System.err.println("----------\n");
            }

    //----------------------------------------------------

    // ----- same length tuples

    //       ascending values

    static int [] []  tuples01=
    { { 3,2,1 }, { 6,5,4 }, { 9,8,7 } };
```

```
//        descending values

static int [] [] tuples02=
{ { 9,8,7 }, { 6,5,4 }, { 3,2,1 } };


//        "V" pattern values

static int [] [] tuples03=
{ { 19,20,21 }, { 10,11,12 }, { 7,8,9 }, { 1,2,3  },
  { 4,5,6 }, { 13,14,15 }, { 16,17,18 } };


//        inverse "V" pattern values

static int [] [] tuples04=
{ { 4,5,6 }, { 10,11,12 }, { 16,17,18 }, { 19,20,21 },
  { 13,14,15 }, { 7,8,9 }, { 1,2,3 } };


//        random values

static int [] [] tuples05=
{ { 2, 71, 3 }, { 67, 5, 61 }, { 7, 59, 11 },
   { 57, 13, 53 },  { 17, 47, 23 }, { 43, 29, 41 },
   { 31, 37, 71 } };


// ----- random length tuples

//        ascending values

static int [] [] tuples06=
{ { 2, 3 }, { 5, 7, 11, 13 },
  { 17, 19, 23, 29, 31, 37 },  { 41, 43, 47 },
  { 53, 57, 59, 61, 67 },
  { 71, 73, 79, 83, 87, 89, 97 },
  { 101, 103, 107, 109, 111, 113, 127, 131 } };


//        descending values

static int [] [] tuples07=
{ { 131, 127, 113 },
  { 111, 109, 107, 103, 101, 97, 89 },
```

```
      { 87, 83, 79, 73, 71 },
      { 67, 61, 59, 57, 53, 47, 43 },
      { 41, 37, 31, 29, 23 }, { 19, 17, 13 },
      { 11, 7, 5, 3, 2 } };

//        "V" pattern values

static int [] [] tuples08=
{ { 109, 103, 97 }, { 87, 79, 71, 61 }, { 57, 47 },
  { 43, 53, 59 },    { 2, 3, 5, 7, 11, 13 },
  { 17, 19, 23 }, { 29, 31, 37, 41 },
  { 67, 73, 83, 89, 101, 107 }, { 111, 113, 127, 131 } };

//        inverse "V" pattern values

static int [] [] tuples09=
{ { 5, 7, 17, 19, 31, 37, 47, 53},
  { 61, 67, 79, 83, 97, 101 },
  { 109, 111, 113, 127, 131 }, { 57, 87, 89, 103, 107 },
  { 73, 59, 71, 41 }, { 43, 23, 29, 11 }, { 13, 2, 3 } };

//        random values

static int [] [] tuples10=
{ {43, 29, 41, 31, 37 }, {2, 71 }, {3, 67, 5, 61, 7 },
  {59, 11, 57 }, {13, 53, 17, 47, 23 } };

// ----- ascending length tuples

//        ascending values
static int [] [] tuples11=
{ { 2, 3 }, { 5, 7, 11 }, { 13, 17, 19, 23 },
  { 29, 31, 37, 43, 41 },  { 43, 47, 53, 57, 59, 61 },
  { 67, 71, 73, 79, 83, 87, 89 },
  { 97, 101, 103, 107, 109, 111, 113, 127 } };

//        descending values
static int [] [] tuples12=
{ { 131, 127 }, { 113, 111, 109 },
  { 107, 103, 101, 97 },  { 89, 87, 83, 79, 73 },
  { 71, 67, 61, 59, 57, 53 },
```

```
    { 47, 43, 41, 37, 31, 29, 23 },
    { 19, 17, 13, 11, 7, 5, 3, 2  } };

//      "V" pattern values
static int [] [] tuples13=
{ { 109, 103 }, { 97, 87, 79} , { 71, 61, 57, 47} ,
  { 5, 2, 3, 7, 13} , { 19, 41, 31, 23, 17, 11} ,
  { 29, 37, 43, 53, 59, 67, 73} ,
  { 83, 89, 101, 107, 111, 113, 127, 131 } };

//      inverse "V" pattern values
static int [] [] tuples14=
{ { 5, 7 }, { 17, 19, 31 }, { 37, 47, 53, 61 },
  { 67, 79, 83, 97, 101 }, { 109, 111, 113, 127, 131 },
  { 57, 87, 89, 103, 107 }, { 59, 71, 41, 43, 73 },
  { 23, 29, 11 }, { 13, 2, 3 } };

//      random values
static int [] [] tuples15=
{ { 109, 103, }, { 97, 87, 79, }, { 71, 61, 57, 47 },
  { 5, 2, 3, 7, 13, }, { 19, 41, 31, 23, 17, 11, },
  { 29, 37, 43, 53, 59, 67, 73, },
  { 83, 89, 101, 107, 111, 113, 127 } };

// ----- descending length tuples

//      ascending values

static int [] [] tuples16=
{ { 2, 3, 5, 7, 11, 13, 17, 19 },
  { 23, 29, 31, 37, 43, 41, 43 },
  { 47, 53, 57, 59, 61, 67 }, { 71, 73, 79, 83, 87 },
  { 89, 97, 101, 103 }, { 107, 109, 111 }, { 113, 127 } };

//      descending values

static int [] [] tuples17=
{ { 131, 127, 113, 111, 109, 107, 103, 101 },
  { 97, 89, 87, 83, 79, 73, 71 },
  { 67, 61, 59, 57, 53, 47 }, { 43, 41, 37, 31, 29 },
  { 23, 19, 17, 13 }, { 11, 7, 5 }, { 3, 2 } };
```

```
//        "V" pattern values

static int [] [] tuples18=
{ { 109, 103, 97, 87, 79, 71, 61, 57 },
  { 47, 5, 2, 3, 7, 13, 19, 41 },
  { 31, 23, 17, 11, 29, 37 }, { 43, 53, 59, 67, 73 },
  { 83, 89, 101, 107 },
  { 111, 113, 127 } };

//        inverse "V" pattern values

static int [] [] tuples19=
{ { 5, 7, 17, 19, 31, 37, 47, 53},
  { 61, 67, 79, 83, 97, 101 },
  { 109, 111, 113, 127, 131 }, { 57, 87, 89, 103, 107 },
  { 73, 59, 71, 41 }, { 43, 23, 29, 11 }, { 13, 2, 3 } };

//        random values

static int [] [] tuples20=
{ { 83, 89, 101, 107, 111, 113, 127 },
  { 29, 37, 43, 53, 59, 67, 73, },
  { 19, 41, 31, 23, 17, 11, }, { 5, 2, 3, 7, 13, },
  { 71, 61, 57, 47 }, { 97, 87, 79, }, { 109, 103, } };

// ----- duplicates

static int [] [] tuples21=
{ { 109, 103, 97 }, { 87, 79, 71, 61 },
  { 89, 101, 107, 111 },{ 57, 47, 41 },
  { 31, 23, 17, 11 }, { 5, 2, 3 }, { 7, 13, 19, 29 },
  { 57, 47, 41 }, { 37, 43, 53 }, { 59, 67, 73, 83 },
  { 109, 103, 97 }, { 89, 101, 107, 111 } };

// ----- singleton

static int [] [] tuples22=
{ { 109, 103, 97, 87, 79, 71, 61, 57, 47, 41, 31, 23,
    17, 11, 5, 2, 3, 7, 13, 19, 29, 37, 43, 53, 59,
    67, 73, 83, 89, 101, 107, 111 } };
}
```

10.1.5.5   **Final source**

The code for the final program is listed as follows:

```java
import java.util.Vector;


//=======================================================
// Sort
// this class contains specialized sorting methods to
// be called statically
//=======================================================


public final class Sort {


//-------------------------------------------------------
// Input:
//    A sequence of string (tuples),
//     A[0], A[1], .. A[n-1],
//    whose components are integers in the range 0 to
//     m-1. Let l[i] be the
//    length of A[i] = (a[il], a[i2], ., a[il,i]).
// Output:
//    A permutation B[1], B[2], ., B[n]
//    of the A[i]'s such that B[1] <= B[2] <= ... <= B[n]
//
//-------------------------------------------------------

    public static Vector lexSortTuples(
                        int [][] tupleList) {

        // find the length of the longest tuple

        int maxLen= -1;
        int tupleListLen= tupleList.length;
        for ( int j= 0; j<tupleListLen; ++j ) {
            int [] tuple= tupleList[j];
            maxLen= Math.max(maxLen, tuple.length);
        }

        // make list of value/location pairs that
        // appear in the tuples
```

```
int maxVal= -1;
Vector pairList= new Vector();
for ( int j=0; j<tupleListLen; ++j ) {
    int [] tuple= tupleList[j];
    int tupleLen= tuple.length;
    for ( int k=0; k<tupleLen; ++k ) {
        int value= tuple[k];
        maxVal= Math.max(maxVal, value);
        int [] pair= new int[2];
        pair[0]= k+1;
        pair[1]= value;
        pairList.addElement(pair);
    }
}

// bucket sort lists of value/location pairs

Vector bucket2= new Vector(1+maxVal);
for ( int i=0; i<bucket2.capacity(); ++i ) {
    bucket2.addElement(new Vector());
}
Vector bucket1= new Vector(1+maxLen);
for ( int i=0; i<bucket1.capacity(); ++i ) {
    bucket1.addElement(new Vector());
}

for ( int j=0; j<pairList.size(); ++j) {
    int [] pair= (int [])pairList.
                    elementAt(j);
    Vector bucket= (Vector)bucket2.
                    elementAt(pair[1]);
    bucket.addElement(pair);
    bucket2.setElementAt(bucket, pair[1]);
}
for ( int j=0; j<bucket2.size(); ++j) {
    pairList= (Vector) bucket2.elementAt(j);
    for ( int k=0; k<pairList.size(); ++k) {
        int [] pair= (int [])pairList.
                        elementAt(k);
        Vector bucket= (Vector)bucket1.
                        elementAt(pair[0]);
```

```
                    bucket.addElement(pair);
                    bucket1.setElementAt(bucket, pair[0]);
            }
    }

    // create lists of unique values at
    // each location

    Vector unique= new Vector(1+maxLen);
    for ( int i= 0; i<unique.capacity(); ++i ) {
        unique.addElement(new Vector());
    }
    for ( int j= 0; j<bucket1.size(); ++j ) {
        pairList= (Vector)bucket1.elementAt(j);
        int [] prev= new int[2];
        prev[0]= -1;
        prev[1]= -1;
        for ( int k= 0; k < pairList.size(); ++k ) {
            int [] curr= (int [])pairList.
                            elementAt(k);
            if ( prev[1] != curr[1] ) {
                Vector update= (Vector)unique.
                                elementAt(j);
                update.addElement(new Integer(
                                curr[1]));
                unique.setElementAt(update, j);
            }
            prev= curr;
        }
    }

    // make lists of all strings of same length

    Vector sameLen= new Vector();
    for ( int i= 0; i<maxLen+1; ++i ) {
        sameLen.addElement(new Vector());
    }
    for ( int j=0; j<tupleListLen; ++j ) {
        int [] tuple= tupleList[j];
        int tupleLen= tuple.length;
        Vector update= (Vector)sameLen.
```

```
                        elementAt(tupleLen);
        update.addElement( tuple );
        sameLen.setElementAt(update, tupleLen);
}


Vector buckets= new Vector(maxVal);
for ( int i=0; i<buckets.capacity(); ++i ) {
    buckets.addElement(new Vector());
}


Vector queue= new Vector();

// process each group of tuples of the
// same length from longest to shortest

for ( int k=maxLen; k>=1; --k ) {

    // add to the queue tuples of length k

    Vector tupleSet= (Vector)sameLen.
                    elementAt(k);
    for ( int i=0; i<tupleSet.size(); ++i) {
        queue.addElement( (int [])tupleSet.
                    elementAt(i) );
    }

    // sort tuples in queue into buckets
    // according to value at this position

    while ( 0 != queue.size() ) {
        int [] tuple= (int []) queue.
                    elementAt(0);
        int index= tuple[k-1] - 1;
        queue.removeElementAt(0);
        Vector update= (Vector)buckets.
                    elementAt(index);
        update.addElement(tuple);
        buckets.setElementAt(update, index);
    }

    // read tuples from buckets that contain
```

```
                        // partially sorted tuples and write them
                        // to the queue for more processing

                        Vector group= (Vector)unique.elementAt(k);
                        for ( int j=0; j<group.size(); ++j ) {
                            int index= ((Integer)group.
                                        elementAt(j)).intValue() - 1;
                            tupleSet= (Vector) buckets.
                                            elementAt(index);
                            for ( int i=0; i<tupleSet.size(); ++i) {
                                queue.addElement( (int [])tupleSet.
                                            elementAt(i) );
                            }
                            buckets.setElementAt(new Vector(),
                                            index);
                        }
                    }
                    return queue;
                }
            }
```

10.2   Case Study 3

10.2.1   The Program

This example presents an algorithm that matches partial or whole expression trees against a database of idiomatic expressions. The original design for this algorithm can be found in the article "Recognition and Selection of Idioms for Code Optimization" by Lawrence Snyder [Sn82]. The implementation is written in C++.

Snyder defines an *idiom* as "a construction used by programmers for a logically primitive operation for which no language primitive exists." Twenty years ago, when Snyder wrote his paper, APL was the only language that was an obvious candidate for the approach to optimization he proposed. Other researchers had collected lists of idioms that commonly occurred in APL applications. Some APL language processors performed extremely limited recognition of a couple of these idioms.

Snyder proposes that an APL language processor (compiler or interpreter) should recognize idioms and evaluate the benefits of replacing them with library calls. He provides an algorithm that can recognize multiple idioms in a single expression and select which idioms should be replaced to achieve maximum benefit. Snyder's recognition algorithm works in $\mathbf{O}(n \log n)$ time, and the selection algorithm works in $\mathbf{O}(n)$ time.

The chief benefit of recognizing a complex expression and replacing it with a call to a runtime library procedure came from eliminating memory allocations and type conversions that were done "under the covers." Every operation in an APL interpreter causes the allocation of storage for results. Since APL works best on arrays, large blocks of memory are continually being allocated and freed. In addition, there are frequent conversions between different data types (integer, real, etc.) and special representations of certain data structures (arithmetic progressions, sets, etc.).

While APL is not used much anymore, other languages have become popular, which can have similar characteristics. Both C++ and Java can cause frequent memory allocations and conversions to occur "behind the programmer's back." Thus, while Snyder's algorithm is interesting on its own, it may also be useful to adapt to languages popular today.

The following technical details highlight Snyder's approach. Idioms can overlap, and the algorithm handles this correctly. Variable operands of idioms are "free variables." They can match constants, variables, or expressions. The algorithm handles these cases. Constants required for the correctness of an idiom are treated as functions with no arguments. Expression trees are assumed to be binary; however, the code would easily extend to trees having nodes of arbitrary degree.

The algorithm performs two passes over an expression tree. The first pass visits the nodes of the tree bottom-up and marks all the nodes with integers. The second pass visits the nodes top-down and performs the recognition and selection. The first pass assigns unique numbers to the roots of all identical subtrees.

Prior to the numbering phase, the expression is preprocessed into a form that makes rapid handling possible. All the nodes in the tree have been placed on linked lists such that nodes that have the same height are on the same list. Nodes at height 0 (i.e., the leaves) have been given integer codes that identify each distinct operand uniquely. Entries into a symbol table or constant table for these operands would be available and suitable for this purpose.

The constructor for the *Expr* class reads in the expression and puts it into a suitable binary form. Each node in the expression tree is represented by an instance of the *Tree* class.

The numbering phase processes all the nodes of the same height together. All nodes with the same height are sorted first on the assigned code of their left descendant, and then similarly on their right descendant, using a bucket sort. The numbering algorithm is found in the file *number.c*.

The database of idioms is stored in a table. Each entry is represented in prefix notation, without parentheses. The first and subsequent occurrences of an operand are represented by distinct codes. The constructor for the *IdiomTable* class reads in the table and puts it into a suitable binary form.

The matching phase performs a depth-first traversal of the expression tree. It performs all matches simultaneously, using a match descriptor to track the progress of a match. The descriptors are represented by instances of the *Desc* class. The descriptor tracks the initial node of the subtree that is matched and the identifiers of the nodes that are operands of the idiom.

Each time the *match* function is called on a node of the tree, it initiates descriptors for all idioms that might match the current node. Then it updates the descriptors for all matches in progress. Then it calls itself recursively to process the left and right children of that node. After returning from the recursive call, it determines which idioms matched the node and which to select. The match algorithm is found in the file *match.c*.

The code for the original program is listed as follows. The original algorithm uses origin-1 array indexing, while C++ uses origin-0 indexing. We tried to work around this issue by padding the arrays with an extra null element at the beginning. While this largely worked, it introduced several bugs, which are discussed in the sequel. The original algorithm also had ambiguous or undefined notation, as well as an inconsistent use of keyword delimiters and indenting to show control flow.

```
/* Bucket.h */

#ifndef _Bucket_h_
#define _Bucket_h_

struct _bucket {
    int link;
    int head;
};
typedef struct _bucket Bucket;
extern int numBuckets;
#endif
```

```
/* Select.h */

#ifndef _Select_h_
#define _Select_h_

class Select {
public:
    // constructors and destructors
    Select();
    Select(int);

    // accessors
    inline int getVertex() { return _vertex; }
    inline Select * getNext() { return _next; }

    // mutators
    inline void setVertex(int x) { _vertex= x; }
    inline void setNext(Select * x) { _next= x; }

private:
    int _vertex;
    Select * _next;
};
#endif
```

```
/* Opcode.h */

#ifndef _Opcode_h_
#define _Opcode_h_

extern char ** tagList;
extern int tagCount;
extern int lookupTag(char *);

/*--------------------------------------------------*/

#define NONE -1
```

```
#define F_FIRST 1
#define F_plus 1
#define F_minus 2
#define F_times 3
#define F_divide 4
#define F_mod 5
#define F_exp 6
#define F_log 7
#define F_and 8
#define F_or 9
#define F_nand 10
#define F_nor 11
#define F_lt 12
#define F_lteq 13
#define F_gt 14
#define F_gteq 15
#define F_eq 16
#define F_neq 17

#define F_plus_scan 18
#define F_times_scan 19
#define F_and_scan 20
#define F_or_scan 21
#define F_lt_scan 22
#define F_lteq_scan 23
#define F_eq_scan 24
#define F_neq_scan 25

#define F_plus_red 26
#define F_times_red 27
#define F_and_red 28
#define F_or_red 29

#define F_and_eq 30
#define F_plus_times 31

#define F_cprs 32
#define F_xpnd 33
#define F_rev 34
#define F_rot 35
#define F_form 36
```

```
#define F_shape 37
#define F_get 38
#define F_iota 39
#define F_ravel 40
#define F_splice 41
#define F_flip 42
#define F_trans 43
#define F_upgr 44
#define F_dngr 45
#define F_rep 46
#define F_value 47
#define F_find 48
#define F_memb 49

#define F_not 50

#define C_int 51
#define C_real 52
#define C_char 53

#define F_LAST 53

#define V_first_1 54
#define V_first_2 55
#define V_first_3 56
#define V_first_4 57
#define V_first_5 58

#define V_dup_1 59
#define V_dup_2 60
#define V_dup_3 61
#define V_dup_4 62
#define V_dup_5 63

#define DUP_FIRST 59
#define DUP_LAST 63
#define VARB_COUNT 5

#endif
```

```
/* Desc.h */

#ifndef _Desc_h_
#define _Desc_h_

class Desc {
public:
    // constructors and destructors
    Desc();
    Desc(int, int, int, int, Select *);
    ~Desc();

    // accessors
    inline int getRow() { return _row; }
    inline int getCol() { return _col; }
    inline int getVertex() { return _vertex; }
    inline int getBenefit() { return _benefit; }
    inline Select * getChain() { return _chain; }
    inline Desc * getNext() { return _next; }
    inline Desc * getPrev() { return _prev; }

    // mutators
    inline void setRow(int x) { _row= x; }
    inline void setCol(int x) { _col= x; }
    inline void setVertex(int x) { _vertex= x; }
    inline void setBenefit(int x) { _benefit= x; }
    inline void setChain(Select * x) { _chain= x; }
    inline void setNext(Desc * x) { _next= x; }
    inline void setPrev(Desc * x) { _prev= x; }

private:
    int _row;
    int _col;
    int _vertex;
    int _benefit;
    Select * _chain;
    Desc * _next;
    Desc * _prev;
};
```

```
#endif
```

```
/* Tree.h */

#ifndef _Tree_h_
#define _Tree_h_

class Tree {
public:
    // constructors and destructors
    Tree();
    Tree(int, int, int, int, int, char *, int,
        Select *);
    ~Tree();

    // accessors
    inline int getLeft() { return _left; }
    inline int getRight() { return _right; }
    inline int getLink() { return _link; }
    inline int getNumber() { return _number; }
    inline int getOpType() { return _opType; }
    inline char * getOpName() { return _opName; }
    inline int getBenefit() { return _benefit; }
    inline Select * getSelect() { return _select; }

    // mutators
    inline void setLeft(int x) { _left= x; }
    inline void setRight(int x) { _right= x ; }
    inline void setLink(int x) { _link= x; }
    inline void setNumber(int x) { _number= x; }
    inline void setOpType(int x) { _opType= x; }
    inline void setOpName(char *x) { _opName= x; }
    inline void setBenefit(int x) { _benefit= x; }
    inline void setSelect(Select *x) { _select= x; }

private:
    int _left;
    int _right;
    int _link;
    int _number;
```

```
        int _opType;
        char *_opName;
        int _benefit;
        Select *_select;
};

#endif
```

```
/* Expr.h */

#ifndef _Expr_h_
#define _Expr_h_

class Expr {
public:
        // constructors and destructors
        Expr(char *);
        Expr(int, int, Tree *, int *);
        ~Expr();

        // accessors
        inline int getSize() { return _size; }
        inline int getDepth() { return _depth; }
        inline int getUnique() { return _unique; }
        inline Tree * getTree() { return _tree; }
        inline int * getHeight() { return _height; }

        // mutators
        inline void setSize(int x) { _size= x; }
        inline void setDepth(int x) { _depth= x; }
        inline void setUnique(int x) { _unique= x ; }
        inline void setTree(Tree * x) { _tree= x; }
        inline void setHeight(int * x) { _height= x; }

private:
        int _size;
        int _depth;
        int _unique;
        Tree * _tree;
        int * _height;
```

```
};
#endif
```

```c
/* IdiomTable.h */

#ifndef _IdiomTable_h_
#define _IdiomTable_h_

class IdiomTable {
public:
    // constructors and destructors
    IdiomTable();
    IdiomTable(char *);
    ~IdiomTable();

    // accessors
    inline int ** getTable() { return _table; }
    inline int getCount() { return _count; }
    inline int getSize() { return _size; }
    inline int getDepth() { return _depth; }

    // mutators
    inline void setTable(int **x) { _table= x; }
    inline void setCount(int x) { _count= x; }
    inline void setSize(int x) { _size= x; }
    inline void setDepth(int x) { _depth= x; }

    // workers
    int idiomPayoff(int,int);
    int isOpRepeated(int);
    int isOpFunction(int);

    int firstOccur(int);

private:
    int ** _table;
    int _count;
    int _size;
    int _depth;
    int * _payoff;
```

```
        int lookup(char *);

};
#endif
```

```
/* Select.c */

#include "Select.h"

Select::Select() {
    Select(0);
}

Select::Select(int vertex) {
    _vertex= vertex;
    _next= 0;
}
```

```
/* Opcode.c */
#include <string.h>

int tagCount= 60;

char * tagList[] = { "NONE",
"F_plus", "F_minus", "F_times", "F_divide", "F_mod",
"F_exp", "F_log", "F_and", "F_or", "F_nand",

"F_nor", "F_lt", "F_lteq", "F_gt", "F_gteq",
"F_eq", "F_neq", "F_plus_scan", "F_times_scan",
"F_and_scan",

"F_or_scan", "F_lt_scan", "F_lteq_scan", "F_eq_scan",
"F_neq_scan", "F_plus_red", "F_times_red", "F_and_red",
"F_or_red", "F_and_eq",

"F_plus_times", "F_cprs", "F_xpnd", "F_rev", "F_rot",
"F_form", "F_shape", "F_get", "F_iota", "F_ravel",

"F_splice", "F_flip", "F_trans", "F_upgr", "F_dngr",
```

```
"F_rep", "F_value", "F_find", "F_memb", "F_not",

"C_int", "C_real", "C_char", "V_first_1", "V_first_2",
"V_first_3", "V_dup_1", "V_dup_2", "V_dup_3"
};

int lookupTag(char * token) {
    int index= -1;
    for ( int i= 0; i < tagCount; ++i ) {
        if ( 0 == strcmp(token,tagList[i]) ) {
            index= i;
            break;
        }
    }
    return index;
}
```

```
/* Desc.c */

#include "Select.h"
#include "Desc.h"

Desc::Desc() {
    Desc(0,0,0,0,0);
}

Desc::Desc(int vertex, int row, int col, int bene,
           Select *chain) {

    _vertex= vertex;
    _row= row;
    _col= col;
    _benefit= 0;
    _next= 0;
    _prev= 0;
    _chain= chain;
}

Desc::~Desc() {
}
```

```
/* Tree.c */

#include "Select.h"
#include "Tree.h"
#include "Opcode.h"

Tree::Tree() {
    Tree(0,0,0,0,0,0,0,0);
}

Tree::Tree( int left, int right, int link, int number,
    int opType, char * opName, int benefit,
    Select * select ) {

    _left= left;
    _right= right;
    _link= link;
    _number= number;
    _opType= opType;
    _opName= opName;
    _benefit= benefit;
    _select= select;
}

Tree::~Tree() { }
```

```
/* Expr.c */

#include <stdio.h>
#include <stdlib.h>
#include <string.h>

#include "Select.h"
#include "Tree.h"
#include "Expr.h"
#include "Opcode.h"

Expr::Expr(char * fileName) {
```

```
int bufSize= 256;
char buffer[256];
char *tokens[128];

FILE * file= fopen(fileName,"r");
if( file == 0 ) {
    fprintf(stderr,"Unable to open %s\n",fileName);
    fflush(stderr);
    exit(1);
}

fscanf(file, "%d\n", &_size);
fscanf(file, "%d\n", &_depth);
fscanf(file, "%d\n\n", &_unique);
_tree= new Tree[_size]; // need to add +1

_height= new int[_depth+1];
int tokenCtr= 0;
fgets(buffer, bufSize, file);
char * token= strtok(buffer, " ");
_height[tokenCtr++]= atoi(token);
while( token= strtok(NULL, " \n") ) {
    _height[tokenCtr++]= atoi(token);
}

int row= 0;
tokenCtr= 0;
while ( 0 != fgets(buffer, bufSize, file) ) {
    token= strtok(buffer, " ");
    tokens[tokenCtr++]= token;
    int k=0;
    while( token= strtok(NULL, " \n") ) {
        tokens[tokenCtr++]= token;
    }
    _tree[row].setLeft(atoi(tokens[0]));
    _tree[row].setRight(atoi(tokens[1]));
    _tree[row].setLink(atoi(tokens[2]));
    _tree[row].setNumber(atoi(tokens[3]));
    _tree[row].setOpType(lookupTag(tokens[4]));
    _tree[row].setOpName(tokens[5]);
```

```
        }
        fclose(file);
}

Expr::Expr(int depth, int unique, Tree * tree, int * height)
        { }

Expr::~Expr() { }
```

```
/* IdiomTable.c */

#include <stdio.h>
#include <string.h>
#include <stdlib.h>

#include "IdiomTable.h"
#include "Opcode.h"

IdiomTable::IdiomTable(char *fileName) {

    int bufSize= 256;
    char buffer[256];
    char * tokens[128];

    FILE * file= fopen(fileName,"r");
    if ( file == 0 ) {
        fprintf(stderr,"Unable to open %s\n",fileName);
        fflush(stderr);
        exit(1);
    }

    fscanf(file, "%d\n", &_count);
    fscanf(file, "%d\n", &_size);

    _table= new (int *)[_count+1];
    for ( int i=0; i < _count; ++i ) {
        _table[i]= new int[_size+1];
    }

    _payoff= new int[_count+1];
```

```
            int tokenCtr= 0;
            fgets(buffer, bufSize, file);
            char * token= strtok(buffer, " ");
            _payoff[tokenCtr++]= atoi(token);
            while( token= strtok(NULL, " \n") ) {
                _payoff[tokenCtr++]= atoi(token);
            }

            int j= 0;
            while ( 0 != fgets(buffer, bufSize, file) ) {
                token= strtok(buffer, " ");
                tokens[tokenCtr++]= token;
                int k=0;
                _table[j][k++]= lookupTag(token);
                while( token= strtok(NULL, " \n") ) {
                    tokens[tokenCtr++]= token;
                    _table[j][k++]= lookupTag(token);
                }
                ++j;
            }

            for( int i=0; i<_count; ++i ) {
                for( int j=0; j<_size; ++j ) {
                    fprintf(stderr,"%d ",_table[i][j]);
                }
                fprintf(stderr,"\n");
            }
            fclose(file);
    }

    int IdiomTable::idiomPayoff(int x, int y) {
        return _payoff[x];
    }

    int IdiomTable::isOpRepeated(int x){
        return 0;
    }

    int IdiomTable::isOpFunction(int x){
        if( x >= F_FIRST && x <= F_LAST) {
            return 1;
```

```
        } else {
            return 0;
        }
    }

    int IdiomTable::firstOccur(int x){
        return 0;
    }
```

```
    /* number.c */

    #include <stdio.h>

    #include "Select.h"
    #include "Tree.h"
    #include "Bucket.h"
    #include "Expr.h"

    void numberTree( Expr * expr ) {

        Tree *tree= expr->getTree();
        int depth= expr->getDepth();
        int * height= expr->getHeight();
        int unique= expr->getUnique();

        Bucket * bucket1= new Bucket[depth+1];
        Bucket * bucket2= new Bucket[depth+1];

        int b1, b2, left, right, node, lNum, rNum;
        int b1Chain= 0;
        int b2Chain= 0;

        // for all levels of the tree
        for( int i= 1; i <= depth; ++i ) {

            // Bucket sort on left descendant
            while( height[i] != 0 ) {

                // for all nodes in one level
                node= height[i];
```

```
            // save ID of next node to process
            height[i]= tree[node].getLink();

            // if we have a left descendant get its
            // leaf number
            left= tree[node].getLeft();
            if( left != 0 ) {
                lNum= tree[left].getNumber();

                // if there aren't any nodes in the
                // chain of buckets yet
                // then initialize the chain
                if( bucket1[lNum].head == 0 ) {
                    bucket1[lNum].link= b1Chain;
                    b1Chain= lNum;
                }

                // Put node in bucket for nodes having
                // this left son
                tree[node].setLink(bucket1[lNum].head);
                bucket1[lNum].head= node;
            }
        }
    }

    // Bucket sort on right descendant
    while( b1Chain != 0 ) {
        b1= b1Chain;
        b1Chain= bucket1[b1].link;
        while( bucket1[b1].head != 0 ) {
            node= bucket1[b1].head;

            // save ID of next node to process
            bucket1[b1].head= tree[node].getLink();

            // if we have a right descendant get
            // its leaf number
            right= tree[node].getRight();
            if( right != 0 ) {
                rNum= tree[right].getNumber();
                // if there aren't any nodes in
                // the chain of buckets
```

```
                    // yet then initialize the chain
                    if( bucket2[rNum].head == 0 ) {
                        bucket2[rNum].link= b2Chain;
                        b2Chain= rNum;
                    }

                    // Put node in bucket for nodes
                    // having this right son
                    tree[node].setLink(
                            bucket2[rNum].head);
                    bucket2[rNum].head= node;
                }
            }
        }

        // Assign unique numbers for each
        // non-empty bucket
        while( b2Chain != 0 ) {
            b2= b2Chain;
            b2Chain= bucket2[b2].link;
            unique += 1;
            while( bucket2[b2].head != 0 ) {
                node= bucket2[b2].head;
                tree[node].setNumber(unique);
                bucket2[b2].head= tree[node].getLink();
            }
        }
    }
}
```

```
/* match.c */

#include <stdio.h>
#include <stdlib.h>

#define max(a,b)  (((a)>(b))?(a):(b))

#include "Select.h"
#include "Desc.h"
#include "Tree.h"
```

```
#include "IdiomTable.h"
#include "Expr.h"

Desc activeHead;
Desc *active;
Desc accumHead;
Desc *accum;

void match(int vertex, Expr *expr, IdiomTable *table) {

    Tree * tree= expr->getTree();
    int ** idiomTable= table->getTable();
    int numIdioms= table->getCount();

    int i, row, col, current, bene, best;
    Desc suspendHead;
    Desc *suspend;
    Select selectHead;
    Select *select;
    Desc *newDesc, *desc;
    Select *newSel, *chain, *link;

    // descriptors of matches in progress that
    // have reached a leaf
    suspendHead.setNext(0);
    accumHead.setNext(0);

    // create match descriptors for all idioms that
    // begin with the same op as the first op
    // in the expression

    for(i= 1; i <= numIdioms; ++i) {
        if( idiomTable[i][0] == tree[vertex].
                                getOpType() ) {
            newDesc= new Desc(vertex,i,1,0,0);
            if( accumHead.getNext() == 0 ) {
                accum= newDesc;
                accumHead.setNext(accum);
            } else {
                accum->setNext(newDesc);
            }
```

```
            }
        }

        // update matches in progress
        while( (desc= activeHead.getNext()) != 0 ) {
            row= desc->getRow();
            col= desc->getCol();
            current= desc->getVertex();
            bene= desc->getBenefit();
            chain= desc->getChain();

            // three possible cases: the next token
            // in the idiom is
            // 1) a function matching the vertex
            if( table->isOpFunction(idiomTable[row]
                                            [col+1]) ) {
                if( idiomTable[row][col+1] == tree[vertex].
                                            getOpType() ) {

                    // put new descriptor on
                    // accumulated list
                    newDesc= new Desc(current,row,col+1,
                                    bene,chain);
                    accum->setNext(newDesc);
                    newDesc->setPrev(accum);
                }

            // 2) a repeated operand matching the vertex
            } else if ( table->isOpRepeated(idiomTable[row]
                                            [col+1]) ) {
                if( tree[vertex].getNumber() ==
                    tree[table->firstOccur(vertex)].
                                            getNumber() ) {

                    // put new descriptor on the
                    // suspended list
                    newDesc= new Desc(current,row,
                                    col+1,bene,chain);
                    if( suspendHead.getNext() == 0 ) {
                        suspend= newDesc;
                        suspendHead.setNext(suspend);
```

```
            } else {
                suspend->setNext(newDesc);
            }
        }

    // 3) the first instance of an operand
    } else {

        // put vertex at the end of the chain
        // for this descriptor
        newSel= new Select(vertex);
        if( chain == 0 ) {
            chain= newSel;
        } else {
            for( link=chain; link->getNext() != 0;
                    link=link->getNext())
            { }
            link->setNext(newSel);
        }

        // put new descriptor on the suspended list
        newDesc= new Desc(current,row,col+1,
                        bene,chain);
        if( suspendHead.getNext() == 0 ) {
            suspend= newDesc;
            suspendHead.setNext(suspend);
        } else {
            suspend->setNext(newDesc);
        }
    }
    activeHead.setNext(desc->getNext());
    free((char *)desc);
}

activeHead.setNext(accumHead.getNext());
best= 0;
select= new Select(0);
selectHead.setNext(select);
// depth first traversal of descendants
// in expression
if( tree[vertex].getLeft() != 0 ) {
```

```
            match(tree[vertex].getLeft(), expr, table);
            best= tree[tree[vertex].getLeft()].getBenefit();
            newSel= new Select(tree[vertex].getLeft());
            if( selectHead.getNext() == 0 ) {
                select= newSel;
                selectHead.setNext(newSel);
            } else {
                select->setNext(newSel);
            }
        }
        if( tree[vertex].getRight() != 0 ) {
            match(tree[vertex].getRight(), expr, table);
            best= tree[tree[vertex].getRight()].
                                getBenefit();
            newSel= new Select(tree[vertex].getRight());
            if( selectHead.getNext() == 0 ) {
                select= newSel;
                selectHead.setNext(select);
            } else {
                select->setNext(newSel);
            }
        }

        accum= 0;
        accumHead.setNext(accum);
        while( (desc= activeHead.getNext()) != 0 ) {
            row= desc->getRow();
            col= desc->getCol();
            bene= desc->getBenefit();
            current= desc->getVertex();
            chain= desc->getChain();

            // was this descriptor initiated by this vertex?
            if( current == vertex ) {

                // yes, we have matched an idiom
                if( best < table->idiomPayoff(vertex,row) +
                                bene ) {
                    select= new Select(row);
                    selectHead.setNext(select);
                    select->setNext(chain);
```

```
        }
        best= max(best, table->idiomPayoff(vertex,
                                       row)+bene);
    } else {

        // no
        newDesc= new Desc(current,row,col,
                                    bene,chain);
        if( accumHead.getNext() == 0 ) {
            accum= newDesc;
            accumHead.setNext(accum);
        } else {
            accum->setNext(newDesc);
        }
    }

    tree[vertex].setBenefit(best);
    tree[vertex].setSelect(select);

    activeHead.setNext(accumHead.getNext());

    // reactivate suspended descriptors
    while( (desc= suspendHead.getNext()) != 0 ) {

        // update benefit field and move to
        // active list
        desc->setBenefit( desc->getBenefit() +
                                    best);
        if( activeHead.getNext() == 0 ) {
            activeHead.setNext(desc);
        } else {
            active->setNext(desc);
        }
        suspendHead.setNext(desc->getNext());
    }
    activeHead.setNext(desc->getNext());
    free((char *)desc);
  }
}
```

```
/* main.c */

#include <stdio.h>
#include <stdlib.h>

#include "IdiomTable.h"
#include "Select.h"
#include "Desc.h"
#include "Tree.h"
#include "Opcode.h"
#include "Expr.h"

void numberTree(Expr *);
void match(int, Expr *, IdiomTable *);

int main(int argc, char **argv ) {

    Expr * expr= new Expr("test1.txt");
    numberTree(expr);
//    IdiomTable * table= new IdiomTable("table.txt");
//    match(1, expr, table );
}
```

10.2.2 Bug 1

10.2.2.1 The evidence

The first debugging session began by running the application. The test input and idiom database are shown as follows. The input expression in the first listing should match the first idiom in the database.

```
9
6
3
-1 8 6 5 3 2 1
-1 -1 -1 -1 NONE "***"
2 9 0 0 F_cprs ""
3 4 9 0 F_trans ""
```

```
0 0 4 1 C_int "(1 1)"
5 0 0 0 F_lt_scan ""
6 7 0 0 F_and_eq ""
0 0 7 2 V_first_1 "M"
8 0 0 0 F_flip ""
0 0 0 2 V_dup_1 "M"
0 0 0 2 V_dup_1 "M"



8
13
-1 5 4 5 7 6 5 5 6
NONE NONE NONE NONE NONE NONE NONE NONE NONE NONE NONE NONE NONE
NONE F_cprs F_trans C_int F_lt_scan F_and_eq V_first_1 F_flip
     V_dup_1 V_dup_1
NONE F_rot F_plus_red F_and_scan F_eq C_char V_first_1 V_dup_1
NONE F_cprs F_or F_neq V_first_1 C_char F_neq V_dup_1 F_rot
     C_int V_dup_1 V_dup_1
NONE F_get V_first_1 F_upgr F_value F_plus C_int F_shape
     V_first_2 F_trans F_find V_dup_2 V_dup_1
NONE F_plus V_first_1 F_plus_red F_and_scan F_not F_and_eq
     V_first_2 F_trans V_dup_2
NONE F_times V_first_1 F_trans F_form F_rev F_shape V_dup_1
     V_first_2
NONE F_cprs F_eq F_find V_first_1 V_dup_1 F_iota F_shape
     V_dup_1 V_dup_1
NONE F_cprs F_ravel F_splice V_first_1 C_int F_ravel F_splice
     V_dup_1 F_not V_dup_1
```

We inserted some debugging output in the code to be able to observe the progress of the computation. In addition, we inserted code at the end of the numbering phase to see the values in the data structure.

```
A: node 8
A: node 6
A: node 5
A: node 3
A: node 2
A: node 1
```

```
NODE  LINK  NUMBER
   0     0       2
   1     0       0
   2     0       0
   3     0       0
   4     0       0
   5     0       0
   6     0       0
   7     0       0
   8     0       0
   9     0       0
  10     0       0
```

10.2.2.2   **The investigation**

Since we have inserted trace code with labels A through J, and only the output with label A is displayed, most of the function is not being executed. Not surprisingly, the final output of the numbering phase is almost all zeros, since nothing happened.

We begin at the beginning and start by verifying that the input to the application is being read correctly. We insert the following code into the function that is reading the test case to find out if the data is being read correctly. It displays the values as they are extracted from a line of text and converted to integers.

```
fprintf(stderr,"%d %d %d %d %d %s\n",
    _tree[row].getLeft(), _tree[row].getRight(),
    _tree[row].getLink(), _tree[row].getNumber(),
    _tree[row].getOpType(), _tree[row].getOpName() );
```

When we rerun the application, we get the following additional output:

```
EXPR
-1 -1 -1 -1 0  "***"
2 11 0 0 32   ""
3 4 11 0 43   ""
0 0 4 1 51   "1,1"
5 10 0 0 22   ""
6 7 10 0 30   ""
0 0 7 2 53   "M"
```

```
8 9 0 0 42    " "
0 0 9 2 53    "M"
0 0 0 3 0     " "
0 0 0 3 0     " "
0 0 0 2 53    "M"
```

We compare this listing to the original test file and find everything satisfactory. So, we insert similar code at the end of the procedure to display the entire data structure as it will be seen by the numbering function. What we see is the following. Obviously, nothing is being stored into this structure.

```
EXPR
0 0 0 0 0 (null)
0 0 0 0 0 (null)
0 0 0 0 0 (null)
0 0 0 0 0 (null)
0 0 0 0 0 (null)
0 0 0 0 0 (null)
0 0 0 0 0 (null)
0 0 0 0 0 (null)
0 0 0 0 0 (null)
0 0 0 0 0 (null)
```

10.2.2.3   The fault and correction

The data that is being correctly read in and converted is not being stored as it should. We review the loop that performs the conversions and assignments and discover that the variable used to index the array of *Tree* nodes is never incremented. We insert the following statement to correct this oversight:

```
row++;
```

We review all the code that creates and handles this data structure.

We observe that the allocation of the array of *Tree* nodes does not include space for an extra pad element to compensate for the origin-1 indexing of the original algorithm. So, we adjust the allocation statement accordingly:

```
tree= new Tree[_size+1];
```

After we make these changes, we recompile and rerun the application. We are now storing the data correctly.

In this round of debugging, we applied the following methods from Chapter 9:

■ Generate a flow trace.

■ Generate a variable snapshot.

We found two defects that had the following root causes, which are explained in Chapter 11:

■ Missing operation—statement missing

■ Initialization errors—aggregate allocated wrong size

10.2.3   Bug 2

10.2.3.1   The evidence

The next debugging session began by running the application again.

We turn off the debugging output in the *Expr* constructor, since it is now working. We get the following results from the next run:

```
A: node 8
A: node 9
A: node 6
A: node 7
B: left 8, lNum 2
C: tree[7].link= 0
D: bucket1[2].head= 7
E: node 7
F: right 9, rNum 3
G: tree[7].link= -1
H: bucket2[3].head= 7
A: node 5
B: left 6, lNum 2
C: tree[5].link= 0
D: bucket1[2].head= 5
A: node 10
E: node 5
```

```
F: right 7, rNum 0
G: tree[5].link= 1075519240
H: bucket2[0].head= 5
A: node 3
A: node 4
B: left 5, lNum 0
C: tree[4].link= 1075519600
D: bucket1[0].head= 4
A: node 2
B: left 3, lNum 1
C: tree[2].link= 0
D: bucket1[1].head= 2
A: node 11
E: node 2
F: right 4, rNum 0
G: tree[2].link= 5
H: bucket2[0].head= 2
A: node 1
B: left 2, lNum 0
C: tree[1].link= 4
D: bucket1[0].head= 1
```

NODE	LINK	NUMBER
0	-1	-1
1	4	0
2	5	0
3	4	1
4	1075519600	0
5	1075519240	0
6	7	2
7	-1	0
8	9	2
9	0	3
10	0	3

We are pleased to see some progress. The distribution of the letters in the trace shows that we are executing much of the numbering algorithm.

10.2.3.2   **The investigation**

Upon further investigation, we see that an invalid value of -1 is being assigned at the trace point G. All of our indices must be positive integers, so we know something has gone wrong by the time we reach this point.

The value being assigned comes from this expression:

```
bucket2[rNum].head
```

Since it has an invalid value, we search backward from this point in the function to places where the *head* field of a *bucket* is assigned.

We insert the following code after each trace point near a statement that modifies this field:

```
for( k=0; k<depth+1; ++k )
fprintf(stderr,"%d ",bucket2[k].head);
fprintf(stderr,"\n");
```

Adding this code quickly uncovers a problem. Here is the output of running the application. The program terminates when it attempts to use the huge value for the *node* variable that is printed on the last line.

The values that are printed after each trace point are the values in the *bucket2* variable. These are random values, which are the result of not initializing the array.

```
A: node 8
A: node 2
B: left 3, lNum 0
1075519240 -1 0 -1 0 0 0
C: tree[2].link= 1075519600
1075519240 -1 0 -1 0 0 0
D: bucket1[0].head= 2
1075519240 -1 0 -1 0 0 0
A: node 6
A: node 2
B: left 3, lNum 0
1075519240 -1 0 -1 0 0 0
C: tree[2].link= 2
1075519240 -1 0 -1 0 0 0
```

```
D: bucket1[0].head= 2
1075519240 -1 0 -1 0 0 0
A: node 1075519600
```

We insert code to initialize the bucket arrays (see next page), but we still have a problem with this data structure. The buckets are used to sort the nodes in the tree, and there must be as many bucket entries as there are nodes. The bucket values are all displaying as initialized to zero now, but there are not enough of them.

10.2.3.3   The fault and correction

There are two problems. First, the two bucket arrays are allocated to the depth of the expression tree, rather than the size of the tree. Second, those elements that are allocated are never properly initialized. The following code corrects the problem:

```
Bucket * bucket1= new Bucket[size+1];
for( int k=0; k<=depth; ++k ) {
    bucket1[k].head= 0;
    bucket1[k].link= 0;
}
Bucket * bucket2= new Bucket[size+1];
for( k=0; k<=depth; ++k ) {
    bucket2[k].head= 0;
    bucket2[k].link= 0;
}
```

In this round of debugging, we applied the following methods from Chapter 9:

- Generate a flow trace.
- Display data structures.

We found two defects that had the following root causes, which are explained in Chapter 11:

- Initialization error—aggregate allocated wrong size

■ Initialization error—aggregate always uninitialized

10.2.4   Bug 3

10.2.4.1   The evidence

The next debugging session began by running the application again. Since we are making progress, we select a different test case to exercise the code.

```
11
6
3
-1 7 6 5 4 2 1
-1 -1 -1 -1          NONE       "***"
 2    3   0   0      F_times    ""
 0    0   3   1      V_first_1  "M"
 4   11   0   0      F_trans    ""
 5   10  11   0      F_form     ""
 6    9  10   0      F_rev      ""
 7    8   9   0      F_shape    ""
 0    0   8   1      V_dup_1    "M"
 0    0   0   2      NONE       ""
 0    0   0   2      NONE       ""
 0    0   0   3      V_first_2  "V"
 0    0   0   2      NONE       ""
```

When we run the application, we obtain the following results:

```
A: node 7
A: node 6
B: left 7, lNum 8
C: tree[6].link= 0
D: bucket1[8].head= 6
E: node 6
F: right 8, rNum 0
G: tree[6].link= 0
H: bucket2[0].head= 6
A: node 5
B: left 6, lNum 9
C: tree[5].link= 0
D: bucket1[9].head= 5
```

```
E: node 5
F: right 9, rNum 0
G: tree[5].link= 6
H: bucket2[0].head= 5

0 -1 -1
1 0 0
2 0 3
3 1 0
4 0 11
5 6 10
6 0 9
7 0 8
8 0 0
9 0 0
10 0 0
11 0 0
```

The trace of the activities seems rather short. The final dump of the data structure shows that the link field (column 2) has hardly been touched, and the number field (column 3) has been corrupted from the original values in the test case.

10.2.4.2 The investigation

Since values that were read in correctly seem to have been overwritten, we suspect a memory corruption problem. We choose to link in a special library for dynamic memory allocation that may help us find the problem. We use the *mpatrol* system, which is an open-source library and a set of related open-source tools, available on a wide variety of systems. See Chapter 14 for more information about this tool.

We add the following statement to our source files:

```
#include <mpatrol.h>
```

We also change our *Makefile* to link in some extra libraries with this line:

```
allmp: $(OBJ)
      g++ -g $(OBJ) -lmpatrol -lbfd -liberty -o snyder.exe
```

We recompile our application, rerun it, and get the following results:

```
A: node 7
A: node -1
```

This does not provide us with much information, so we rerun the application under the debugger.

```
(gdb) run
Starting program: snyder.exe
A: node 7
A: node -1

Program received signal SIGSEGV, Segmentation fault.
0x0805f616 in getNumber__4Tree (this=0xb2b1a3d0) at Tree.h:19
19     inline int getNumber() { return _number; }
(gdb) bt
#0  0x0805f616 in getNumber__4Tree (this=0xb2b1a3d0) at Tree.h:19
#1  0x0804ac0b in numberTree__FP4Expr (expr=0x806f1b8) at number.c:53
#2  0x0804bcd8 in main (argc=1, argv=0xbffff9ac) at main.c:19
....
(gdb) q
```

We need to find out why the value assigned to the *node* variable is -1, which is invalid. We run the application in the debugger and set a breakpoint just before the trace output that identifies the incorrect value.

```
(gdb) b number.c:42
Breakpoint 1 at 0x804ab84: file number.c, line 42.
(gdb) run
Breakpoint 1, numberTree__FP4Expr (expr=0x806f1b8) at number.c:42
42     node= height[i];
(gdb) p i
$1 = 1
(gdb) p height[i]
$2 = 7
(gdb) cont
A: node 7
Breakpoint 1, numberTree__FP4Expr (expr=0x806f1b8) at number.c:42
42     node= height[i];
(gdb) p i
$3 = 2
(gdb) p height[i]
$4 = -1
(gdb) p height[0]
$5 = -1
```

```
(gdb) p height[1]
$6 = 0
(gdb) p height[2]
$7 = -1
(gdb) p height[3]
$8 = 6
(gdb) p height[4]
$9 = -1
(gdb) p height[5]
$10 = 5
(gdb) p height[6]
$11 = -1
(gdb) p height[7]
$12 = 0
(gdb) q
```

It appears that the values being inserted into the *height* array are being interspersed with incorrect values, or alternatively, that locations are being skipped as the values are being stored.

We look over the code in *Expr.c* and discover that the counter that tracks the location to store values is incremented twice each time a value is extracted from the input line.

We correct this problem (see following) and continue. We rebuild and rerun the application standalone, obtaining the following output:

```
A: node 7
A: node 6
B: left 7, lNum 8
C: tree[6].link= 0
D: bucket1[8].head= 6
E: node 6
F: right 8, rNum 0
G: tree[6].link= 0
H: bucket2[0].head= 6
A: node 5
B: left 6, lNum 9
C: tree[5].link= 0
D: bucket1[9].head= 5
E: node 5
F: right 9, rNum 0
G: tree[5].link= 6
H: bucket2[0].head= 5
```

```
A: node 4
B: left 5, lNum 10
C: tree[4].link= 0
D: bucket1[10].head= 4
E: node 4
F: right 10, rNum 0
G: tree[4].link= 5
H: bucket2[0].head= 4
A: node 2
A: node 1
B: left 2, lNum 3
C: tree[1].link= 0
D: bucket1[3].head= 1
E: node 1
F: right 3, rNum 0
G: tree[1].link= 4
H: bucket2[0].head= 1
0 -1 -1
1 4 0
2 0 3
3 1 0
4 5 11
5 6 10
6 0 9
7 0 8
8 0 0
9 0 0
10 0 0
11 0 0
```

The trace looks more interesting, and there are no more obviously incorrect values.

10.2.4.3 The fault and correction

The problem is corrected simply by removing the following statement from the processing of the *height* array:

```
++tokenCtr;
```

In this round of debugging, we applied the following methods from Chapter 9:

- Display data structures.

- Generate a flow trace.

- Use runtime heap checking.

We found one defect that had the following root causes, explained in Chapter 11:

- Initialization errors—aggregate variable partially uninitialized

- Control-flow problems—statement executed too many times

10.2.5 Bug 4

10.2.5.1 The evidence

The next debugging session began by running the application. We modify the main program so that it now reads in and constructs the *IdiomTable* object. We also insert code to display this data structure after it is constructed.

Here is the initial output:

```
0 0 0 0 0 0 0 0 0 0 0 0 0 -1
0 32 43 51 22 30 53 42 56 56 0 0 0 -1
0 35 26 20 16 52 53 56 0 0 0 0 0 -1
0 32 9 17 53 52 17 56 35 51 56 56 0 -1
0 38 53 44 47 1 51 37 54 43 48 57 56 -1
0 1 53 26 20 50 30 54 43 57 0 0 0 -1
0 3 53 43 36 34 37 56 54 0 0 0 0 -1
0 32 16 48 53 56 39 37 56 56 0 0 0 -1
0 32 40 41 53 51 40 41 56 50 56 0 0 -1
```

10.2.5.2 The investigation

All the numbers look correct except the last columns. We hypothesize that we have made the same mistake we made before, which is to dimension the array for origin-0 indexing. We review the code that allocates the storage for the *Idiom Table* class and find three statements where this is true.

10.2.5.3   The fault and correction

The original algorithm used origin-1 indexing, but C++ naturally uses origin-0 indexing. We had tried to avoid problems in converting the algorithm by padding the arrays with an extra element. We did an incomplete job and did not pad the arrays in the *Idiom Table* object. We make the following changes:

```
_table= new (int *)[_count+1];
...
_table[i]= new int[_size+1];
...
_payoff= new int[_count+1];
```

In this round of debugging, we applied the following method from Chapter 9:

- Display data structures.

We found several defects that all had the following root cause, explained in Chapter 11:

- Initialization errors—aggregate allocated wrong size

10.2.6   Bug 5

10.2.6.1   The evidence

The next debugging session began by reviewing code that we are about to enable. Before turning on the matching algorithm, we decide to read the whole function through, looking for problems. We start with the loop that creates match descriptors that begin with the same operation as the first operation in the expression.

```
for(i= 1; i <= numIdioms; ++i) {
    if( idiomTable[i][1] == tree[vertex].getOpType() ) {
```

```
newDesc= new Desc(vertex,i,1,0,0);
if( accumHead.getNext() == 0 ) {
    accum= newDesc;
    accumHead.setNext(accum);
} else {
    accum->setNext(newDesc);
}
        }
    }
```

10.2.6.2   The investigation

What catches our eye is that we are mostly using doubly linked lists in this
application, and yet this code does not invoke a method to set a back pointer.
In addition, the variable that tracks the leading edge of the list, *accum,* gets
set only once, when the pointer that tracks the head of the list is null.

10.2.6.3   The fault and correction

We recall that we used the same head variable/frontier variable method for
representing several linked lists used by the *match* algorithm: the accumulate list, the active list, the suspend list, and the selection chain. We review
all the code that appends to one of these lists and find seven places that all
have the same problem.

We change five of them from the structure listed next to the one that
follows it. The other two update a list that does not have a back pointer, so
the assignment to the previous field is not used.

```
newObject= new Object(arguments);
if( listHead.getNext() == 0 ) {
    listHead.setNext(frontier);
} else {
    frontier->setNext(newObject);
}

newObject= new Object(arguments);
if( listHead.getNext() == 0 ) {
    listHead.setNext(newObject);
} else {
    frontier->setNext(newObject);
```

```
          newObject->setPrev(frontier);
     }
     frontier= newObject;
```

In this round of debugging, we applied the following method from Chapter 9:

- Read the source code.

We found several defects that had the following root causes, explained in Chapter 11:

- Reference errors—variable not assigned
- Control-flow problems—statement controlled by wrong control-flow condition

10.2.7 Bug 6

10.2.7.1 The evidence

The next debugging session began by running the application under the debugger, with the special memory allocation library linked in. We immediately run into a problem.

```
(gdb) run
Starting program: snyder.exe

Program received signal SIGABRT, Aborted.
0x4010d801 in __kill () from /lib/i686/libc.so.6
(gdb) bt
#0  0x4010d801 in __kill () from /lib/i686/libc.so.6
#1  0x4010d5da in raise (sig=6) at ../sysdeps/posix/raise.c:27
#2  0x4010ed82 in abort () at ../sysdeps/generic/abort.c:88
#3  0x080547fc in __mp_checkinfo () at main.c:22
#4  0x0804c2b6 in __mp_fini () at main.c:22
#5  0x0805f786 in _fini ()
#6  0x4011022b in exit (status=0) at exit.c:54
#7  0x400fc180 in __libc_start_main (main=0x804bae0 <main>, argc=1,
    ubp_av=0xbffff9ac, init=0x80498d8 <_init>, fini=0x805f768
<_fini>, rtld_fini=0x4000e184 <_dl_fini>, stack_end=0xbffff99c)
```

```
    at ../sysdeps/generic/libc-start.c:129
(gdb) q
```

10.2.7.2   The investigation

The application is dying in the memory allocation library. This is almost guaranteed to be some sort of memory corruption problem. Our first step is to change the test driver and turn off some of the processing steps. We will add them back in as we develop more confidence in them.

```
int main(int argc, char **argv ) {
    Expr * expr= new Expr("test1.txt");
//     numberTree(expr);
//     IdiomTable * table= new IdiomTable("table.txt");
//     match(1, expr, table );
}
```

When we comment out everything but the construction of the *Expr* object, the application runs to completion normally. The same is true when we put the call to the *numberTree* function back in. When we put the construction of the *IdiomTable* object back in, we get the original symptom. So, the problem is likely occurring in the function before the place where the symptom manifests itself (e.g., in *numberTree*). We take the call to the constructor for *IdiomTable* back out and turn on the display of the data structure on exit from *numberTree*. This results in the following output:

```
exit numberTree()
0 -1 -1
1 4 0
2 0 3
3 1 0
4 5 11
5 6 10
6 0 9
7 0 8
8 0 0
9 0 0
10 0 0
11 0 0
```

The nonzero values in the original test case in column three (the unique node numbers) should be preserved on exit from this function. They are not being preserved, so we decide to check whether they were available on entry to the function. We add an identical display at the start of the *numberTree* function.

```
enter numberTree()
0 -1 -1
1 0 0
2 0 3
3 1 0
4 0 11
5 0 10
6 0 9
7 0 8
8 0 0
9 0 0
10 0 0
11 0 0
```

It is now clear that the input to this function was not what the original test case contained. So, we need to determine whether the data structure was ever created correctly. We insert code at the end of the constructor for the *Expr* object to display the data coming from the file as it is converted, and later to display the entire tree structure.

```
exit Expr()
0 -1 -1
1 0 0
2 0 3
3 1 0
4 0 11
5 0 10
6 0 9
7 0 8
8 0 0
9 0 0
10 0 0
11 0 0
```

We have located the problem. The data is being read and converted correctly but is not being stored where it belongs.

10.2.7.3   The fault and correction

How could the data be read in and converted correctly, but not stored in the data structure correctly? The answer is that as each line is read in and tokens are identified, those tokens are stored in a temporary array until they can all be converted and stored, and the location of the next place to save a token is kept in a variable *tokenCtr*.

As written, the counter is initialized to zero at the beginning of the outer loop, which processes one line of input per iteration. Unfortunately, it needs to be initialized at the beginning of the inner loop, which recognizes the tokens. The result of the error is that subsequent to the first iteration, tokens were being saved into memory following the temporary array, and the tokens from the first input line were being converted over and over. The problem is corrected simply by moving the following statement inside the loop that processes lines of input:

```
tokenCtr= 0;
```

In this round of debugging, we applied the following methods from Chapter 9:

■ Generate a flow trace.

■ Display data structures.

■ Use runtime heap checking.

We found one defect that had the following root causes, explained in Chapter 11:

■ Dynamic data-structure problems—array subscript out of bounds

■ Control-flow problems—statement controlled by wrong control-flow condition

10.2.8   10.2.8 Bug 7

10.2.8.1   The evidence

The next debugging session began by running the application. We use the same test input and test driver as before. We obtain the following output, and then the program seems to go into an infinite loop:

```
<number
[ 0]  -1  -1  -1  -1
[ 1]   2  11   0   8
[ 2]   3   4   0   7
[ 3]   0   0   4   1
[ 4]   5  10   0   6
[ 5]   6   7   0   5
[ 6]   0   0   7   2
[ 7]   8   9   0   4
[ 8]   0   0   9   2
[ 9]   0   0   0   3
[10]   0   0   0   3
[11]   0   0   0   2


Table
0 0 0 0 0 0 0 0 0 0 0 0 0
0 32 43 51 22 30 54 42 57 57 0 0 0
0 35 26 20 16 53 54 57 0 0 0 0 0
0 32 9 17 54 53 17 57 35 51 57 57 0
0 38 54 44 47 1 51 37 55 43 48 58 57
0 1 54 26 20 50 30 55 43 58 0 0 0
0 3 54 43 36 34 37 57 55 0 0 0 0
0 32 16 48 54 57 39 37 57 57 0 0 0
```

10.2.8.2   The investigation

We turn on the control-flow trace statements in the *match* function and rerun the application in the debugger. Here is a portion of the trace output:

```
(gdb) run
Starting program: /home/metzger/src/idiom/evolve/b07/snyder.exe
....
match: vertex= 1, tree[vertex].getOpType= 32
```

```
A: vertex= 1, row= 1, col= 1, bene= 0, chain= 0
A: vertex= 1, row= 3, col= 1, bene= 0, chain= 0
A: vertex= 1, row= 7, col= 1, bene= 0, chain= 0
A: vertex= 1, row= 8, col= 1, bene= 0, chain= 0
C: tree[1].getLeft()= 2, best= 0

match: vertex= 2, tree[vertex].getOpType= 43
B: curr= 1, row= 1, col= 1, bene= 0, chain= 0
0) idiomTable[1][2]= 43, isOpFunction= 1
1) curr= 1, row= 1, col+1= 2, bene= 0, chain= 0
B: curr= 1, row= 3, col= 1, bene= 0, chain= 0
0) idiomTable[3][2]= 9, isOpFunction= 1
B: curr= 1, row= 7, col= 1, bene= 0, chain= 0
0) idiomTable[7][2]= 16, isOpFunction= 1
B: curr= 1, row= 8, col= 1, bene= 0, chain= 0
0) idiomTable[8][2]= 40, isOpFunction= 1
C: tree[2].getLeft()= 3, best= 0

match: vertex= 3, tree[vertex].getOpType= 51
B: curr= 1, row= 1, col= 2, bene= 0, chain= 0
0) idiomTable[1][3]= 51, isOpFunction= 1
1) curr= 1, row= 1, col+1= 3, bene= 0, chain= 0
G: curr= 1, row= 1, col= 3, bene= 0, chain= 0; vertex= 3
K: tree[3]: benefit= 0, select= 804d370
G: curr= 1, row= 1, col= 3, bene= 0, chain= 0; vertex= 3

.... [infinite loop]

Program received signal SIGINT, Interrupt.
0x0804aa68 in match__FiP4ExprP10IdiomTable (vertex=3, expr=0x804cf78,
     table=0x804d060) at match.c:306
306          while (0 != (desc = suspendHead.getNext ())) {
(gdb) bt
#0  0x0804aa68 in match__FiP4ExprP10IdiomTable (vertex=3,
expr=0x804cf78, table=0x804d060) at match.c:306
#1  0x0804a2f1 in match__FiP4ExprP10IdiomTable (vertex=2,
expr=0x804cf78, table=0x804d060) at match.c:179
#2  0x0804a2f1 in match__FiP4ExprP10IdiomTable (vertex=1,
expr=0x804cf78, table=0x804d060) at match.c:179
#3  0x0804aef6 in main (argc=1, argv=0xbffff9ac) at main.c:22
....
(gdb) q
```

We try executing in the debugger several times. Each time we generate an interrupt from the keyboard, we are somewhere in the loop that contains the two flow trace statements that are repeating infinitely.

We read the source code very carefully, comparing it to the algorithm design in the original paper.

We notice something disturbing. The author uses a pseudocode notation with Pascal-like keywords and indentation. Since he does not enclose every control-flow construct with delimiters, dangling *else* clauses could be subject to more than one interpretation. Nowhere in the paper does he define or reference the definition of the semantics of his notation. We had assumed that syntactic entities with the same level of nesting should be treated as being parallel. The more we read the pseudocode for this loop, the more we are convinced that this assumption is false.

10.2.8.3 The fault and correction

We rewrite the nested *if-then-else* statements in the loop that is running infinitely with the other interpretation of dangling *else* clauses. This changes the conditions under which the computation of the best-selection value was made. It also makes the code that saves the computation of the best-selection value independent of the match between the current node and the root of the matched idiom.

Since the dangling *else* problem occurs more than once in the algorithm design, we also modify conditions under which vertices are appended to the match descriptor.

In this round of debugging, we applied the following methods from Chapter 9:

- Read the source code.
- Generate a flow trace.

We found several defects that had the following root cause, explained in Chapter 11:

- Control-flow problems—statements controlled by wrong control-flow condition

10.2.9   **Bug 8**

10.2.9.1   **The evidence**

The next debugging session began by running the application. We used the same test input and driver. The results are listed as follows.

```
match: vertex= 1, tree[vertex].getOpType= 3
A: vertex= 1, row= 6, col= 1, bene= 0, chain= 0
C: tree[1].getLeft()= 2, best= 0
match: vertex= 2, tree[vertex].getOpType= 54
B: curr= 1, row= 6, col= 1, bene= 0, chain= 0
0) idiomTable[6][2]= 54, isOpFunction= 1
1) curr= 1, row= 6, col+1= 2, bene= 0, chain= 0
G: curr= 1, row= 6, col= 2, bene= 0, chain= 0; vertex= 2
K: tree[2]: benefit= 0, select= 804d3d0
D: vertex= 1, best= 0
D1: 2
E: tree[1].getRight()= 3, best= 0
match: vertex= 3, tree[vertex].getOpType= 43
C: tree[3].getLeft()= 4, best= 0
match: vertex= 4, tree[vertex].getOpType= 36
C: tree[4].getLeft()= 5, best= 0
match: vertex= 5, tree[vertex].getOpType= 34
C: tree[5].getLeft()= 6, best= 0
match: vertex= 6, tree[vertex].getOpType= 37
C: tree[6].getLeft()= 7, best= 0
match: vertex= 7, tree[vertex].getOpType= 57
D: vertex= 6, best= 0
D1: 7
E: tree[6].getRight()= 8, best= 0
match: vertex= 8, tree[vertex].getOpType= 0
F: vertex= 6, best= 0
F1: 8
D: vertex= 5, best= 0
D1: 6
E: tree[5].getRight()= 9, best= 0
match: vertex= 9, tree[vertex].getOpType= 0
F: vertex= 5, best= 0
F1: 9
D: vertex= 4, best= 0
```

```
D1: 5
E: tree[4].getRight()= 10, best= 0
match: vertex= 10, tree[vertex].getOpType= 55
F: vertex= 4, best= 0
F1: 10
D: vertex= 3, best= 0
D1: 4
E: tree[3].getRight()= 11, best= 0
match: vertex= 11, tree[vertex].getOpType= 0
F: vertex= 3, best= 0
F1: 11
F: vertex= 1, best= 0
F1: 3
```

We are not going into an infinite loop anymore. Unfortunately, we do not seem to be going into the loop that had the problem. The trace records with labels "G" and "K" occur only once each, and "H," "I," "J," and "L" do not occur at all.

10.2.9.2   The investigation

We rerun the application under the debugger and set a breakpoint at the entry to the loop. It goes into the loop, so we set additional breakpoints at the *if* statement and the *while* loop that control almost all of the contents of the loop. The *if* statement is never true, and the w*hile* is never executed. The former symptom is the really worrisome one, since this code detects a match and computes the selection of the best match among several.

We decide to investigate the reason that the *while* loop is not being executed. Upon careful investigation of its body, we discover that we did not implement the fix for bug 5 in this loop. This is not keeping the loop from executing, of course, but at least we have fixed the bug without having to search for it. We also notice that this is the only loop that modifies an existing match descriptor, rather than creating a new one. We decide to make it work the same, in the interest of consistency.

Now we need to find out why the loop is not executing the key segments. We note that this loop processes items on the *suspend* list and that there are never any such items. We look at the code that should be putting items on this list. There are no trace records for the code that puts items on the *suspend* list.

10.2.9.3   The fault and correction

We compare the code to the original algorithm. We conclude that we have found yet two more places where we have been bitten by inconsistent indentation and dangling *else* clauses. We restructure the code with the other interpretation of conditional nesting and move on.

In this round of debugging, we applied the following methods from Chapter 9:

- Read the source code.
- Generate a flow trace.

We found two defects that had the following root cause, explained in Chapter 11:

- Control-flow problems—statements controlled by wrong control-flow condition

10.2.10   Bug 9

10.2.10.1 The evidence

The next debugging session began by running the application. We continue with the same test input and test driver. This is the control-flow trace we get from the *match* algorithm:

```
match: vertex= 1, tree[vertex].getOpType= 3
A: vertex= 1, row= 6, col= 1, bene= 0, chain= 0
C: tree[1].getLeft()= 2, best= 0
match: vertex= 2, tree[vertex].getOpType= 54
B: curr= 1, row= 6, col= 1, bene= 0, chain= 0
D: vertex= 1, best= 0
D1: 2
E: tree[1].getRight()= 3, best= 0
match: vertex= 3, tree[vertex].getOpType= 43
C: tree[3].getLeft()= 4, best= 0
match: vertex= 4, tree[vertex].getOpType= 36
C: tree[4].getLeft()= 5, best= 0
```

```
match: vertex= 5, tree[vertex].getOpType= 34
C: tree[5].getLeft()= 6, best= 0
match: vertex= 6, tree[vertex].getOpType= 37
C: tree[6].getLeft()= 7, best= 0
match: vertex= 7, tree[vertex].getOpType= 57
D: vertex= 6, best= 0
D1: 7
E: tree[6].getRight()= 8, best= 0
match: vertex= 8, tree[vertex].getOpType= 0
F: vertex= 6, best= 0
F1: 8
D: vertex= 5, best= 0
D1: 6
E: tree[5].getRight()= 9, best= 0
match: vertex= 9, tree[vertex].getOpType= 0
F: vertex= 5, best= 0
F1: 9
D: vertex= 4, best= 0
D1: 5
E: tree[4].getRight()= 10, best= 0
match: vertex= 10, tree[vertex].getOpType= 55
F: vertex= 4, best= 0
F1: 10
D: vertex= 3, best= 0
D1: 4
E: tree[3].getRight()= 11, best= 0
match: vertex= 11, tree[vertex].getOpType= 0
F: vertex= 3, best= 0
F1: 11
F: vertex= 1, best= 0
F1: 3
```

10.2.10.2 The investigation

We have grown tired of dealing with inconsistent indentation and dangling *else* problems. We decide to strip out all the debugging scaffolding, run the source through the *indent* utility, and compare the control structure to the published algorithm. When we do so, we decide that we now have control structures consistent with our new interpretation of the published notation.

Unfortunately, we are also convinced that the control flow of the published algorithm is wrong. The last part of the algorithm is supposed to move descriptors from the suspended list. This action occurs inside a loop that executes when there are items on the active list. If there is nothing on the active list, this loop will not execute, and no descriptors from the suspended list will be moved to the active list. No more active tasks means no more resumption of suspended tasks, which would become active. It is a catch-22.

10.2.10.3 **The fault and correction**

We move the enclosing brace so that the movement of items on the suspended list always occurs, even when the active list is empty.

Having found yet another error due to our problems interpreting the notation of the original algorithm, we decide to go over the entire listing one more time. We find two more problems.

The original algorithm has a statement in which the selection list is assigned the value "(0)." Everywhere else in this algorithm, items are put inside of parentheses to denote the creation of a list. We originally interpreted this as meaning "create a list with the integer 0 in it." We note that every other value that is appended to this list is a valid node index. Zero is not a valid node index when origin-1 indexing is in use. Putting zero at the head of this list makes no sense, so we decide that either the author made a typographical error—")" and "0" are on the same key—or he used his notation inconsistently. We change the assignment to be a null pointer.

The original paper presents two versions of the algorithm. The earlier one only performs matching. The later one performs matching and selection based on benefit analysis. The nodes that are appended to the suspended list are different in the first and second versions of the algorithm. We started with the first version and now decide to try the second one instead. The first version refers to variables "v" and "u" (our "vertex" and "current"); the second version refers to "u" and "u."

In this round of debugging, we applied the following methods from Chapter 9:

- Read the source code.
- Generate a flow trace.

We found three defects that had the following root causes, which are explained in Chapter 11:

- Control-flow problems—statements controlled by wrong control-flow condition
- Initialization errors—simple variable initialized with wrong value
- Reference errors—wrong variable referenced

10.2.11 Bug 10

10.2.11.1 The evidence

The next debugging session began by running the application. The test output is shown as follows:

```
match: vertex= 1, tree[vertex].getOpType= 3
A: vertex= 1, row= 6, col= 1, bene= 0, chain= 0
C: tree[1].getLeft()= 2, best= 0

match: vertex= 2, tree[vertex].getOpType= 54
B: curr= 1, row= 6, col= 1, bene= 0, chain= 0
4) curr= 1, row= 6, col+1= 2, bene= 0, chain= 804d150
L: current= 1, row= 6, col= 2, bene= 0, chain= 804d150

D: vertex= 1, best= 0
D1: 2
E: tree[1].getRight()= 3, best= 0

match: vertex= 3, tree[vertex].getOpType= 43
B: curr= 1, row= 6, col= 2, bene= 0, chain= 804d150
0) idiomTable[6][3]= 43, isOpFunction= 1
1) curr= 1, row= 6, col+1= 3, bene= 0, chain= 804d150
C: tree[3].getLeft()= 4, best= 0

match: vertex= 4, tree[vertex].getOpType= 36
B: curr= 1, row= 6, col= 3, bene= 0, chain= 804d150
0) idiomTable[6][4]= 36, isOpFunction= 1
1) curr= 1, row= 6, col+1= 4, bene= 0, chain= 804d150
C: tree[4].getLeft()= 5, best= 0
```

```
match: vertex= 5, tree[vertex].getOpType= 34
B: curr= 1, row= 6, col= 4, bene= 0, chain= 804d150
0) idiomTable[6][5]= 34, isOpFunction= 1
1) curr= 1, row= 6, col+1= 5, bene= 0, chain= 804d150
C: tree[5].getLeft()= 6, best= 0

match: vertex= 6, tree[vertex].getOpType= 37
B: curr= 1, row= 6, col= 5, bene= 0, chain= 804d150
0) idiomTable[6][6]= 37, isOpFunction= 1
1) curr= 1, row= 6, col+1= 6, bene= 0, chain= 804d150
C: tree[6].getLeft()= 7, best= 0

match: vertex= 7, tree[vertex].getOpType= 57
B: curr= 1, row= 6, col= 6, bene= 0, chain= 804d150
2) curr= 1, row= 6, col+1= 7, bene= 0, chain= 804d150

D: vertex= 6, best= 0
D1: 7
E: tree[6].getRight()= 8, best= 0

match: vertex= 8, tree[vertex].getOpType= 0

F: vertex= 6, best= 0
F1: 8

D: vertex= 5, best= 0
D1: 6
E: tree[5].getRight()= 9, best= 0

match: vertex= 9, tree[vertex].getOpType= 0

F: vertex= 5, best= 0
F1: 9

D: vertex= 4, best= 0
D1: 5
E: tree[4].getRight()= 10, best= 0

match: vertex= 10, tree[vertex].getOpType= 55

F: vertex= 4, best= 0
```

```
F1: 10

D: vertex= 3, best= 0
D1: 4
E: tree[3].getRight()= 11, best= 0

match: vertex= 11, tree[vertex].getOpType= 0

F: vertex= 3, best= 0
F1: 11

F: vertex= 1, best= 0
F1: 3
```

We are very pleased with this listing. Nodes are being visited in the right order. Auxiliary linked lists are being created. The control-flow trace shows that many of the critical code sections are being executed when processing the nodes.

There are still two obvious problems. First, all the benefit calculations are yielding a result of zero. Second, significant portions of the algorithm are not being executed. In particular, the trace points G, H, I, J, K, and L are not found in the listing.

10.2.11.2 The investigation

We begin by looking at the statement that controls the first section that is not executed. The *if* statement includes a call to the function *firstOccur*. We have not looked at this before.

```
int IdiomTable::firstOccur(int x) {
    return 0;
}
```

10.2.11.3 The fault and correction

This is an obvious omission. We decide that the function belongs in the *Expr* class, rather than the *IdiomTable* class, since it requires access to the elements of that class.

Here we provide an implementation to replace the stub:

```
int Expr::firstOccur(int opcode) {
    opcode -= VARB_COUNT;
    int first= -1;
    for( int i= 0; i <= _size; ++i ) {
        if( opcode == _tree[i].getOpType()) {
            first= i;
            break;
        }
    }
    return first;
}
```

In this round of debugging, we applied the following methods from Chapter 9:

- Generate a flow trace.
- Read the code.

We found one defect that had the following root cause, explained in Chapter 11:

- Missing operation—statements are missing

10.2.11.4 Final test

The debugging process is not complete until the changes have been thoroughly tested. Listed as follows are eight test cases we ran and the output of the program resulting from those cases.

```
9
6
3
-1 8 6 5 3 2 1
-1 -1 -1 -1 NONE "***"
2 9 0 0 F_cprs ""
3 4 9 0 F_trans ""
0 0 4 1 C_int "(1 1)"
5 0 0 0 F_lt_scan ""
```

```
6 7 0 0 F_and_eq ""
0 0 7 2 V_first_1 "M"
8 0 0 0 F_flip ""
0 0 0 2 V_dup_1 "M"
0 0 0 2 V_dup_1 "M"


IDIOM: 1
VARBS: 6 8 9




7
5
3
-1 5 4 3 2 1
-1 -1 -1 -1 NONE ""
2 7 0 0 F_rot ""
3 0 7 0 F_plus_red ""
4 0 0 0 F_and_scan ""
5 6 0 0 F_eq ""
0 0 6 1 C_char " "
0 0 0 2 V_first_1 "V"
0 0 0 2 V_dup_1 "V"


IDIOM: 2
VARBS: 6 7




11
5
4
-1 9 4 3 2 1
-1 -1 -1 -1 NONE "***"
2 11 0 0 F_cprs ""
3 6 11 0 F_or ""
4 5 6 0 F_neq ""
0 0 5 1 V_first_1 "V"
0 0 7 2 C_char " "
```

```
7 8 0 0 F_neq ""
0 0 8 1 V_dup_1 "V"
9 10 0 0 F_rot ""
0 0 10 3 C_int "1"
0 0 0 1 V_dup_1 "V"
0 0 0 1 V_dup_1 "V"


IDIOM: 3
VARBS: 4 7 10 11




12
6
4
-1 8 6 5 4 2 1
-1 -1 -1 -1 NONE "***"
2 3 0 0 F_get ""
0 0 3 1 V_first_1 "M"
4 0 0 0 F_upgr ""
5 9 0 0 F_value ""
6 7 9 0 F_plus ""
0 0 7 2 C_int "1"
8 0 10 0 F_shape ""
0 0 11 3 V_first_2 "K"
10 0 0 0 F_trans ""
11 12 0 0 F_find ""
0 0 12 3 V_dup_2 "K"
0 0 0 1 V_dup_1 "M"

IDIOM: 4
VARBS: 2 8 11 12




9
7
4
-1 9 7 6 5 4 2 1
-1 -1 -1 -1 NONE "***"
```

```
2 3 0 0 F_plus ""
0 0 3 1 V_first_1 "Qio"
4 0 0 0 F_plus_red ""
5 0 0 0 F_and_scan ""
6 0 0 0 F_not ""
7 8 0 0 F_and_eq ""
0 0 8 2 V_first_2 "M"
9 0 0 0 F_trans ""
0 0 0 2 V_dup_2 "M"


IDIOM: 5
VARBS: 2 7 9




8
6
3
-1 7 6 5 4 2 1
-1 -1 -1 -1 NONE "***"
2 3 0 0 F_times ""
0 0 3 1 V_first_1 "M"
4 0 0 0 F_trans ""
5 8 0 0 F_form ""
6 0 8 0 F_rev ""
7 0 0 0 F_shape ""
0 0 0 1 V_dup_1 "M"
0 0 0 3 V_first_2 "V"


IDIOM: 6
VARBS: 2 7 8




9
5
2
-1 8 4 3 2 1
-1 -1 -1 -1 NONE "***"
```

```
2 9 0 0 F_cprs ""
3 6 9 0 F_eq ""
4 5 6 0 F_find ""
0 0 5 1 V_first_1 "V"
0 0 7 1 V_dup_1 "V"
7 0 0 0 F_iota ""
8 0 0 0 F_shape ""
0 0 0 1 V_dup1 "V"
0 0 0 1 V_dup_1 "V"


IDIOM: 7
VARBS: 4 5 8 9



10
5
3
-1 10 4 3 2 1
-1 -1 -1 -1 NONE "***"
2 6 0 0 F_cprs ""
3 0 6 0 F_ravel ""
4 5 7 0 F_splice ""
0 0 5 1 V_first_1 "B"
0 0 8 2 C_int "1"
7 0 0 0 F_ravel ""
8 9 0 0 F_splice ""
0 0 9 1 V_dup_1 "B"
10 0 0 0 F_not ""
0 0 0 1 V_dup_1 "B"


IDIOM: 8
VARBS: 4 8 10
```

10.2.11.5 Final source

The code for the final program is listed as follows. In the interest of brevity, we have omitted the source for the following files since we did not change them during our debugging activities:

- *Bucket.h*
- *Select.h*
- *Opcode.h*
- *Desc.h*
- *Tree.h*
- *IdiomTable.h*
- *Select.c*
- *Opcode.c*
- *Desc.c*

```
/* Expr.h */

#ifndef _Expr_h_
#define _Expr_h_

class Expr {
public:
    // constructors and destructors
    Expr(char *);
    Expr(int, int, Tree *, int *);
    ~Expr();

    // accessors
    inline int getSize() { return _size; }
    inline int getDepth() { return _depth; }
    inline int getUnique() { return _unique; }
    inline Tree * getTree() { return _tree; }
    inline int * getHeight() { return _height; }

    // mutators
    inline void setSize(int x) { _size= x; }
    inline void setDepth(int x) { _depth= x; }
    inline void setUnique(int x) { _unique= x ; }
    inline void setTree(Tree * x) { _tree= x; }
    inline void setHeight(int * x) { _height= x; }

    // workers
```

```
        int firstOccur(int);
        void solution();

    private:
        int _size;
        int _depth;
        int _unique;
        Tree * _tree;
        int * _height;
};

#endif
```

```
/* Tree.c */

#include "Select.h"
#include "Tree.h"
#include "Opcode.h"

Tree::Tree() {
    Tree(0,0,0,0,0,0,0,0);
}

Tree::Tree( int left, int right, int link, int number,
    int opType, char * opName, int benefit,
    Select * select ) {

    _left= left;
    _right= right;
    _link= link;
    _number= number;
    _opType= opType;
    _opName= opName;
    _benefit= benefit;
    _select= select;
}

Tree::~Tree() {
    delete _opName;
```

```
        Select *p, *q;
        for( p= _select; p != 0 ; p= q ) {
            q= p->getNext();
            delete p;
        }
}
```

```
/* Expr.c */

#include <stdio.h>
#include <stdlib.h>
#include <string.h>
#include <ctype.h>

#include "Select.h"
#include "Tree.h"
#include "Expr.h"
#include "Opcode.h"


//----------------------------------------------------

Expr::Expr(char * fileName) {

    int bufSize= 256;
    char buffer[256];
    char *tokens[128];

    FILE * file= fopen(fileName,"r");
    if( file == 0 ) {
        fprintf(stderr,"Unable to open %s\n",fileName);
        fflush(stderr);
        exit(1);
    }

    fscanf(file, "%d\n", &_size);
    fscanf(file, "%d\n", &_depth);
    fscanf(file, "%d\n\n", &_unique);
    _tree= new Tree[_size+1];

    _height= new int[_depth+1];
```

```
            int tokenCtr= 0;
            fgets(buffer, bufSize, file);
            char * token= strtok(buffer, " ");
            _height[tokenCtr++]= atoi(token);
            while( token= strtok(NULL, " \n") ) {
                if( !isdigit(token[0]) ) {
                    continue;
                }
                _height[tokenCtr++]= atoi(token);
            }

            int row= 0;
            while ( 0 != fgets(buffer, bufSize, file) ) {
                tokenCtr= 0;
                buffer[strlen(buffer)-1]= '\0';
                token= strtok(buffer, " ");
                tokens[tokenCtr++]= token;
                int k=0;
                while( token= strtok(NULL, " \n") ) {
                    tokens[tokenCtr++]= token;
                }
                _tree[row].setLeft(atoi(tokens[0]));
                _tree[row].setRight(atoi(tokens[1]));
                _tree[row].setLink(atoi(tokens[2]));
                _tree[row].setNumber(atoi(tokens[3]));
                _tree[row].setOpType(lookupTag(tokens[4]));
                _tree[row].setOpName(tokens[4]);
                _tree[row].setBenefit(0);
                _tree[row].setSelect(0);
#ifdef DEBUG
fprintf(stderr,"%d %d %d %d %d %s\n",
        _tree[row].getLeft(), _tree[row].getRight(),
        _tree[row].getLink(), _tree[row].getNumber(),
        _tree[row].getOpType(), _tree[row].getOpName() );
#endif
                row++;
            }

            fclose(file);
        }
```

```
//-------------------------------------------------------

Expr::Expr(int depth, int unique, Tree * tree, int * height) {
    _depth= depth;
    _unique= unique;
    _tree= tree;
    _height= height;
}

//-------------------------------------------------------

Expr::~Expr() {
     delete _height;
     delete _tree;
}

//-------------------------------------------------------

int Expr::firstOccur(int opcode) {

    opcode -= VARB_COUNT;
    int first= -1;
    for( int i= 0; i <= _size; ++i ) {
        if( opcode == _tree[i].getOpType() ) {
            first= i;
            break;
        }
    }
    return first;
}
```

```
/* IdiomTable.c */

#include <stdio.h>
#include <string.h>
#include <stdlib.h>

#include "IdiomTable.h"
#include "Opcode.h"
```

```
//--------------------------------------------------------

IdiomTable::IdiomTable(char *fileName) {

    int bufSize= 256;
    char buffer[256];
    char * tokens[128];

    FILE * file= fopen(fileName,"r");
    if ( file == 0 ) {
        fprintf(stderr,"Unable to open %s\n",fileName);
        fflush(stderr);
        exit(1);
    }

    fscanf(file, "%d\n", &_count);
    fscanf(file, "%d\n", &_size);

    _table= new (int *)[_count+1];
    for ( int i=0; i <= _count; ++i ) {
        _table[i]= new int[_size+1];
    }

    _payoff= new int[_count+1];
    int tokenCtr= 0;
    fgets(buffer, bufSize, file);
    char * token= strtok(buffer, " ");
    _payoff[tokenCtr++]= atoi(token);
    while( token= strtok(NULL, " \n") ) {
        _payoff[tokenCtr++]= atoi(token);
    }

    int j= 0;
    while ( 0 != fgets(buffer, bufSize, file) ) {
        token= strtok(buffer, " ");
        tokens[tokenCtr++]= token;
        int k=0;
        _table[j][k++]= lookupTag(token);
        while( token= strtok(NULL, " \n") ) {
            tokens[tokenCtr++]= token;
            _table[j][k++]= lookupTag(token);
```

```
            }
            ++j;
        }


#ifdef DEBUG
        fprintf(stderr,"Table\n");
        for( int i= 0; i < _count; ++i ) {
            for( int j= 0; j < _size; ++j ) {
                fprintf(stderr,"%d ",_table[i][j]);
            }
            fprintf(stderr,"\n");
        }
#endif
        fclose(file);
}


//------------------------------------------------------


IdiomTable::~IdiomTable() {
    delete _payoff;
    for ( int i=0; i <= _count; ++i ) {
        delete _table[i];
    }
    delete _table;
}


//------------------------------------------------------


int IdiomTable::idiomPayoff(int x, int y) {
    return _payoff[y];
}


int IdiomTable::isOpRepeated(int x){
    return x >= DUP_FIRST && x <= DUP_LAST;
}


int IdiomTable::isOpFunction(int x){
    if( x >= F_FIRST && x <= F_LAST) {
        return 1;
    } else {
        return 0;
```

```
        }
}
```

```
/* number.c */

#include <stdio.h>

#include "Select.h"
#include "Tree.h"
#include "Bucket.h"
#include "Expr.h"


//------------------------------------------------------

void numberTree( Expr * expr ) {

    Tree *tree= expr->getTree();
    int depth= expr->getDepth();
    int size= expr->getSize();
    int * height= expr->getHeight();
    int unique= expr->getUnique();

#ifdef DEBUG_IN
    fprintf(stderr,">number\n");
    for( int i= 0; i<= expr->getSize(); ++i )
        fprintf(stderr,"[%2d] %2d %2d %2d %2d\n",
                       i, tree[i].getLeft(),
                       tree[i].getRight(),
                       tree[i].getLink(),tree[i].
                       getNumber());
    fprintf(stderr,"\n");
#endif

    int k, b1, b2, left, right, node, lNum, rNum;
    int b1Chain= 0;
    int b2Chain= 0;

    Bucket * bucket1= new Bucket[size+1];
    for( int k=0; k<=size; ++k ) {
        bucket1[k].head= 0;
```

```
                    bucket1[k].link= 0;
        }
        Bucket * bucket2= new Bucket[size+1];

        for( k=0; k<=size; ++k ) {
            bucket2[k].head= 0;
            bucket2[k].link= 0;
        }

        // for all levels of the tree
        for( int i= 1; i <= depth; ++i ) {

#ifdef DEBUG_TRACE
fprintf(stderr,
        "A: height[%d]= %d\n", i, height[i]);
#endif
            // Bucket sort on left descendant
            while( height[i] != 0 ) {

                // for all nodes in one level
                node= height[i];
#if 0
fprintf(stderr,
        "A: node %d\n", node);
#endif

                // save ID of next node to process
                height[i]= tree[node].getLink();

                // if we have a left descendant get
                // its leaf number
                left= tree[node].getLeft();
#ifdef DEBUG_TRACE
fprintf(stderr,
        "A2: tree[%d].getLeft = %d\n", node, left);
#endif
                if( left != 0 ) {
                    lNum= tree[left].getNumber(); // *
#ifdef DEBUG_TRACE
fprintf(stderr,
        "B: left %d, lNum %d\n", left, lNum);
```

```
#endif

                    // if there aren't any nodes in
                    // the chain of buckets yet
                    // then initialize the chain
                    if( bucket1[lNum].head == 0 ) {
                        bucket1[lNum].link= b1Chain;
                        b1Chain= lNum;
                    }

                    // Put node in bucket for nodes having
                    // this left son
                    tree[node].setLink(bucket1[lNum].head);
#ifdef DEBUG_TRACE
fprintf(stderr,
        "C: tree[%d].link= %d\n",
        node, bucket1[lNum].head);
#endif
                    bucket1[lNum].head= node;
#ifdef DEBUG_TRACE
fprintf(stderr,
        "D: bucket1[%d].head= %d\n", lNum, node);
#endif
                }
            }

        // Bucket sort on right descendant
        while( b1Chain != 0 ) {
            b1= b1Chain;
            b1Chain= bucket1[b1].link;
            while( bucket1[b1].head != 0 ) {
                node= bucket1[b1].head;
#ifdef DEBUG_TRACE
fprintf(stderr,
        "E: node %d\n", node);
#endif

                // save ID of next node to process
                bucket1[b1].head= tree[node].getLink();

                // if we have a right descendant get
```

```
                          // its leaf number
                     right= tree[node].getRight();
                         if( right != 0 ) {
                             rNum= tree[right].getNumber();
#ifdef DEBUG_TRACE
fprintf(stderr,
        "F: right %d, rNum %d\n", right, rNum);
#endif

                             // if there aren't any nodes in
                             // the chain of buckets yet then
                             // initialize the chain
                             if( bucket2[rNum].head == 0 ) {
                                 bucket2[rNum].link= b2Chain;
                                 b2Chain= rNum;
                             }

                             // Put node in bucket for nodes
                             // having this right son
                             tree[node].setLink(bucket2[rNum].head);
#ifdef DEBUG_TRACE
fprintf(stderr,
         "G: tree[%d].link= %d\n",
         node, bucket2[rNum].head);
#endif
                             bucket2[rNum].head= node;
#ifdef DEBUG_TRACE
fprintf(stderr,
        "H: bucket2[%d].head= %d\n", rNum, node);
#endif
                         }
                     }
                 }

            // Assign unique numbers for each
            // non-empty bucket
            while( b2Chain != 0 ) {
                b2= b2Chain;
                b2Chain= bucket2[b2].link;
                unique += 1;
                while( bucket2[b2].head != 0 ) {
```

```
                node= bucket2[b2].head;
                tree[node].setNumber(unique);
#ifdef DEBUG_TRACE
fprintf(stderr,
        "I: tree[%d].number= %d\n",node,unique);
#endif
                bucket2[b2].head= tree[node].getLink();
#ifdef DEBUG_TRACE
fprintf(stderr,
        "J: bucket2[%d].head= %d\n",
        b2,tree[node].getLink());
#endif
            }
        }
    }

#ifdef DEBUG_OUT
    fprintf(stderr,"<number\n");
    for( int i= 0; i<= expr->getSize(); ++i )
        fprintf(stderr,
                "[%2d] %2d %2d %2d %2d\n",
                i, tree[i].getLeft(),
                tree[i].getRight(),
                tree[i].getLink(),
                tree[i].getNumber());
    fprintf(stderr,"\n");
#endif
}
```

```
/* match.c */

#include <stdio.h>
#include <stdlib.h>

#define max(a,b)  (((a)>(b))?(a):(b))

#define DEBUG_OUT 1

#include "Select.h"
#include "Desc.h"
```

```
#include "Tree.h"
#include "IdiomTable.h"
#include "Expr.h"

Desc activeHead;
Desc *active= 0;
Desc accumHead;
Desc *accum= 0;


//-------------------------------------------------------

void match(int vertex, Expr *expr, IdiomTable *table) {

    Tree * tree= expr->getTree();
    int ** idiomTable= table->getTable();
    int numIdioms= table->getCount();

#ifdef DEBUG_IN
fprintf(stderr,
    "\nmatch: vertex= %d, tree[vertex].getOpType= %d\n",
        vertex, tree[vertex].getOpType() );
#endif

    int row, col, current, bene, best;
    Desc *newDesc, *desc;
    Select *newSel, *chain;

// descriptors of matches in progress that have
// reached a leaf

    Desc suspendHead;
    suspendHead.setNext(0);
    Desc *suspend= 0;

// create match descriptors for all idioms that begin
// with the same op as the first op in the expression

    accumHead.setNext(0);
    for(int i= 1; i <= numIdioms; ++i) {
        if( idiomTable[i][1] == tree[vertex].getOpType() ) {
```

```
#ifdef DEBUG_TRACE
fprintf(stderr,
"A: vertex= %d, row= %d, col= %d,bene= %d, chain= %x\n",
        vertex,i,1,0,0);
#endif

            newDesc= new Desc(vertex,i,1,0,0);
            if( accumHead.getNext() == 0 ) {
                accumHead.setNext(newDesc);
            } else {
                accum->setNext(newDesc);
                newDesc->setPrev(accum);
            }
            accum= newDesc;
        }
    }


// update matches in progress

    while( 0 != (desc= activeHead.getNext() )) {
        activeHead.setNext(desc->getNext());

        current= desc->getVertex();
        row= desc->getRow();
        col= desc->getCol();
        bene= desc->getBenefit();
        chain= desc->getChain();
        delete desc;

#ifdef DEBUG_TRACE
fprintf(stderr,
"B: curr= %d, row= %d, col= %d, bene= %d, chain= %x\n",
        current,row,col,bene,chain);
#endif

        int opcode= idiomTable[row][col+1];

        if( table->isOpFunction(opcode) ) {

#ifdef DEBUG_TRACE
fprintf(stderr,
```

```
                   "0) idiomTable[%d][%d]= %d, isOpFunction= %d\n",
                          row, col+1, opcode,
                          table->isOpFunction(opcode));
          #endif

          // 1) a function or constant matching the vertex

                       if( opcode == tree[vertex].getOpType() ) {

          #ifdef DEBUG_TRACE
          fprintf(stderr,
          "1)curr= %d, row= %d, col+1= %d, bene= %d, chain= %x\n",
                   current,row,col+1,bene,chain);
          #endif

          // put new descriptor on accumulated list

                          newDesc= new Desc(current,row,col+1,
                                            bene,chain);
                          if( accumHead.getNext() == 0 ) {
                             accumHead.setNext(newDesc);
                          } else {
                             accum->setNext(newDesc);
                             newDesc->setPrev(accum);
                          }
                          accum= newDesc;
                      }

          // 2) a repeated operand matching the vertex

                   } else if ( table->isOpRepeated(opcode) ) {

          #ifdef DEBUG_TRACE
          fprintf(stderr,
          "2)curr= %d, row= %d, col+1= %d, bene= %d, chain= %x\n",
                   current,row,col+1,bene,chain);
          #endif

                       if( tree[vertex].getNumber() ==
                           tree[expr->firstOccur(opcode)].
                                   getNumber() ) {
```

```
// put new descriptor on the suspended list

                newDesc= new Desc(current,row,col+1,
                                   bene,chain);
                if( suspendHead.getNext() == 0 ) {
                    suspendHead.setNext(newDesc);
                } else {
                    suspend->setNext(newDesc);
                    newDesc->setPrev(suspend);
                }
                suspend= newDesc;

#ifdef DEBUG_TRACE
fprintf(stderr,
"3)curr= %d, row= %d, col+1= %d, bene= %d, chain= %x\n",
        current,row,col+1,bene,chain);
#endif
            }
        } else {

// put vertex at the end of the chain for
// this descriptor

                newSel= new Select(vertex);
                if( chain == 0 ) {
                    chain= newSel;
                } else {
                    Select * link;
                    for( link=chain; link->getNext() != 0;
                        link=link->getNext())
                    { }
                    link->setNext(newSel);
                }

// put new descriptor on the suspended list

                newDesc= new Desc(current,row,col+1,
                                  bene,chain);
                if( suspendHead.getNext() == 0 ) {
                    suspendHead.setNext(newDesc);
                } else {
```

```
                            suspend->setNext(newDesc);
                            newDesc->setPrev(suspend);
                    }
                    suspend= newDesc;

#ifdef DEBUG_TRACE
fprintf(stderr,
"4)curr= %d, row= %d, col+1= %d, bene= %d, chain= %x\n",
        current,row,col+1,bene,chain);
#endif


            }
        }
        activeHead.setNext(accumHead.getNext());

        best= 0;
        Select * select= 0;
        Select selectHead;
        selectHead.setNext(select);

// depth first traversal of descendants in expression

        int left= tree[vertex].getLeft();
        if( left != 0 ) {

#ifdef DEBUG_TRACE
fprintf(stderr,
        "C: tree[%d].getLeft()= %d, best= %d\n",
        vertex, left, best);
#endif

            match(left, expr, table);
            best= tree[left].getBenefit();

#ifdef DEBUG_TRACE
fprintf(stderr,
        "\nD: vertex= %d, best= %d\n",
        vertex,best);
#endif
            newSel= new Select(left);
            if( selectHead.getNext() == 0 ) {
```

```
                     selectHead.setNext(newSel);
              } else {
                     select->setNext(newSel);
              }
              select= newSel;
#ifdef DEBUG_TRACE
fprintf(stderr,"D1: ");
for( Select *p= select; p != 0; p= p->getNext() ) {
fprintf(stderr,"%d ",p->getVertex()); }
fprintf(stderr,"\n");
#endif
       }


       int right= tree[vertex].getRight();
       if( right != 0 ) {

#ifdef DEBUG_TRACE
fprintf(stderr,
       "E: tree[%d].getRight()= %d, best= %d\n",
       vertex, right, best);
#endif

              match(right, expr, table);
              best += tree[right].getBenefit();

#ifdef DEBUG_TRACE
fprintf(stderr,
       "\nF: vertex= %d, best= %d\n",
       vertex,best);
#endif
              newSel= new Select(right);
              if( selectHead.getNext() == 0 ) {
                  selectHead.setNext(newSel);
              } else {
                  select->setNext(newSel);
              }
              select= newSel;
#ifdef DEBUG_TRACE
fprintf(stderr,"F1: ");
for( Select *p= select; p != 0; p= p->getNext() ) {
fprintf(stderr,"%d ",p->getVertex()); }
```

```
fprintf(stderr,"\n");
#endif
    }

    accum= 0;
    accumHead.setNext(accum);

    while( 0 != ( desc= activeHead.getNext()) )  {
        activeHead.setNext(desc->getNext());

        current= desc->getVertex();
        row= desc->getRow();
        col= desc->getCol();
        bene= desc->getBenefit();
        chain= desc->getChain();
        delete desc;

#ifdef DEBUG_TRACE
fprintf(stderr,
"G: curr= %d, row= %d, col= %d, bene= %d, \
        chain= %x; vertex= %d\n",
        current,row,col,bene,chain,vertex);
#endif

// was this descriptor initiated by this vertex?

        if( current == vertex ) {

#ifdef DEBUG_TRACE
fprintf(stderr,
        "H: MATCH idiom= %d, vertex= %d\n",
        row,vertex);
#endif

            if( best < table->idiomPayoff(vertex,row) + bene ) {

#ifdef DEBUG_TRACE
fprintf(stderr,
    "I: best= %d, idiomPayoff(%d,%d) = %d, bene= %d\n",
    best, vertex, row,
    table->idiomPayoff(vertex,row), bene);
```

```
#endif

                  select= new Select(row);
                  selectHead.setNext(select);
                  select->setNext(chain);
                  best= max(best, table->idiomPayoff(
                            vertex,row)+bene);
          }

#ifdef DEBUG_TRACE
fprintf(stderr,
"J: curr= %d, row= %d, col= %d, bene= %d, chain= %x\n",
        current,row,col,bene,chain);
#endif
        } else {

              newDesc= new Desc(current,row,col,
                                bene,chain);
              if( accumHead.getNext() == 0 ) {
                  accumHead.setNext(newDesc);
              } else {
                  accum->setNext(newDesc);
                  newDesc->setPrev(accum);
              }
              accum= newDesc;
        }
        tree[vertex].setBenefit(best);
        tree[vertex].setSelect(select);
#ifdef DEBUG_TRACE
fprintf(stderr,
        "K: tree[%d]: benefit= %d, select= %x\n",
        vertex,best,select);
#endif
#ifdef DEBUG_OUT
if( select != 0 && select->getNext() != 0 ) {
fprintf(stderr, "IDIOM: %d\n",select->getVertex());
fprintf(stderr, "VARBS: ");
for( select= select->getNext(); select != 0;
     select= select->getNext()) {
    fprintf(stderr,"%d ",select->getVertex()); }
fprintf(stderr,"\n");
```

```
        }
#endif
        }

    activeHead.setNext(accumHead.getNext());
    active= accum;

// reactivate suspended descriptors

    while( 0 != (desc= suspendHead.getNext()) ) {
        suspendHead.setNext(desc->getNext());

        current= desc->getVertex();
        row= desc->getRow();
        col= desc->getCol();
        bene= desc->getBenefit();
        chain= desc->getChain();
        delete desc;

#ifdef DEBUG_TRACE
fprintf(stderr,
"L:current= %d, row= %d, col= %d, bene= %d, chain=%x\n",
        current,row,col,bene,chain);
#endif

// update benefit field and move to active list

        newDesc= new Desc(current,row,col,
                          bene+best,chain);
        if( activeHead.getNext() == 0 ) {
            activeHead.setNext(newDesc);
        } else {
            active->setNext(newDesc);
            desc->setPrev(active);
        }
        active= newDesc;
    }
}
```

```
/* main.c */

#include <stdio.h>
#include <stdlib.h>

#include "IdiomTable.h"
#include "Select.h"
#include "Desc.h"
#include "Tree.h"
#include "Opcode.h"
#include "Expr.h"

void numberTree(Expr *);
void match(int, Expr *, IdiomTable *);

int main(int argc, char **argv ) {

    Expr * expr= new Expr(argv[1]);
    numberTree(expr);
    IdiomTable * table= new IdiomTable("table.txt");
    match(1, expr, table );
}
```

The Way of the Safety Expert

Cause and effect are two sides of one fact.

—Ralph Waldo Emerson

11.1 Preview

This chapter views finding defects from the perspective of the safety expert. The first section explains the worldview of the safety expert.

The second section of this chapter explains the concept of root-cause analysis. It asserts that the root cause of a defect is the earliest cause that describes the problem in terms of the program's definition, not in terms of the programmer's behavior.

The third section of this chapter explains an approach to collecting root-cause analysis information. This information is separated into four parts. General information is collected for every defect, as is a categorization of the defect symptom. The root cause of a defect is either a design error or a coding error in this approach. An exhaustive list of root causes is provided for both of these categories.

The fourth section of this chapter describes the process of causal-factor charting.

The fifth section of this chapter describes the method of fault-tree analysis.

11.2 Worldview of the safety expert

In this chapter, we make an analogy between accidents or critical events, which are the concern of the quality or safety manager, and software defects. The defect is considered a critical event, and the programmer is the safety analyst. The safety expert seeks to prevent future problems by analyzing the causes of significant events, such as accidents, near misses, and potential problems.

11.3   Root-cause analysis

There is a variety of bug-tracking systems available today, both commercial and open-source. Bug-tracking systems are necessary for any organization that maintains medium- to large-scale systems. While they're useful, however, bug-tracking systems merely record the process through which a defect report goes.

The really valuable information generated by this process is only gleaned at the end of that process and often isn't recorded. The most valuable information to be gained from diagnosing a bug is why the problem occurred.

The process of determining the earliest point in the design and implementation of a program that a defect was introduced is called **root-cause analysis.**

Doing root-cause analysis is important for several reasons. First, it keeps you from fixing symptoms. Second, it enables you to improve the quality-evaluation methods for the phase of the development cycle in which the defect was introduced. Finally, it makes it easier to find similar bugs sooner in the future.

Programmers are sometimes unwilling to record this information because they fear that authority figures may abuse it. In some situations, this fear may be justified.

Managers looking for programmers to downsize may decide to choose staff based on false conclusions derived from root-cause-analysis data. For example, they might choose to terminate those programmers who have the most root-cause records logged against software they worked on. Or, they might withhold raises from those programmers who submit the most root-cause records.

These are both foolish choices, since these phenomena may be explained by reasons other than programmer incompetence. In the first case, uneven test coverage can cause one part of a system to look more defective than others, even though the opposite might actually be the truth. In the second case, the programmer who submits the most records may in fact be the most diligent tester in his group.

As a result of the potential for these abuses, organizations that attempt to collect root-cause-analysis data sometimes promise *not* to keep individual records, but statistical summaries of the information. After a programmer enters root-cause information, it's immediately aggregated with totals, counts, averages, and so forth. Management can see trends, but can't evaluate the work of individuals.

As you develop a database of root-cause-analysis records, you will be able to focus a debugging search on the errors you make most frequently. Another value of this database is being able to recall problems you have fixed that were similar to the problem you're currently working on. This will enable you to diagnose more quickly and thereby fix more defects over a fixed period of time. See Chapter 8 for further discussion on similar problems.

Statistical summaries of your root-cause analyses can also be useful. They can tell you where you need to brush up your skills or employ additional "defensive programming" tactics to avoid the problem in the future.

If the people who supervise you aren't asking for this information, you can keep it anyway and become more productive than your peers. As a student, you should get better grades by completing your assignments with less effort and with greater quality. As an employee, if your employer rewards you based on performance, you should earn more by getting your software to market earlier than the competition and with fewer customer complaints.

11.4 Software-defect root causes

This section documents an approach to categorizing software-defect root causes. It is a synthesis of the best of several approaches used in different software-development organizations.

11.4.1 General information

If you're going to keep records on the root causes of individual defects, you need to keep some general information for identification purposes.

The first kind of general information that it's valuable to track is who reported the defect. Keeping individual names isn't necessary. Just track them by the following categories:

- Original developer
- Project colleague

- Internal partner
- External customer

How can you use this information? Consider the situation where you have many memory-allocation problems. If they aren't being caught until they reach external customers, the cost to assist the customer and the potential for lost business is considerable. A wise manager could easily make the case for investing a significant sum for licensing a tool that finds such problems automatically.

The second kind of general information that is valuable to track is the method or tool that was used to identify the defect. Here is a list of categories of methods and tools to track:

- User report
- Code review
- Unit testing
- System testing
- Periodic testing
- Release testing
- Static analysis tools
- Dynamic analysis tools

How can you use this information? Consider the situation where you're detecting most of your defects by periodically rotating testing through parts of a very large test suite. This may consume most or all of your machine resources at night or on the weekends. If it's effective, but the rotation has a long period, defects remain in the product until the rotation completes. A wise manager could easily make the case for investing in additional hardware resources to reduce the period of the rotation.

The third kind of general information that is valuable to track is the scope of the defect. The particular names used for these levels depend on the programming language you're using. You can categorize the scope of a defect using these categories for a large number of popular languages:

- Methods/functions/procedures
- Classes/modules/files
- Packages/components/relocatables
- Archives/libraries/executables

How can you use this information? Consider the situation where you're asked to assess the risk of a change to fix a given defect. The wider the scope, the more risk there is in accidentally breaking something else while making a correction.

The fourth kind of general information that is valuable to track is how long it took to diagnose and correct the defect. You can categorize these times into the following orders of magnitude:

- One hour or less
- Several hours
- One day
- Several days
- One week
- Several weeks

How can you use this information? Consider the situation where you're assigned a very high-priority defect submitted by a customer. Your supervisor wants to know when you will have it fixed. If you have a reasonably large database of analyses, you should be able to give him or her the average time, with two standard deviations added for safety, for the defect based on the symptom. Once you have diagnosed the root cause, you can update your estimate for the time remaining with a high degree of precision.

11.4.2   Symptom description

The first kind of symptom description that is valuable to track is the character of runtime problems. Most defects show up when the application is executed. Here is a list of categories of symptoms that show up at run time:

- The application generates all correct values but in incorrect order.

- The application generates only some correct values.

- The application generates some incorrect values.

- The application generates all correct values but with cosmetic display problems.

- The application accepts bad input.

- The application rejects good input.

- The application runs indefinitely.

- The application terminates prematurely.

These symptom categories are valuable in estimating the time it's likely to take to diagnose and correct a defect. Problems with display cosmetics and input validation tend to be highly localized and more easily fixed. Problems where an application silently generates wrong results, or never terminates, or terminates prematurely, tend to be much more difficult to track down.

The second kind of symptom description that is valuable to track is the character of link-time problems. Some defects show up when an application is linked. These defects are more likely to be in other people's software, particularly libraries and middleware. If these problems aren't with other people's software, they're often a result of a faulty build process. Here is a list of categories of symptoms that show up at link time:

- Procedure calls across components don't match procedure interfaces.

- System calls don't match system call interfaces.

- Generated code was targeted at incompatible hardware architectures.

- A symbol doesn't have a definition.

- A symbol has more than one definition.

The third kind of symptom description that is valuable to track is the character of compile-time problems. Some defects show up when an application is compiled. These defects are more likely to be in other people's software, particularly compilers and programming tools. Here is a list of categories of symptoms that show up at compile time:

- The compiler accepts this invalid program.

- The compiler rejects this valid program.

- The compiler runs indefinitely.

- The compiler terminates prematurely.

- The compiler generates bad information for downstream tools.

11.4.3 Design errors

Now we get into the actual root-cause descriptions. We divide these into two major categories: design and coding errors. The first section describes errors that occur during the design phase.

We don't consider problem reports that originated in erroneous requirement specifications. Our view of software defects is that a defect occurs when there is a difference between what the user or customer or his representative asked for and what the software actually does. The requirements are what was asked for; by definition, there can be no difference between requirements and themselves. If user requirements don't match what is communicated to the people developing the software, the methods described in this book won't help with diagnosing the resulting problems.

11.4.3.1 Data structures

The first category of design defects includes those caused by a deficient data-structure design. Here is a list of possible data-structure design defects:

- A data definition is missing.

- A data definition is incorrect.

- A data definition is unclear.

- A data definition is contradictory.

- A data definition is out of order.

- A shared-data access control is missing.

- A shared-data access control is incorrect.

- A shared-data access control is out of order.

In problems with data definitions, these categories refer both to individual data elements and to complex data aggregates. The following are examples of data-structure errors.

A data definition is missing when it's referred to in an algorithm but isn't defined. A data definition is incorrect when it must have a different data type, domain, or structure than the one specified for references to this entity in an algorithm to be meaningful. A data definition is unclear when it can be implemented in more than one way and at least one of the ways will cause an algorithm to work incorrectly. A data definition is contradictory when it's contained in more than one other data structure in inconsistent ways. Data definition items are out of order when two or more algorithms depend on different orderings of the items.

In problems with shared-data access, these categories refer to synchronization required by multithreading, multiprocessing, or specialized parallel execution. A shared-data access control is missing when two independent streams of instructions can update a single data item, and there is no access control on the item. A shared-data access control is incorrect when two independent streams of instructions can update a single data item, and the access control can cause deadlock. A shared-data access control is out of order when two independent streams of instructions can update a single data item, and the access control allows updates to occur in invalid order.

11.4.3.2   Algorithms

The second category of design defects includes those caused by a deficient algorithm design. Here is a list of possible algorithm design defects:

- A logic sequence is missing.
- A logic sequence is superfluous.
- A logic sequence is incorrect.
- A logic sequence is out of order.
- An input check is missing.
- An input check is superfluous.
- An input check is incorrect.
- An input check is out of order.
- An output definition is missing.
- An output definition is superfluous.
- An output definition is incorrect.
- An output definition is out of order.

- A special-condition handler is missing.

- A special-condition handler is superfluous.

- A special-condition handler is incorrect.

- A special-condition handler is out of order.

The following are examples of algorithm errors. A logic sequence is missing if a possible case in an algorithm isn't handled. A logic sequence is superfluous if it's logically impossible for a case in an algorithm to be executed. A logic sequence is incorrect if it doesn't compute values as described in the requirements specification. A logic sequence is out of order if it attempts to process information before that information is ready.

An input check is missing if invalid data can be received from a user or a device and it isn't rejected by the algorithm. An input check is superfluous if it's logically impossible for input data to fail the test. An input check is incorrect if it detects some, but not all, invalid data. An input check is out of order if invalid data can be processed by an algorithm, prior to being checked for validity.

An output definition is missing if information specified in the requirements document isn't displayed. An output definition is superfluous if it's logically impossible for the output to ever be generated. An output definition is incorrect if values displayed to the user aren't in the correct format. An output definition is out of order if information specified in the requirements document isn't displayed in a sequence that is useful to the user.

A special-condition handler is missing if it's possible for an exception to be generated and there is no handler, implicit or explicit, to receive it. A special-condition handler is superfluous if it's logically impossible for an exception to be generated that would activate the handler. A special-condition handler is incorrect if it doesn't resolve the cause of an exception and continues processing. A special-condition handler is out of order if a handler for a more general exception is executed before a handler for a more specific exception.

11.4.3.3   User-interface specification

Here is a list of possible user-interface specification defects:

- An assumption about the user is invalid.

- A specification item is missing.

- A specification item is superfluous.

- A specification item is incorrect.

- A specification item is unclear.

- Specification items are out of order.

The following are examples of user-interface specification errors. A user-interface specification item is missing if there is no way for a user to select or enter a required value. A user-interface specification item is superfluous if it allows the user to select or enter a value that is ignored. A user-interface specification item is incorrect if it specifies the display of information in a format that is incompatible with the data type.

A user-interface specification item is unclear if it's possible to implement in two different ways, such that one will cause the user to enter or select the wrong information. User-interface specification items are out of order if the target users speak a language that is read left to right, and the user must work right to left or bottom to top.

11.4.3.4   **Software-interface specification**

Here is a list of possible software-interface specification defects:

- An assumption about collateral software is invalid.

- A specification item is missing.

- A specification item is superfluous.

- A specification item is incorrect.

- A specification item is unclear.

- Specification items are out of order.

The following are examples of software-interface specification errors. A software-interface specification item is missing if the name, the data type, the domain, or the structure of a parameter to a procedure or system call has been omitted. A software-interface specification item is superfluous if the parameter is never used in one of the algorithms of the design. A software-interface specification item is incorrect if the name, the data type, the domain, or the structure of a parameter to a procedure or system call is inconsistent with the usage of that parameter in another part of the design.

A software-interface specification item is unclear if a parameter to a procedure or system call can be implemented in more than one way and at least one of the ways will cause an algorithm to work incorrectly. Software-interface specification items are out of order if the parameters to a procedure or system call are permuted from their usage in one or more algorithms.

11.4.3.5 Hardware-interface specification

Here is a list of possible hardware-interface specification defects:

- An assumption about the hardware is invalid.
- A specification item is missing.
- A specification item is superfluous.
- A specification item is incorrect.
- A specification item is unclear.
- Specification items are out of order.

Hardware-interface specification errors are analogous to their software counterparts.

11.4.4 Coding errors

In this section, we describe errors that occur during the coding phase. We have used general terms to describe programming constructs wherever possible. We have also collected the union of the sets of coding errors possible in a number of programming languages. This means that if you're only familiar with one language, such as Java, some of the descriptions may not be familiar to you.

11.4.4.1 Initialization errors

Here is a list of possible initialization errors:

- A simple variable is always uninitialized.
- A simple variable is sometimes uninitialized.

- A simple variable is initialized with the wrong value.
- An aggregate variable is always uninitialized.
- An aggregate variable is sometimes uninitialized.
- An aggregate variable is initialized with the wrong value.
- An aggregate variable is partially uninitialized.
- An aggregate variable isn't allocated.
- An aggregate variable is allocated the wrong size.
- A resource isn't allocated.

In these cases, a simple variable refers to a variable that can be stored in a hardware data type, to an element of an array, or to a member of an inhomogeneous data structure, such as a structure or class. An aggregate variable refers to composite data structures, whose members are referred to by ordinal number, such as arrays, or by name, such as a C **struct** or C++ **class**. When either a simple or aggregate variable is sometimes uninitialized, there is some control-flow path along which the variable isn't initialized.

11.4.4.2   Finalization errors

Here is a list of possible finalization errors:

- An aggregate variable isn't freed.
- A resource isn't freed.

11.4.4.3   Binding errors

Here is a list of possible binding errors:

- A variable is declared in the wrong scope.
- A procedure call is missing arguments.
- A procedure call has the wrong argument order.
- A procedure call has extra arguments.
- The actual argument-passing mechanism doesn't match the usage of the formal argument.
- A procedure returns no value.

■ A procedure returns the wrong value.

The following are examples of binding errors. A variable is declared in the wrong scope when a variable of local scope hides a variable of more global scope.

Using procedure calls with the wrong number of arguments is possible in older languages such as Fortran 77 or C. Fortran 95 and C++ provide the means to prevent this error.

The two most common argument-passing mechanisms are call-by-reference and call-by-value. In languages that use call-by-reference, such as Fortran, it's possible to pass a constant as an actual argument and assign it to the corresponding formal parameter. This can result in constants having varying values!

It is possible to define functions that don't return values in Fortran 77 or C. Fortran 95 and C++ provide the means to prevent this error as well.

11.4.4.4   Reference errors

Here is a list of possible reference errors:

■ The wrong procedure is called.

■ The wrong variable is referenced.

■ The wrong constant is referenced.

■ The wrong variable is assigned.

■ A variable isn't assigned.

In the first four cases, the statement was syntactically correct, but the programmer referred to a different procedure or variable than he or she meant. In the last case, a reference did not occur.

11.4.4.5   Static data-structure problems

Here is a list of possible errors with static data structures:

■ A simple variable has the wrong data type.

■ An element of an aggregate variable has the wrong data type.

- An aggregate variable has the wrong aggregate size.

The following are examples of static data-structure errors. An item has the wrong data type when it doesn't have sufficient precision to accommodate all legitimate values. An aggregate has the wrong size when it doesn't have sufficient capacity to accommodate all generated values.

11.4.4.6   Dynamic data-structure problems

Here is a list of possible errors with dynamic data structures:

- An array subscript is out of bounds.
- An array subscript is incorrect.
- An uninitialized pointer has been dereferenced.
- A null pointer has been dereferenced.
- A pointer to freed memory has been dereferenced.
- An uninitialized pointer has been freed.
- A pointer stored in freed memory has been dereferenced.
- A null pointer has been freed.
- A pointer to freed memory has been freed.
- A pointer to static memory has been freed.
- A pointer to automatic (stack) memory has been freed.

The following are examples of dynamic data-structure problems. An array subscript is out of bounds when it's nonintegral, is less than the lower bound on a given dimension, or is greater than the upper bound on a given dimension. An array subscript is incorrect when it's a valid subscript but isn't the element that should have been referenced.

Dereferencing or freeing uninitialized pointers, null pointers, and pointers to free memory are all errors because only pointers to allocated blocks of memory can be dereferenced or freed. Freeing pointers to static or automatic memory is an error because only dynamic memory, allocated on the heap, can be explicitly freed.

11.4.4.7 Object-oriented problems

Here is a list of possible errors that occur in object-oriented code:

- A class containing dynamically allocated memory doesn't have required methods.
- A base class has methods declared incorrectly for derived class to override.
- The wrong method signature has been used to invoke an overloaded method.
- A method from the wrong class in the inheritance hierarchy has been used.
- A derived class doesn't completely implement the required functionality.

The following are examples of object-oriented problems. In C++, all classes that contain references or pointers need an ordinary constructor, a copy constructor, an assignment operator, and a destructor. It is a common error to omit the copy constructor or assignment operator. In Java, classes that contain references need an ordinary constructor and a copy constructor. In C++, a base class should provide destructors that are virtual.

In Java, it's possible to provide all the method signatures required to implement an interface without actually providing the semantic content they must have. Similar problems can occur in Java and C++ with abstract and derived classes.

11.4.4.8 Memory problems

Here is a list of possible memory problems:

- Memory is corrupted.
- The stack is corrupted.
- The stack overflows.
- The heap is corrupted.
- A pointer is invalid for the address space.
- An address has an invalid alignment.

Memory, stack, and heap corruption are normally symptoms of problems from the dynamic data-structure section (incorrect use of pointers or array subscripts). Occasionally these are problems in their own right. In these cases, there is a related problem in the underlying hardware or operating system.

Some systems have a segmented address space, and in these systems, it's possible to create a pointer that is invalid for a particular address space. Similarly, some systems have special requirements for the alignment of items addressed by a pointer, and it's possible to create a pointer to a piece of data that isn't addressable because of alignment.

11.4.4.9   Missing operations

Here is a list of possible missing operations:

- The return code or flag hasn't been set.
- The return code or flag hasn't been checked.
- An exception hasn't been thrown.
- The exception thrown hasn't been handled.
- The event sequence hasn't been anticipated.
- The program state hasn't been anticipated.
- Statements are missing.
- Procedure calls are missing.

Return codes or flags are normally associated with operating system calls and C functions. Most operating system calls are defined as if they were written in C, even if they were actually compiled with a C++ compiler. Because C doesn't have exception handling, it's necessary to return status codes. A return code of 0 usually means the operation was successful. Statements or procedure calls can be missing because they weren't included in the algorithm design or because they were simply omitted during coding.

11.4.4.10 Extra operations

Here is a list of possible extra operations:

- A return code or flag is set when not needed.
- An exception is thrown when not valid.
- Extraneous statements are executed.
- Extraneous procedure calls are executed.

Statements or procedure calls can be extraneous because they were included in the algorithm design under assumptions that are no longer valid or because they were duplicated during coding.

11.4.4.11 Control-flow problems

Here is a list of possible control-flow problems:

- Statements are controlled by the wrong control-flow condition.
- Loop iterations are off by one.
- A loop terminates prematurely.
- A loop runs indefinitely.
- A case in a multiway branch is missing.
- A multiway branch takes the wrong case.
- A statement is executed too many times.
- A statement is executed too few times.

The following are examples of control-flow problems. Statements are controlled by the wrong condition when the sense of an *if* test is reversed. Loop iterations are off by one when either too few or too many iterations are executed. A loop terminates prematurely when the condition that controls it changes its truth value at the wrong time. A loop never terminates when the condition that controls its truth value never changes. A case is missing in a multiway branch when the default case is applied to a situation that should have special handling. A wrong case is taken in a multiway branch when flow of control falls through from one case to another because a **break** statement is missing.

11.4.4.12 Value-corruption problems

Here is a list of possible value-corruption problems:

- Arithmetic operation has underflow or overflow.

- Precision is lost.

- Signed and unsigned integers are mixed.

- Floating-point numbers are compared incorrectly.

Arithmetic overflow occurs either when an integer result exceeds the largest representable integer or when the exponent of a floating-point result is positive and the value of the exponent is too large to fit in the exponent field of the floating-point representation being used. Arithmetic underflow occurs when the exponent of a floating-point result is negative and the absolute value of the exponent is too large to fit in the exponent field of the floating-point representation being used.

Precision loss occurs in floating-point computations because floating-point numbers are a finite precision approximation of real numbers. When a program performs millions of floating-point operations, if it doesn't manage the precision loss due to this approximation carefully, the resulting values can be meaningless. An invalid floating-point comparison occurs when a floating-point number is compared for equality without a tolerance factor.

11.4.4.13 Invalid expressions

Here is a list of possible invalid expression problems:

- The wrong variable is used.

- The operator input is invalid.

- The wrong arithmetic operator is used.

- The wrong arithmetic expression order is used.

- The wrong relational operator is used.

- The wrong relational expression order is used.

- The wrong Boolean operator is used.

- The wrong Boolean expression order is used.

- There is a missing term.

- There is an extra term.

The following are examples of invalid expression problems. When a wrong variable is used, the expression is syntactically correct, but you referred to a different variable than you meant. Operator input is invalid when providing an argument that isn't in the domain of the operator, such as dividing by zero. An arithmetic operator is wrong when you used addition but should have used subtraction. A relational operator is wrong when you reverse the sense of a comparison.

Arithmetic expression order is wrong when you use arithmetic operator precedence, associativity, or parentheses incorrectly. Relational expression order is wrong when you use relational operator precedence, associativity, or parentheses incorrectly. A Boolean operator is wrong when you use logical OR when you should have used logical AND. Boolean expression order is wrong when you use Boolean operator precedence, associativity, or parentheses incorrectly.

A term is an operator and its corresponding inputs. Inputs can be constants, variables, or function calls.

11.4.4.14 Typographical errors

Here is a list of possible typographical errors:

- There are missing characters.
- There are extra characters.
- Characters are out of order.

These are low-level mistakes that usually result in one of the other root causes listed previously. They are the direct cause, however, when they occur in data that is embedded in a program. If the data is used to control the logic of the program and isn't there merely for printing so a human can read it, these typographical errors can cause significant problems in program execution.

11.4.4.15 External software problems

Two classes of problems arise from using software written by other people. The first class occurs when we use their software incorrectly. The second class occurs when the problem is actually in the other software.

Here is a list of possible problems with using other people's software:

- The compiler has been used incorrectly to build the application.

- A software tool has been used incorrectly to build the application.

- A system library bound with the application has been used incorrectly.

- A third-party library bound with the application has been used incorrectly.

The following are examples of using other software incorrectly. A compilation is wrong when the code generation options selected are a mismatch for the target hardware architecture. A linker can be used incorrectly by binding the wrong versions of libraries to an application. The build of a program using a tool like the UNIX™ *make* or an Integrated Development Environment (IDE) can be wrong if not all of the dependencies have been acknowledged. In this case, some parts of the application may not be rebuilt when they should be. A library can be used incorrectly by selecting the wrong Application Programming Interface (API) call or by structuring that call incorrectly.

Here is a list of possible problems within other people's software:

- The compiler used to build the application has a defect.

- A software tool used to build the application has a defect.

- The operating system used to execute the application has a defect.

- A system library bound with the application has a defect.

- A third-party library bound with the application has a defect.

11.4.4.16 Root-cause analysis tools

You can download an interactive tool that implements the root-cause classification scheme described in this section from the supporting Web site for this book at www.debuggingbythinking.com.

It allows the programmer to enter new items from any of the categories, which are added to the current classification scheme. Every time the program terminates, it sorts the items in each category by frequency or by recency and writes the counts and dates to the file. The detailed records are stored in a standard comma-delimited ASCII file, which can be imported into any spreadsheet program for analysis.

11.5 **Cause-and-event charting**

The first part of this chapter explained how to record root-cause information, with much of the chapter devoted to a taxonomy of root causes for software defects. This is what most software-development organizations mean when they say that they do root-cause analysis. It is not, however, root-cause analysis according to the definition commonly used by safety experts. All we have done so far from the perspective of the safety expert is to provide a method for categorizing and recording the final results of root-cause analysis.

Cause-and-event charting produces a graphic display of the relationship between events, conditions, changes, and causal factors. Standard symbols borrowed from the ancient method of flowcharting are used to draw the diagram. We present here a simplified version of the method as described in *The Root Cause Analysis Handbook* by Max Ammerman [Am98].

The following symbols are used to construct the cause-and-event chart:

- *Event:* An action or circumstance that was observed to occur. Events are represented by rectangles drawn with a solid line.

- *Presumed event:* An action or circumstance that was not observed to occur, but that is presumed by logical deduction to have happened. Presumed events are represented by rectangles drawn with a dashed line.

- *Critical event:* An undesirable event that was critical to the problem you're analyzing. Critical events are represented by diamonds drawn with a solid line. Critical events should occur only on the primary event line; otherwise they aren't critical events.

- *Terminal event:* The starting and ending events of the analysis. Terminal events are represented by circles drawn with a solid line. Terminal events should occur at the beginning and end of the primary event line.

- *Condition:* Circumstances that may have influenced the events in the diagram. Conditions are represented by ellipses drawn with a solid line. Circumstances should be connected to the related event with a dashed line.

Describe all events with a simple sentence. The subject should refer to an entity in the program or the real world. Events should be described by action verbs, not being verbs. If you can't describe an event with an action verb, it probably isn't an event. Put dates and times on events wherever possible.

Describe all conditions with a simple sentence. The subject should refer to an entity in the program or the real world. The verb should generally be a being verb, normally with a predicate adjective. If you can't describe a condition with a being verb and an adjective, or equivalent grammatical construct, it probably isn't a condition.

To make the charts readable, label each symbol with a number or letter. Create a legend at the bottom of the chart that spells out what the contents of that symbol are.

You can construct a cause-and-event chart by performing the following steps:

1.   Draw the primary event line with the terminal events.

2.   Review the defect report to identify the critical events. Add them to the chart on the primary event line, chronologically from left to right.

3.   Place all primary events on the primary event line.

4.   Add secondary events and conditions to the chart. They will be off the primary event line.

5.   Review the critical events and determine what conditions or causes allowed or forced the critical event to occur. Add the conditions to the chart.

6.   For each condition on the chart, determine why it occurred. Recursively analyze each condition as if it were a critical event until the original critical event is fully explained.

7.   Make a list of actions to take to remedy the root cause and prevent it from occurring again.

11.6   Fault-tree analysis

Fault-tree analysis produces a graphic display of an event that shows the contributing factors to each event. It is primarily used to analyze complex problems with several causes. We present here a simplified version of the method as described in *Root Cause Analysis: A Tool for Total Quality Management* by P. F. Wilson, L. D. Dell, and G. F. Anderson [WDA93].

This formalism is an effective way to analyze problems that involve multiple processes, multiple users, multiple platforms, and sequences of events that occur over longer periods of time. It is probably overkill for problems that involve only a single process, single user, single platform, and very short periods of time.

The following symbols are used to construct the cause-and-event chart:

- *Rectangle:* Rectangles symbolize events or causal factors. Place the description of the event inside the rectangle.

- *Semicircle:* Semicircles symbolize a logical AND connection. All of the conditions that feed it must be true for this part of the tree to be a cause of the problem. This symbol is used to represent AND gates in electronics.

- *Tri-arc:* Polygons created from three arcs of equal length symbolize a logical OR connection. If any of the conditions that feed it are true, then this part of the tree could be a cause of the problem. This symbol is used to represent OR gates in electronics.

- *Triangle:* Triangles represent sections of the fault tree that have been described separately. These can occur because they're repeated or because of space requirements. Place an identifier in the triangle.

- *Ellipse:* Ellipses symbolize conditions or constraints on a logical connection. Place the description of the condition inside the ellipse.

- *Diamond:* Diamonds symbolize a terminal event whose cause hasn't been determined. Place the description of the event inside the ellipse.

As with cause-and-event charts, describe all events with a simple sentence that contains an active verb; describe conditions with a simple sentence that contains a being verb.

Begin constructing the fault tree by putting the defect symptom in an event rectangle. Connect this rectangle to a logical OR connector. The inputs to this OR should reflect the independent centers of control in the system. The following sets of control centers are useful:

- User, client, server

- Several clients and a server
- Several processes
- Several platforms

Continue constructing the fault tree by adding in causes that are relevant to each particular type of control center. Consult the earlier parts of this chapter for relevant lists of causes.

Continue branching the tree by putting conditions or causal factors under the relevant nodes of the tree. Where all of the conditions or causal factors are required for an event to happen, connect them with an AND connector. Where any one of them is sufficient for an event to happen, connect them with an OR connector.

Once you have constructed the tree, you must validate it. You do this by following each path through the tree and evaluating whether that path fits the facts known about the defect. Start at each of the leaves, and trace a path to the root. Consider whether the combination of conditions and causes attributed to the particular control center would be sufficient to cause the observed symptoms. If a subset of the path seems to recur as a possibility through several control centers, this is a good candidate for a root-cause explanation.

11.7 Review

General information to keep with a root-cause-analysis record includes the type of person who reported the problem, the method or tool used to identify the problem, the scope of the defect, and the order of magnitude of the time required to diagnose the defect. Symptom descriptions can be categorized as runtime problems, link-time problems, and compile-time problems.

We don't consider problem reports that originated in erroneous requirement specifications. Our view of software defects is that a defect occurs when there is a difference between requirements and actual behavior.

Design errors can be categorized as data-structure problems, algorithm problems, and problems with user-interface specifications, software-interface specifications, and hardware-interface specifications.

Coding errors can be categorized as initialization and finalization errors, binding and reference errors, data-structure problems and violations, memory problems, missing operations, control-flow problems, value-corruption problems, invalid expressions, typographical errors, and other people's problems.

Cause-and-event charting is a method for analyzing complex software defects. While it can be quite valuable for dealing with complex problems, it's more method than is necessary for analyzing many common software defects.

Fault-tree analysis is another method for analyzing complex software defects. As with cause-and-event charting, it can be quite valuable for dealing with complex problems, but is more method than is necessary for analyzing many common software defects.

Cause-and-event charting is a diachronic (through time) method, in which the chronological order of events is made explicit. Cause-and-event charting is concerned with the dynamic view of a situation.

Fault-tree analysis is a synchronic (with time) method, in which the logical relationship of events is made explicit. Fault-tree analysis is concerned with the static view of a situation.

The Way of the Psychologist

The most dangerous error is failure to recognize our own tendency to error.

—*B. H. Liddell Hart*

12.1 Preview

This chapter views finding defects from the perspective of cognitive psychology. The first section explains the worldview of the psychologist. It suggests that psychology is about modeling human behavior and that the mindset of the psychologist can be applied to the process of preventing and detecting bugs.

The second section of this chapter summarizes the approach of cognitive psychologists to the issues of how humans make errors. It begins with common distinctions between errors occurring during the cognitive stages of planning, storage, and execution. It then explains more sophisticated models, which distinguish errors as skill-based, rule-based, and knowledge-based.

The third section of this chapter reviews experimental research on programmers doing debugging. It presents the published research in terms of experiment subjects, programming language used, program size, defect type, experimental procedures, and conclusions.

12.2 Worldview of the psychologist

When we follow the way of the psychologist, we recognize that software defects are the result of human error. Human error has relatively recently become an area of study for cognitive psychologists.

There are two major contributing factors in the study of human error by psychologists. First, in the 1970s and 1980s, a number of cognitive psychologists developed *information-processing models* of human intelligence. These models have many common or similar features. They provide sufficient detail about how the human mind seems to work that they have enabled psychologists to explain many types of observed human error.

The second contributing factor to the development of the study of human error is the proliferation of highly complex automated systems: nuclear power plants, jet airliners, medical devices, and so forth. All have the power to do great good, but they also have the power to cause great harm, including loss of property and life, because of human failures in design or in operation.

12.3   Models of human cognition

Since the 1970s, cognitive psychologists have been proposing various models of human cognition. They all differ in detail, but there has also been convergence on some broad themes. This isn't surprising, as they must all deal with a growing collection of experimental results.

These researchers don't claim that the human mind is physically structured as the information-processing models suggest. They have presented a great deal of experimental evidence, however, that these models do describe the apparent behavior of the human mind. Most importantly, these models are becoming increasingly effective at predicting the behavior of the human mind under particular circumstances.

The first common idea is the notion of multiple control modes. Conscious controlled thought is one mode. Subconscious automatic thought is another mode. Both modes of thought occur simultaneously and independently.

Conscious thought, which is the focus of our attention, is relatively slow. It requires effort to sustain, and one thought activity follows another sequentially. When we use conscious thought, we set goals, select the means for achieving those goals, and monitor our progress. This type of thought can perform the type of inference associated with classical logic.

Subconscious thought, which doesn't require our attention, seems to proceed more quickly. This type of thought processes familiar information quickly, in parallel, and without conscious effort. This type of thought matches activation conditions with sensory input or intentional input.

The second common idea is the concept of cognitive structures. Working memory is used by the activities of conscious thought. The knowledge base is used by the activities of subconscious thought.

Working memory has a very limited storage capacity, typically judged to be less than ten items. Items are stored in working memory according to the recency of their arrival. They depart from working memory as other items arrive and push them out. The capacity of working memory can be leveraged by hierarchical structure.

The knowledge base contains logical data structures. Some theorists assert that the knowledge base contains two types of information: declarative and procedural. Declarative knowledge seems to include propositions, lists, and images. People learn such information quite quickly.

The procedural part of the knowledge base contains interrelated data structures with a uniform format. Many theorists assert that the procedural data is structured as rules. The rules have a set of conditions (the *if* part) and actions (the *then* part). If the current state of processing matches the conditions in a rule, the actions are executed. Actions can activate other rules, which cause us actually to do some physical action, move information into working memory for conscious processing, and so forth. People learn procedural information more slowly.

Based on this model, many cognitive psychologists believe that human thought is mostly pattern matching the activation conditions of rules, rather than logical deduction. These rules are generated by past experience. The common situations that we encounter are recorded. When exceptions to these situations are encountered, they're recorded in separate rules. Memory is biased toward generalization and regularization of common situations and emphasizing exceptional properties.

12.4　Defining and classifying human error

12.4.1　Defining human error

In their summary of 1980 and 1983 Conferences on the Nature and Source of Human Error, Senders and Moray [SM91] document a number of different ways of defining human error. The consensus definition is that errors are all those occasions in which a planned sequence of mental or physical activities fails to achieve its intended outcome, and these failures can't be attributed to the intervention of some chance agency.

There were considerable differences in the terminology used to define errors at the conference Senders and Moray documented. The most popular terminology comes from the definition of error itself. Slips and lapses are defined as failures in the execution, storage, or both of an action sequence, regardless of whether the guiding plan was adequate to achieve its objective. Mistakes are defined as failures in judgment or inference processes involved in the selection of an objective or in the specification of the means to achieve it. Thus, slips and lapses are execution problems, and mistakes are planning problems.

12.4.2   Classifying different errors

Senders and Moray discuss a number of different ways of classifying errors that were discussed at the conference they documented. The phenomenological approach is useful for computing reliability rates. It distinguishes omissions, substitutions, and so forth. The internal processes approach is useful for understanding decision errors. It describes errors in terms of capture, overload, and so forth. The neuropsychological approach is useful for organizational engineering. It describes errors in terms of forgetting, stress, and attention. The neurological events approach was deemed useless. The external events approach is useful for designing systems. It correlates human error with equipment design, user interfaces, and so forth.

It would seem obvious that errors in execution (slips) and errors in planning (mistakes) should correspond to different cognitive operations. Experimental evidence contradicts this assumption. Both slips and mistakes can take the same form. Numerous well-documented errors have been shown to have properties of both slips and mistakes. These observations led Reason [Re90] to adopt Rasmussen's [Ra86] three-level hierarchy of human cognition.

Reason developed Rasmussen's ideas and distinguished between skill-based slips and lapses, rule-based mistakes, and knowledge-based mistakes. This is a refinement of the slips/mistakes dichotomy that was popularized both by Norman [No90] and Reason.

Rasmussen developed a three-level classification of human performance from the study of errors in emergency situations in hazardous-process industrial facilities. He first observed the distinction in studying the behavior of technicians who were troubleshooting electronic systems. The analogy between diagnosing problems in electronic hardware and debugging computer software is obvious. The hierarchy has become widely used in the analysis of systems reliability.

The lowest level of human performance is skill-based. At this level, behavior is controlled by stored sequences of actions in time and space. Errors that occur when people are engaging in skill-based performance are related to coordination of space, time, and force.

The middle level of human performance is rule-based. At this level, behavior is controlled by stored *if-then* rules. Errors that occur when people are engaging in rule-based performance happen under two general categories. In some errors, the conditions in the *if* part of the selected rule aren't completely matched to the actual problem at hand. In other errors, the procedures in the *then* part of the rule aren't the best means of handling the conditions.

The highest level of human performance is knowledge-based. At this level, behavior is controlled by conscious logical and analytical reasoning. Errors that occur when people are engaging in knowledge-based performance fall into two general categories. In some errors, resource limitations of the conscious mind cause problems. In other errors, the actor applies incomplete or incorrect knowledge.

12.4.2.1 Skill-based behavior

The lowest level of behavior is skill based. An experienced programmer can type any number of low-level programming constructs without conscious thought. The constructs are lexical constructs of the language and the most stereotypical low-level syntactic constructs.

Novices have to think about how to compose these constructs. In contrast, an experienced programmer can type an array reference or a procedure call, for example, without thinking about where the punctuation goes or where the indices or argument values are placed.

12.4.2.2 Rule-based behavior

Much of an experienced programmer's routine behavior is rule-based. The rules encode the experience of the programmer in a way that can be applied with much less effort than a novice will apply to solving the same problem.

The rules that programmers apply vary with the language they're using. Rules may not cover all possible cases. They may be based on incorrect information or lack of information. They are always dependent on the expertise of the programmer, which varies greatly, both between novices and experts and between experts of varying degree. Rules are normally implicit, and a given programmer almost certainly hasn't articulated them.

The following rules for representing sets would be appropriate for C programmers:

- *If* the sets are subsets of a fixed universal set of counting or whole numbers and the most frequent operations will be **union, intersection**, and **difference**,
  Then represent the sets as vectors of bits, in which a given bit is true if the corresponding integer is in the set.

- *If* the sets are homogeneous collections of integers, reals, or character strings, and the most frequent operations will be **union, intersection**, and **difference**,
  Then represent the sets as sorted linked lists.

- *If* the sets are homogeneous collections of integers, reals, or character strings, and the most frequent operations will be **membership, insertion**, and **deletion**,
  Then represent the sets as red-black trees.

This set of rules, while far from perfect, is quite reasonable. It provides good performance and covers a wide number of cases.

A C++ programmer who isn't familiar with the Standard Template Library (STL) might use the same set of rules. If he or she is familiar with the STL, he or she might use the following rules:

- *If* the sets are subsets of a fixed universal set of counting or whole numbers,
  Then represent the sets using the STL *Bitset* class.

- *If* the sets are homogeneous collections of integers, reals, or character strings,
  Then represent the sets using the STL *Set* class.

Note that the rules don't cover all cases. Sets that are inhomogeneous collections of integers, reals, and strings aren't covered. Sets whose members can be other sets aren't covered. Neither are sets whose members can't be enumerated, but must be described by an expression, and which are potentially infinite in size. If the programmer encounters a situation in which such sets are required, he or she will move from rule-based reasoning to knowledge-based reasoning.

12.4.2.3 **Knowledge-based behavior**

The relationship between skill-based errors, rule-based errors, and knowledge-based errors, as described by Reason, is presented in Table 12.1.

Table 12.1 *Distinctions between Skill-Based, Rule-Based, and Knowledge-Based Errors*

	Skill-Based Errors	**Rule-Based Errors**	**Knowledge-Based Errors**
Type of activity	Routine actions	Problem-solving activities	Problem-solving activities
Focus of attention	Elsewhere than problem	Problem-related issues	Problem-related issues
Control mode	Schemata	Schemata	Conscious processes
Predictability of error types	Predictable: Actions	Predictable: Rules	Variable
Ratio of error to opportunity	Numbers high, opportunity small	Numbers high, opportunity small	Numbers small, opportunity high
Influence of situational factors	Intrinsic factors dominate	Intrinsic factors dominate	Extrinsic factors dominate
Ease of detection	Usually rapid and effective	Difficult	Difficult
Relationship to change	Departure from routine	Anticipated changes	Unanticipated changes

From Reason, p. 62. Reprinted with the permission of Cambridge University Press.

When people make skill-based errors, they're performing routine actions, but when they make rule-based errors or knowledge-based errors, they're engaged in problem-solving activities. When people make skill-based errors, their focus of attention is elsewhere, but when they make rule-based errors or knowledge-based errors, their attention is focused on problem-related issues. When people make skill-based errors or rule-based errors, their thoughts are controlled by stored pattern-matching schemata, but when they make knowledge-based errors, they're engaged in conscious logical thought.

When people make skill-based errors or rule-based errors, the numbers of errors are relatively high, but the opportunities are few; when they make knowledge-based errors, the number of these errors is small, but the opportunities are many. When people make skill-based errors or rule-based errors, intrinsic factors are dominant; when they make knowledge-based errors, extrinsic factors are dominant. When people make skill-based errors, they usually find the errors quickly and correct them effectively; when they make rule-based errors or knowledge-based errors, the errors are much harder to detect and correct.

12.5 Explaining error causes

There are many possible causes of errors, and the relationship between them is complex. The result is that predicting error timing isn't possible. It is possible to identify circumstances that increase the probability of errors. When novices in a given competence domain make errors, these errors result from incompetence and are mostly random. When experts in a given competence domain make errors, they result mostly from misplaced competence.

Experts have a lower probability of making planning-oriented mistakes and a higher probability of making an execution-oriented skilled slip. It is easier to prevent an error that is the result of the conjunction of many causes than it is to prevent an error that has a single cause. All you have to do is break the causal chain anywhere to prevent the error from occurring.

12.5.1 Skill-based errors

Most errors that occur at the skill-based level fall into two categories. *Inattention* occurs when you fail to make an attention check at an important point while executing a routine sequence of actions. These types of errors often occur when the sequence is about to deviate from a standard pattern. *Overattention* occurs when you make an attention check at an inappropriate point while executing a routine sequence of actions.

12.5.2 Inattention failures

12.5.2.1 Interrupt sequence, start another sequence

Reason refers to these types of errors as double-capture slips, while Norman refers to them as capture errors, and Silverman [Si92] refers to them as capture slips.

These errors occur when the majority of your attention resources is claimed by internal or external distraction at a critical point in the execution of a sequence of actions. When it's time to continue execution of the sequence, a sequence that has stronger weight and the same initial set of steps hijacks the execution.

The conditions for this error are the following:

- You are doing an activity that you have practiced often.

- You intend to perform some variation on this activity.

- The standard form of the activity and the variation have a common initial sequence of steps.

- You fail to pay attention at the place where the two sequences of steps diverge.

The following is a programming example of this type of error. Almost all counted loops use a step value of one. In C++ or Java, most counted loops begin with an initial value of zero. Experienced programmers write such loops as a single idiom without conscious thought. If you need to make the loop step in increments of two, rather than one, and you're distracted as you begin writing the increment step, you may end up with the following code, rather than the intended version below it:

```
// actual
for( counter=0; counter<limit; ++counter )

// intended
for( counter=0; counter<limit; counter += 2 )
```

12.5.2.2   Interrupt sequence, omit step

Reason refers to these types of errors as omissions following interruptions, while Silverman refers to them as omissions due to interruptions.

These errors occur when the majority of your attention resources is claimed by internal or external distraction at a critical point in the execution of a sequence of actions. When your attention returns to executing the sequence, you omit one or more steps from the sequence and continue on. These errors are more likely if you performed some action that will be treated as a substitute for the next step of the sequence.

The following is a programming example of this type of error. Coding **switch** compound statements in C++ and Java involves a double set of repetitions. The construct as a whole requires the **switch** keyword, an opening brace, a sequence of case statements, and a closing brace. Within a given case, you must provide the **case** keyword, an integer value followed by a semicolon, a block of one or more statements, and a **break** statement.

It is very easy to lose your place in a nested set of repetitions. It is easy to be distracted by some event on your computer, such as a task running in the background, which suddenly pops up a window. If this happens, you may unconsciously substitute the response to that window as the next action you should have taken in composing the **switch** statement. This may cause you to omit an entire case, or even more unfortunately, omit the **break** statement. In either case, your **switch** will be syntactically correct and won't be rejected by the compiler.

12.5.2.3   Interrupt sequence, repeat step

Silverman refers to these types of errors as repetitions due to interruptions. These errors occur when the majority of your attention resources is claimed by internal or external distraction at a critical point in the execution of a sequence of actions. When your attention returns to executing the sequence, you repeat the step you last executed from the sequence and continue on.

The following is a programming example of this type of error. There are several constructs in C and Java where it's possible to stutter at the keyboard and not have the error caught by the compiler. The simplest is entering the digits of a numeric constant or any character within a literal constant.

Under certain circumstances, it's possible to add an additional asterisk "*" in a pointer declaration or a pair of brackets "[]" in an array declaration and create a source file that will compile. The likelihood of this error increases in C, particularly if the variable is local and not passed in function calls that would be subject to prototype checking.

12.5.2.4   Sequence interrupted, loss of control

Reason refers to these types of errors as reduced intentionality, while Norman refers to them as loss-of-activation errors, and Silverman refers to them as loss of schema activation.

These errors occur because a delay intervenes between the time you decide to do something and the time you're in a position to start executing the sequence of actions. If you have ever gone into another room in your home and forgotten why you were there, this is the type of error you have experienced.

The following is a programming example of this type of error. Often as we write the code for one C++ function or Java method, we realize that we need to add or modify the code in another class, which is usually in a different source file. If you have ever found yourself in this situation, opened the source file for the second class, and then wondered what you wanted to change in that file, this is the type of error you experienced.

12.5.2.5   Multiple matches, incorrect choice

Reason refers to these types of errors as perceptual confusions, while Norman refers to them as description errors. These errors occur because the recognition schemata accept a match for an object that looks similar, is in a similar place, or does a similar job. Many of the anecdotal cases of this error involve putting things into, or taking things out of, the wrong container. They occur most often when the right and wrong objects aren't only similar in appearance but also adjacent to each other.

The following is a programming example of this type of error. The metaphor of the desktop and the use of icons to represent objects to be directly manipulated makes it possible for software users to commit these types of errors.

Programmers used to be counseled to put Exit and Help function keys at the opposite ends of the keyboard. Since the action (pressing the key) is the same, the target location should be quite different to avoid errors. The same principle applies to putting similar icons next to one another on toolbars. If two icons look very similar, the action of clicking the mouse on them is the same, and buttons are right next to each other, the probability is high that users will click the wrong button some of the time.

12.5.2.6   Multiple sequences active, steps mixed

Reason refers to these types of errors as interference errors, and Norman refers to them as associative activation errors. Silverman refers to them as associative schema activation, but also distinguishes two additional categories: spoonerisms and schema binding slips. He considers the first an issue of information acquisition, while the other two are information-processing issues.

These errors occur when two currently active sequences or two elements of a sequence become entangled. This can occur because the current sequence triggers others with which it is associated or because attentional resources are being divided between two sequences that are both being executed at the same time.

This type of error is the famous Freudian slip—you think about something that you shouldn't say and then you say it. The spoonerism, which is a ludicrous transposition of the sounds of two or more words, is also included in this category.

The following is a programming example of this type of error. The idiom for swapping two values is

```
temp= left
left= right
right= temp
```

The relationship between pointer dereferences and array element references in C++ is the following:

```
*(a+i) == a[i]
```

If a programmer is trying to swap two values and cleverly minimize typing by using the relationship between array references and pointers, two different sequences are active. This can result in erroneous code like the following:

```
*a = a[1]
a[1] = a[2]
a[0] = a[1]
```

12.5.2.7 Sensory input interferes with active sequence

Norman refers to these as data-driven errors, while Silverman refers to them as data-driven schema activation. Automatic actions that are skill-based are normally driven by the arrival of data from the five senses. Sometimes, however, the arrival of sensory data can intrude into an active action sequence.

The following is a programming example of this type of error. If you're typing in literal or numeric data that will be used to initialize arrays, files, and so forth, you should be careful not to expose yourself to sources of similar input. It is very easy to get distracted while doing such menial work and for your mind to slip in the other data as an item to be entered.

People most frequently experience this error while absentmindedly dialing a phone number and including digits from some other source they're looking at or thinking about. It is just as possible to do this while keying data, and there will be no wrong number message to warn you of your error.

12.5.3   Overattention failures

Overattention occurs when you make an attention check at an inappropriate point while executing a routine sequence of actions. If you're a touch typist, try typing while concentrating on how your fingers are moving over the keyboard as you type. Or, if you play the piano, focus on the movement of a single finger as you play a piece that you know by heart. You will likely experience a greater error rate than normal. This is due to the intrusion of attention on skill-based behavior.

Reason notes that these types of overattention errors can manifest themselves as omissions, repetitions, and reversals. He suggests that overattention errors are particularly likely when the task at hand involves a series of steps mixed with periods of waiting between the steps. The waiting periods increase the likelihood that extra attention will be focused on the task when it should be performed automatically.

12.5.4   Memory failures

Silverman documents a number of errors that occur during skill-based reasoning.

- *Forgetting a goal:* You execute an action sequence but forget why you're doing it.

- *Order memory error:* You temporarily forget the order in which actions in a sequence should be performed.

- *Spacing memory error:* You temporarily forget the physical or chronological spacing between actions in a sequence.

- *Coordinating memory error:* You temporarily forget the motions of physical objects required in the action sequence.

- *Remembering incorrectly:* You forget how proficient you actually are in executing a specific action sequence.

- *Not remembering:* You forget the actual steps of a sequence and need to relearn the skill.

These skill-based errors can all occur when a programmer is performing a sequence of actions that are part of a learned skill.

12.5.5   Rule-based errors

Most errors that occur at the rule-based level fall into two categories:

1.   Misapplication of good rules occurs when a rule that has proven to be effective in the past is applied in a situation that has the indicated conditions, but also contains additional conditions that require the execution of a different rule.

2.   Application of bad rules occurs when not all of the conditions of a situation are represented correctly or when the action corresponding to a set of conditions will result in an ineffective or inefficient action.

When a person is performing rule-based problem solving, more than one rule will be competing to represent the solution. Which rule is selected depends on several factors:

- The conditions of the rule must be satisfied.

- The rule with a stronger weight will be preferred, where the weight is determined by the past success of this rule in solving the problem.

- The more specific rule will be preferred.

- The rule with support from other rules being evaluated will be preferred.

Rules are organized into a hierarchy, with the most general rules evaluated first. Rules that handle exceptions to the general cases are found in lower levels of the hierarchy.

Consider the following set of rules, which is a representation of how a typical programmer might handle the problem of selecting a representation for a dictionary data structure.

- *If* every entry to be looked up in a dictionary occurs exactly once,
  Then use a hash table.

- *If* the same key can have multiple values in a dictionary,
  Then use a tree.

- *If* the same key can have multiple values in a dictionary, but only the most recent is visible,
  Then use a series of hash tables chained together.

This set of rules doesn't cover all possible uses of a dictionary data structure. It does cover several major applications of that structure (sets, natural languages, symbol tables in block-structured languages). When the current set of rules doesn't cover a new situation, the problem solver goes into knowledge-based thinking.

12.5.6 Misapplication of good rules

12.5.6.1 General rule, exception condition

A rule that has been successful in the past acquires greater strength. The first time a person runs into an exception to a general rule, especially when that rule has been an effective solution to the problems encountered, the more likely it's that he or she will choose the general rule, despite the exceptional condition.

The cognitive psychologists theorize that these situations cause the mind to generate rules to handle exceptions. The first time the exception is encountered, the general rule is tried, and the solution fails. This failure results in an exception rule being generated. Reason refers to these types of errors as first exceptions.

The following is a programming example of this type of error. Consider the following set of rules, which is a representation of how a typical programmer might handle the problem of selecting a sorting algorithm:

- *If* the number of items to be sorted will always be relatively small,
  Then use *Shellsort*.

- *If* the number of items to be sorted will always be unknown,
  Then use *Quicksort.*

This is a reasonable rule set that might serve a programmer well. The first time he or she comes upon a sorting situation that requires a stable sort of a large number of items, a bug will result. *Quicksort* isn't a stable sort. Another rule covering this exception condition is needed.

12.5.6.2   Conflicting signals

In a complex problem-solving situation, a person may be exposed to a variety of information as he or she evaluates rules. There will be "signs," or inputs that satisfy some aspect of the conditions of a potential rule. There will also be "countersigns," or inputs that suggest using a more general rule. Finally, there will be "nonsigns," or inputs not relating to any existing rule, which are basically just background noise.

The countersigns can influence the choice of a general rule over a specific one, and the nonsigns can cause problems just by distraction.

The following is a programming example of this type of error. Consider the following set of rules, which is a representation of how a programmer might handle the problem of selecting a sorting algorithm:

- *If* the number of items to sort is unknown.
  Then use *Quicksort.*

- *If* the number of items to sort is less than twenty-five,
  Then use *Shellsort.*

If the requirements indicate that maximum performance is necessary, then the general rule should be matched, since a properly implemented *Quicksort* will use $O(2 * N * \ln N)$ comparisons on average. If the requirements also include optimal sorting of short files, then there is a conflict.

12.5.6.3   Excess information, multiple rule match

The storage capacity of the human conscious memory is extremely limited. If a number of conditions are relevant to the problem being analyzed, it's possible that some of them will simply fall out of consideration due to capacity problems.

One of the possible results of information loss is that several rules will match. This happens because not all of the context information is available and being used. If the choice between the matching rules is made without the missing context information, an error can result. Reason refers to these types of errors as informational overload.

12.5.6.4   **Rule strength versus rule conditions**

A rule that has been successful in the past has greater strength. The first time a person runs into an exception to a general rule, especially when that rule has been an effective solution to the problems encountered, it's likely that he or she will choose the general rule, despite the exceptional condition. Reason refers to this as rule strength.

The following is a programming example of this type of error. Consider the following set of rules, which is a representation of how a typical programmer might handle the problem of selecting a sorting algorithm:

- *If* characteristics of the input data are unknown,
  Then use *Quicksort*.

- *If* a stable sort is required,
  Then use *Mergesort*.

- *If* it is likely that the input data is mostly sorted,
  Then use *Shellsort*.

If the programmer has achieved many satisfactory results using *Quicksort*, he or she may be inclined to use it, even when input is probably mostly sorted. This decision is easy to make, despite the fact that an insertion sort like *Shellsort* operates in linear time on mostly sorted data and that *Quicksort* is much slower in such cases. While this easy decision won't cause the application to produce incorrect results, it may make it significantly slower.

12.5.6.5   **Other rule problems**

There is a natural conflict between general rules and exception rules. General rules often gain greater weight because they're exercised successfully so frequently. On the other hand, exception rules match the circumstances of the problem more precisely. Sometimes people apply the general rule when they should apply an exception rule, because the weight of the general rule is so strong. Reason refers to these types of problems as general rules errors.

As people formulate rules to solve problems, they learn to focus on the key indicators of the circumstances. This means that they also learn to treat the other indicators as redundant information and not use that information. If this information is ignored when it's important, an error occurs. Reason refers to these types of problems as redundancy errors.

Studies show when people develop habits for solving problems, those habits can overshadow the condition-matching thought process. Humans are strongly biased to apply techniques that worked in the past, even though the current circumstances are no longer the same. Reason refers to these types of problems as rigidity errors.

12.5.7   Application of bad rules

Rules can be incorrect because they don't match the right combination of circumstances, or because they don't perform the right actions when the circumstances are matched.

12.5.7.1   Incorrect rule conditions

The condition part of rules can be incorrect in several ways. Aspects of the problem to be solved may be not represented at all in the condition part of a rule that is intended to address the problem.

Other aspects of the problem may be represented inaccurately. A state may be Boolean and represented as a multiple choice, or vice versa. A threshold value may be considered as a discrete integer, when it really is a function of a continuous set of real numbers. Components of the condition may be treated as mutually exclusive when they're not, or vice versa. Components of the condition may be connected by disjunction when they should be connected by conjunction, and vice versa.

An erroneous general rule may be effectively nullified by a series of valid exception rules that prevent its activation. Reason refers to errors caused by these problems as encoding deficiencies.

The following is a programming example of this type of error. Consider the following set of rules, which is a representation of how a programmer might handle the problem of selecting a sorting algorithm:

- *If* comparisons are relatively expensive, but exchanges are inexpensive, *Then* use an insertion sort.

- *If* comparisons are relatively inexpensive, but exchanges are expensive,
  Then use a selection sort.

Selection sorts use about $O(N^{2}/2)$ comparisons and N exchanges. Insertion sorts use about $O(N^{2}/4)$ comparisons and $O(N^{2}/8)$ exchanges, on average [Se90]. Given these bounds, the rule set is helpful when $N = 8$. Thus, the rules that govern the selection of a sorting algorithm are only correct under certain circumstances.

12.5.7.2 Incorrect rule actions

Rule actions can be wrong because someone learned how to do something incorrectly or how to do something that is no longer, or is only sometimes, correct. Reason refers to these as action deficiencies.

12.5.7.3 Frequently ineffective rules

Sometimes people just learn things incorrectly. When the algorithms they use generate nondeterministic results, they may be shielded from their mis-understanding for a long time. Reason refers to these as wrong rules.

The following is a programming example of this type of error. Consider the following set of rules, which is a representation of how a programmer might handle the problem of selecting a sorting algorithm for a C program:

- *If* the values to be interchanged are the values to be compared,
  Then call the library *qsort* routine.
- *If* the values to be interchanged aren't the values to be compared,
  Then write a *Quicksort* that generates a permutation vector, which is applied to the values to be interchanged after sorting.

If these are the only rules for selecting sorting algorithms, the programmer will be quite unhappy with the results the first time a stable sort is required and *Quicksort*'s lack of stability becomes obvious. It may take thousands or millions of executions of a program before it happens.

12.5.7.4 Formerly effective rules

There are often many ways to solve a programming problem. Sometimes the rules we learn to solve one problem later introduce other problems.

Reason refers to these as inelegant or clumsy rules. He notes that these rules are often introduced to achieve economies of effort that are later counterproductive.

The following is a programming example of this type of error. In the 1970s and 1980s, it was common for programmers to manually unroll the loops that they wrote. Loop unrolling replicates the loop body in the source code and divides the number of iterations of the loop by the number of times the body was replicated.

Programmers did this because the overhead of a loop was considered high, and the compilers did not perform automatic loop unrolling. In the 1990s, automatic loop unrolling became an essential optimization for Reduced Instruction Set Computers (RISC) processors, and optimizing compilers frequently performed loop unrolling automatically.

Unfortunately, the factor to which a loop is unrolled is highly machine dependent. This means that the manually unrolled loops in older code usually had the wrong unrolling factor and actually were slower on newer machines. Loop rerolling is possible for partially unrolled loops, but very few compilers perform this optimization. As a result, the rules programmers followed for manually unrolling loops to speed up applications actually had the opposite effect over time.

12.5.7.5   Occasionally effective rules

These rule sets are sufficient to achieve the goal under normal circumstances, but occasionally cause problems. Reason refers to these as inadvisable rules.

The following is a programming example of this type of error. Consider the following set of rules, which is a representation of how a programmer might handle the problem of selecting a stable sorting algorithm:

- *If* auxiliary storage is an issue,
  Then use *Quicksort*.

- *If* auxiliary storage is an issue, and the sort must be stable,
  Then use *Quicksort*, and add a secondary key to preserve stability.

- *If* auxiliary storage isn't an issue, and the sort must be stable,
  Then use *Mergesort*.

The auxiliary memory required by *Mergesort* grows linearly with the size of the input. What some programmers forget is that if *Quicksort* is implemented using recursion, rather than using an explicit stack, and if the file is already sorted, the stack size grows linearly with the input. This is quite different from the **O(lg *N*)** size that is required without recursion. To add insult to injury, the *Quicksort* solution has added a secondary key to preserve stability.

If the programmer is developing software for a system with limited memory, the auxiliary storage requirements of algorithms become a major concern. This rule set will work for many situations. It will, however, use much more storage than necessary if a stable sort is required and the file is already largely sorted.

12.5.8 Knowledge-based errors

Based on the preceding sections, it should be clear that debugging itself is a knowledge-based problem-solving activity. In this section, we explain various types of knowledge-based errors and how to avoid encountering them during the debugging process.

12.5.8.1 Misdirected focus

Research has shown that people tend to focus on those aspects of a problem that are emotionally or psychologically interesting, rather than those that are logically important. A common cause of reasoning errors is giving attention to the wrong aspects of the problem, or not giving attention to the right aspects. Reason refers to these types of errors as selectivity.

A significant part of the debugging process involves knowledge-based reasoning. The programmer must deal with novel situations, since we rarely make exactly the same type of nontrivial mistake in the same context. The previous chapters have introduced methods for enabling programmers to perform knowledge-based reasoning about program defects more effectively.

How can we avoid this error during the debugging process? We have previously recommended keeping a record of the symptoms under investigation. We can enhance this approach by recording the reason why we choose to investigate a particular symptom during our debugging efforts. If we make explicit our reasons for our choices, we may be less likely to choose the symptoms that are appealing, rather than those that are important.

12.5.8.2   Storage limitations

Research has shown that the storage capacity of the conscious mind performing knowledge-based reasoning is extremely limited. Researchers have also observed that storage in the short-term memory works on the first-in, first-out principle. In addition, people tend to place greater emphasis on the first and last items in a set of information.

This means that the presentation of a problem can have a great impact on the ability of the conscious mind to store all the relevant information as it reasons through a problem. Reason refers to these types of errors as workspace limitations, while Silverman discusses order effects.

How can we avoid these errors during the debugging process? Once again, the written record of our debugging efforts is an important technique for avoiding reasoning errors. Whether we record observations, hypotheses, and experiments on paper, in a file on our workstation, or on a handheld computer, our view of the problem is much more likely to be comprehensive if it's recorded.

12.5.8.3   Information availability

Research has shown that people give too much weight to facts that readily come to their minds. In addition, they have the tendency to ignore information that isn't immediately accessible.

Reason refers to these types of errors as out of sight, out of mind, while Silverman distinguishes two variations of this problem: availability and ease of recall. The former refers to using only widely available information, which is external to the problem solver. The latter refers to using only easily recallable information, which is necessarily internal to the problem solver.

How can we avoid this error during the debugging process? A written record of observations can reduce the possibility of this error during debugging.

12.5.8.4   Hypothesis persistence

Research has shown that preliminary hypotheses formed on the basis of incomplete data early on in a problem-solving process are retained in the face of additional, more complete data available later.

Reason refers to these types of errors as confirmation bias, while Silverman sees three variations on this theme: confirmation, selective perception, and expectations. The first variation refers to failing to judge hypotheses that might nullify a previously held conclusion. The second refers to seeking only information that confirms the previously held conclusion. The third refers to attaching greater weight to information that supports the previously held conclusion.

How can we avoid this error during the debugging process? Unlike the first three knowledge-based errors, this problem needs more than just a written record of the investigation.

The information needs to be structured so that the supporting evidence for different hypotheses can be reviewed in parallel. The same is true for the rebutting evidence. One way to build such a structure is to use an outline editor. Put a pro and con branch under each hypothesis. To review the supporting evidence for multiple hypotheses, expand the pro section of each outline point, but leave the con section collapsed. Review both the supporting and rebutting evidence for competing hypotheses at regular intervals when you're assessing your progress.

12.5.8.5 Selective support

Research has shown that problem solvers are often overconfident about the correctness of what they know. Not only do they tend to justify their plans by focusing on the information that supports the plan, but also they will even ignore information that doesn't support the plan.

How can we avoid this error during the debugging process? Unlike the first three knowledge-based errors, this problem needs more than just a written record of the investigation.

The information needs to be structured so that the supporting evidence for different hypotheses can be reviewed in parallel. The same is true for the rebutting evidence. Use the same approach as described in the previous section on hypothesis persistence. A structure that can show the supporting and rebutting evidence for a hypothesis can be valuable here as well.

Cognitive psychology research also shows that the likelihood of this error increases with the expertise of the problem solver. This error is compounded if the plan is very detailed, was created with a great deal of work and emotional investment, or was created by a group of people working together.

Reason refers to these types of errors as overconfidence, and Silverman refers to them similarly. The way to avoid this error during the debugging process is the same as that for the previous error type. It is particularly important to give as much consideration to the opposing evidence as to the supporting evidence. Assigning numerical weights to each evidence item and summing the weights might be an effective way to treat both sides evenly.

12.5.8.6   Limited reviewing

Research has shown that when problem solvers review a planned course of action, they often do an incomplete job. The problem is that people don't consider all of the factors that are relevant to their plan, and they only consider them one or two at a time, instead of in combination. Reason refers to these types of errors as biased reviewing.

How can we avoid this error during the debugging process? The methods described in Chapter 11 are very good at showing the relationship between contributing conditions to a problem. Both cause-and-event charting and fault-tree analysis could be used to avoid this mental error.

For a simpler approach, write a little program that prints all the lines of a file taken in all possible combinations. Describe all the possible contributing factors to the problem in a single sentence and put each in a separate line in a file. Run your program on your file and review all the combinations separately.

For example, for a problem with four contributing factors, first consider the six combinations of factors taken two at a time. Next, consider the four combinations of factors taken three at a time. Finally, consider the combination of all factors together.

12.5.8.7   Inadequate data

People often come to conclusions based on inadequate information. Information can be inadequate for several reasons. It can be preliminary or cover only a limited period of the total time that can be observed. It can also be an inadequate sample size for the actual population being analyzed. It has been shown that people are very likely to draw conclusions from completely inadequate samples.

We can avoid inadequate data collection in several ways. If we're collecting data over a fraction of the time that a process or event occurs, we should be able to justify why that small time period is representative.

For example, if we're observing the memory usage of a program, we must be able to characterize the memory allocation and deallocation behavior across the time period and across the total program execution. As a check on our tendency toward rationalization, it's good to describe our sampling period as a percentage of the total time.

If we're collecting data for a large population, we must be able to defend the sampling method used. For example, if we're sampling the hardware program counter to create an execution profile, the rate of sampling must be frequent enough that short procedures have a chance to be represented. As a check on our tendency toward rationalization, it's good to describe our sample size as a percentage of the total population.

12.5.8.8   Multiple variables

Research has shown that problem solvers do a very poor job of dealing with variables that are partially related. Statistics teaches that in the case where two variables are partially related, when one of the variables takes on an extreme variable, the other variable tends to take on less extreme values. This is called the regression effect.

Unfortunately, when people are asked to predict the future values of variables that are partially related to other variables, they tend to choose the extreme values, rather than those that tend toward the mean. This explains why so many people invest in stocks or mutual funds that did very well in the previous year (an extreme), only to be disappointed by more average performance in the following year. Reason refers to these types of errors as illusory correlation, while Silverman refers to them as illusion of correlation.

12.5.8.9   Misplaced causality

People tend to have problems correctly attributing causality. Studies have shown that people are likely to judge causality based on their perception of the similarity between a potential cause and its effect. Reason and Silverman refer to this type of error as the representativeness problem.

How can we avoid problems with incorrectly assigning causality? The cause-and-event-charting and fault-tree-analysis methods described in Chapter 11 are very good at showing the relationship between contributing conditions to a problem. An objective diagram showing cause and effect is a good counter to assigning causality based upon faulty intuitions.

12.5.8.10 Dealing with complexity

People tend to have trouble working with complex processes that occur over time and prefer to deal with a single moment. They also have problems coping with processes that have exponential growth or decay and think in terms of linear change. People have problems thinking about multiple side effects of an action or event, which spread in a manner analogous to a network. They prefer to think in linear sequences of cause and effect instead.

How can we avoid problems with dealing with complex situations? Once again, the cause-and-event-charting and fault-tree-analysis methods are very helpful in exposing change over time and showing nonlinear relationships between causes and effects.

12.5.8.11 Decisions and probability

A number of studies have shown that people don't make good decisions in circumstances that require assessing probabilities. We don't currently see an application of these knowledge-based errors to debugging, since the causes of software defects are deterministic. Either something is a cause of a defect, or it's not.

For completeness, we survey these errors briefly, in the hopes that future studies on debugging might find applications for them. They demonstrate that people commit many different types of knowledge-based errors when making decisions. Readers who are interested in pursuing these topics further should read M. Piatelli-Palmarini's *Inevitable Illusions* [Pi94] and T. Gilovich's *How We Know What Isn't So* [Gi91].

Ease of representation

People tend to assign a higher likelihood to events that are easier to remember or easier to imagine. They decide to take precautions against negative events based primarily not on their likelihood, but on their emotional impact.

Framing of choices

People tend to select a choice that is described in terms of the likelihood of positive outcome rather than a choice that is described in terms of negative outcome. Positive outcomes are situations like succeeding, winning, or being cured of an illness. Negative outcomes are situations like failing, losing, or succumbing to an illness. This tendency is observed even when the probability of the negative outcome is just the probability of the positive outcome subtracted from one:

$$P_{(\text{negative})} = 1 - P_{(\text{positive})}$$

Conjunction effect

People tend to rate as more probable those circumstances that they find easier to imagine or that seem more typical. This behavior becomes problematic when a circumstance is the simultaneous occurrence of several items, each of which isn't a certainty. Mathematics teaches us that the probability of two or more events is the product of their individual probabilities. In the situation described above, none of individual items is a certainty, which has probability of one. Thus, the product will be smaller than the individual probabilities, and the conjunction will be less likely than any of the individual items.

Base rates

When they assess probabilities, people tend to give lesser weight to, even to ignore, general or abstract information than they do to concrete or specific case data. This phenomenon is known to psychologists as neglect of base rates. This problem occurs most often in situations in which a person must make a decision about an individual object or person that is part of a large population of individuals belonging to some particular class.

Certainty effect

People tend to be willing to incur greater costs than are justified by the economic benefit to achieve illusory certainty about taking risks. Similarly, they expect to receive a greater payback for taking risks to achieve illusory certainty. An example of this problem is the great desire on the part of the general public to seek laws and regulations that purport to reduce to zero the probability of certain accidents, diseases, and so forth.

Disjunction effect

People tend to have trouble making decisions when they're faced with two more choices, one of which will occur with certainty some time in the future. What starts out as prudence in the face of uncertainty often becomes paralysis.

Gambler's fallacy

The basic problem that this item covers is the notion that the occurrence of a run of some event affects the likelihood of that event occurring again. In the world of gaming, players assume that a series of outcomes increases the likelihood of that outcome recurring. In the world of sports, players assume that a series of successes (or failures) increases the likelihood of the same result again. If the events are truly independent, such as the roll of an honest pair of dice, there is no relationship between past and future outcomes.

12.6   Research review

In the previous sections, we have considered how skill-based and rule-based errors result in program bugs and how we can avoid making knowledge-based errors during debugging. In this section, we present a brief review of experimental research on how programmers think when they're debugging.

12.6.1   Youngs, 1974

Citation: "Human Errors in Programming" [Yo74]

Subjects: Thirty novices and twelve professional programmers

Programming language: Algol, Basic, COBOL, Fortran, and PL/1

Program size: Between twenty and eighty statements

Defect type: Introduced by the subjects during the experiment

Experimental procedure: The subjects implemented various simple numerical algorithms. During their work, compilation logs and execution output were saved automatically. The researcher analyzed questionnaires, compile logs, and execution logs after completion. The analysis of the programs was done by manually working backward from the final correct version to an initial faulty version. At each step, the errors corrected were grouped according to language construct and were classified as syntactic, semantic, logical, or clerical.

Conclusions: The decline in the number of bugs fits an exponential decay curve, with different constants for novice and experienced programmers. Experts eliminated syntactic and semantic errors quickly, while beginners were slower in correcting semantic errors.

12.6.2   Gould, 1975

Citation: "Some Psychological Evidence on How People Debug Computer Programs" [Go75]

Subjects: Ten expert programmers

Programming language: Fortran

Program size: Four statistical programs from a commercial subroutine library

Defect type: Introduced by the researcher beforehand

Experimental procedure: The researcher modified existing Fortran programs to contain bugs. A single line in each program was changed to introduce an error in an arithmetic expression, an invalid array subscript, or an incorrect loop limit. This produced a total of twelve erroneous programs.

The subjects were told to debug each of the programs. They were given labeled, formatted output, and were allowed to use an interactive debugger. The subjects were told to work as fast as possible, and they had a maximum of forty-five minutes on any given program. Their work was assessed based on the number of correct diagnoses, false diagnoses, and the time required to find the problem.

Conclusions: The subjects improved their time in debugging different versions of the same program. There was significant variation in the quality, quantity, and efficiency of the results produced by the programmers.

12.6.3 Brooke and Duncan, 1980

Citation: "Experimental Studies of Flowchart Use at Different Stages of Program Debugging" [BD80]

Subjects: Twenty high-school and college students

Programming language: "Warehouse" language for simple two-dimensional movement

Program size: Twenty to thirty statements in listings or flowcharts

Defect type: Inserted by researcher beforehand

Experimental procedure: The subjects were instructed to locate the procedure in a program that contained the error. Programs simulated the movement of a truck in a warehouse, which could pick up items and deliver them to one of four loading bays. Some subjects were given program listings; others received detailed flowcharts with equivalent content.

Conclusions: Flowcharts were found to be more useful than simple program listings when the debugging task primarily requires following execution paths. Errors in identifying defect causes were equally likely with flowcharts and source listings.

12.6.4 Gilmore and Smith, 1984

Citation: "An Investigation of the Utility of Flowcharts during Computer Program Debugging" [GS84]

Subjects: Twenty-four psychology students, twenty-one of whom had taken a five-week course in POP11

Programming language: POP11

Program size: Twenty to thirty statements

Defect type: Introduced by the researcher beforehand

Experimental procedure: The programs that were debugged were a set of instructions for moving an object through a maze. The subjects were divided into three groups, each of which was given a program listing, a hierarchical diagram of the program (Bowles diagram), or a flowchart of the program. The subjects in each group attempted to debug six different versions of an algorithm. There was one error in each program in a conditional statement. The activities of the subjects were measured in terms of the time required to find the bug and the number of traces they needed to solve it.

Conclusions: The availability of flowcharts did not significantly improve the performance of the subjects. The authors suggest a number of areas needing further research, including choice of debugging strategies by programmers, cognitive style demonstrated by subjects, and the way differences in problem context (reading or writing programs) affect the best way to represent programs.

12.6.5 Anderson and Jeffries, 1985

Citation: "Novice LISP Errors: Undetected Losses of Information from Working Memory" [AJ85]

Experiments 1 and 2

Subjects: Thirty out of seventy-five undergraduates in a class on artificial intelligence

Programming language: LISP

Program size: Single LISP expression

Defect type: Introduced by the subjects during the experiment

Experimental procedure: Subjects evaluated the result of complete expressions; completed expressions in which a result was given, but an input was missing; and completed expressions in which a result was given, but a function name was missing. Expressions were presented in three forms: (1) basic, (2) with extraneous parentheses, and (3) with arguments provided through invoking the list reversal function.

Conclusions: Subjects who showed a general weakness in the subject matter experienced greater difficulty processing the more complex, but equivalent, expressions. Proper use of parentheses caused more problems than the semantics of the functions.

Experiment 3

Subjects: Twenty students

Programming language: LISP

Program size: Single LISP expression

Defect type: Introduced by the subjects during the experiment

Experimental procedure: Subjects were taught four basic LISP functions and given 336 LISP expressions to evaluate. Subjects worked at a CRT with keyboard and were told to work as quickly as possible.

Conclusions: Errors were primarily due to the misuse of parentheses, rather than the semantics of the functions used. Extra or missing pairs of parentheses were more frequent than unbalanced pairs of parentheses.

Experiment 4

Subjects: Twenty-six undergraduate students, half with no knowledge of LISP, the other with minimal training

Programming language: LISP

Program size: Single LISP expression

Defect type: Introduced by the researchers beforehand

Experimental procedure: Subjects were given 180 expressions to assess for correctness, 120 of which did contain errors.

Conclusions: The subjects who had received fifteen minutes of training in list structures did moderately better at detecting errors than the untrained group, but not significantly so.

12.6.6 Spohrer, Soloway, and Pope, 1985

Citation: "A Goal/Plan Analysis of Buggy Pascal Programs" [SSP85a]; "Where The Bugs Are" [SSP85b]

Subjects: About two hundred college students in an introductory programming class

Programming language: Pascal

Program size: Seventy to eighty lines

Defect type: Introduced by the subjects during the experiment

Experimental procedure: The researchers automatically collected each syntactically valid program that students compiled when solving a tax calculation programming assignment. The programs were analyzed manually to map them to a goal-and-plan tree representation of possible solutions to the assigned programming problem.

Conclusions: Student programmers often write programs in which code to achieve multiple logical goals is merged into a single physical source code unit. Those merged code sections include merge-related bugs in addition to bugs found in nonmerged versions. The merged versions contain more bugs than the nonmerged versions. Bugs peculiar to merged versions include loss of a goal and loss of constraints on achieving a goal.

12.6.7   Vessey, 1985, 1986

Citation: "Expertise in Debugging Computer Programs: A Process Analysis" [Ve85]; "Expertise in Debugging Computer Programs: An Analysis of the Content of Verbal Protocol" [Ve86]

Subjects: Sixteen professional programmers

Programming language: COBOL

Program size: A sales reporting program of about one hundred lines

Defect type: Introduced by the researcher beforehand

Experimental procedure: Prior to the experiment, half of the subjects were rated as novice and half as expert by their manager. The subjects were told to find the bug in a COBOL program by looking at a listing. The bug was a logic error inserted into one of two different locations in the program control structure.

They were told to verbalize their thoughts as they worked. These protocols were recorded and transcribed. The subjects were rated on the time they took to debug the program and the number of mistakes they made. After the experiment, the researcher rated the subjects as novice or expert, based on their demonstrated ability to absorb the meaning of a section of code and not return to it. The researcher's rating system correlated more closely with the subjects' performance than did the manager's rating.

Conclusions: Expert programmers followed a breadth-first approach to program comprehension, while novices tended to follow a depth-first approach. Experts weren't as committed to their hypotheses as novices and were more open to using new information. Expert programmers developed a mental model of the program structure and function, while novices were less likely to do so. The researcher believes that the main difference between novices and experts is that experts spend their time understanding the program while novices focus on finding a solution.

12.6.8 Gugerty and Olson, 1987

Citation: "Comprehension Differences in Debugging by Skilled and Novice Programmers" [GO87]

Experiment 1

Subjects: Eighteen novices taking a first Pascal course and six computer science graduate students

Programming language: Logo

Program size: Fifteen to fifty lines

Defect type: Introduced by the researchers beforehand

Experimental procedure: Subjects were trained in Logo programming. They were given three defective programs, as well as a drawing of what each program should generate. They were given a maximum of thirty minutes to debug each program. Subjects were told to think out loud, and their verbal protocols were recorded.

Experiment 2

Subjects: Ten novices completing a first Pascal course and ten computer science graduate students

Programming language: Pascal

Program size: Forty-six lines

Defect type: Introduced by the researchers beforehand

Experimental procedure: All subjects were familiar with Pascal. They were given a program listing, a listing of the input data file, a listing of the expected output, and a description of the program purpose, all of which were also available online. The subjects were given forty minutes to correct the program. An observer monitored what the subjects looked at and what they were keying.

Conclusions: Novices and experts use the same techniques for exploring a new program. Experts generate better hypotheses about the cause of defects, thus having fewer hypotheses to validate and correcting the defect in less time. Novices were more likely to add bugs in the process of trying to diagnose the original problem.

12.6.9 Kessler and Anderson, 1987

Citation: "A Model of Novice Debugging in LISP" [KA87]

Subjects: Eight undergraduate students with no LISP experience, at most a Pascal course

Programming language: LISP

Program size: Single-line LISP expressions

Defect type: Introduced by the researchers beforehand

Experimental procedure: Subjects were given a first lesson in LISP using an online tutorial. Subjects were presented with eighteen functions, twelve of which contained defects. The subjects would say whether they thought the function had a defect and then would invoke it. Then they would correct the function if necessary. The subjects were encouraged to talk aloud about their analysis as they worked. These protocols were recorded.

Conclusions: Most subjects began by trying to understand the code, and then they proceeded to execute it. The next phase of localization was difficult and time-consuming. The final repair of the problem was also challenging. Educators should teach students the skills of evaluating expressions, localizing problems, and correcting them, in addition to teaching them how to write programs.

12.6.10 Spohrer and Soloway, 1987

Citation: "Analyzing the High Frequency Bugs in Novice Programs" [SS87]

Subjects: Sixty-one students enrolled in an introductory Pascal programming class

Programming language: Pascal

Program size: Sixty to one hundred statements

Defect type: Introduced by the subjects during the experiment

Experimental procedure: The researchers automatically collected each syntactically valid program students compiled when solving three programming assignments. The programs were analyzed manually to map them to a goal-and-plan tree representation of possible solutions to the assigned programming problem. A total of 183 programs were collected; 25 were excluded because the program was significantly incomplete. The researchers developed explanations for the causes of 11 of 101 defect types that comprised over one-third of all the defects identified.

Conclusions: Some defect types occur much more frequently than others in the work of novice programmers. Many of these defects aren't related to the semantics of a particular programming language construct, but rather to more general programming issues. Instructors should teach students to recognize these types of errors.

12.6.11 Katz and Anderson, 1988

Citation: "Debugging: An Analysis of Bug-Location Strategies" [KA88]

Experiment 1

Subjects: Groups of thirteen, twenty, and eighteen undergraduates taking a LISP course

Programming language: LISP

Program size: Fewer than twenty lines

Defect type: Introduced by the subjects during the experiment

Experimental procedure: The first two groups of subjects solved exercises from an introductory programming class with the assistance of an automatic tutor program, which provided feedback when they made errors. This tutor also collected data on the subjects' efforts as they worked. The third group wrote functions in an open environment, with a human tutor available. Both verbal protocols and a complete record of the keyboard activities were collected.

Conclusions: Errors were classified as goal errors, misunderstandings of the problem, intrusions of previous solutions, misconceptions about LISP features, and syntax errors. No defects spanned more than one line. Subjects did not generally repeat the same bug within or between programs.

Experiment 2

Subjects: Eight undergraduate students taking a LISP course, who had previously taken a Pascal course

Programming language: LISP

Program size: Three programs of less than twenty lines

Defect type: Introduced by the subjects during the experiment

Experimental procedure: The subjects wrote three LISP functions with the aid of a tutor. Subjects were encouraged to talk aloud as they worked, and these verbal protocols were recorded.

Conclusions: Locating the problem was the most difficult part of the debugging process. Subjects had little problem correcting identified problems. Subjects used three strategies to locate bugs: mapping from error messages to the location of the defect in the program, manually executing the program with sample values, and reasoning from the (incorrect) output back to the program.

Experiment 3

Subjects: Thirty-six undergraduate students taking introductory LISP

Programming language: LISP

Program size: Fewer than twenty lines

Defect type: Introduced by the subjects during the experiment

Experimental procedure: Subjects wrote and debugged four LISP functions that they wrote and four that were written by other subjects. One-third of the students completed the assignments in an open environment; the others used the LISP tutor. Both verbal protocols and a complete record of the keyboard activities were collected.

Conclusions: At the start of a debugging session, subjects spent less time looking at programs they had written than those written by others. They also were significantly less successful in locating the bugs in programs written by others than those they wrote themselves. Subjects debugging their own functions tended to use backward-reasoning strategies (mapping errors to program lines, reasoning from incorrect output to program location), whereas those debugging functions written by others tended to use forward-reasoning strategies (building a mental model of the program, manual execution).

Experiment 4

Subjects: Twenty-seven undergraduates taking a LISP class; all had one or two other programming classes

Programming language: LISP

Program size: Fewer than twenty lines

Defect type: Introduced by the researchers beforehand

Experimental procedure: Every subject worked with two sets of six programs. Eight of the programs had one bug, two programs had two bugs, and two programs had no bugs. The subjects were divided into three groups. With the first set of programs, the first group used forward-reasoning strategies, the second using backward-reasoning strategies, and the third group could use any strategy. The use of strategies was forced by using an interactive tool. With the second set of programs, all subjects could use any strategy.

Conclusions: When the subjects were allowed to use any debugging strategy, they still used the one they had trained on with the first set of programs. The subjects allowed to use any strategy worked the fastest but made the most mistakes. The subjects forced to use working backward were the slowest but most accurate.

12.6.12   Vessey, 1989

Citation: "Toward a Theory of Computer Program Bugs: An Empirical Test" [Ve89]

Subjects: Seventy-eight students and thirty-eight professionals

Programming language: COBOL

Program size: A sales reporting program of about one hundred lines

Defect type: Introduced by the researcher beforehand

Experimental procedure: The same logic error was introduced in each of four levels of the program's control-flow hierarchy. Subjects were told to verbalize their thoughts as they worked. These protocols were recorded and transcribed. The subjects were rated on the time they took to debug the program and the number of mistakes they made.

Conclusions: The time to locate and correct a bug wasn't related to the location of the bug in the control-flow hierarchy. Expert programmers debugged more quickly and with fewer mistakes than the novices.

12.6.13   Carver, 1989

Citation: "Programmer Variations in Software Debugging Approaches" [Ca89]

Subjects: Three experienced programmers

Programming language: Not specified

Program size: A billing system of thirteen modules

Defect type: Introduced by the subjects during the experiment

Experimental procedure: Each programmer worked on a different part of the same system. The purpose of the study was to analyze the volume of changes to a program that a programmer makes before testing those changes.

Conclusions: The researcher observed consistent patterns of behavior in each programmer, but no generalizations could be drawn because of the limited sample size and the fact that each programmer worked on different problems.

12.6.14 Stone, Jordan, and Wright, 1990

Citation: "The Impact of Pascal Education on Debugging Skill" [SJW90]

Experiment 1

Subjects: 124 students in five COBOL courses

Programming language: COBOL

Program size: 319-line unstructured, 362-line poorly structured, 417-line well-structured versions

Defect type: Introduced by the researcher beforehand

Experimental procedure: The three versions of the program were randomly distributed to the subjects. All subjects received a program listing and an output listing with the erroneous output clearly marked. The subjects were given twenty minutes to locate and correct the error.

Experiment 2

Subjects: Forty-two students in an introductory COBOL course

Programming language: COBOL

Program size: 319-line unstructured, 417-line well-structured versions

Defect type:

Experimental procedure: Two versions of the program were randomly distributed to the subjects. All subjects received a program listing and an output listing with the erroneous output clearly marked. The subjects were given thirty minutes to locate and correct the error.

Conclusions: Pascal education was strongly correlated with the ability to diagnose and correct errors. Pascal education was also strongly correlated with computer science majors, a greater number of previous programming courses, and previous professional programming experience. Pascal education wasn't correlated with the ability to maintain structured programs.

12.6.15 Allwood and Bjhorhag, 1991

Citation: "Novices' Debugging When Programming in Pascal" [AB91]

Subjects: Eight novices taking a Pascal programming class

Programming language: Pascal

Program size: Not given

Defect type: Introduced by the subjects during the experiment

Experimental procedure: The subjects were given a written specification of a numerical programming problem. They were told to think out load, and their verbal protocols were written down. All activity was recorded on video. The researchers manually analyzed the recorded protocols. Errors were distinguished as syntactical, semantic, and logical errors. The researchers analyzed the triggers, durations, and actions of so-called evaluative episodes.

Conclusions: Subjects spent most of the time debugging. They would have spent an even greater amount of time debugging if they hadn't been stopped by the observers when time expired. Even though they were working on programs they wrote, the subjects spent much of their time interpreting and understanding the program.

12.6.16 Ebrahami, 1994

Citation: "Novice Programmer Errors: Language Constructs and Plan Composition" [Eb94]

Experiment 1

Subjects: Eighty undergraduate students, with four groups of twenty each taking one of the four languages

Programming language: Pascal, C, Fortran, and LISP

Program size: Fewer than ten statements

Defect type: Introduced by the researcher beforehand

Experimental procedure: The subjects were asked to evaluate program segments manually with the specified input data. After processing all of the segments, the subjects were interviewed and asked to think through the problems aloud. The researcher classified the errors made by the subjects according to the programming constructs used.

Experiment 2

Subjects: Eighty undergraduate students, with four groups of twenty each taking one of the four languages

Programming language: Pascal, C, Fortran, and LISP

Program size: Fewer than one hundred statements

Defect type: Introduced by the subjects during the experiment

Experimental procedure: The subjects were given a written problem definition. They wrote programs to implement the specification. The researcher evaluated the programs submitted and recorded the errors. The researcher classified the errors in the programs, comparing the correct plan and the actual plan used by the student to solve the problem.

Conclusions: The language constructs most frequently misused were loop termination conditions, logical operators in conditional statements, and language-specific features. The plan element most frequently missing or in error was a conditional statement serving as a guard.

12.6.17   Summary

Performing experimental research on programmers doing debugging is difficult for several reasons. The subjects available to university researchers are usually novice programmers. Novice and expert programmers don't exhibit the same behaviors. The economic cost of using enough professional programmers in psychological experiments whose results have statistical significance is high. Debugging actually involves a number of skills and behaviors, which are difficult to separate in a controlled experiment.

Previous experimental research in debugging has limited value to the professional programmer. Researchers tested programming languages and development techniques that are no longer used in modern computing environments. Most experiments were performed on tiny programs that aren't typical of the complex software that professional programmers develop.

Some of the experimental work is also difficult to assess because of the limited sample size, the design of the experiment, or the subjects used. Most of the subjects in the experiments were complete novices taking a first or second programming course. The related topic of program comprehension has interested researchers more recently, but a survey of that literature is beyond the scope of this section.

12.7 Review

Our brief survey has shown that a number of cognitive psychologists have developed similar models of human thought processes. While they don't claim that the human mind is physically structured as the information-processing models suggest, they have presented a great deal of experimental evidence that these models do describe the apparent behavior of the human mind.

One point of similarity among these models is the notion of conscious controlled thought and subconscious automatic thought as different modes of mental activity. Conscious thought is slow, effortful, and sequential. Subconscious thought is fast, effortless, and parallel.

A second point of similarity among these models is the notion of cognitive structures. Working memory is the domain of conscious thought, while the knowledge base is the domain of subconscious thought.

The procedural part of the knowledge base contains interrelated data structures with a uniform format. One popular format for these structures to take is a set of rules, each with a set of conditions to be satisfied, and a set of actions to perform if the rule holds. Many cognitive psychologists believe that human thought is mostly pattern matching the activation conditions of rules, rather than logical deduction.

The study of human error is a relatively recent phenomenon. Researchers have developed several similar taxonomies of human error. The initial similarity developed from common definitions of basic terms. Further similarities developed from Rasmussen's hierarchy of human problem-solving activities and resulted in cataloging failure modes observed in research about specific issues.

Errors occur when a planned sequence of mental or physical activities fails to achieve its intended outcome. Slips and lapses are problems that occur when a plan is executed incorrectly. Mistakes are problems that occur due to formulating a plan incorrectly.

Rasmussen developed a three-level classification of human performance: skill-based behavior is controlled by stored sequences of actions in time and space; rule-based behavior is controlled by stored *if-then* rules; knowledge-based behavior is controlled by conscious logical and analytical reasoning.

An experienced programmer performs skill-based actions to type any number of low-level programming constructs without conscious thought. Novices have to think about how to compose these constructs. Rules encode the experience of an expert programmer in a way that can be applied with much less effort than a novice will apply to solving the same problem.

When novices in a given competence domain make errors, they come from incompetence and are mostly random. When experts in a given competence domain make errors, they mostly come from misplaced competence.

Inattention occurs when you fail to make an attention check at an important point while executing a routine sequence of actions. Overattention occurs when you make an attention check at an inappropriate point while executing a routine sequence of actions.

Capture errors occur when your attention is claimed by an internal or external distraction at a critical point in the execution of a sequence of actions. When it's time to continue execution of the sequence, a sequence that has stronger weight and has the same initial set of steps hijacks the execution.

Interruption errors occur when your attention is claimed by an internal or external distraction at a critical point in the execution of a sequence of actions. When your attention returns to executing the sequence, you omit one or more steps from the sequence and continue on.

Delay errors occur because a delay intervenes between the time you decide to do something and the time you're in a position to start executing the sequence of actions. When your attention returns to the task at hand, it's no longer in control, and you stop doing the planned action.

Multiple match errors occur because the recognition schemata accept a match for an object that looks similar, is in a similar place, or does a similar job. Many of the anecdotal cases of this error involve putting things into, or taking things out of, the wrong container.

Mixed sequence errors occur when two currently active sequences or two elements of a sequence become entangled. This can occur because the current sequence triggers others with which it's associated or because attentional resources are being divided between two sequences that are both being executed at the same time.

Sensory interference errors occur when you're performing an action sequence and the arrival of sensory data intrudes into the active action sequence. Overattention errors manifest themselves as omissions, repetitions, and reversals. They are more likely when the task at hand involves a series of steps mixed with periods of waiting between the steps. Silverman documents a number of errors that occur during skill-based reasoning.

Misapplication of good rules occurs when a rule that has proven to be effective in the past is applied in a situation that has the indicated conditions, but also contains additional conditions that require the execution of a different rule. Application of bad rules occurs when not all of the conditions of a situation are represented correctly or when the action corresponding to a set of conditions will result in an ineffective or inefficient action.

The first time a person runs into an exception to a general rule, especially when that rule has been an effective solution to the problems encountered, the more likely it's that they will choose the general rule, despite the exceptional condition. The cognitive psychologists theorize that these situations cause the mind to generate rules to handle exceptions.

In a complex problem-solving situation, a person may be exposed to a variety of information as he or she evaluates rules. Contrary indicators can influence the choice of a general rule over a specific one, and the irrelevant information can cause problems just by distraction.

If a number of conditions are relevant to the problem being analyzed, it's possible that some of them will simply fall out of consideration due to capacity problems. One of the possible consequences of information loss is that several rules will match, and the wrong one will be chosen.

A rule that has been successful in the past has greater strength. The first time a person runs into an exception to a general rule, it's more likely that he or she will choose the general rule, despite the exceptional condition. This is especially true when that rule has been an effective solution to the problems encountered.

Sometimes people apply a general rule when they should apply an exception rule because the weight of the general rule is so strong. As people formulate rules to solve problems, they learn to focus on the key indicators of the circumstances. If they ignore other information when it's important, an error occurs. Humans are strongly biased to apply techniques that worked in the past, even though the current circumstances are no longer the same.

The condition part of rules can be incorrect in several ways. Aspects of the problem to be solved may be not represented at all in the condition part of a rule that is intended to address the problem. Other aspects of the problem may be represented inaccurately. An erroneous general rule may be effectively nullified by a series of valid exception rules that prevent its activation.

Rule actions can be wrong because someone learned how to do something incorrectly or how to do something that is no longer, or is only sometimes, correct. Sometimes people just learn things incorrectly. When the algorithms they use generate nondeterministic results, they may be shielded from their misunderstanding for a long time.

There are often many ways to solve a programming problem. Sometimes the rules we learn to solve one problem later introduce other problems. There are also rule sets that are sufficient to achieve the goal under normal circumstances, but that occasionally cause problems.

People tend to focus on those aspects of a problem that are emotionally or psychologically interesting, rather than those that are logically important. If we explicitly record the reasons for our choices, we may be less likely to choose the symptoms that are appealing, rather than those that are important.

Research has shown that the storage capacity of the conscious mind performing knowledge-based reasoning is extremely limited. Once again, a written record of our debugging efforts is an important resource for avoiding reasoning errors due to memory capacity limitations. We also know that people give too much weight to those facts that readily come to their minds. The written debugging log can balance selective memory.

Research has shown that preliminary hypotheses formed on the basis of incomplete data early on in a problem-solving process are retained in the face of additional, more complete data available later. If we structure the information that supports and rebuts our hypotheses, we can review both at regular intervals as we assess our progress.

People are often overconfident about the correctness of what they know when they solve problems. This problem can be mitigated as well by giving full consideration to the information recorded in a supporting or opposing structure.

When people review a planned course of action, they often do an incomplete job, not considering all the factors that are relevant to their plan, or not considering those factors in combination. The methods described in Chapter 11 are very good at showing the relationship between contributing conditions to a problem.

People often come to conclusions based on inadequate information. We must ensure that samples are representative in terms of time period and quantity.

Research has shown that problem solvers do a very poor job of dealing with variables that are partially related. Unfortunately, when people are asked to predict the future values of variables that are partially related to other variables, they tend to choose the extreme values, rather than those that tend toward the mean.

People tend to judge causality based on their perception of the similarity between a potential cause and its effect. People also tend to have trouble working with complex processes that occur over time and prefer to deal with a single moment. The cause-and-event-charting and fault-tree-analysis methods are helpful in avoiding theses type of errors.

A number of studies have shown that people don't make good decisions in circumstances that require assessing probabilities. We don't currently see an application of these knowledge-based errors to debugging, since the causes of software defects are deterministic.

Performing experimental research on programmers doing debugging is difficult. Much previous research has focused on programming languages and development techniques that are no longer in use. Almost all published research on debugging has used complete novices as subjects, which raises questions about its relevance to professional programmers.

The Way of the Engineer

I believe that the concept of failure . . . is central to understanding engineering, for engineering design has as its first and foremost objective the obviation of failure.

—*Henry Petroski [Pe92]*

13.1 Preview

This chapter views finding defects from the perspective of engineering. The first section of this chapter explains the worldview of the engineer. It suggests that engineering is about designing reliable structures and that the mindset of the engineer can be applied to the process of preventing and detecting bugs. It quotes several key statements from works by Henry Petroski [Pe92] and James L. Adams about the nature of the engineering process and relates them to the process of building and debugging software.

The second section of this chapter describes how programming errors can be classified by the development stage in which they occur. It proposes three stages of program development: conception, expression, and transcription. It defines each of these stages and provides lists of errors that are commonly committed during that stage.

The third section of this chapter describes how programming errors can be avoided according to the development stage in which they occur. It explains that there are two main ways to avoid conception-stage errors and shows how to use them. It continues by describing several ways to avoid expression-stage errors. It concludes by explaining several ways to avoid transcription-stage errors.

The fourth section of this chapter explains how to avoid programming errors by using coding conventions. It presents a general approach to programming conventions. It starts out with a general approach to object-oriented programming and structures a coding convention into six areas.

For each of these areas, it recommends choosing a set of conventions that implement a set of metarules.

The fifth section of this chapter suggests adding debugging infrastructure to a program as it's developed. It recommends the use of augmented data structures, augmented procedures, specialized debuggers, and assertions.

13.2 Worldview of the engineer

When we follow the way of the engineer, we use an analogy between the design of reliable material objects and the design of reliable immaterial software. Engineers follow a standard process for creating physical objects. We note the methods that can prevent or identify defects that are introduced during phases of the software-development process. Engineers design useful objects by following standards, and we suggest ways to prevent software defects by following standards.

James Adams provides in his book *Flying Buttresses, Entropy, and O-Ring: The World of an Engineer* [Ad91] a diagram that shows the engineering process having the following stages (p. 39):

- Problem definition
- Preliminary design
- Detail design
- Development
- Production
- Dissemination
- Maintenance
- Disposal

The three stages that are of most interest to us are preliminary design, detail design, and development. Adams defines these stages as follows ([Ad91], pp. 44–45):

- *Preliminary design:* Various ways of solving the problem are conjured up and compared. Toward the end of the process, a decision is made as to which design to pursue, and the overall configuration of the product is defined.

- *Detail design:* The product is completely defined in its final form. This means that each component of the product is described so that it can be produced and so that the whole will fit together into a balanced and integrated product.

- *Development:* Prototype products are brought to a functional and economic level that will satisfy customers, whoever they may be, and the producers.

These three stages correspond to the software-development phases of design, coding, and testing. There are significant differences, however, between the development of software and the engineering of tangible objects.

One of the most important results of the preliminary design of an object is a mathematical analysis of whether it will operate safely and serve the purpose for which it was designed. This isn't always done. Sometimes the scientific theory doesn't exist to resolve these issues. In other situations, the computation required to apply the theory to the product in question is beyond current computers.

In *Invention by Design: How Engineers Get from Thought to Thing,* Henry Petroski [Pe96] states, "The ability to calculate is the ability to predict the performance of a design before it is built and tested. . . . Calculations that indicate failure conditions in the design enable the engineer to modify and remodify the design until it is ready to be realized."

The designer of a software system has no opportunity to apply the laws of physics to validate his design mathematically. One can validate the design of disks and memory that will store software and circuits that will execute it. The software itself, however, has no tangible referent to which the laws of physics apply. This makes software infinitely malleable. Unfortunately, it also places the software designer at a severe disadvantage vis-à-vis his or her engineering counterpart when it comes to validating a design.

In *To Engineer is Human: The Role of Failure in Successful Design,* Henry Petroski [Pe92] states the following:

Engineers . . . make mistakes in their assumptions, in their calculations, in their conclusions. That they make mistakes is forgivable;

that they catch them is imperative. Thus, it is the essence of modern engineering not only to be able to check one's own work, but also to have one's work checked and to be able to check the work of others.

Software designs are typically validated by peer review. The same is true of designs for tangible objects. The opinions of experts are often useful in identifying flaws in a design, but they're no substitute for mathematics.

Discussion of the peer review methodology is beyond the scope of this work. See the bibliography for recommended books on this topic.

The output of the detailed design phase of a tangible object is pictorial representations and textual descriptions of the object and the process for manufacturing or building it. The output of the coding phase of software development is a textual description of the software and instructions necessary for building a representation of that description in a form that can be executed by hardware.

Another aspect of the relationship between the detailed design phase of a tangible object and the coding phase of software development is the use of standards. For tangible objects, a variety of standards must be followed.

Some standards come from manufacturer's groups that wish their products to be able to work together. Other standards come from government regulatory bodies or insurance underwriting organizations. Professional societies also recommend various standards for engineers who work in a particular field. There are also internal standards that a given organization imposes upon itself. These standards all serve to channel detail-design decisions in certain directions, resulting in products that are safer, more reliable, and more useful.

There are no universal required standards for software. Nonetheless, wise software developers use standard methods for coding to improve reliability and maintainability.

Thus, the first major aspect of the engineering worldview that is valuable in the debugging enterprise is the attitude of defect prevention. The engineer designing a tangible object uses analytical, experimental, and methodological means to identify and remove potential sources of failure. The remainder of this chapter is devoted to explaining methods for preventing defects that are applicable during the coding phase of software development.

Defect prevention is also important during the design phase of software development. Using object-oriented analysis and design methodology is a good way to prevent defects during the design phase. Discussion of this methodology is beyond the scope of this work. See the bibliography for recommended books on this topic.

Of course, thorough testing is critical to defect prevention in software. Discussion of testing methodology is beyond the scope of this work. See the bibliography for recommended books on this topic.

The second major aspect of the engineering worldview that is valuable in the debugging enterprise is the attitude of leveraging failure to achieve future success. Henry Petroski does an excellent job of advocating this mindset in several of his books. In *Invention by Design: How Engineers Get from Thought to Thing,* he states, "It is the analysis of failures or of limitations of a design that leads to improved understanding and thus to improved products."

The entirety of Chapter 11 is devoted to explaining methods for analyzing the root causes of software defects. The purpose of this analysis is to ensure that one identified defect can be leveraged into many defects prevented.

The third major aspect of the engineering worldview that is valuable in the debugging enterprise is expecting unexpected failures. Engineers who build physical objects provide a safety factor in their designs. They acknowledge that there are limits to the strength of their designs and that unknown factors might make the design weaker than their analysis shows.

While software developers can't specify extra structural or material integrity, they can include debugging infrastructures in their programs as they develop them. By acknowledging that there will be flaws in their design that they haven't anticipated, they can prepare to make it easier to debug when those flaws are revealed.

13.3 Classifying errors by development stage

When looking for ways to prevent and diagnose bugs, it's helpful to consider the stages of writing a program and how defects are introduced in each of those stages. We identify three stages of writing a program:

- Conception
- Expression
- Transcription

For each stage, we identify the particular causes of errors that occur during that stage. This division of stages is logical rather than physical. Programmers can pass from one stage to another without conscious thought. This set of stages defines the coding phase of software development.

13.3.1 Conception stage

13.3.1.1 Conception-stage definition

In the **conception stage**, a program is couched in a language-independent notation such as pseudocode or structure charts. Nonessential details are omitted.

The effort involved in the conception stage can be entirely mental. In fact, the results of the conception stage may never be written down. Errors occur in the conception stage due to the programmer not fully understanding the problem to be solved.

13.3.1.2 Conception-stage errors

Here is a list of errors that commonly occur during the conception stage:

- An algorithm makes invalid assumptions about the input.
- An algorithm makes invalid assumptions about the program state.
- An algorithm omits coverage of logical possibilities.
- An algorithm omits actions that must be performed.
- An algorithm performs actions that aren't needed.
- An algorithm applies wrong action when it detects a condition.
- An algorithm performs actions in the wrong order.
- An algorithm has a time complexity that prevents it from completing in a time acceptable in an interactive or real-time situation.
- A data structure doesn't have capacity to handle the volume of input.
- A data structure uses a representation that will cause loss of information.
- A data structure omits storage for input items or intermediate results.
- A data structure doesn't facilitate data access in an acceptable time.

13.3.2   Expression stage

13.3.2.1   Expression-stage definition

In the **expression stage**, the programmer encodes the algorithm in a specific programming language. The programmer has filled in all the details necessary to compile and execute the program.

Once again, the effort involved in the expression stage can be entirely mental. It is possible not to commit the results of this stage to writing.

13.3.2.2   Expression-stage-error causes

There are two possible reasons for expression-stage errors. First, the programmer writes a program that is invalid in the target programming language. Language translators (compilers, interpreters) normally find these problems, particularly if the problem is lexical or syntactic.

Second, the programmer writes a valid program that doesn't say what he or she meant to write. Since even the best language translator can't analyze intentions, these problems aren't normally detected until further on in the software-development process.

13.3.2.3   Recognizing expression errors

To know how to recognize expression errors, it's useful to consider the analogous errors made by people speaking a language that isn't their native language. Grammatical mistakes can give away a speaker who has excellent pronunciation and vocabulary in the second language. Here are some of the more common mistakes of this kind:

- Using appropriate words but putting them in the wrong order
- Conjugating verbs, particularly irregular verbs, incorrectly
- Selecting the wrong case endings for nouns and adjectives
- Omitting items not required in the speaker's native language, such as being verbs and definite and indefinite articles

These mistakes are interesting to us because programmers who use more than one language often make analogous mistakes in programming. They are also interesting because they reflect the kind of errors that experienced programmers make when writing code.

13.3.2.4 Expression-stage errors

The following errors occur during the expression stage:

- Unintended expression evaluation order is caused by operator precedence rules.

- Loss of precision is caused by mixed data types and implicit conversions.

- Unintended statement order of execution is caused by control-flow default rules.

- Incompatible operand types in dynamically typed languages are caused by attribute derivation and inheritance rules.

The following code segments show typical expression errors of the second type. The comment says what the programmer meant to say, and the code says something else.

```
C count positive values:
C compare each value to zero
C if greater, then increment counter
      DO I = 1, N
        IF( X(I) .LT. 0 ) THEN
          C = C + 1
        ENDIF
      ENDDO
```

```
// count positive values:
// compare each value to zero
// if greater, then increment counter
      for ( i=0; i< 0 ) {
          c += 1;
        }
      }
```

13.3.2.5 Expression errors and permissive languages

Some languages, such as Fortran, C, and PL/I, require the language translator to accept implausible or questionable source code. Such programs that are accepted by the translator often have problems like loss of precision in conversions, wrong type of pointer for the object pointed to, and so forth.

The language translator will handle these codes by making assumptions or adding hidden code. The language translator may accept the program without complaint. Language translators use several mechanisms to cope with questionable code:

- Adding conversions between data types
- Assuming equality of operand width and pointer sizes
- Generating code regardless of precision loss

13.3.2.6   Expression errors and strict languages

Language translators for languages such as C++, Ada, and Java are normally much stricter about their language interpretations. They require matching types between formal and actual arguments, between left- and right-hand sides of assignments, and between pointers and the objects to which they point. This strictness prevents certain types of expression errors from resulting in an executable program that doesn't do what the programmer intended.

13.3.3   Transcription stage

13.3.3.1   Transcription-stage definition

In the **transcription stage**, the programmer embodies the program in a machine-readable medium. In the ancient past of computing, professional typists would create decks of cards by key-punching the code written by hand on a standard form by the programmer. Today, programmers do their own data entry on workstations or PCs, and program text is stored directly on disk.

When the transcription stage is complete, the program is in a form that the language translator will process.

13.3.3.2   Transcription-stage errors

The following errors occur during the transcription stage:

- Omitting characters or words

- Inserting extra characters or words

- Substituting characters or words

- Transposing adjacent characters or words

13.3.3.3   **Transcription-stage-error causes**

Some transcription errors are caused by difficulty reading the previous version of the program. Others are simply typing mistakes.

Transcription mistakes are trivial to correct, but they can result in valid programs that don't express the intent of the programmer. If the language processor doesn't catch them, they can be very difficult to isolate.

13.3.3.4   **Transcription-stage-error examples**

Some of computing's most infamous bugs have been caused by transcription errors. Omitting or inserting a blank or period for a comma can be very expensive, even fatal. In the following Fortran statements, a period has been inadvertently substituted for a comma in the second statement. This change results in the intended loop control statement becoming a simple assignment. Since the code that was the body of the loop is only executed once, the results are quite unexpected.

```
DO 10 I = 1,100
DO10I=1.100
```

13.4   Avoiding errors by development stage

13.4.1   Avoiding conception-stage errors

In the conception stage, errors happen when the programmer doesn't fully understand the problem to be solved. In the expression stage, errors are due to not following the rules of the programming language or not writing what you meant. In the transcription stage, errors are due to hand-eye coordination problems, spelling misconceptions, and so forth.

There are two main ways to avoid conception-stage errors. The first is to write out the design in a textual or graphical format. The second is to implement a prototype.

13.4.1.1 Write out the design

In this section, we aren't discussing the design of the system as a whole, which includes classes, methods, interfaces, and so forth, but rather the design of individual procedures, functions, and methods. There are several good books on the topic of object-oriented analysis and design that cover the design of classes, methods, and interfaces. They don't cover the design of individual methods, since the structured programming era handled this satisfactorily.

Start avoiding errors in your code by writing out the design in some design medium. Designs need to be reviewed. This seems obvious to many people, but there are reasons related to debugging that are important. Human memories are fallible, so you can't review a design you haven't written down. Your colleagues can't read your mind, so a written design is essential to peer review. Writing down designs has the desirable side effect of delaying coding. As soon as you start coding, you start introducing bugs into your software.

After you code and execute your procedure, if testing reveals the existence of defects, you can compare the design with the procedure source to see if you really coded what you meant. All AI systems for finding bugs work by comparing a design and its realization. You need to be able to use the same technique to find bugs in your programs.

There are several notations suitable for writing out the design of a procedure. They all date back to the structured programming era. Some of them are as follows:

- Structured pseudocode
- Nassi-Shneiderman diagrams
- Warnier-Orr diagrams

See the bibliography for recommended books on this topic.

In these design notations, data structures aren't fully declared but are described in terms of high-level data structures, such as dynamic arrays, trees, sets, and so forth. Low-level structures used to implement these high-level structures, such as fixed-length arrays, linked lists, and hash tables, are not normally used. In addition, we recommend that only structured control constructs be used. For this reason, we haven't included the venerable flow-chart in our list of design notations.

Here is a small list of questions to use in reviewing the design of a procedure:

- What assumptions are being made about the input and program state? Are they valid?

- Are other logical possibilities not being handled?

- Is there code to handle all default cases?

- Is there any other action that must be taken at this point in the algorithm?

- Is it always necessary to perform this action at this point in the algorithm?

- Is this action the correct one to perform when this condition occurs?

- Are these actions performed in the correct order?

13.4.1.2 Implement a prototype

An alternative to traditional design methods is to code and execute your algorithm in a VHLL. Such languages allow the programmer to omit details, often at the expense of range of expression and execution efficiency. APL, LISP, Scheme, and SETL are examples of languages useful for this work. They provide implied control structures and high-level data structures. Scripting languages such as Perl and Tcl can also be used for prototyping.

Rapid prototyping has all the advantages of a written design plus an additional one: You can execute it to find design flaws. This creates a higher level of confidence than does a reviewed design.

Two approaches are useful in this context:

1. Disciplined use of simplifying assumptions, developed by Rich and Waters [RW82]

2. The concept of scale models, explained by Weiser [We82a]

Simplifying assumptions

Assumptions must simplify the problem in a significant way without changing the essential character of the problem. The designer must keep track of the assumptions made so that they can later be retracted in the full-scale system.

Good simplifying assumptions have the qualities of consistency and continuity. A consistent assumption permits the prototype to work correctly for at least some real inputs. Ignoring invalid inputs is a consistent assumption. A continuous assumption makes it possible to modify the prototype so that it increasingly performs as a real system. Building a prototype of a parallel system without synchronization isn't a continuous assumption.

Scale models

A scale model is accurate in some ways but inaccurate in others. Different kinds of scale models have a different set of attributes that are scaled down. The model must interact with the real world in a limited, but natural, way.

A **functional prototype** does the critical system computations with the input domain scaled down. Special restricted formats for input are allowed, and only valid inputs need to be processed. The user interface is scaled down. The output format may only be adequate for manually validating the computations.

A **user-interface prototype** shows the user the following:

- Options that will be available
- Mechanisms to access those options
- Messages generated by the system
- Displays and reports that will be shown

Computation is scaled down, and output may be canned, rather than computed. Performance is scaled down as well. Tools that generate the dialog may be used, even though they create slower interfaces.

A **performance prototype** demonstrates whether a system can meet time or space limitations. It implements the features of the system that consume the most resources. The system features are scaled down so that computations known not to be resource intensive are omitted. User interfaces are scaled down, so that only those features that have response time requirements are implemented.

13.4.2   Avoiding expression-stage errors

There are several ways to avoid expression-stage errors:
- Exploit redundancy in your program.

- Use tools that pick at programming nits.

13.4.2.1   Exploit redundancy

We exploit redundancy differently in software development than we do in the design of tangible objects. With tangible objects, redundancy is largely used to provide a margin of safety that will cover unintended stresses on the object. It also covers for simplifications and assumptions made during the mathematical modeling. Thus, an engineer will specify additional material to be used beyond the minimum required for proper functioning to provide a safety factor. This type of redundancy masks failures in the original design.

With software, we include redundancy to expose failures as early as possible. Some of the redundant information we recommend will expose errors at compile time. Other information will uncover problems when the application is executed, hopefully during testing, rather than after the product is completed.

There are two other types of redundancy, which we don't discuss further. These types of redundancy provide the same masking of failures as that used in the design of tangible objects.

Execution redundancy provides for executing the same program on multiple, identical platforms. This type of redundancy is found in fault-tolerant systems, used primarily in commercial environments where downtime results in severe financial losses.

Computational redundancy provides for executing different programs on multiple identical platforms. These different programs, developed independently, are supposed to compute the same result. When the results differ, a majority vote determines the correct result. The development and hardware resources required for this kind of redundancy are very expensive. This kind of redundancy is only used in situations where failure would be catastrophic, such as in space shuttles or nuclear reactors.

Embed redundant information in declarations

Providing data a compiler doesn't need to generate a correct program enables it to identify some incorrect programs. In Fortran, both the type of a variable and its initial value have defaults, depending on the first letter of the name. If a name begins with the letters "I," "J," "K," "L," "M," or "N," then the type defaults to **INTEGER**; otherwise it defaults to **REAL**. In PL/I, all attributes have a default value. In C and C++, **external** and **static** variables are initialized by default to 0. Rather than use defaults, specify values explicitly.

Make full use of user-defined data types. Define numeric variables in terms of a unit of measure or the set of values they take on. Only programming artifacts, such as loop counters, are exempt from the possibility of typing in this way.

13.4.2.2   Use nitpicking tools

Permissive languages often have nitpicking tools to complement their compilers. These languages include Fortran, C, PL/I, and Scheme.

Strict languages require compilers to find the sort of problems that nitpicking tools find. These languages include Pascal, Ada, C++, and Java. There are such tools for these languages, but they look for a very small set of possible problems.

One way to perform nitpicking is to convert to a stricter variant of the language or just to use the compiler for a stricter variant. For example, you can convert from Fortran 77 to Fortran 95, or use a C++ compiler on a program that was originally written in C.

It is important to maximize the benefit and minimize the cost of using nitpicking tools. There are several ways to do this:

- Keep a record of which messages turn up errors.
- Use the tool's control knobs to turn off messages that never uncover errors in your code.
- Write a program to filter out the noise, if necessary.
- Check your code regularly to make the task less burdensome.
- Adopt a zero-tolerance policy for warnings.

See Chapter 14 for further details on nitpicking tools.

13.4.3   Avoiding transcription-stage errors

There are several ways to avoid transcription-stage errors:

- Compensate for human psychology.
- Exploit redundancy in your program.

13.4.3.1   Compensate for human psychology

There are at least three ways to compensate for human psychology to avoid transcription stage errors:

1.   Overcome psychological set.

2.   Maximize psychological distance.

3.   Prevent typographical errors.

Overcome psychological set

Psychological "set" reduces the ability of programmers to find errors [Uz66]. In our context, set causes the brain to see what it expects to see, rather than what the eye actually perceives. A transcription error may be completely masked by the set of the author. He or she knows what the program is supposed to say and is incapable of seeing what it actually says.

One way to overcome your psychological set is to have another person read your program. That person won't come to the text with the same assumptions you have. If you're working alone, leave the workplace and do something that has nothing to do with programming. When you return, your change of venue will often have broken your set.

A second way to overcome your psychological set is to display the program in a different format than that in which you're accustomed to viewing it. Here is a list of different ways to look at a program listing:

- Look at a paper listing instead of a video display.

- Display one token per line.

- Display a blank space after each token.

- Display the listing with the comments deleted.

- Display everything in reverse video.

- Display different lexical categories in various formats. Lexical categories include keywords, numeric literals, string literals, user names, and those glyphs that aren't numbers or letters. Different formats include all uppercase, italics, boldface, different colors for each category, and so forth.

- Display numbers in equivalent formats. Show them in hexadecimal notation, scientific notation, or spelled out in words.

- Display the program nesting structure in varying colors.

A third way to overcome your psychological set is to listen to the program being read. You can ask another programmer to read it to you. You can also have a voice synthesis program read it to you. In both cases, read along as the program is read aloud. You will notice that other human readers will separate and group items differently than you do.

Maximize psychological distance

All misreadings aren't created equal. Information theory says that messages have a distance that is computed by counting the number of positions in which they differ [SW49].

The distance between "word" and "work" is one. The distance between "word" and "warm" is two. To reduce the likelihood of transcription errors, maximize the distance between characters and words that may be confused.

The number of different characters is only a starting point. Some pairs of letters and digits are much easier for the brain to misread than others. Easily confused pairs include the following:

- 0 and O
- k and x
- i and l
- w and v
- m and n

The positions of differing characters are also important. When words differ in the first or last positions, people are less likely to misread them. Consider how likely you might be to confuse the following pairs of words:

- "word" versus "ward"
- "word" versus "cord"
- "word" versus "worm"

Prevent typographical errors

Errors in keying must be considered when selecting names for constructs in a program. Names that differ only in characters adjacent on the keyboard are more likely to be mistyped. Touch typists are more likely to mistype characters that are reached by the same fingers on opposite hands.

13.4.3.2 Minimize transcription errors

Choose names according to the following rules:

- Prefer names that have a minimum distance of two characters from other names.

- One of the differing characters should be at the beginning or end of the word.

- Prefer names that aren't likely to be misread as another name.

- Avoid names that differ only in characters that have similar shapes.

- Prefer names that aren't likely to be mistyped as another name.

- Avoid names that differ only in characters that are next to each other on the keyboard, or are on the same fingers of opposite hands.

13.4.3.3 Exploit redundancy

Make programming constructs do double duty. It is a common error in C to mistype or confuse equality (two equals signs) with assignment (one equals sign). C allows assignments to be embedded anywhere in expressions. Some compilers will warn about every embedded assignment that feeds a conditional. While this can be helpful, embedding assignments in loop controls in C is common and efficient. Looking through hundreds of false alarm messages is discouraging and unproductive.

```
(var == 1)
(var = 1) /* error missed */
(1 == var)
(1 = var) /* error found */

C error unnoticed
DO 10 I=1.100
C compiler sees
DO10I=1.10
C error detected
DO 10 I=1.100,1
```

13.5 Avoiding errors by coding conventions

A programming convention is a set of choices. An individual or group of programmers decides to code in a certain style to achieve their goals. Programming conventions can make bugs less likely. They also can make it easier to diagnose problems when they do occur and easier to modify them once the problems are found.

We prefer the term "programming convention" to "programming standard." Programming standards tend to be imposed on programmers by managers. Programming conventions tend to be agreements among peers that are largely self-enforcing.

Programming conventions aren't the Ten Commandments. They are selected by people, rather than dictated by God. There is no justification for breaking a divine commandment. There may be, however, occasions when it's appropriate to ignore a tenet of a programming convention to achieve some other purpose. Most programming standards or conventions presented in the literature tend to be a bit arbitrary or idiosyncratic.

There is rarely only one reasonable choice for any given coding style issue. While our suggestions are carefully thought out, you could achieve similar results by a consistent set of different choices. Almost any programming convention is better than no convention at all. Consistency rewards its practitioners.

How does consistent coding reduce the number of bugs in an application? Consistency enables the programmer to code with less mental effort. If a given construct is always written the same way, the programmer will learn to do so without conscious thought. Since every conscious effort presents the chance for making an error, making coding a mechanical task reduces errors. It also makes it possible to automate certain programming tasks.

How does consistent coding make it easier to diagnose problems when they do occur? Consistency enables the programmer to understand the code more quickly. For example, if a programmer sees a name written in a certain way, he or she will be able to infer certain information about the object to which it refers. He can do this without having to look at its definition, which is likely to be on a different screen or page of the program source.

How does consistent coding make it easier to correct erroneous code? Consistency enables the programmer to identify all sections of code related to the change he or she wants to make. If a given construct is always written in the same way, the programmer can have confidence that if these sections are changed, nothing will have been omitted.

The purpose of this section is to present a general approach to programming conventions. This approach applies to a variety of programming languages, including those that aren't "O-O kosher." The organizing concept for our approach to programming conventions is object-oriented programming. The phrase "object-oriented" has been applied to every computing activity imaginable. This overuse shouldn't cause us to lose sight of an important concept.

13.5.1   Object-oriented programming

You can think of object-oriented programming as designing and programming an application-specific computer architecture. Such architectures are often referred to as "virtual machines." A computer architecture has a set of primitive data types, such as integers and floating-point numbers. The operations are defined on the primitive data types, such as addition and comparison. Anything the computer can do must ultimately be defined in terms of these types and operations. A virtual machine has the same features as a real machine. The difference is that the virtual machine's features are defined in software.

Object-oriented programming involves three steps:

1.   Find those data types and operations that are fundamental to a given application.

2.   Implement those types and operations.

3.   Code the application in terms of those types and operations.

The application only refers to the data structures that implement the objects through the procedures that implement the fundamental operations. The application need not know how the basic data types are implemented. Access to the data structures is made only through the interface provided. The implementation of an object can be completely replaced without harming the application.

Our approach to programming conventions structures them into the following sections:

- The structure and format of source files

- The structure and format of classes

- The structure and format of procedures

- The structure and format of statements

- Consistent construction of names

- Constructs that should be avoided

13.5.2   Programming convention

Each of the sections of the convention consists of a set of metarules for deriving specific standards and a commentary on the metarules.

13.5.2.1   Source-file metarules

- Recommend a consistent file-naming convention.

- Recommend a helpful line-length limit.

- Recommend a block of comments that describe the most important aspects of a class before the definition of the class.

- Recommend a block of comments that describe the most important aspects of a procedure before the definition of the procedure.

- Avoid mandating comments that can become easily outdated or that are readily discerned from reading the text.

- Recommend a method for distinguishing the beginning of new class definitions and new procedure definitions.

13.5.2.2   Source-file metarules commentary

Both programming languages and platforms impose constraints on the names that programmers can give to source files. Java requires that the name of a file correspond in spelling and capitalization with the public class that it contains. Back in the bad old days, many operating systems restricted the length of file names, often to eight characters. Fortran 77 restricted the length of procedure names to six characters.

The most common line-length limits correspond to the form factors of video displays and printer paper. Don't assume that everyone who looks at your program will have a wide display or wide paper.

The most useful information about a procedure is a one-sentence description of its purpose. References to published literature, such as where the algorithm comes from, are also quite useful.

Code changes, so why encourage the comments to get out of date by putting information in comments that is readily obtained from the source as well? This includes the name of the procedure, the names and types of the arguments, and the type of the return values.

Delineating the definitions of procedures and objects makes it easier for a reader to scan your source code looking for items of interest. White space or comments containing a separating line are the most common ways to achieve this goal.

13.5.2.3   Source-file convention examples

Listed as follows is a set of conventions for C++ that address the issues of file structure. There are other choices that are reasonable and effective in preventing bugs.

- Do name include files with an extension of "H".

- Do name implementation files with an extension of "C".

- Do name the include file for a class the same as the name of the class.

- Do use upper- and lowercase letters in file names as they're used for class names in source code.

- Do use "//" to denote comments. Don't use "/* . . . */" to denote comments.

- Do write comments at the beginning of an include file that describe the purpose of the class defined.

- Do write comments before a function definition that describes the purpose of the function defined.

- Do put all data members, member functions, and friend functions with each other in the source file. Separate each group with the following comment:

    ```
    //====================================================
    ```

- Do separate each function with the following comment:

    ```
    //----------------------------------------------------
    ```

- Do provide all include files with some means of preventing multiple inclusion of that file.

- Do break source lines of more than eighty characters over multiple lines.

- Don't put more than one class definition in an include file.

- Don't define functions in the class header file.

- Don't put names of formal arguments in function definitions in header files.

Listed as follows is a set of conventions for Java that address the issues of file structure. There are other choices that are reasonable and effective in preventing bugs.

- If a nonpublic class supports only one public class, put it in the same file as the public class; otherwise, put it in a separate file.

- Do use *javadoc* conventions to describe the purpose of each class.

- Do use *javadoc* conventions to describe the purpose and contents of instance and class (static) variables.

- Do use *javadoc* conventions to describe the purpose, assumptions, and effects of methods.

- Do use "/* */" for block comments.

- Do use "//" for inline comments.

- Do put two blank lines between major sections of a source file.

- Do put one blank line between method definitions.

- Do put one blank line between the local variables of a block and the first statement.

- Do put one blank line before a block or single-line comments.

- Do put one block line between logical sections of a method.

13.5.2.4 Class structure metarules

- Recommend ways to hide the implementation of procedures and the internal representation of data from the user of a class.

- Recommend ways to provide a full set of operations for each data type to be defined.

- Recommend ways to employ polymorphism to achieve maximum code reuse.

- Recommend ways to use inheritance to share the common features between classes.

13.5.2.5 Class structure metarules commentary

Data hiding isn't object-oriented programming per se. Some authors refer to encapsulation and data abstraction as object-based programming. They distinguish this from object-oriented programming, by which they mean the use of inheritance and polymorphism.

13.5.2.6 Class structure convention examples

Listed as follows is a set of conventions for C++ that address the issues of class structure. There are other choices that are reasonable and effective in preventing bugs.

- Do encapsulate global variables, global constants, and enumerations in a separate class.

- Do declare **public**, **protected**, and **private** sections of a class in that order.

- Don't create **public** or **protected** data members in a class.

- Do declare as **inline** all accessor member functions.

- Do declare as **inline** all mutator member functions. Mutators assign their argument to a data member.

- Don't declare as **inline** constructors or destructors.

- Do declare as **const** a member function that doesn't change the values of data members.

- Do define a virtual destructor for classes used as base classes that have virtual functions.

- Do define a copy constructor for classes that contain pointer or reference data members.

- Do define an assignment operator for classes that contain pointer or data reference members.

- Do define assignment operators to return a **const** reference to the assigning object.

- Don't return non-**const** references or pointers to data members from **public** member functions.

- Do give derived classes access to data members by providing **protected** accessor functions.

- Do use the Standard Template Library wherever possible.

Listed as follows is a set of conventions for Java that address the issues of class structure. There are other choices that are reasonable and effective in preventing bugs.

- Do put the items in the definition of a class in the following order:
  - Class (static) variables: **public**, **protected**, **private**
  - Instance variables: **public**, **protected**, **private**
  - Constructors
  - Other methods

- Do declare each class and instance variable on a separate line.

- Don't make instance variables **public**.

- Don't make class (static) variables **public** unless they're constants.

- Do access class (static) variables or methods through the class name, not the name of an instance.

- Do initialize class (static) and instance variables in the constructor.

- Do use the Java Collections Framework classes wherever possible.

13.5.2.7 Procedure metarules

- Recommend a consistent method for listing and aligning the return types and argument lists of procedures.

- Recommend using language features to ensure type-safe procedure linkage.

- Recommend a consistent method for locating the placement of local name definitions within a procedure.

- Recommend a procedure length limit based on the semantic complexity of the procedure.

- Recommend a control structure nesting limit based on the semantic complexity of the statements.

- Recommend inserting blank lines to group related lines of text.

13.5.2.8 Procedure metarules commentary

Defining local variables where they're first assigned or initialized reduces the total number of lines of code. It also reduces the need to look back up the page for declarations. Some people prefer to find all local variable definitions in one place. Consistency is the key here.

The cyclomatic complexity of a procedure describes the control-flow graph that can be induced from that procedure. For most programming languages, it can be computed by adding one to the number of control-flow decisions. People have difficulty understanding procedures with greater complexity. The depth of nesting of control structures is another measure of the complexity of a procedure.

13.5.2.9 Procedure convention examples

Listed as follows is a set of conventions for C++ that address the issues of procedure structure. There are other choices that are reasonable and effective in preventing bugs.

- Do specify a return type for all functions.

- Do put the return type of a function on a separate line from the name of the function.

- If a function has one argument, put it on the same line as the function name.

- If a function has more than one argument, put the argument list on the line following the function name.

- Don't use unspecified function arguments with ellipsis notation.

- Do declare local variables as near to their first assignment as possible.

- Do declare all local variables in separate statements.

- Do assign a value to local variables where they're declared.

- Do prefer initializing local variables over assigning values to them.

- Do insert blank lines to group logically related statements.

Listed as follows is a set of conventions for Java that address the issues of procedure structure. There are other choices that are reasonable and effective in preventing bugs.

- Do put the return type on the same line as the method name.

- Do put the argument list on a line following the method name.

- Do put the parenthesis immediately after the method name.

- Do declare each local variable on a separate line.

- Do initialize variables where they're declared.

- Do declare variables at the beginning of the block that delimits their scope.

- Do insert blank lines to group logically related statements.

13.5.2.10 Statement metarules

- Recommend indenting and aligning nested control structures.

- Recommend safe handling of default cases for multiway branches.

- Recommend testing loops at the top whenever possible.

- Recommend starting each statement on a new line.

- Recommend writing no more than one simple statement per line.

- Recommend a method for breaking compound statements over multiple lines.

- Recommend an approach for placing blank spaces within a statement.

- Recommend an approach for using parentheses in expressions where operators have different precedence.

13.5.2.11 Statement metarules commentary

Indenting is a powerful way to show someone what control statements control other statements, if it's used consistently. Placing blank lines between groups of related statements allows the reader to "chunk" blocks of code and aids reading and comprehension.

Providing a default case for multiway branches and testing a loop at the top both make a procedure more robust. The former handles cases not explicitly listed, while the latter handles the case in which the loop shouldn't be executed.

Putting more than one statement on a line can make it difficult to stop and step in some source-level debuggers. Blank spaces are most helpful to readers when they separate groups of related characters, like a word, rather than separating individual characters. Believe it or not, the use of blank spaces between words did not occur for over a thousand years after the Phoenicians invented the alphabet.

If you're writing expressions so complicated that a few extra parentheses makes the expression spill over a line, you're probably writing expressions that should be broken into pieces. C statements with several predecrement and postincrement operators may be cute but are no longer necessary to cause a C compiler to generate efficient code. Compilers have advanced quite a bit in two decades.

13.5.2.12 Statement convention examples

Listed as follows is a set of conventions for C++ that address the issues of statement structure. There are other choices that are reasonable and effective in preventing bugs.

- Do indent four spaces for nested control-flow constructs.

- Do indent four spaces for nested class members.

- Do split lines that run over eighty characters:
  - Break after a comma.
  - Break before an operator.
  - Indent eight spaces from the left edge of the beginning of the statement.

- Do put opening braces on the same line as the keyword they're associated with.

- Do put closing braces on a separate line, indented to the same level as the associate keyword.

- Do follow the **if**, **else**, **while**, **for**, and **do** keywords with a compound statement block, rather than a simple statement, even if the block contains only one or even zero statements.

- Don't put spaces around the reference operators "." and "->" or between unary operators and their operands.

- Do put spaces between binary operators and their operands.

- Do conclude the code after a **case** statement with a **break** statement.

- Do include a **default** case in a **switch** statement.

- Avoid using **do while** loops.

- Do put each simple statement on a separate line.

- Don't assign more than one variable in a statement.

- Do parenthesize expressions with more than one operator, so that the default precedence rules are made plain.

Listed as follows is a set of conventions for Java that address the issues of statement structure. There are other choices that are reasonable and effective in preventing bugs.

- Do split lines that run over eighty characters:
  - Break after a comma.
  - Break before an operator.
  - Break after a parenthesis.

- Do indent one tab stop for nested control constructs.

- Do indent one tab stop for nested class members.

- Do put an open brace on the same line as the declaration statement.

- Do put a closing brace on a separate line, indented to the same level as the first keyword of the declaration statement.

- Do put each simple statement on a separate line.

- Don't put extra parentheses in a return statement.

- Do indent statements in a compound statement one level.

- Do put braces around the statements of a compound statement, even if there is only one statement in the block.

- Do put an open brace on the same line as a control-flow statement.

- Do put a closing brace on a separate line, indented to the same level as the first keyword of the control-flow statement.

- Do put **case** statements at the same level of indentation as the **switch** statement that controls them.

- Do indent the statements of a case one level.

- Either put a **break** statement or a comment that the case falls through at the end of every case.

- Don't assign more than one variable in an assignment statement.

- Do parenthesize the first operand of the ternary conditional operator.

- Do put a blank space after keywords that are followed by parentheses (**while, if, for, switch**).

- Do put a blank space after commas in argument lists.

- Do put a blank space between binary operators and their operands, except for the dot operator.

- Do put a blank space after semicolons in compound statements.

- Do put a blank space after cast operators.

- Avoid using **do while** loops.

13.5.2.13 Naming-convention issues

The following issues must be dealt with when considering a convention for the selection of names for program entities:

- How should nonalphabetic characters be used?

- How should upper- and lowercase letters be used?

- How should compound names be formed?

- How should acronyms and abbreviations be used?

- Under what circumstances should names be reused?

13.5.2.14 Naming-convention metarules

General issues

- Recommend choosing names that are meaningful in the application context.

- Recommend choosing names that suggest their use in the program.

- Recommend spelling names according to the rules for minimizing mistyping or misreading names.

Glyph choice

- Recommend using special characters in names only to convey extra information to a person reading your code.

- Recommend using upper- and lowercase letters to form names that help a person understand your code more quickly.

Compound names

- A compound name is formed by chaining several words from a natural language together to form a name.

- Recommend using noun phrases to create names for data, such as variables or files.

- Form noun phrases from adjectives and nouns.

- Recommend using verb phrases to create names for procedures.

- Form verb phrases by beginning with an action verb that modifies an object noun.

- Recommend forming compound names so they're easy to read and understand.

Abbreviations and acronyms

- Recommend consistent abbreviations.

- Recommend using one way to abbreviate a word in all contexts.

- Don't abbreviate a word in some places and spell it out in others.

- Recommend condensing instead of truncating abbreviations.

- Recommend condensing words by removing duplicate letters and removing easy-to-infer sounds.

Name reuse

- Don't use the same name for distinct objects in the same procedure.

13.5.2.15 Naming-convention metarules commentary

Some languages allow one or more nonalphabetic characters in user names. The underscore character is commonly used to separate words in a compound name, particularly if the name is written in all capital letters. The downside of this practice is that it makes names longer.

Some languages make no distinction between upper- and lowercase letters. Other languages do treat upper- and lowercase letters as distinct. Use upper- and lowercase letters to form names that help a person understand your code more quickly. A common use is to capitalize the first letter of each word in a compound name. Words composed of multiple adjacent capital letters are harder to read. Use capitals sparingly.

The human mind is adept at filling in missing vowels when a name is condensed by removing them. There are languages, such as Hebrew, that are written without vowels, and readers have no problem supplying them mentally.

The problem with acronyms is knowing the context in which to interpret them. CIA could mean Central Intelligence Agency or Culinary Institute of America. If you use acronyms, provide a dictionary.

Some languages, like C, allow programmers to create distinct instances of variables with the same name by using a block-structured scope. Weakly typed languages like APL allow different variables to be assigned to the same name in a single function.

13.5.2.16 Naming-convention examples

Listed as follows is a set of conventions for C++ that address the issues of name selection. There are other choices that are reasonable and effective in preventing bugs.

- Do begin the names of classes, structures, typedefs, and enumerations with an uppercase letter.

- Do begin the names of functions, variables, and constants with a lowercase letter.

- Don't begin names with an underscore.

- Do name variables with nouns or noun phrases that suggest the data that they contain.

- Do name functions with verbs or verb phrases that suggest the process they perform.

- Do use an uppercase letter for the first letter of each word after the first word in a multiword name.

- Do name accessor functions with the prefix *get* and mutator functions with the prefix *set*.

- Do name functions that return a Boolean return with the prefix *is*.

Listed as follows is a set of conventions for Java that address the issues of name selection. There are other choices that are reasonable and effective in preventing bugs.

- Do name packages with all lowercase letters. The uniquely identifying prefix should begin with *com, edu, gov, mil, net, org*, or one of the two-letter country codes.

- Do name classes and interfaces with nouns or noun phrases. The first letter of each internal word should be capitalized, including the first letter.

- Do name methods with verbs or verb phrases. The first letter of each word (except the first, which should be in lowercase) should be capitalized.

- Do name variables with nouns or noun phrases. The first letter of each word (except the first, which should be in lowercase) should be capitalized.

- Do name constants with all uppercase letters. Each word in a phrase should be separated with an underscore.

- Do name accessor functions with the prefix *get* and mutator functions with the prefix *set.*

- Do name functions that return a Boolean return with the prefix *is.*

13.5.2.17 Language-construct avoidance metarules

- Recommend avoiding language features whose implementation is platform dependent.

- Recommend avoiding language features that will be removed from a future standard.

- Recommend avoiding language features that have been superceded by constructs that are less error prone.

13.5.2.18 Language-construct avoidance metarules commentary

In almost every language, there are a few ill-considered constructs you should avoid. Most programming languages evolve. While language evolution is incremental, new ideas sometimes make old approaches obsolete.

Modern programming languages have few uses for the **goto** statement. C and C++ don't have any means to exit from inner loops other than a **goto**. If you need to implement high-level control structures, such as finite-state machines or decision tables, you will need to code them using a **goto**.

Some constructs should be avoided because they're proven error generators.

13.5.2.19 Language-construct avoidance examples

Listed as follows is a set of conventions for C++ that address the issues of construct avoidance. There are other choices that are reasonable and effective in preventing bugs.

- Don't use **goto** except to break out of loops that are multiply nested.
- Don't use **malloc**, **realloc**, or **free**.
- Don't assume that an **int** is thirty-two bits wide.
- Don't assume that pointers and integers are the same width.
- Do use **inline** functions instead of **#define** with arguments.
- Do use enumerations instead of **#define** for groups of named constants.
- Do use **const** instead of **#define** for individual named constants.
- Do use **typedef** to simplify declaration of function pointers.
- Do use the preprocessor only to compile code conditionally.

Java is a recent language without the long-term legacy of features that C or C++ have. We don't typically find lists of features to avoid in Java programming standards.

13.6   Building debugging infrastructure

13.6.1   Augmented data structures

If you know that you will have to debug a program you're developing, consider augmenting your data structures with information that will make the debugging task easier. Several different types of data can be added.

One way to augment data structures is to provide identification information that connects the data structure to the user input or the outside world.

Compiler developers normally insert the source-file name, line number, and column number into the internal representations the compiler builds while parsing a program. This enables the compiler to generate error messages that relate back to the element of the user program that is erroneous.

Optimizing compilers normally use additional representations, such as control-flow graphs, derived from the representation generated during parsing. The source-file, line, and column information must be consistently transferred to these intermediate representations. When a problem in the compiler occurs, the compiler writer can more easily trace the problem in his data structures to the user program and often create a minimal test case.

Programs that process discrete transactions can include timestamp information in data structures that are related to the transactions. Timestamps can be collected in several ways. Sometimes the most valuable information is the time of the original transaction. In other situations, it's useful to collect a string of timestamps that identify each occasion when a data structure was updated. In other situations, just the time of the most recent update is useful.

Another way to augment data structures is to provide structural redundancy. Linked lists and B-trees can be augmented to include redundant structural information. Research into augmented data structures was motivated by the desire to build fault tolerance into software. The bibliography contains several references on this subject.

When data structures have been afflicted by memory corruption, debugging can be very difficult. Data structures that contain sufficient information to detect corruption, and even to correct the problem automatically, make this task much easier. Designers of such robust structures take care to minimize both the extra space and extra time required to use them.

13.6.2   Augmented procedures

If you know that you will have to debug a program you're developing, consider augmenting your procedures with code you can use to help with debugging. Chapter 9 begins with the following tactics that involved augmenting procedures:

- Display variable values.
- Display execution messages.
- Display procedure arguments.

The refined versions of these tactics all included variants that place the output generation under the control of a preprocessing statement or a conditional statement that is evaluated at runtime. The conditional statement could either test a state variable or check whether a command-line option was used.

Besides building in the ability to display variable values, execution points, and procedure arguments, you can also consider adding the ability to store important values. In the simplest case, you may want just to assign the intermediate results of a complex calculation to a variable. This may simplify using an interactive debugger.

When debugging programs that run for a long time, such as a database system or an operating system kernel, it can be useful to accumulate a log of actions performed by the program. Normally, this log is written to a memory area for efficiency reasons. You may want to inspect the log while the program is running. To do so, you can attach an interactive debugger to the running program and display the contents of the log area. Alternatively, the logging code can provide calls that flush the log to disk when the area is full or upon request.

13.6.3 Specialized interactive debuggers

If you know that you will have to debug a program with complex data structures, consider implementing a specialized debugger. You invoke the specialized debugger by executing a procedure while running the application under a standard interactive debugger. The special debugger takes commands from the keyboard and executes procedures that implement the commands.

The Convex Application Compiler [LM94] created a Program Data Base (PDB) to represent all of the information that it collected or deduced about an application. The PDB contained a modest number of root objects, such as a programwide symbol table and a procedure call graph. A graph that represented the *contains* relationship for objects in the PDB was over ten deep for some of the root objects. The program had five phases, each of which read from and wrote to the PDB.

The Convex Application Compiler included a specialized internal debugger. Programmers typically debugged this compiler by running one or more phases of the compiler and then inspecting the PDB. At each level, the programmer could select any data member of the active object. This would reveal the data members of the selected member, and so the entire database could be traversed recursively. For members that were container objects (usually vectors), the programmer could select any item in the container.

Each object that was a part of the database was required to have several standard methods. The sketch method would display the contents of the object without recursively traversing the contents of the contained objects. Pointers were simply shown as hexadecimal numbers. The dump method would recursively display the object and all the contained objects, using the most human-readable form possible. For example, enumeration constants were shown with literal tags, rather than integer values.

13.6.4 Assertions

An assertion is a test to confirm the truth condition that should be true. If the test is true, nothing happens. If the test is false, a message is printed, and the program stops. Assertions prevent programs from executing when the assumptions they make aren't valid.

Some people practice contractual programming. This doesn't refer to how the programmer is paid, but the relationship between calling procedures and called procedures. The language Eiffel has built-in features that support the concept of the contract. The calling procedure promises that certain conditions will be true when it makes a call. The called procedure promises that certain conditions will be true when it has completed.

There is no real need for language features to support assertions, since a simple conditional test and I/O statement provide the necessary support. You can assert the assumptions a procedure makes before it starts work and assert the conditions it guarantees to be true before it returns. Be careful not to include any code in an assertion that causes side effects, such as assignments or input/output. If you include these, and turn off assertion checking, the behavior of your program will change in mystifying ways.

13.7 Review

Two important values that traditional engineering and software development share are their emphasis on defect prevention and learning from past failures. The software-development phases of design, coding, and testing correspond to the engineering stages of preliminary design, detail design, and development.

Engineers designing tangible objects apply mathematical analysis of physical laws to determine the reliability of an object. Software developers don't have an analogous method. They both do peer reviews of their work.

Engineers designing tangible objects produce pictorial and textual descriptions of the object to be built or manufactured. Software developers also generate pictorial and textual descriptions of programs and the methods for building them.

Engineers designing tangible objects follow standards and codes when implementing a detailed design. Software developers should also follow standards when they are coding programs.

We can identify the three stages of coding a program as conception, expression, and transcription. In the conception stage, a program is couched in a language-independent notation. In the expression stage, the programmer encodes the algorithm in a specific programming language. In both of these stages, the activity may be entirely in the programmer's mind, with no physical embodiment.

Expression-stage errors can occur in two ways: (1) the programmer can write a program that is invalid in the target programming language or (2) write a valid program that doesn't say what he or she meant to write. Expression-stage errors that aren't caught by the compiler are analogous to the subtle grammatical mistakes made by someone speaking in a second language. Languages that require the compiler to accept questionable source code mask many expression-stage errors. Languages that require the compiler to reject such code expose these errors at compile time.

In the transcription stage, the programmer embodies the program in a machine-readable medium. Transcription mistakes are trivial to correct, but they can result in valid programs that don't express the intent of the programmer.

There are two main ways to avoid conception-stage errors: (1) you can write out the design in a textual or graphical format or (2) you can implement a prototype. Avoid errors in your code by writing out the design in some design medium. Without a design to compare to an implementation, there is really no objective way to assess whether a behavior is a conception-stage bug. An alternative to traditional design methods is building a prototype. A prototype can be thought of as an implementation with a set of simplifying assumptions or as a scale model of the implementation.

There are two main ways to avoid expression-stage errors: (1) you can exploit redundancy by adding information that will show errors at compile or execution time; and (2) you can also use nitpicking tools to identify potential problems that compilers must overlook.

There are two main ways to avoid transcription-stage errors: (1) you can exploit redundancy by adding information that will show errors at compile or execution time and (2) you can also compensate for human psychology by a variety of methods.

A programming convention is a set of choices made by an individual or group of programmers to code in a certain style to achieve their goals. There is rarely only one reasonable choice for any given coding style issue. Consistency in coding reduces the creation of errors and makes it easier for a programmer to diagnose and correct problems in a program.

The organizing principle for our approach to programming conventions is object-oriented programming. Rather than provide a set of specific conventions, we specify metarules from which a variety of consistent conventions may be generated. We divide our rules into the following categories: objects, source files, procedures, statements, names, and avoided constructs.

Data structures can be augmented for debugging with identification information that connects the data structure to the user input or the outside world. They can also be augmented with redundant structural information that makes it possible to detect and recover from memory corruption problems.

Procedures can be augmented for debugging with output that is generated when a preprocessor includes the code, or when a conditional statement evaluates to true at runtime. They can also be augmented by accumulating a log of actions performed by the program, which is stored in memory or written to disk.

Applications that have complex data structures can include a specialized debugger. This debugger is invoked from a standard interactive debugger and enables the programmer to navigate and display recursive data structures.

Assertions prevent programs from executing when the assumptions that they make aren't valid. You can assert the assumptions a procedure makes before it starts to work and assert the conditions it guarantees to be true before it returns.

14

The Way of the Computer Scientist

> *The power of using abstractions is the essence of intellect, and with every increase in abstraction the intellectual triumphs are enhanced.*
>
> —*Bertrand Russell*

14.1 Preview

This chapter views finding defects from the perspective of computer science. The first section explains the worldview of the computer scientist.

The first section of this chapter describes how programming errors can be classified by linguistic formalisms. It presents the classic definition of the Chomsky hierarchy. It defines each of the levels of the hierarchy and explains the phase of a compiler that might employ techniques from that level.

The second section of this chapter describes how programming errors can be detected by linguistic formalisms. It explains that the front end of a compiler performs lexical, syntactic, and semantic analysis, and not all compilers find the same defects. It considers each of these forms of analysis in turn, noting defects that they can identify.

The third section of this chapter introduces a number of tools that can be used in the process of debugging. This section motivates those who have access to such tools and encourages their use; it motivates those who don't have access to such tools to get them. In each case, examples are provided for the relevant tools. The common thread that runs through this section is examining the kinds of information required for the tool to work. This section extends the information presented in Chapter 8 on debugging tactics by showing how debugging tools can enhance a programmer's effectiveness.

14.2   The worldview of the computer scientists

When we follow the way of the computer scientist, we treat defective software as processes that fail to manipulate symbols correctly. Computer science studies symbol manipulation by digital electronics. Some of the theoretical concepts of computer science for classifying and analyzing information can be applied to the process of debugging. Computer scientists advance their discipline by inventing layers of tools that can be composed into larger systems. When we follow the way of the computer scientist, we will also consider tools that can automatically diagnose software defects.

14.3   Classifying errors by linguistic formalism

14.3.1   Chomsky hierarchy

A grammar is a set of rules that define how to generate valid sentences in a language. Noam Chomsky defined a hierarchy of increasingly complex grammars and corresponding methods for recognizing the sentences that those grammars generate. Grammars are defined by four sets:

1.   Terminals are the strings of characters used in the language.

2.   Nonterminals are names to associate with sequences of strings and other nonterminals.

3.   The start symbol is the name given to the nonterminal that includes all other nonterminals.

4.   The rules define the legitimate sequences for the language. Rules have left- and right-hand sides. Rules determine possible substitutions.

14.3.1.1   The Chomsky hierarchy

Type	Grammar	Recognizer
3	Regular	Finite-state automaton
2	Context-free	Push-down automaton
1	Context-sensitive	Turing machine
0	Phrase-structure	None

14.3.1.2   Regular grammars

It is possible to describe the valid words in most high-level programming languages using regular grammars. The phase of a compiler that determines the valid sequences of strings or words is the lexical analyzer (or lexer). Lexical analyzers for languages that can be analyzed with regular grammars are usually created with special tools that generate the analyzer. Handwritten lexical analyzers are sometimes preferred, either for performance reasons or because the language contains some features that make it impractical to use a generated lexical analyzer.

14.3.1.3   Context-free grammars

It is possible to describe the valid sentences in most high-level programming languages using context-free grammars. The phase of a compiler that determines the valid sequences of strings or words is the syntactic analyzer (or parser). Syntactic analyzers for languages that can be analyzed with context-free grammars are usually created with special tools that generate the analyzer. Handwritten syntactic analyzers are sometimes preferred, either for performance reasons or because the language contains some features that make it impractical to use a generated syntactic analyzer.

14.3.1.4   Context-sensitive grammars

Context-sensitive grammars can be used to describe valid programs in many languages. It is difficult to write them and computationally expensive to use them.

Because of the drawbacks of context-sensitive grammars, most modern compilers use a context-free grammar to describe the valid syntax of a procedure, augmented with various techniques to handle the context-sensitive issues.

To verify the context-sensitive aspects of a program, some compilers use a hand-coded program that checks the results of performing the syntactic analysis. Other compilers use a combination of a hand-coded program and an attribute grammar. The phase of a compiler that determines the valid procedures is the semantic analyzer.

The semantic analyzer performs context-sensitive analysis by referring to additional data structures as it examines its representation of the program:

- Symbol tables

- Control-flow information
- Data-flow information

Each of these data structures can represent information for a single procedure or for the entire program.

14.3.1.5   Phrase-structure grammar

Writing these grammars is very difficult. Executing tools that parse these grammars is very intensive computationally. We know of no practical use for them at the present time.

14.4   Detecting programming errors by linguistic formalism

The front end of a compiler performs lexical, syntactic, and semantic analysis. Not all compilers find the same defects. The more information a compiler has, the more defects it can find. Some compilers operate in a "forgiving" mode but have a "strict" or "pedantic" mode, if you request it.

14.4.1   Regular grammars

Lexical analyzers can find the following errors:

- Characters in the source that aren't in the alphabet of the language
- Words in the source that aren't in the vocabulary of the language

14.4.2   Context-free grammars

Syntactic analyzers for fixed-form languages such as Fortran and COBOL can find the following errors:

- Required fields that haven't been used
- Incorrect values in a field
- Invalid continuations of statements across multiple lines
- Keywords that have been misspelled
- Required punctuation that is missing
- Delimiters such as parentheses that are missing

- Blank or tab characters that are missing

- Blank or tab characters that shouldn't occur where they're found

Syntactic analyzers for free-form languages such as C++ and Java can find the following errors:

- Comment delimiters that have been put in the wrong place or omitted

- Literal delimiters that have been put in the wrong place or omitted

- Keywords that have been misspelled

- Required punctuation that is missing

- Construct delimiters such as parentheses or braces that have been misplaced

- Blank or tab characters that are missing

- Blank or tab characters that shouldn't occur where they're found

14.4.3   Semantic analysis

If a semantic analyzer has a symbol table for each separate procedure, it can find semantic errors that occur because of the following mistakes:

- Names that aren't declared

- Operands of the wrong type for the operator they're used with

- Values that have the wrong type for the name to which they're assigned

If a semantic analyzer has a symbol table for the program as a whole, it can find semantic errors that occur because of the following mistakes:

- Procedures that are invoked with the wrong number of arguments

- Procedures that are invoked with the wrong type of arguments

- Function return values that are the wrong type for the context in which they're used

If a semantic analyzer has control-flow and data-flow information for each separate procedure, it can find semantic errors that occur because of the following mistakes:

- Code blocks that are unreachable

- Code blocks that have no effect

- Local variables that are used before being initialized or assigned

- Local variables that are initialized or assigned but not used

If a semantic analyzer has control-flow and data-flow information for the program as a whole, it can find semantic errors that occur because of the following mistakes:

- Procedures that are never invoked

- Procedures that have no effect

- Global variables that are used before being initialized or assigned

- Global variables that are initialized or assigned, but not used

14.5   Static-analysis tools

Chapter 9 discussed debugging tactics that can be used with the tools that every programmer has available. These include a text editor and a language translator, either a compiler, interpreter, or assembler. In addition, most programmers have access to an interactive debugger, either at the high-level-language or assembly-language level. This section, and the following one, complement that chapter. They discuss advanced debugging techniques that can only be done with the aid of sophisticated tools.

We want to find bugs beyond those that can be identified by compilers. Compilers use semantic analysis augmented with symbol tables and control-flow and data-flow information to find the defects described previously. To find additional bugs, it's necessary to develop additional information about the behavior of the program.

There are two main approaches to developing this information. The first approach is static analysis. Static analysis derives information prior to execution, usually at compile time.

There are two techniques used in static analysis: rule evaluation and symbolic execution. Rule evaluation first matches parts of the representation of the program with representations of problem program fragments. It executes a set of instructions for each match. Symbolic execution first creates an abstract representation of some aspect of the computation. It then evaluates each part of that representation in an order derived from the application.

Symbolic execution can be flow sensitive or insensitive. Flow-sensitive execution means that the flow of control of the original program is simulated in some fashion. Flow-insensitive execution means that the simulation is sequential, without the possibility of conditional or iterative execution. Flow-sensitive symbolic execution is normally more expensive, both in time and space.

The other approach to developing extra information about the behavior of a program is dynamic analysis. Dynamic analysis derives information at application runtime.

Dynamic information can be collected by modifying the source files, modifying the object files, linking in different libraries, modifying the application executable, or running a separate process to monitor the behavior of the original.

14.5.1 Static analysis

There are several reasons why static analysis may be more effective than dynamic analysis in diagnosing a problem. Static analysis evaluates all code in an application. It can find defects in code not exercised by a particular test run. Actually running an application may take significant resources in a production environment. Sometimes those resources aren't available to developers. Static analysis can be done offline in a development environment.

On the other hand, static evaluation isn't without its drawbacks. Static analysis requires source code, which normally excludes system and third-party libraries from the analysis. Static analysis often takes more time than dynamic analysis.

14.5.2 Splint

Splint is an open-source tool for statically checking C programs. It is available for download from www.splint.org. *Splint* is a derivative of *LCLint*, which was developed by MIT and DEC SRC [GH93].

It can be used as a substitute for UNIX™ *lint.* By adding annotations to programs, it can perform stronger checks than any standard *lint* can. Annotations are stylized comments that document assumptions about functions, variables, arguments, and types.

14.5.2.1 Features

The following problems, among others, can be detected by *Splint* with just source code:

- Unused declarations

- Type inconsistencies

- Variables used before being assigned

- Function return values that are ignored

- Execution paths with no return

- Switch cases that fall through

- Apparent infinite loops

The following problems, among others, can be detected by *Splint* with annotation information:

- Dereferencing pointers with possible null values

- Using storage that is undefined or partly undefined

- Returning storage that is undefined or partly defined

- Type mismatches

- Using deallocated storage

- Memory leaks

- Inconsistent modification of caller visible states

- Unexpected aliasing or data-sharing errors

- Inconsistent use of global variables

- Violations of information hiding

- Undefined program behavior due to evaluation order, incomplete logic, infinite loops, statements with no effect, and so on

- Problematic uses of macros

14.5.2.2   **Technology**

Special comments, called annotations, are used to provide extra information about types, variables, and functions. These comments start and end with the "at" sign (@).

Splint provides several hundred command-line options to control its error checking:

- Global options control initialization.

- Message format options control message display.

- Mode selectors provide coarse control of checking.

- Checking options select checks and the classes of reported messages.

Global options are used on the command line or in initialization files. The other options can be used in control comments in the source as well.

Splint detects null pointer dereferences by analyzing pointers at procedure interface boundaries. If this checking is turned on, the program must protect all dereferences to possible null pointers with either guard statements or annotations that declare the safety of various pointer constructs.

Splint detects local variable references that may occur before a valid value is assigned to the variable. Unless references are annotated, the storage referred to by global variables, function arguments, and function return values must be defined before and after function calls.

Instead of treating user-defined enumeration as integers, *Splint* treats each enumeration as a distinct type. Similarly, instead of treating **char** data as integers, *Splint* treats it as a distinct type. *Splint* also provides a Boolean type that is treated differently from integers, making it possible to check for common errors in control-flow statements.

Splint detects memory leaks and the use of invalid pointers with annotations that document the assumptions about function interfaces, pointer variables, type definitions, and structure fields. It uses the concept of deallocation obligations, which occur at certain points in the program, to detect deallocation problems. If the assumptions about pointers are completely documented, the tool can assure the programmer that some memory management errors never occur. In contrast, dynamic tools can only provide the assurance that those errors don't occur when executing specific test cases.

While C++ provides built-in language features for object-oriented programming, those who must use C can also benefit from some of its features through the use of *Splint*. It detects when the representation of an abstract type is exposed, which occurs when a user of an object has a pointer to storage that is part of an object instance. Not only can it identify these types of information-hiding violations, but it can also detect other related problems such as modifications of string literals.

Splint takes the concept of the prototype in ANSI C to its logical conclusion. It enables the programmer to specify what global variables a function uses and what side effects it can cause. It also provides a general-purpose facility for describing predicates that must be true on entry to or exit from a function.

14.5.2.3   Usage

Under what circumstances does it make sense to use *Splint*? First, *Splint* only handles C source code, not C++ or Java. There are still many large programs written in C. In some cases, there is a large prior investment in code. In other cases, a C++ compiler isn't available for the target hardware. In still other cases, the C++ development environment may not be competitive with the C development environment in some respect.

The second constraint on *Splint* usage is the investment in annotations. If the program will be in use for a relatively long time, the extra effort required to add annotations will pay off in quicker diagnosis of defects. If there will be more than one person doing maintenance on the program, the explanatory benefit of the annotations can be significant.

The third constraint on *Splint* usage is the relative priority of security. If the application being checked will be in wide public usage in a way that could be used to attack system security, the investment in annotation is easily justified. *Splint* is supported by a research group that specializes in security issues. It is particularly effective at finding certain kinds of problems that are commonly exploited by hackers.

14.5.3   CodeSurfer

14.5.3.1   Features

CodeSurfer is a product of GrammaTech for statically analyzing C programs. It is available on Windows™ platforms, Solaris™, and Linux™.

A **slice** is a collection of all the code that contributes to the computation of a value. A slice can be computed strictly from static data-flow graphs, or it can be constrained by actual statements executed. Research going back twenty years shows that programmers think in terms of slices when they debug [We82b].

CodeSurfer analyzes the application as a whole to generate the following information:

- Data predecessors are those assignments whose values may be used by a statement.

- Control predecessors are the control statements that may affect whether a statement is executed.

- Data successors are those program elements that may use the values assigned by a statement.

- Control successors are the statements whose execution depends on control-flow choices made by a statement.

- Backward slicing shows all the program elements that may affect a specified statement.

- Forward slicing shows all the program elements that may be affected by executing a specified statement.

- Chopping shows all the ways one set of program elements affects another set of program elements.

CodeSurfer doesn't currently perform dynamic slicing, which is sometimes called **dicing.** This would require the use of an execution profile.

The results of analysis can be used both from an interactive tool (*CodeSurfer*) and through an API for the Scheme programming language. The interactive tool supports queries of the developed analyses from the perspective of selected variables, selected variables used in particular program elements, and selected functions. You can create complex queries through the use of a set calculator.

The interactive tool creates a number of graphs that you can navigate. This navigation is done in a manner analogous to using a Web browser. The links between program elements aren't inserted into program text. Instead, they're collected into property sheets, which you can activate by clicking the appropriate program element.

14.5.3.2 Technology

Interprocedural control- and data-flow analysis are essential to compute useful slices. *CodeSurfer* does both. To understand C programs, it's essential to do pointer-target analysis, which *CodeSurfer* also does [LMSS91].

You can increase the performance of pointer-target analysis, as well as the other dependency analysis algorithms, by selecting settings that generate less-precise results. Pointer-target analysis in *CodeSurfer* is insensitive to flow of control within a procedure and to function invocation among procedures. The results of flow-sensitive analysis would provide more precise results.

CodeSurfer doesn't currently apply the results of its dependence analysis to do interprocedural constant (or value) propagation [MS93]. This analysis could be fed back into control-flow analysis, resulting in more precise slices.

CodeSurfer doesn't currently apply the results of its dependence analysis to do interprocedural array subscript analysis. This analysis would result in more precise slices.

14.5.3.3 Usage

Chapter 7 describes a strategy for using a slice browser. First, you use a backwards slice to identify those program elements that are related to a given statement. Then you recursively investigate those elements looking for the source of the problem. Once you have identified a change to fix the problem, you use a forward slice from the point of the change to identify those program elements that will be affected by your proposed change.

At the time of this writing, *CodeSurfer* only supports the C language. Hopefully, by the time you read this book, it will also support C++. Currently, the vendor says that 100,000 lines of code is a reasonable limit on the size of the application that *CodeSurfer* can handle. Hopefully, by the time you read this book, this limit will have been increased.

There are some limitations on its effectiveness. Currently, *CodeSurfer* doesn't represent the dependencies introduced by the following features of ANSI C:

- **union**
- **setjmp/longjmp**
- Signals
- Volatile storage

- System calls such as **exec** and **abort** that terminate an application

This means that if your problem is related to the use of these features, *CodeSurfer* won't identify them as dependencies of the statement where you identified the problem.

14.5.4   PC-lint/FlexeLint

PC-lint is a product of Gimpel Software for statically checking C and C++ programs. It is available on all Windows™ platforms. The corresponding tool, *FlexeLint,* is available on UNIX™, Linux™, and other popular operating systems.

14.5.4.1   Features

PC-lint provides the traditional rule-based *lint* features. It also implements value tracking both within and across function boundaries. It provides the means for C programmers to perform strong type checking through the use of **typedef.**

The most recent version of *PC-lint* has more than eight hundred error messages. It also provides more than one hundred command-line options, so you have complete control over the messages you wish to see.

14.5.4.2   Technology

PC-lint employs a number of different methods for identifying errors or likely errors. It uses control-flow and data-flow analysis to find the following errors, which are normally found by optimizing compilers:

- Uninitialized simple and aggregate variables
- Unused variables and functions
- Variables that are assigned, but not used
- Code that is unreachable

PC-lint compares expressions to common error patterns to find the following types of errors:

- Likely problems with operator precedence

- Constant inputs to control-flow statements
- Empty statements in problematic places
- Undefined order of evaluation for expressions
- Insufficient or excessive initializers

PC-lint uses language-specific analyses to find the several dozen different errors in C++ code that aren't detected by some C++ compilers, including the following:

- Constructor misuses
- Destructor misuses
- Initializer misuses
- Exception misuses

PC-lint uses analysis of the numerical types and precision of expressions to find the following types of errors:

- Loss of precision in expressions
- Mixing signed and unsigned integer expressions
- Overflow evaluating constant expressions
- Constant expressions that reduce to zero
- Unsigned comparisons with zero

PC-lint uses a scan of preprocessor macros to find the following types of errors:

- Using an expression as a macro parameter that isn't parenthesized
- Using an expression with side effects as a macro parameter that is repeated
- Macros that are unparenthesized expressions

PC-lint uses an analysis of language constructs that only exist at compile time to find the following types of errors:

- Unused macros, typedefs, declarations, structs, unions, enums, classes, and templates
- Unused header files
- Externals that can be declared static
- Declarations that can be removed from header files

PC-lint uses procedural and interprocedural value tracking to find the following types of errors:

- Boolean expressions that always evaluate to the same result
- Dereferencing a null pointer
- Passing a null pointer to library functions
- Dereferencing a pointer that doesn't point to value memory
- Failure to deallocate dynamic memory
- Incorrect deallocation of dynamic memory

In *PC-lint*, value tracking associates a set of values that are bound to local variables, arguments, and class data members. These values can be bound by assignment, passing arguments, and returning results. Not only are the values associated with the name, but also the source code locations that contributed to generating the value.

While C++ provides built-in language features for object-oriented programming, those who must use C can also benefit from some of its features through the use of *PC-lint*. *PC-lint* provides features that allow the C programmer to use strong typing. Thus, the relationship between **typedef** references are examined strictly by name, rather than by equivalence of implementation. Command-line options are provided to control the nature of type checking, to add array subscripts as special types, and to create an inheritance hierarchy of types.

14.5.4.3   Usage

The best way to use a static checking tool is by continually keeping your source code clean of those messages reported by the tool that you know are more likely to indicate bugs. Some reports from these tools have such a low yield of real bugs that you're better off ignoring them. On the other hand, for those reports that you know have a meaningful possibility of indicating a real bug, you should investigate them immediately and resolve the problem.

If you're starting a new project and plan to use *PC-lint*, decide which of its messages you will be concerned about, turn them on, and resolve them frequently. Some projects do a nightly build of their software, and this is an excellent time to run a static analyzer. First thing in the morning, you can resolve all of the reports, in addition to any bugs turned up by nightly testing. Don't let a backlog develop. The inevitable result of accumulating a backlog is that you will turn off the messages and eventually stop using the tool altogether.

If you're doing maintenance of an existing project and have decided to use *PC-lint* at this point in the project life cycle, it's important to schedule time to resolve all the reports this tool will generate. Once you have decided which reports you will be concerned about, resolve all of them and follow a zero-tolerance policy so they don't creep back in.

In either case, it's instructive to keep a record of the percentage of reports that actually indicate a real defect. Even for the most important messages, this will still be only a modest fraction of the total. Even if only 5 percent of the messages point to a problem, that could translate to dozens of defects that weren't being found by your other methods of testing.

14.6   Dynamic-analysis tools

14.6.1   Dynamic analysis

There are several reasons why dynamic analysis may be more effective than static analysis in diagnosing a bug. Dynamic analysis can include system and third-party libraries. Source code isn't required. Dynamic analysis only evaluates code that is executed. This is likely to take less system time than static analysis. With dynamic analysis, an error is caught right before it occurs.

On the other hand, dynamic analysis isn't perfect. Dynamic analysis only evaluates code that is executed. It won't find defects in code not exercised by your tests. To get the full benefit from a dynamic-analysis tool, you need a comprehensive test suite in place. You should also have a test coverage tool that will enable you to determine whether your test suite actually exercises all parts of your application.

14.6.2   **Insure++**

Insure++ is a product of ParaSoft. It is available on Windows™, as well as on popular versions of UNIX™ and Linux™.

14.6.2.1   **Features**

Insure++ detects the following pointer-reference problems:

- References to null pointers
- References to uninitialized pointers
- References to pointers that don't point to valid memory locations
- Comparison of pointers that point to different memory blocks
- Attempts to execute functions through pointer references that don't actually point to functions

Insure++ detects the following memory-leak problems:

- Freeing blocks of memory that contain pointers to other blocks of memory
- Functions that ignore pointers to storage allocated by a subfunction and returned as a result
- Functions that return without freeing storage pointed to by local pointers

Insure++ detects the following miscellaneous pointer problems:

- Freeing a memory block more than once
- Freeing static memory (global variables)
- Freeing stack memory (local variables)
- Applying **free** or **delete** to an address that isn't the beginning of an allocated memory block
- Applying **free** or **delete** to a null or uninitialized pointer

- Passing invalid arguments to **malloc**, **calloc**, **realloc**, or **free**
- Mismatching invocations of **new []** and **delete []**
- Mixing allocation using **malloc**, **calloc**, **realloc**, or **free**
- Invalid overloading of operators **new** and **delete**

Insure++ detects the following library API errors:

- Mismatched argument types
- Invalid argument values
- Errors returned by library functions

The system knows how to check system calls and X/Motif API calls, as well as other popular libraries.

### 14.6.2.2	Technology

To get the full benefit of *Insure++*, you must recompile your source code, using the tool instead of your normal compiler. If you want to use the tool in *Chaperon* mode, you don't need to recompile or relink. This mode doesn't do error checking as extensively as normal mode. It operates on the executable program. The *Chaperon* mode slows down the application, but not nearly as much as the normal mode. *Insure++* is based on patented technology (U.S. Patents 5,581,696 and 5,842,019), which is the basis for the following description:

The normal mode of operation for *Insure++* is Source Code Instrumentation mode. In this mode, the tool is invoked instead of a compiler. The tool parses your program and identifies constructs that must be tracked at runtime. It generates revised source code for the constructs that must be monitored and passes this code to your regular compiler. When you run your program, the tool checks data values and memory references against a database to verify consistency and correctness.

There are seven types of instrumentation described in U.S. Patent 5,581,696:

1.	Detecting a read of an uninitialized simple variable

2.   Detecting a read or write through an invalid address for an aggregate variable

3.   Detecting a dynamic-memory error while using a pointer variable

4.   Detecting an invalid use of a pointer variable

5.   Detecting a memory leak

6.   Detecting a function call argument error

7.   User-definable instrumentation

To find reads of uninitialized simple variables, *Insure++* places calls to runtime procedures in two places. After space is allocated on the stack for the variable, it calls the runtime library to record its uninitialized state. Before the value of the variable is referenced, it makes another call that checks whether the variable has been assigned since the previous call.

To find reads or writes through an invalid address for an aggregate variable, *Insure++* places calls to runtime procedures in two places. After the declaration of an aggregate variable, *Insure++* places a call to the runtime library to record the length of a homogeneous aggregate (array) or the size of an inhomogeneous aggregate (structure). Before the value of an element is referenced or assigned, it calls a runtime routine that checks whether the address generated is within the bounds of the aggregate.

There are six problems that *Insure++* categorizes as dynamic-memory errors while using a pointer variable:

1.   Reading from or writing through an invalid pointer

2.   Passing an invalid pointer as a function argument

3.   Returning an invalid pointer as a function result

4.   Freeing the same memory block more than once

5.   Freeing addresses that are on the stack

6.   Freeing addresses that don't point to the beginning of a memory block

To find errors using pointer variables, *Insure++* places calls to runtime procedures in several places. After the declaration of a pointer variable, *Insure++* places a call to the runtime library that generates a record of the pointer variable and its contents. After memory allocation operations that are assigned to a pointer variable, it makes a call to record the size and starting address of the memory block, addresses of pointers that point to or are contained by the memory block, and miscellaneous information. After assignments to pointer variables, it makes a call to note that the pointer contents may be changed or invalid.

Once these are set up, it's possible to check for dynamic-memory errors. Before a pointer variable is used to read or write memory, a call is made to check that the pointer contains a valid address. Before a pointer variable is passed as an argument or is returned as a result, it makes a call to check that the pointer contains a valid address. Before a memory deallocation, it makes a call to check that the address being freed isn't already freed, isn't a stack address, and is the start of a memory block.

There are five problems that *Insure++* categorizes as invalid uses of a pointer variable:

1.   Operating on a null pointer

2.   Operating on an uninitialized pointer

3.   Operating on a pointer that doesn't point to valid data

4.   Comparing pointers that point to different objects

5.   Invoking a function through a pointer that doesn't point to a function

To find errors operating on pointer variables, *Insure++* places calls to runtime procedures in two places. After the declaration of a pointer variable, *Insure++* places a call to the runtime library that generates a record of the pointer variable and its contents. Before operations on the value of a pointer variable, *Insure++* places a call to the runtime library that checks that none of the five problems mentioned above occur.

There are three problems that *Insure++* categorizes as memory-leak errors:

1.   An assignment to the only variable containing the address of a memory block before that block is freed

2.   Returning the address of a memory block as a function result and not assigning that return value to a pointer variable

3.   Returning from a function before freeing all memory blocks that are pointed to by local pointer variables

To find memory-leak errors, *Insure++* places calls to runtime procedures in two places. After the declaration of a pointer variable, *Insure++* places a call to the runtime library that generates a record of the pointer variable and its contents. Before operations that decrease the stack size, *Insure++* places a call to the runtime library to note that local variables have gone out of scope. When these calls are evaluated, the runtime library checks to see if any memory blocks were only pointed to by local pointer variables. To increase the effectiveness of its leak tracking, *Insure++* supplements the tracking described above with a reference count for memory blocks. *Insure++* uses both a dynamic search for leaked blocks and a static scan through allocated memory at the end of program execution.

14.6.2.3   Usage

As with all dynamic techniques, the checking done by *Insure++* is only as good as the coverage of the code that results from the test suite you use. *Insure++* can be licensed with an optional module that does test coverage analysis. Use this optional module to increase your confidence level with the problem reports *Insure++* generates.

14.6.3   BoundsChecker

BoundsChecker is a product of Compuware Corporation. It is available on Windows™ operating systems. It checks memory error and API calls in C and C++ source code.

14.6.3.1   Features

You can use *BoundsChecker* in two modes. In *ActiveCheck* mode, you use *BoundsChecker* with Microsoft Visual Studio. When you run your program in Visual Studio, *BoundsChecker* will run in the background checking for errors. When the tool finds a bug, it stops your application and displays the error description, the call stack, and the source line where the problem occurred.

In *FinalCheck* mode, you use *BoundsChecker* with standalone Windows™ applications. As you build your application, *BoundsChecker* inserts error-detection code into the intermediate representation used by the

Visual C++ compiler. When your application runs, the inserted code finds memory and pointer errors as before.

BoundsChecker finds pointer errors and memory leaks in the usage of static, automatic (stack), and dynamic (heap) memory.

BoundsChecker validates calls to Windows™, ODBC, ActiveX, DirectX, COM, and Internet APIs. It will check for the following API errors:

- Invalid parameters

- Invalid return codes

- Wrong number of parameters

- Out-of-range parameters

- Invalid flags

- Uninitialized fields

- Invalid pointers

You can extend it to check calls to custom libraries (DLLs) that you produce.

You can customize the analysis and output of *BoundsChecker* to fit your needs. You can control which types of errors to check for, which files and modules to check, and which reports to suppress. You can also control which Windows™ version should be used to check for API errors.

14.6.3.2 **Technology**

BoundsChecker instruments the intermediate representation generated by the Visual C++ compiler. Modifying this representation is faster than generating modified source code. *BoundsChecker* doesn't have to write and read the modified source file or analyze the lexical and syntactic structure of the modified program. These time savings can speed up the edit-compile-run cycle significantly in a large program.

Modifying the compiler's internal representation provides more context information than modifying the object code. Tools that modify object code can't relate an error back to source code without extra annotations provided by the compiler, which may or may not be available.

These points are advantages over the competitors of *BoundsChecker*, *Insure++*, and *Purify*. The downside of its tight integration with the Visual

C++ compiler is that it is only available on Windows™ platforms. In addition, version 7.0 and beyond of *BoundsChecker* don't support Windows 98.

14.6.3.3 Usage

As with all dynamic techniques, the checking done by *BoundsChecker* is only as good as the coverage of the code that results from the test suite you use. *BoundsChecker* can be licensed with an optional module, *TrueCoverage,* which does test coverage analysis. Use this optional module to increase your confidence level with the problem reports *BoundsChecker* generates.

14.6.4 Purify

Purify is a product of the Rational Corporation. It is available on Windows™ and UNIX™ operating systems. It checks memory errors and API calls in C and C++ source code, and garbage-collection problems in Java code.

14.6.4.1 Features

The following problems are found by *Purify:*

- Reading or writing beyond memory block bounds

- Reading or writing freed memory

- Freeing memory multiple times

- Reading uninitialized memory

- Reading or writing through invalid or null pointers

- Reading or writing beyond stack end

- Overflowing the stack

- Memory leaks

- File descriptor leaks

- Windows™ API usage errors

- COM API usage errors

The Windows™ product is integrated with Microsoft Visual Studio, and the UNIX™ product provides a GUI. The level of checking can be set to minimal or precise.

14.6.4.2 **Technology**

Purify works by modifying the object code used to build your application. This means that it's useful for debugging assembly code, as well as code generated by compilers. It will even modify object code that comes from system libraries. Of course, there isn't much you can do with problems for which you don't have the source code, except report them to someone else. *Purify* is based on patented technology (U.S. Patent 5,335,344), which is the basis for the following description:

Purify modifies object files, which originate from compiled code, assembled code, or archive libraries. It inserts instructions in front of every instruction that accesses data from memory. These instructions call functions from a special library. After inserting the instructions, it performs necessary changes to symbol tables, instruction-relocation structures, or data-relocation structures as needed.

Purify monitors the state of memory with two bits of state per byte of accessible memory. One bit refers to the allocation status of the memory; the other bit refers to the initialization status. The extra instructions that are inserted before the original set read these bits to detect invalid memory accesses.

Purify also modifies the data sections of object files to insert dummy storage around the original application variables. It notes that these dummy variables are unallocated and uninitialized, as far as the original application is concerned, and thus any attempt to read or write them is an error.

To check access to stack memory, *Purify* inserts code before instructions that change the stack pointer. Increasing the stack is treated as a memory allocation, and decreasing it as a deallocation. *Purify* uses the same checking methods for heap and stack memory. Rather than look up each byte in the stack, *Purify* uses a shortcut convention where it compares the address to be accessed with the current stack pointer. If the address is beyond the stack pointer, the memory is treated as unallocated.

To track the allocation and deallocation of heap memory, *Purify* replaces references to **malloc** and **free** with references to functions in the *Purify* library. These functions call the original library functions after they record information in the *Purify* data structures about the memory allocated or freed.

Purify provides for watch points to be set on monitored memory by recording a state of unallocated and uninitialized for the address and putting the address on a special list. When a reference to the address is detected, the address is looked up on the list of watch points; if it's found, the watch point procedure is called instead of normal error reporting.

14.6.4.3 Usage

Under what circumstances does it make sense to use *Purify*? *Purify* handles C and C++ source code. Most of its features aren't relevant to Java because of error-checking features built into that language. It does, however, provide support for the analysis of garbage-collection issues in Java.

The *Purify* literature says that it performs checks for "array bound read and write errors." It defines an array as a block of contiguous memory. This isn't the same as array-subscript checking. *Purify* doesn't deal with array subscripts, but with addresses.

Purify will find array-subscript errors for simple arrays, which are the vast majority of arrays used in typical C and C++ code. It is possible, however, to have array-subscript errors in arrays of arrays, in which the address generated from subscript calculations is wrong, but is within the bounds of the memory block. *Purify* will not, in general, find these errors.

14.6.5 mpatrol

mpatrol is an open-source memory allocation library that can help you find runtime memory problems. A comprehensive set of tools is provided with the library to make it useful for a variety of memory debugging tasks. It will work with both C and C++ memory allocation functionality. It has been ported to Windows™, Linux™, and numerous UNIX™ implementations. It is available for download from several Web sites, including SourceForge (sourceforge.net/projects/*mpatrol*) and FreshMeat (freshmeat.net.projects.*mpatrol*).

14.6.5.1 Features

The level of modification that you must make to your application depends on the operating system you're using. In some cases, you must relink your application to use *mpatrol*. In other cases, you can attach it to your application when it executes. To use it as a substitute for the other dynamic tools described in this section, you must recompile your sources, including a single *mpatrol* header file.

mpatrol creates a comprehensive log of all dynamic memory operations that occur while a program is executing. *mpatrol* performs extensive runtime checking for invalid operations performed on dynamically allocated memory.

Numerous library settings can be changed at runtime through environment variables and command-line options.

mpatrol includes a complete set of replacements for those C and C++ library functions that allocate and manipulate memory. This includes C dynamic-memory-allocation functions, C++ dynamic-memory-allocation operators, and C memory-manipulation functions.

mpatrol can produce a summary of memory-allocation statistics. An accompanying tool can read and summarize this information and generate profile reports.

mpatrol can produce a concise trace of all memory allocations, reallocations, and deallocations. An accompanying tool can read this file and generate a trace of the memory events in a tabular or graphical format.

14.6.5.2   **Technology**

mpatrol coexists with the *gcc* command-line option *-fcheck-memory-usage*. This option tells the compiler to place calls to functions that check each memory access. This option supports the GNU *Checker* tool. The *Checker* tool itself doesn't coexist with *mpatrol*.

Memory operation logging includes a call stack traceback wherever possible. Since these logs can be quite large, you can request that memory-allocation events be recorded in a very concise format suitable for analysis by tracing.

When you log allocation information, you can specify that allocations are recorded in a special leak table. The leak table records the memory-allocation behavior between two points in a program. The library provides functions that can dynamically start and stop recording in the leak table.

You can have all allocated and freed memory filled with special bytes to track operations that are using uninitialized or freed memory. You can also keep some or all freed memory blocks to track these type of errors.

You can have special buffers placed on either side of each block of allocated memory, prefilled with a special value, to catch code that is running off either end of a memory block. *mpatrol* also provides features to allocate these buffers in write-protected memory.

mpatrol provides convenient symbols that you can use to set breakpoints in the allocation library and procedures for printing information about memory allocations. It also provides hooks so that you execute your own procedures when the library starts up and shuts down and each time a memory block is allocated or freed. There are functions to query for detailed information about any memory block, to iterate over every allocated or freed memory block, and to check the library's data structures. There are numerous functions that can be called to generate output to the log file.

There are a number of utility programs included with the library. *mleak* checks the log file for memory leaks. *mprof* is analogous to the popular UNIX™ *gprof* command and generates summaries of allocation behavior on a call graph basis. *mptrace* can be used to trace the history of every memory allocation and can generate output in graphical or tabular form on systems that support X Windows.

14.6.5.3 Usage

Under what circumstances does it make sense to use *mpatrol?* It supports both C and C++ sources. It has been ported to more operating systems and hardware platforms than any other tool in this chapter. It is well integrated with the GNU program development environment. It can be built as a thread-safe library on a number of platforms, although the serialization is done at a somewhat coarse level.

It provides more information about memory allocation than the other dynamic tools, but collecting this information comes with a runtime performance penalty. If you need a high degree of flexibility and control for your analysis, this penalty will be justified.

The method of placing buffers around allocated blocks is useful for detecting writes off the ends of blocks, but doesn't catch reads off the ends. The method of using protected virtual memory pages to detect these errors can be prohibitively expensive in terms of memory space. If you think that your problem is reading or writing past the end of a block, *mpatrol* may not be the best way to find your problem, unless you can use the **gcc** compiler with the *-fcheck-memory-usage* option.

14.6.6 Examples

The following listings show the relevant output of *mpatrol* when used to diagnose the bugs described.

14.6.6.1 *mpatrol* output for case 1, bug 3

```
@(#) mpatrol 1.4.8 (02/01/08)
Copyright (C) 1997-2002 Graeme S. Roy
```

```
...
operating system:       UNIX
system variant:         Linux
processor architecture: Intel 80x86
...
allocation peak:    22 (456907 bytes)
allocation limit:   0 bytes
allocated blocks:   15 (1871 bytes)
marked blocks:      0 (0 bytes)
freed blocks:       0 (0 bytes)
free blocks:        3 (518321 bytes)
internal blocks:    35 (573440 bytes)
total heap usage:   1093632 bytes
total compared:     0 bytes
total located:      0 bytes
total copied:       0 bytes
total set:          594984 bytes
total warnings:     0
total errors:       0

ERROR: [ILLMEM]: illegal memory access at address 0x00000008
    0x00000008 not in heap

    call stack
0x08049FA9 insert__4Heap+53
0x08049F3C __4HeapiPi+212
0x0804B5CF main+75
0x400FC177 __libc_start_main+147
0x08049D51 _start+33
```

14.6.6.2   *mpatrol* output for case 2, C++ version, part 1

```
@(#) mpatrol 1.4.8 (02/01/08)
Copyright (C) 1997-2002 Graeme S. Roy
...
operating system:       UNIX
system variant:         Linux
processor architecture: Intel 80x86
...
MEMCOPY: memmove (0x08076BF4, 0x08079A0C, 10572 bytes, 0x00) [-|-|-]
0x08062BAD __copy_trivial__H1Zi_PCX01T0PX01_PX01+33
```

```
0x080623CE copy__t15__copy_dispatch3ZPCiZPiZ11__true_typePCiT1Pi+26
0x080615DA copy__H2ZPCiZPi_X01X01X11_X11+26
0x08062786
__uninitialized_copy_aux__H2ZPCiZPi_X01X01X11G11__true_type
        _X11+30
0x08061FE3 __uninitialized_copy__H3ZPCiZPiZi_X01X01X11PX21_X11+35
0x08060821 uninitialized_copy__H2ZPCiZPi_X01X01X11_X11+45
0x0805F5F4
__t6vector2ZiZt9allocator1ZiRCt6vector2ZiZt9allocator1Zi+120
0x0804B0C8 lexSortTuples__FGt6vector2ZPt6vector2ZiZt9allocator1ZiZt9
        allocator1ZPt6vector2ZiZt9allocator1Zi+3192
0x0804BC87 test__FiPiT1+67
0x0804BE1E main+30
0x400FC177 __libc_start_main+147
0x0804A371 _start+33


ERROR: [RNGOVF]: memmove: range [0x08076BF4,0x0807953F] overflows
        [0x080768FC,0x08076E13]
0x080768FC (1304 bytes) {malloc:80:0} [-|-|-|-]
0x08063607 _S_chunk_alloc__t24__default_alloc_template2b1i0UiRi+239
0x08063388 _S_refill__t24__default_alloc_template2b1i0Ui+28
0x08062F6E allocate__t24__default_alloc_template2b1i0Ui+122
0x08062751
allocate__t12simple_alloc2ZiZt24__default_alloc_template2b1
        i0Ui+25
0x08061FA5
_M_allocate__t18_Vector_alloc_base3ZiZt9allocator1Zib1Ui+21
0x08061397 _M_insert_aux__t6vector2ZiZt9allocator1ZiPiRCi+179
0x0805FDAF push_back__t6vector2ZiZt9allocator1ZiRCi+83
0x0804BB15 makeTuples__FiPiT1+305
0x0804BC5C test__FiPiT1+24
0x0804BE1E main+30
0x400FC177 __libc_start_main+147
0x0804A371 _start+33
```

14.6.6.3 *mpatrol* output for case 2, C++ version, part 2

```
allocation count:   121
allocation peak:    54 (456907 bytes)
allocation limit:   0 bytes
allocated blocks:   54 (25427 bytes)
```

```
marked blocks:        0 (0 bytes)
freed blocks:         0 (0 bytes)
free blocks:          3 (494765 bytes)
internal blocks:      38 (622592 bytes)
total heap usage:     1142784 bytes
total compared:       0 bytes
total located:        0 bytes
total copied:         1852 bytes
total set:            609144 bytes
total warnings:       0
total errors:         1

ERROR: [ILLMEM]: illegal memory access at address 0x00000007
    0x00000007 not in heap

    call stack
        0x08060499 size__Ct6vector2Zt6vector2ZiZt9allocator1ZiZt9
                    allocator1Zt6vector2ZiZt9allocator1Zi+17
        0x0806011E __t6vector2Zt6vector2ZiZt9allocator1ZiZt9allocator1

Zt6vector2ZiZt9allocator1ZiRCt6vector2Zt6vector2ZiZt9

allocator1ZiZt9allocator1Zt6vector2ZiZt9allocator1Zi+42
        0x0804B136
lexSortTuples__FGt6vector2ZPt6vector2ZiZt9allocator1
                    ZiZt9allocator1ZPt6vector2ZiZt9allocator1Zi+3302
        0x0804BC87 test__FiPiT1+67
        0x0804BE1E main+30
        0x400FC177 __libc_start_main+147
        0x0804A371 _start+33
```

14.6.6.4   *mpatrol* output for case 3, bug 3

```
@(#) mpatrol 1.4.8 (02/01/08)
Copyright (C) 1997-2002 Graeme S. Roy
...
operating system:      UNIX
system variant:        Linux
processor architecture: Intel 80x86
...
allocation count:   94
allocation peak:    26 (456907 bytes)
```

```
allocation limit:   0 bytes
allocated blocks:   26 (3079 bytes)
marked blocks:      0 (0 bytes)
freed blocks:       0 (0 bytes)
free blocks:        4 (517113 bytes)
internal blocks:    36 (589824 bytes)
total heap usage:   1110016 bytes
total compared:     0 bytes
total located:      0 bytes
total copied:       0 bytes
total set:          596664 bytes
total warnings:     0
total errors:       0


ERROR: [ILLMEM]: illegal memory access at address 0x00000000
    0x00000000 not in heap

call stack
    0x0804C109 main+137
    0x400FC177 __libc_start_main+147
    0x08049DE1 _start+33
```

14.7   Analysis comparison

A helpful way to put all of these tools in perspective is to consider what additional information they develop beyond that of a traditional procedural compiler. The Chomsky hierarchy categorizes some of the types of information that such a compiler can develop. We have summarized the types of errors that such information can uncover. In addition, procedural compilers develop symbol tables and control-flow and data-flow information on a per-procedure basis.

Whole-program compilers are relatively rare. The author led the development of the first multilanguage, interprocedurally optimizing compiler available as a commercially supported product over a decade ago [LMSS91]. There have only been a few such compilers developed since then. See the bibliography for additional information on compiler techniques for interprocedural analysis.

The additional compile time required for interprocedural analysis is usually justified for compute-intensive applications. A side benefit of such compilers, however, is that they develop symbol tables and control-flow and

data-flow information on a whole-program basis. The users of the afore-
mentioned compiler liked it as much for its additional error-checking capa-
bilities as for its optimizing ability!

14.7.1   Static-analysis tools

CodeSurfer does both intraprocedural and interprocedural pointer-target
analysis. Static pointer-target analysis associates the names of variables
whose address is taken with pointer variables. *CodeSurfer* doesn't do any
type of constant propagation. Constant propagation is the use of control-
flow and data-flow information to determine that a variable must have a
particular constant value at a specific point in the program. *PC-lint* does
both intraprocedural and interprocedural value tracking. Value tracking
includes both constant propagation and pointer-target analysis. Pointer-target analysis makes it possible to catch a variety of misuses of dynamic memory statically.

Splint does error checking beyond that of procedural compilers by using
annotations supplied by the user. These annotations, when provided, make
it possible to perform strict type checking, to enforce information hiding of
user-defined types, and to check the side effects of calling functions. *PC-lint*
also employs supplemental information when it's provided by the user for
similar purposes.

14.7.2   Dynamic-analysis tools

Insure++ uses modified source code to track the status of memory blocks
and verify the correctness of arguments to API calls. *BoundsChecker* uses
modified intermediate code to track the status of memory blocks and verify
the correctness of arguments to API calls. *Purify* uses modified object code
to track the status of memory blocks and verify the correctness of arguments to API calls.

Insure++ and *BoundsChecker* use calls embedded in the program to
record information relating pointer variables and addresses of memory.
Other embedded calls check that information to validate the status of the
pointer variables and make sure that operations on the memory addresses
are valid.

Purify uses calls embedded in the program to record whether memory
locations are writable (allocated) and readable (initialized). Other embedded calls check that information to make sure that operations on the memory addresses are valid. Unlike *Insure++* and *BoundsChecker,* *Purify* has no

concept of pointer variables, since it works without high-level-language source code. It tracks memory usage purely in terms of addresses.

mpatrol uses special versions of libraries to track the status of memory blocks. Like *Purify*, it can insert special buffers around dynamically allocated memory so that there is a record of aberrant pointer behavior at runtime.

Insure++, BoundsChecker, and *Purify* all check the correctness of arguments to API calls at runtime. If the APIs that they check were all written in a language with strict typing, it wouldn't be necessary to check their arguments at runtime.

Unfortunately, many of these APIs are written in C, and so these tools are useful for catching API errors. The information needed from a strictly typed language to provide full static checking would include the following:

- A true Boolean type that couldn't be converted to and from integers

- Types derived from integers with ranges of allowable values

- Enumeration types that couldn't be converted to and from integers

- Character types that couldn't be converted to and from integers

- Array types composed from the types listed above with specified bounds

14.8 **Review**

A grammar is a set of rules that defines how to generate valid sentences in a language. Noam Chomsky defined a hierarchy of increasingly complex grammars and corresponding methods for recognizing the sentences that those grammars generate. It is possible to describe the valid words in most high-level programming languages, except Fortran and COBOL, using regular grammars. Similarly, it's possible to describe the valid sentences in most high-level programming languages, except Fortran and COBOL, using context-free grammars. Rather than use context-sensitive grammars, most compilers either use a hand-coded program to verify the context-sensitive aspects of a program or a combination of a hand-coded program and an attribute grammar.

The more information a compiler has, the more defects it can find. The types of syntactic and semantic errors that a compiler can find depend on the language being compiled. The semantic analyzer performs context-sensitive analysis by referring to additional data structures as it examines its representation of the program. These additional data structures include symbol tables, control-flow information, and data-flow information, each at either the procedure or whole-program level.

Static analysis evaluates all code in an application. It can find defects in code not exercised by a particular test run. Static analysis requires source code and is likely to take more time than dynamic analysis.

Splint is a tool for statically checking C programs. Special comments called annotations are used to provide extra information about types, variables, and functions. By adding annotations to programs, it can perform stronger checks than any standard *lint*-like tool. *Splint* provides several hundred command-line options to control its error checking.

Splint detects memory leaks, the use of invalid pointers, and null pointer dereferences. It provides C programmers with tools to check object-oriented implementations by checking for violations of information hiding. It provides for complete type checking of Boolean, **enum**, and **char** data types. It extends the notion of C prototypes by enabling the programmer to identify global variables and side effects. *Splint* is particularly useful in identifying defects in C programs that are commonly used by hackers to attack network applications.

PC-lint/FlexeLint is a tool for statically checking C and C++ programs. It uses a number of different types of analysis to detect potential problems. Like other *lint*-type programs, it uses control-flow analysis, data-flow analysis, and the comparison of expressions to known problematic patterns. It performs special analyses of preprocessor macros and of all programming language constructs that don't correspond to generated code or data. One of its strong features is procedural and interprocedural value tracking. It also provides features for C programmers to get some of the benefits of object-oriented programming.

CodeSurfer is a slice browsing tool for statically analyzing C programs. A slice is a collection of all the code that contributes to the computation of a value. *CodeSurfer* does both intraprocedural and interprocedural control and data-flow analysis, as well as pointer-target analysis. *CodeSurfer* provides the following analysis results in an interactive tool: data predecessors, control predecessors, data successors, control successors, backward slicing, forward slicing, and chopping. The interactive tool enables you to view these analyses from the perspective of specific variables, specific variables used in particular program elements, and specific functions.

Dynamic analysis can include system and third-party libraries, since source code isn't required. Dynamic analysis only evaluates code that is executed. While this may mean that it will take less time than static analysis, it also means you must have a comprehensive test suite to get the full benefit from doing it.

Insure++ is a tool for dynamically checking C and C++ programs. *Insure++* detects pointer-reference problems, memory-leak problems, miscellaneous pointer problems, and library API problems. It is used in place of your normal compiler. It parses your source code, generates revised source code that contains monitoring calls, and passes this code to your compiler. When you run your program, the runtime part of the tool checks data values and memory references for correctness.

Purify is a tool for dynamically checking C and C++ programs. It finds references to heap and stack memory that are unallocated or uninitialized. *Purify* works by modifying the object code used to build your application. It inserts instructions in front of every instruction that accesses data from memory. These instructions call functions that track the state of memory addresses in terms of allocation and initialization. When unallocated addresses are read or written or uninitialized addresses are read, *Purify* signals an error. After the object code of an application is processed by *Purify*, it can be linked in the normal way. When the application is executed, the *Purify* runtime library will report errors that it finds.

mpatrol is a library for dynamically checking C and C++ programs on a wide variety of platforms. It can generate a readable log file, summary profile, and history trace of dynamic-memory operations. It includes a complete set of replacements for those C and C++ library functions that allocate and manipulate memory. It also provides a complete API for controlling and examining the behavior of the memory allocator while it's running. It provides multiple methods for diagnosing common memory-allocation and -manipulation problems.

All of these tools are very valuable in detecting bugs. If you're programming in C or C++, we strongly recommend that you get both a static- and a dynamic-analysis tool. If you're programming in C and can't afford commercial tools, get *Splint* and *mpatrol*. If you're programming in C++ and have a tools budget, get one of the dynamic-analysis tools first and then consider adding one of the static-analysis tools.

15

Get Back to Work

Far and away the best prize that life offers is the chance to work hard at work worth doing.

—Theodore Roosevelt

You have done us the courtesy of reading this book all the way through. I appreciate that.

Now it's time for you to transfer the ideas you have been exposed to in this book into the realm of practice. We have several suggestions on how to do this.

15.1   Review the methods

15.1.1   Review now

Now is a good time to evaluate whether you have learned anything from reading this book and what you want to put into practice. The tables in this section list all the techniques described in this book. If you don't know how to use a technique, go back and reread the corresponding section.

The columns give you space to decide how to apply the technique. If you're already using the technique, check the first column. If you would like to use the technique at the next opportunity, check the second column. If you would like to use the technique at some future time, check the third column. Put more checks in the third column than the second one. You can't use everything first. If you don't think the technique is applicable to your work, check the last column.

Table 15.1   *Debugging Techniques, Part 1*

Technique	Already Using	Use Soon	Use Later	No Plans
Use cross-disciplinary knowledge				
Focus on facts				
Pay attention to unusual details				
Gather facts before hypothesizing				
State the facts to someone else				
Start by observing				
Don't guess				
Exclude alternative explanations				
Reason in both directions				
Watch for red herrings				
Use alibis as clues				
Eliminate impossible causes				
Exercise curiosity				
Reason based on facts				
Enumerate possibilities				
Use the power of logic				
Use a system for organizing facts				
Exercise caution when searching				
Use gestalt understanding				
Show how something could be done				
Don't look for it				
It isn't lost—you are				

Debugging Techniques, Part 2

Technique	Already Using	Use Soon	Use Later	No Plans
Remember the three c's				
It's where it's supposed to be				
Look for domestic drift				
You're looking right at it				
The camouflage effect				
Think back				
Look once, look well				
The eureka zone				
Tail thyself				
It wasn't you				
Use a binary search strategy				
Use a greedy search strategy				
Use a breadth-first search strategy				
Use a depth-first search strategy				
Use a program slice strategy				
Use a deductive-analysis strategy				
Use a inductive-analysis strategy				
Stabilize the program				
Create a test case				
Reduce the required input				
Categorize the problem				
Describe the problem				
Explain the problem to someone else				

Debugging Techniques, Part 3

Technique	Already Using	Use Soon	Use Later	No Plans
Recall a similar problem				
Draw a diagram				
Choose a hypothesis from historical data				
Read the code				
Write unit tests				
Display variable values				
Display execution messages				
Display procedure arguments				
Generate a flow trace				
Generate a variable snapshot				
Generate a memory dump				
Force a variable value				
Assert assumptions				
Check data structures				
Display data structures				
Use runtime subscript checking				
Use runtime stack checking				
Use runtime heap checking				
Initialize global variables				
Initialize local variables				
Change storage class				
Use a different compiler				
Compile to an intermediate level				
Execute on a different platform				

15.1.2   Review later

Keep the list near you when you're doing debugging work. When you're working on a difficult bug, look over the list and see if any of the techniques might help you. If you use one of the techniques for the first time, write the date in the table.

15.2   Measure your work

If you're going to get serious about improving your debugging productivity, you need to keep records. We have already described several ways of keeping logs or journals about your debugging efforts. If you want to measure whether your productivity is improving, all you need to add to those records are the dates and times when you started and finished working on the bugs.

15.3   Visit our Web site

You can obtain ongoing value from this book by visiting our Web site at www.debuggingbythinking.com.

We guarantee that there are no irritating pop-up ads or other distractions. You can register to have e-mail sent to you when there are major additions to the content, if you so desire.

15.3.1   Download new debugging tools

The Web site contains the latest editions of tools that we produce to help people debug software. For example, the latest version of the root-cause analysis tool demonstrated in Chapter 11 can be found on our site. It is written in Java and will run on any platform with a Java Runtime Environment installed on it.

The Web site also contains links to or copies of open software produced by other people that we consider valuable. For example, there are links to the open-source tools mentioned in Chapter 14.

15.3.2   Springboard to other sites

The Web site also contains links to a variety of other sites that provide information, methods, or tools useful in debugging and related phases of software development. For example, there are links to the Web sites of the vendors who sell the commercial tools mentioned in Chapter 14.

15.3.3 Read reviews of other publications

It wasn't possible to put all the bibliographic information developed for this book into the hard copy. The Web site includes expanded reviews of books about debugging, as well as abstracts and reviews of academic papers about debugging.

Obviously, the book is static and the Web site is dynamic. We update the Web site regularly with reviews of the latest publications related to debugging.

15.3.4 Contact the author

You can contact the author through the Web site. I would be delighted to hear about how you debug software, how this book helped you, or how this book or the Web site can be improved.

Glossary

bug: Synonymous with "defect."

code block: A group of sequentially executed statements with a single exit point.

conception stage: The phase in which the programmer embodies his or her plan in a language-independent notation such as pseudocode or structure charts, which omit nonessential implementation details.

control-flow graph: A directed graph in which executed statements (or procedures) are represented by the nodes and control-flow is represented by the arcs.

data-flow graph: A directed graph in which assignments to and references to variables are represented by the nodes and information flow is represented by the arcs.

debugging: The process of determining why a given set of inputs causes a nonacceptable behavior in a program and what must be changed to cause the behavior to be acceptable.

defect: That aspect of the design or implementation that will result in a symptom.

desk checking: The process of manually evaluating each statement in a program in the order in which they would be executed by a computer.

diachronic: Literally, "through time." A diachronic approach observes the evolution of something over a period of time.

expression stage: The phase in which the programmer encodes the algorithm in a specific programming language, which includes all details necessary to compile and execute the program.

failure: Synonymous with "symptom."

fault: Synonymous with "defect."

filter: A program that takes all of its input from the operating system standard input and sends all of its output to the operating system standard output.

heuristics, debugging: Techniques for making progress on unfamiliar problems or rules of thumb for effective problem solving.

intraprocedural analysis: An evaluation of some aspect of the semantics of an individual procedure in which the evaluation is performed across the boundaries of individual statements and on all of the statements of that procedure.

interprocedural analysis: An evaluation of some aspect of the semantics an executable program in which the evaluation is performed across the boundaries of individual procedures and on all of the procedures of that program.

program slice: The set of statements and predicates in a program that may affect the value of the variables referenced at a specific location in that program.

root-cause analysis: The process of determining the earliest point in the design and implementation of a program at which a defect was introduced.

strategies, debugging: Global decisions regarding the selection and implementation of heuristics and tactics.

symptom: An observable difference between the actual behavior and the planned behavior of a software unit.

synchronic: Literally, "with time." A synchronic approach observes a situation in an instance of time.

tactics, debugging: Programming skills that produce information, which can be applied automatically without requiring contemplation.

testing: The process of determining whether a given set of inputs causes a nonacceptable behavior in a program.

topological sort: A listing of the nodes of a directed graph such that if one node directly or indirectly precedes another node in the graph, the first node is listed before the second node in the listing.

transcription stage: The phase in which the programmer embodies the program in a machine-readable medium.

Root-Cause Checklist

A.1 Design errors

A.1.1 Data structures

- A data definition is missing.
- A data definition is incorrect.
- A data definition is unclear.
- A data definition is contradictory.
- A data definition is out of order.
- A shared-data access control is missing.
- A shared-data access control is incorrect.
- A shared-data access control is out of order.

A.1.2 Algorithms

- A logic sequence is missing.
- A logic sequence is superfluous.
- A logic sequence is incorrect.
- A logic sequence is out of order.
- An input check is missing.
- An input check is superfluous.
- An input check is incorrect.
- An input check is out of order.

- An output definition is missing.
- An output definition is superfluous.
- An output definition is incorrect.
- An output definition is out of order.
- A special-condition handler is missing.
- A special-condition handler is superfluous.
- A special-condition handler is incorrect.
- A special-condition handler is out of order.

A.1.3 User-interface specification

- An assumption about the user is invalid.
- A specification item is missing.
- A specification item is superfluous.
- A specification item is incorrect.
- A specification item is unclear.
- Specification items are out of order.

A.1.4 Software-interface specification

- An assumption about collateral software is invalid.
- A specification item is missing.
- A specification item is superfluous.
- A specification item is incorrect.
- A specification item is unclear.
- Specification items are out of order.

A.1.5 Hardware-interface specification

- An assumption about the hardware is invalid.
- A specification item is missing.
- A specification item is superfluous.
- A specification item is incorrect.

- A specification item is unclear.
- Specification items are out of order.

A.2   Coding errors

A.2.1   Initialization errors

- A simple variable is always uninitialized.
- A simple variable is sometimes uninitialized.
- A simple variable is initialized with the wrong value.
- An aggregate variable is always uninitialized.
- An aggregate variable is sometimes uninitialized.
- An aggregate variable is initialized with the wrong value.
- An aggregate variable is partially uninitialized.
- An aggregate variable is not allocated.
- An aggregate variable is allocated the wrong size.
- A resource is not allocated.

A.2.2   Finalization errors

- An aggregate variable is not freed.
- A resource is not freed.

A.2.3   Binding Errors

- A variable is declared with the wrong scope.
- A procedure call is missing arguments.
- A procedure call has the wrong argument order.
- A procedure call has extra arguments.
- The actual argument passing mechanism does not match the usage of the formal argument.
- A procedure returns no value.
- A procedure returns the wrong value.

A.2.4 Reference errors

- The wrong procedure is called.
- The wrong variable is referenced.
- The wrong constant is referenced.
- The wrong variable is assigned.
- A variable is not assigned.

A.2.5 Static data-structure problems

- A simple variable has the wrong data type.
- An element of an aggregate variable has the wrong data type.
- An aggregate variable has the wrong aggregate size.

A.2.6 Dynamic data-structure problems

- An array subscript is out of bounds.
- An array subscript is incorrect.
- An uninitialized pointer has been dereferenced.
- A null pointer has been dereferenced.
- A pointer to freed memory has been dereferenced.
- An uninitialized pointer has been freed.
- A pointer stored in freed memory has been dereferenced.
- A null pointer has been freed.
- A pointer to freed memory has been freed.
- A pointer to static memory has been freed.
- A pointer to automatic (stack) memory has been freed.

A.2.7 Object-oriented problems

- A class containing dynamically allocated memory does not have the required methods.
- A base class has methods declared incorrectly for the derived class to override.

- The wrong method signature is used to invoke an overloaded method.
- A method from the wrong class in the inheritance hierarchy is used.
- A derived class does not completely implement the required functionality.

A.2.8 Memory problems

- Memory is corrupted.
- The stack is corrupted.
- The stack overflows.
- The heap is corrupted.
- A pointer is invalid for the address space.
- An address has an invalid alignment.

A.2.9 Missing operations

- A return code or flag has not been set.
- A return code or flag has not been checked.
- An exception has not been thrown.
- An exception thrown has not been handled.
- An event sequence has not been anticipated.
- A program state has not been anticipated.
- Statements are missing.
- Procedure calls are missing.

A.2.10 Extra operations

- A return code or flag is set when not needed.
- An exception is thrown when not valid.
- Extraneous statements are executed.
- Extraneous procedure calls are executed.

A.2.11   Control-flow problems

- Statements are controlled by the wrong control-flow condition.
- Loop iterations are off by one.
- A loop terminates prematurely.
- A loop runs indefinitely.
- A case in a multiway branch is missing.
- A multiway branch takes the wrong case.
- A statement is executed too many times.
- A statement is executed too few times.

A.2.12   Value-corruption problems

- An arithmetic operation has underflow or overflow.
- Precision is lost.
- Signed and unsigned integers are mixed.
- Floating-point numbers are compared incorrectly.

A.2.13   Invalid expressions

- The wrong variable is used.
- Operator input is invalid.
- The wrong arithmetic operator is used.
- The wrong arithmetic expression order is used.
- The wrong relational operator is used.
- The wrong relational expression order is used.
- The wrong Boolean operator is used.
- The wrong Boolean expression order is used.
- A term is missing.
- There is an extra term.

A.2.14   Typographical errors

- Characters are missing.

- There are extra characters.
- Characters are out of order.

A.2.15   Other people's problems

- A compiler has been used incorrectly.
- A software tool has been used incorrectly.
- A system library has been used incorrectly.
- A third-party library has been used incorrectly.
- There is a defect in a system library.
- There is a defect in a compiler.
- There is a defect in a software tool.
- There is a defect in the operating system.
- There is a defect in the third-party software.

B

Books about Debugging

Ag02 Agans, D. *Debugging*. Amacom, 2002.

The book contains 175 pages of general techniques for diagnosing problems, which can be applied to both hardware and software problems. The index is seven pages long; the book contains no bibliography, appendices, or collateral software. This book suggests nine general principles for troubleshooting and debugging. The author presents 45 personal experience anecdotes to motivate readers and illustrate his principles. Most of these are related to debugging electronic hardware or low-level system software.

The most helpful feature of this book is the chapter that contains four extended personal experience anecdotes and explanations of how the nine principles were applied in these situations. The summaries at the end of the chapters are also helpful.

Al02 Allen, E. *Bug Patterns in Java*. APress, 2002.

The book contains 7 pages of language- and platform-independent debugging information, 141 pages of language-dependent debugging information, and 52 pages related to other phases of the software-development process. The bibliography contains 35 URLs for Web pages and 16 annotated book references. The index is 10 pages long; there are 14 pages of appendices, and there is no collateral software. The core of the book is the presentation of 14 bug patterns, one per chapter. The focus of these chapters is to explain the causes and prevention of these bug types, rather than the diagnosis of the bugs.

The most helpful parts of the book are (1) a table of 6 pages that provides an alphabetical list of 120 concepts and the corresponding chapter, and (2) a chapter of 10 pages that provides 121 questions that the book answers, organized by chapter.

FT02 Ford, A. R., and Teorey, T. J. *Practical Debugging in C++*. Prentice Hall, 2002.

The book contains 20 pages of information on common C++ problems, 41 pages of platform-independent debugging information, and 27 pages of tool-specific debugging information. The index is 2 pages long, the bibliography contains 12 entries, there are 4 pages of appendices, and there is no collateral software.

This book would be most helpful to college students who are learning to program in C++. The most valuable feature is the list of the 32 most common bugs in first programs.

Br01 Brown, M. *Debugging Perl*. McGraw-Hill, 2001.

The book contains 114 pages of Perl language information, 4 pages of language- and platform-independent debugging information, 118 pages of language-dependent debugging information, and 71 pages related to other phases of the software-development process. The index is 21 pages long, there is no bibliography, there is one appendix of 48 pages, and there is no collateral software.

The most helpful features of the work are the chapters on the Perl debugging modules and the appendix, which contains a complete list of possible error messages, along with explanations of how each message could be generated.

Mc01 McDowell, S. *Windows 2000™ Kernel Debugging*. Prentice-Hall PTR, 2001.

The book contains 165 pages of platform-dependent debugging information. The index is 6 pages long, there is no bibliography, there are 128 pages of appendices, and there is no collateral software.

The book is aimed at people who support Windows 2000 systems, and programmers who develop device drivers. It would be highly valuable to that audience.

SW01 Scott, P., and Wright E. *Perl Debugged*. Addison-Wesley, 2001.

The book contains 106 pages of Perl language information, 96 pages of language-dependent debugging information, and 14 pages related to other phases of the software-development process. The index is 7 pages long, there is no bibliography, there are 14 pages of appendices, and there is no collateral software.

The most helpful features of the work are the "Perls of Wisdom," collected in a reference card at the back, and the chapters on syntax errors, runtime exceptions, and semantic errors.

TH01 Telles, M., and Hsieh, Y. *The Science of Debugging.* Coriolis Group, 2001.

The book contains 216 pages of language- and platform-independent debugging information, and 230 pages related to other phases of the software-development process. The index is 15 pages long, the bibliography contains 33 entries, there are 10 pages of appendices, and there is no collateral software.

The most helpful feature of the work is the collection of principles in the chapters titled "The General Process of Debugging" and "Debugging Techniques."

JK00 Jung, D. G., and Kent, J. *Debugging Visual Basic.* McGraw-Hill, 2000.

The book contains 35 pages of language- and platform-dependent debugging information, 14 pages of information on the VB language, 247 pages on the Microsoft software environment, and 54 pages related to other phases of the software-development process. The index is 18 pages long, there is no bibliography, there are 9 pages of appendices, and there is no collateral software.

The most helpful feature of the work is the chapter on debugging tools.

Le00 Lencevicius, R. *Advanced Debugging Methods.* Kluwer Academic Publishers, 2000.

The book contains a 13-page summary of current research projects related to runtime debugging and 123 pages describing a query-based tool for debugging object-oriented software systems. The index is 9 pages long, there are 12 pages of appendices, the bibliography contains 204 entries, and there is no collateral software.

The book is a revision of the author's Ph.D. thesis. It might be of interest to computer science researchers, but has no material that can be used by practicing programmers.

W00 McKay, E. N., and Woodring, M. *Debugging Windows Programs.* Addison-Wesley, 2000.

The book contains 38 pages of language- and platform-independent debugging information, 43 pages of C++ language information, and 436 pages of

C++/Microsoft-specific debugging information. The index is 32 pages long, the bibliography contains 49 entries, and there is no collateral software.

The most helpful features of the work are the thorough coverage of Microsoft-specific information and the lists of recommended reading at the end of each chapter.

Unfortunately, the book is marred by numerous incorrect statements and unsubstantiated opinions. For example, the authors assert, "One difficulty with optimizers is that they operate on a small window of code. It's just not feasible for an optimizer to scan the entire body of code and take everything into account to optimize for a loop" (p. 434). This statement was true in the early 1960s. It hasn't been true for decades. Highly effective loop optimization was available in commercial compilers in the late 1960s. Whole procedure optimizers were available in commercial products in the early 1980s, and products containing whole program optimizers became available in the early 1990s.

Let the reader beware.

PM00 Pappas, C. H., and Murray, W. H. *Debugging C++*. Osborne/McGraw-Hill, 2000.

The book contains 7 pages of language- and platform-independent debugging information, 26 pages of C++ language information, 99 pages of Microsoft platform information, 312 pages of C++/Microsoft-specific debugging information, and 49 pages related to other parts of the software-development process. The index is 12 pages long, there is no bibliography, and there is no collateral software.

The detailed examples of debugging Microsoft-specific features are excellent. The publisher should have given the book the title *Debugging C++ on Microsoft Windows* since it doesn't provide any coverage of other platforms, such as UNIX™ or Linux™.

Mi00 Mitchell, W. D. *Debugging Java*. Osborne/McGraw-Hill, 2000.

The book contains 13 pages of language- and platform-independent debugging information, 69 pages of Java language information, 87 pages of Java-specific debugging information, and 172 pages related to other phases of the software-development process. The index is 19 pages long, there are 78 pages of appendices, and there is no bibliography or collateral software.

The most helpful features of the work are the good overview of Java debugging tools and the appendix that lists commercial software tools available for the Java programmer. The publisher should have given the book the title *Java Software Development* since the majority of the book isn't about debugging.

Ro00 Robbins, J. *Debugging Applications.* Microsoft Press, 2000.

The book contains 25 pages of language- and platform-independent debugging information and 402 pages of C++/Microsoft-specific debugging information. The index is 14 pages long, there are 13 pages of appendices, the bibliography contains 23 annotated entries, and collateral software is included on a CD-ROM.

The detailed examples of debugging Microsoft-specific features are excellent. The publisher should have given the book the title *Debugging GUI Applications on Microsoft Windows* since it doesn't provide any coverage of other platforms, such as UNIX™ or Linux™.

Ba98 Ball, S. *Debugging Embedded Microprocessor Systems.* Butterworth-Heineman, 1998.

The book contains 7 pages of language- and platform-independent debugging information and 198 pages of system-dependent debugging information, targeted specifically at embedded microprocessor systems. The index is 9 pages long, there are 25 pages of appendices, and there is no bibliography or collateral software.

The reader should have a working knowledge of microprocessor hardware internals. There aren't many resources for those who debug embedded systems. If you do this type of work, this book is worth reading.

Bu98 Bugg, K. *Debugging Visual C++ Windows.* Miller-Freeman, 1998.

The book contains 16 pages of language- and platform-independent debugging information and 156 pages of C++/Microsoft-specific debugging information. The index is 13 pages long, there are 20 pages of appendices, there is no bibliography, and collateral software is included on a CD-ROM.

The most helpful feature of the work is that it collects useful information about defects on Windows™ systems and tools that might help a programmer debug defects on windows. The work would have been more helpful if it included some examples that show how to use the information or tools presented to diagnose a bug.

Ni96 Nicolaisen, N. *NuMega's Practical Guide to Debugging 32-bit Windows Applications.* IDG Books, 1996.

The book contains 359 pages of language- and platform-dependent debugging information, focusing on the NuMega toolset for C++ applications running on Windows™. The index is 21 pages long, there is no bibliography, there are no appendices, and a demonstration version of NuMega BoundsChecker is included on a CD-ROM.

The most helpful features of the work are the chapters discussing errors on writing to memory, reading from memory errors, pointer errors, and leak errors. A programmer working on Windows™ with Visual C++, but not with the NuMega products, will still find value in the first twelve chapters.

THYS96 Tsai, J. J. P.; Bi, Y.; Yang, S. J. H.; and Smith, R. A. W. *Distributed Real-time Systems.* John Wiley, 1996.

The book contains 71 pages (3 chapters) of language- and platform-independent debugging information related specifically to distributed real-time systems. The index is 3 pages long, there are no appendices, the bibliography has 444 entries, and there is no collateral software.

There aren't many resources for those who debug distributed real-time systems. If you do this type of work, this book is worth reading.

Yo95 Young, D. *Motif Debugging and Performance Tuning.* Prentice Hall, 1995.

The book contains 25 pages of language- and platform-independent debugging information, 57 pages on avoiding software defects, 174 pages of language- and platform-dependent debugging information, 158 pages related to performance tuning, and 145 pages of application case studies. The index is 6 pages long, the bibliography contains 24 entries, and there are no appendices or collateral software.

The most helpful features of the work are the chapters on characterizing bugs, memory bugs, and layout bugs. This is an excellent resource for developers building Motif applications. Developers using other GUI systems might also find some ideas to transfer.

Ne95 Neumann, P.G. *Computer Related Risks.* Addison-Wesley, 1995.

Chapter 1 introduces fundamental concepts, including a notation that is used in the following chapters to summarize the causes of the problems described. The remainder of the book describes hundreds of problems occurring in societies around the world through the use of computers. Some were caused deliberately, others accidentally. The author analyzes and categorizes the problems and presents recommendations on how to build and use systems so that they pose fewer risks to their users and society. The index is 16 pages long, there are 7 pages of appendices, the bibliography has 179 entries, and there is no collateral software.

The value of this work lies in its educating programmers about the repercussions that software defects can have. It doesn't teach debugging techniques per se. Managers of computer programmers should read this book.

Pe95 Peterson, I. *Fatal Defect.* Random House, 1995.

This book is aimed more at the general reading population than Neumann's book. It discusses fewer computer-related problems that have occurred in society. The discussion is organize . around the work of various computer scientists, who are contributing to the analysis and understanding of defective systems. The index is 6 pages long, there are no appendices, the bibliography has 458 entries, and there is no collateral software.

The value of this work lies in its explanations of some of the reasons that software contains defects and of the potential repercussions of serious defects. It doesn't teach debugging techniques per se. The book is suitable for the noncomputer literate. Managers of computer programmers should read this book.

Sp94 Spuler, D. A. *C++ and C Debugging, Testing, and Reliability.* Prentice Hall, 1994.

The book contains 59 pages on generating debugging output and using debugging memory allocators for C and C++, 30 pages on software-development phases other than debugging, 28 pages on exception handling in C++ and C, 32 pages on coding methods that make C++ and C code more robust, 23 pages on debugging and testing tools, and 142 pages on a catalog of 167 errors that C++ and C programmers commonly make. The index is 6 pages long, there are 10 pages of appendices, the bibliography has 61 entries, and a 3.25-inch floppy disk is included as collateral software.

The error catalog would be quite helpful to programmers with limited professional experience in C++ and C. If you program in C or C++, you should read this book. Unfortunately, it's out of print, but if you can find an inexpensive used copy, buy it.

Th92 Thielen, D. *No Bugs! Delivering Error-Free Code in C and C++.* Addison-Wesley, 1992.

The book contains 119 pages on language- and platform-dependent debugging, 25 pages on other phases of the software-development process, and 16 pages on debugging tools (quite obsolete). The index is 8 pages long, there are 31 pages of appendices, there is no bibliography, and there is no collateral software.

If you're a programmer with limited professional experience in C++ and C, you could benefit from reading this book. The examples in this book are all focused on the 80X86 hardware and Microsoft Windows™ software that was popular when the book was written in 1992. Nonetheless, if you skim (or skip) the 80X86/MS-DOS particulars, there are still useful suggestions in this book. Unfortunately, it's out of print, but if you program in C or C++ and you can find an inexpensive used copy, buy it.

St92 Stitt, M. *Debugging: Creatives Techniques and Tools for Software Repair.* John Wiley, 1992.

The book contains 43 pages of language- and platform-independent advice on the debugging process; 136 pages on tools for isolating platform-dependent bugs, including documentation of the software included with the book; 112 pages on methods for isolating platform-dependent bugs, emphasizing MS-DOS and 80X86 systems; 8 pages in an appendix matching problems and methods; 29 pages on system-level knowledge for debugging MS-DOS 80X86 systems; and 50 pages of assembly source code for specialized tools for debugging MS-DOS 80X86 systems. The index is 12 pages long, there is no bibliography, and there is a 5.25-inch floppy disk included as collateral software.

The examples in this book are all focused on the 80X86 hardware and MS-DOS software that was popular when the book was written in 1992. Nonetheless, if you skim (or skip) the 80X86/MS-DOS particulars, there are still a lot of useful suggestions in this book. The chapters have good summaries that omit much of the platform-dependent detail. Unfortunately, the book is out of print, but if you can find an inexpensive used copy, buy it.

Ve91 Vesely, E. G. *COBOL Debugging Diagnostic Manual.* Prentice Hall, 1991.

The book contains 136 pages of language-dependent advice for debugging COBOL programs, 138 pages of source listing of computer-assisted reengineering programs, 36 pages of glossary from ANSI-1974 and ANSI-1985 COBOL manuals, and 8 pages listing annotated COBOL reserved words. The index is 4 pages long, there is no bibliography, and a 5.25-inch floppy disk is included as collateral software. If you're supporting old COBOL programs, you'll find this book helpful.

Ko89 Koenig, A. *C Traps and Pitfalls.* Addison-Wesley, 1989.

The book contains 63 pages of language-dependent common lexical, syntactic, semantic, and linkage bugs; 31 pages of common problems with library functions, the preprocessor, and portability; 3 pages of language-independent advice on the debugging process; and 19 thought questions, distributed over 7 chapters, with answers at the back. The index is 5 pages long, there are 20 pages of appendices, there is no bibliography, and there is no collateral software.

The book would be quite helpful to programmers with limited professional experience in C.

Mu88 Murray, W. R. *Automatic Program Debugging for Intelligent Tutoring Systems.* Morgan Kaufmann, 1988.

The index is 9 pages long, there are 45 pages of appendices, the bibliography has 82 entries, and there is no collateral software.

The book is a revision of the author's Ph.D. thesis. The work is valuable in that it educates programmers about what it would take to automate the debugging process. It makes explicit actions that they do implicitly and, thus, provides ideas about how to think about debugging. It doesn't teach debugging techniques per se.

Jo86 Johnson, W. L. *Intention-Based Diagnosis of Novice Programming Errors.* Morgan Kaufmann, 1986.

The index is 5 pages long, there are 40 pages of appendices, the bibliography has 71 entries, and there is no collateral software.

The book is a revision of the author's Ph.D. thesis. The work is valuable in that it educates programmers about what it would take to automate the debugging process. It makes explicit actions that they do implicitly and, thus, provides ideas about how to think about debugging. It doesn't teach debugging techniques per se.

Wa86 Ward, R. *Debugging C.* Que Corporation, 1986.

The book contains 13 pages of language-independent advice on the debugging process; 24 pages on program testing; 155 pages on how to isolate language-dependent bugs, emphasizing MSDOS and CP/M systems running on microcomputers; 70 pages on how to use source-level debuggers, interpreters, and integrated environments; 25 pages of source code for a machine-level debugger for Wintel machines; and 13 pages of source code for a trace package that works with the debugger. The index is 7 pages long, the bibliography has 29 entries, and there is no collateral software.

The most helpful features of the work are the chapters titled "Why Is Debugging C Difficult?" and "Stabilizing Pointer Bugs." The specifics of dealing with pointer problems differ on modern systems, but the principles are sound. The book is out of print, but if you program in C or C++ and you can find an inexpensive used copy, buy it.

Bi85 Binder, R. *Application Debugging.* Prentice Hall, 1985.

The book contains 13 pages of language-independent advice on the debugging process and 309 pages of IBM-/MVS-specific debugging information, covering COBOL, Fortran, assembly language, and PL/I.

The index is 20 pages long, there are 15 pages of appendices, the bibliography has 9 annotated entries, and there is no collateral software.

Sm84 Smith, T. *Secrets of Software Debugging.* Tab Books, 1984.

The book contains 31 pages of language-independent advice on the debugging process and 29 pages of computing fundamentals aimed at programming novices. Three complete programs, implemented in BASIC, Pascal, and Apple II assembly language, comprise the bulk of the book (175 pages). Problems actually encountered during their development are analyzed and corrected. The index is 3 pages long, there are 8 pages of appendices, the bibliography has 10 entries, and there is no collateral software.

The work targets an obsolete language/environment and is of historical interest only.

Ce84 Cecil, D. R. *Debugging Basic Programs.* Tab Books, 1984.

The book contains 4 pages of language-independent advice on the debugging process. The rest of the book demonstrates errors commonly committed by BASIC programmers. It assumes debugging tools limited to statements available in BASIC language processed by an interpreter. The index is 3 pages long, there are no appendices, and there is no bibliography or collateral software.

The work targets an obsolete language/environment and is of historical interest only.

Ca83 Cassel, D. *The Structured Alternative: Program Design, Style, and Debugging.* Reston Publishing, 1983

The book contains 10 pages of language-independent debugging information. The remainder of the work is devoted to software-development and testing issues. The index is four pages long, there are no appendices, there are three pages of bibliography, and there is no collateral software.

The work confuses testing and debugging and is of limited value.

Cl81 Clary, W. *OS Debugging for the COBOL Programmer.* Mike Murach Associates, 1981.

The book contains 390 pages of system-dependent information about debugging on IBM 360/370 in COBOL. The index is 2 pages long, there are 61 pages of appendices, and there is no bibliography or collateral software.

The work targets an obsolete language/environment and is of historical interest only.

Br80 Bruce, R. C. *Software Debugging for Microcomputers.* Reston Publishing, 1980.

The book contains 339 pages of language-dependent information about debugging in BASIC, intermixed with fundamental software engineering principles.

The index is three pages long, there are eight pages of appendices, and there is no bibliography or collateral software.

The work targets an obsolete language/environment and is of historical interest only.

VT78 Van Tassel, D. *Program Style, Design, Efficiency, Debugging, and Testing.* Prentice Hall, 1978.

The chapter on debugging contains 45 pages of largely language-independent advice on how to diagnose and prevent bugs, as well as 15 pages of questions and problems intended to teach or extend debugging skills. The index is 11 pages long, there are 74 exercises in the appendices, the bibliography has 14 entries, and there is no collateral software.

Despite the age of the work, there is still a lot of good advice in the debugging chapter. The exercises would be useful to students.

Ri76 Rindfleisch, D. H. *Debugging System 360/370 Programs Using OS and VS Storage Dumps.* Prentice Hall, 1976.

The book contains 259 pages of system-dependent information about debugging on IBM 360/370, including information on Fortran and assembly programming. The index is 3 pages long, there are 21 pages of appendices, and there is no bibliography or no collateral software.

The work targets an obsolete language/environment and is of historical interest only.

BS73 Brown, A. R., and Sampson, W. A. *Program Debugging: The Prevention and Cure of Program Errors.* American Elsevier, 1973.

The book contains 16 pages of a language-independent method for debugging based on the Kepner and Tregoe problem-solving method. The remainder of the work is devoted to software-development and testing issues. There is no index, there are 28 pages of appendices, and there is no bibliography or collateral software.

The work confuses testing and debugging and is of limited value.

C

Software Recommendations

C.1   Testing

CAPBAK/X, CAPBAK/MSW - Software Research - X on UNIX(tm) and Windows(tm) — www.soft.com/TestWorks/unix.html

QARun - Compuware — www.compuware.com/qacenter

QC/Replay - Centerline - X on UNIX(tm) — www.centerline.com

QES/Ez - QES — www.qestest.com

Vermont HighTest Plus - Vermont Creative Software - Windows(tm) — www.vtsoft.com

Visual Test - Rational Software - Windows(tm) — www.rational.com

WinRunner - Mercury Interactive - Windows(tm) — www.aptest.com

XRunner - Mercury Interactive - X on UNIX(tm) — www.aptest.com

C.2   Static and Dynamic Analysis

Splint – open source – www.splint.org

CodeSurfer – GrammaTech – www.grammatech.com

PC-lint/FlexeLint – Gimpel Software – www.gimpel.com

Insure++ — ParaSoft – www.parasoft.com

BoundsChecker – Compuware Corporation – www.compuware.com

Purify – Rational Corporation – www.rational.com

mpatrol – open source — www.cbmamiga.demon.co.uk/mpatrol

References

Software Development

Structured Development Techniques

Techniques of Program Structure and Design—Yourdon, Prentice-Hall, 1975

The Elements of Programming Style—Kernighan and Plauger, Addison-Wesley, 1974

Top-Down Structured Programming Techniques—McGowan and Kelly, Mason/Charter, 1975

Structured Systems Development—Orr, Yourdon Press, 1977

Structured Design—Constantine and Yourdon, Prentice-Hall, 1979

Composite/Structured Design—Myers, Van Nostrand Reinhold, 1978

Structured Systems Analysis—Gane and Sarson, Prentice-Hall, 1979

Structured Analysis and System Specification—DeMarco, Prentice-Hall, 1979

Structured Requirements Definition—Orr, Ken Orr Assoc., 1981

Software Testing Techniques—Beizer, Van Nostrand Reinhold, 1982

A Structured Approach to Systems Testing—Perry, QED Information Sciences, 1983

Object-Oriented Development Techniques

Object-Oriented Software Construction—Meyer, Prentice-Hall, 1988

The C++ Programming Language – 2nd ed, Stroustrup, Addison-Wesley, 1991

Object-Oriented Design with Applications—Booch, Benjamin/Cummings, 1991

Object-Oriented Modeling and Design—Rumbaugh et al., Prentice-Hall, 1991

Design Patterns—Gamma, Helm, Johnson, Vlissides, Addison-Wesley, 1995

Object-Oriented Analysis and Design with Applications—Booch, Addison-Wesley, 1994

Object-Oriented Systems Analysis—Shlaer and Mellor, Addison-Wesley, 1989

Object Oriented Software Testing—Siegel, Wiley, 1996

Testing Object-Oriented Systems—Binder, Addison-Wesley, 2000

Prototyping

RW82 Rich, C., and Waters, R. C. "The Disciplined Use of Simplifying Assumptions," *ACM SIGSOFT Software Engineering Notes* 7(5) ACM, 1982.

We82a Weiser, M. "Scale Models and Rapid Prototyping," *ACM SIGSOFT Software Engineering Notes* 7(5) ACM, 1982.

BP91 Bischofberger, W., and Pomberger, G. *Prototyping-Oriented Software Development.* Springer-Verlag, 1991.

Peer Review Methods

Yo79 Yourdon, E. *Structured Walkthroughs,* 2nd ed. Prentice Hall, 1979.

FW82 Freedman, D. P., and Weinberg, G. M. *Handbook of Walkthroughs, Inspections, and Technical Reviews,* 3rd ed. Little, Brown and Co., 1990.

GG93 Gilb, T., and Graham, D. *Software Inspection.* Addison-Wesley, 1993.

Diagramming Methods

NS73 Nassi, I., and Schneiderman, B. "Flowchart Techniques for Structured Programming," *ACM SIGPLAN Notices* 8(8) (1973).

Or77 Orr, K. T. *Structured Systems Development.* Yourdon Press, 1977.

Ma87 Martin, J. *Recommended Diagramming Standards for Analysts and Programmers.* Prentice Hall, 1987.

Testing

My79 Myers, G. J. *The Art of Software Testing.* John Wiley and Sons, 1979.

Be95 Beizer, B. *Black Box Testing.* John Wiley and Sons, 1995.

Ma95 Marick, B. *The Craft of Software Testing.* Prentice Hall, 1995.

Program Analysis

We82b Weiser, M. "Programmers Use Slices When Debugging." *Communications of the ACM* 25(7) (July 1982): 446–452.

GH93 Guttag, J. V., and Horning, J. J. *Larch: Languages and Tools for Formal Specification.* Springer-Verlag, 1993.

LMSS91 Loeliger, J. D.; Metzger, R. C.; Seligman, M.; and Stroud, S. "Pointer Target Tracking: An Empirical Study." In *Proceedings of Supercomputing 1991*, IEEE Computer Society Press, 14–23.

LM94 Loeliger, J. D., and Metzger, R. C. "Engineering an Interprocedural Optimizing Compiler." *SIGPLAN Notices* 29(4) (April 1994): 41–48.

MS93 Metzger, R. C., and Stroud, S. "Interprocedural Constant Propagation: An Empirical Study." *ACM Letters on Programming Languages and Systems* 2(1) (March, 1993): 213–232.

MW00 Metzger, R., and Wen, Z. *Automatic Algorithm Recognition and Replacement: A New Approach to Program Optimization.* MIT Press, 2000.

Wo96 Wolfe, M. *High Performance Compilers for Parallel Computing.* Addison-Wesley, 1996.

AK01 Allen, R., and Kennedy, K. *Optimizing Compilers for Modern Architectures: A Dependence-Based Approach.* Morgan-Kauffman, 2001.

Data Structures and Algorithms

AHU74 Aho, A. V.; Hopcroft, J.; and Ullman, J. D. *The Design and Analysis of Computer Algorithms.* McGraw-Hill, 1974.

Se90 Sedgewick, R. *Algorithms in C.* Addison-Wesley, 1990.

HSR97 Horowitz, E.; Sahni, S.; and Rajasekaran, S. *Computer Algorithms/ C++.* Computer Science Press, 1997.

Se98 Sedgewick, R. *Algorithms in C++,* 3rd ed. Addison-Wesley, 1998.

Robust Data Structures

LCF88 Li, C. C.; Chen, P. P.; and Fuchs, W. K. "Local Concurrent Error Detection and Correction in Data Structures Using Virtual Backpointers," *Proceedings of COMPSAC 1988,* IEEE, 245–251.

TB86 Taylor, D. J., and Black, J. P. "A Locally Correctable B-Tree Implementation." *The Computer Journal,* 29(3) (1986): 269–276.

TMB80 Taylor, D. J.; Morgan, D. E.; and Black, J. P. "Redundancy in Data Structures: Improving Fault Tolerance." *IEEE Transactions on Software Engineering* 6(6) (November 1980): 585–594.

Miscellany

Sn82 Snyder, L. "Recognition and Selection of Idioms for Code Optimization," *Acta Informatica* 17(3) (1982): 327–348.

IEEE94 *IEEE Standard Classification for Software Anomalies.* IEEE Computer Society, 1994.

Be99 Beck, K. *Extreme Programming Explained.* Addison-Wesley, 1999.

Be90 Berliner, B. "CVS II: Parellelizing Software Development." In *Proceedings of the Winter 1990 USENIX Technical Conference,* USENIX, 1990.

Ti85 Tichy, W. F. "RCS—A System for Version Control," *Software—Practice and Experience* 15(7) (July 1985): 637–654.

Books about Supporting Disciplines

Literary Detectives

Do88 Doyle, A. C. *A Study in Scarlet.* Ward, Lock, and Co., 1888.

Do90 Doyle, A. C. *The Sign of the Four.* Spencer Blackett, 1890.

Do92 Doyle, A. C. *The Adventures of Sherlock Holmes.* George Newnes, 1892.

Do93 Doyle, A. C. *The Memoirs of Sherlock Holmes.* George Newnes, 1893.

Do02 Doyle, A. C. *The Hound of the Baskervilles.* George Newnes, 1902.

Do05 Doyle, A. C. *The Return of Sherlock Holmes.* George Newnes, 1905

Do15 Doyle, A. C. *The Valley of Fear.* Smith, Elder, and Co., 1915.

Do17 Doyle, A. C. *His Last Bow.* John Murray, 1917.

Do27 Doyle, A. C. *The Case-Book of Sherlock Holmes.* John Murray, 1927

Sa23 Sayers, D. L. *Whose Body?* Harper and Row, 1923

Sa27a Sayers, D. L. *Clouds of Witness.* The Dial Press, 1927.

Sa27b Sayers, D. L. *Unnatural Death.* Harper and Row, 1927.

Sa28a] Sayers, D. L. *The Unpleasantness at the Bellona Club.* Harper and Row, 1928.

Sa28b Sayers, D. L. *Lord Peter Views the Body.* Harper and Row, 1928.

Sa30 Sayers, D. L. *Strong Poison.* Harper and Row,1930.

Sa31 Sayers, D. L. *The Five Red Herrings.* Harper and Row, 1931.

Sa32 Sayers, D. L. *Have His Carcase.* Harper and Row, 1932.

Sa33a Sayers, D. L. *Murder Must Advertise.* Harper and Row, 1933.

Sa33b Sayers, D. L. *Hangman's Holiday.* Harcount, Brace, Jovanovich, 1933.

Sa34 Sayers, D. L. *The Nine Tailors.* Harcount, Brace, Jovanovich, 1934.

Sa35 Sayers, D. L. *Gaudy Night.* Harper and Row, 1935.

Sa37 Sayers, D. L. *Busman's Honeymoon.* Harper and Row, 1937.

Sa39 Sayers, D. L. *In the Teeth of the Evidence.* Harcount, Brace, Jovanovich, 1939.

SW98 Sayers, D. L with Walsh, J. P. *Thrones, Dominations.* St. Martin's Press, 1998.

SW03 Walsh, J. P., and Sayers. D. L. *A Presumption of Death.* St. Martin's Press, 2003.

Mathematical Problem Solving

Po45 Polya, G. *How to Solve It.* Princeton University Press, 1945.

MBS85 Mason, J.; Burton, L.; and Stacey, K. *Thinking Mathematically,* rev. ed. Addison-Wesley, 1985.

Sc85 Schoenfeld, A. H. *Mathematical Problem Solving.* Academic Press, 1985.

De97 Devlin, K. *Mathematics: The Science of Patterns.* Scientific American Library, 1997.

Cu01 Cupillari, A. *The Nuts and Bolts of Proofs,* 2nd ed. Academic Press, 2001.

So02 Solow, D. *How to Read and Do Proofs,* 3rd ed. John Wiley and Sons, 2002.

Engineering

Ad91 Adams, J. L. *Flying Buttresses, Entropy, and O-Rings: The World of an Engineer.* Harvard University Press, 1991.

Pe92 Petroski, H. *To Engineer Is Human.* Vantage Books, 1992.

Pe96 Petroski, H. *Invention by Design.* Harvard University Press, 1996.

Root Cause Analysis

WDA93 Wilson, P. F.; Dell, L. D.; and Anderson, G. F. *Root Cause Analysis: A Tool for Total Quality Management.* ASQ Quality Press, 1993.

Am98 Ammerman, M. *The Root Cause Analysis Handbook.* Productivity, Inc., 1998.

Psychology of Human Error

SW49 Shannon, C. E., and Weaver, W. *The Mathematical Theory of Communication.* University of Illinois Press, 1949.

Uz66 Uznadze, D. N. *The Psychology of Set,* trans. Basil Haigh. Consultants Bureau, 1966.

We71 Weinberg, G. M. *The Psychology of Computer Programming.* Van Nostrand Reinhold, 1971.

Ra86 Rasmussen, J. *Information Processing and Human-Machine Interaction.* North-Holland, 1986.

No90 Norman, D. *The Design of Everyday Things.* Doubleday, 1990.

Re90 Reason, J. *Human Error.* Cambridge University Press, 1990.

SM91 Senders, J., and Moray, N. *Human Error: Cause, Prediction, and Reduction.* Lawrence Erlbaum Associates, 1991.

Gi91 Gilovich, T. *How We Know What Isn't So.* The Free Press, 1991.

Si92 Silverman, B. *Critiquing Human Error.* Academic Press, 1992.

Pi94 Piatelli-Palmarini, M. *Inevitable Illusions.* John Wiley, 1994.

Books about Thinking Skills

Da89 Dauer, F. W. *Critical Thinking: An Introduction to Reasoning.* Oxford University Press, 1989.

Ne85 Neblett, W. *Sherlock's Logic.* University Press of America, 1985.

Experimental Psychology and Debugging

See our Web site for a complete bibliography of research papers on debugging.

Yo74 Youngs, E. A. "Human Errors in Programming," *Int. J. of Man-Machine Studies* 6 (1974): 361–376.

Go75 Gould, J. D. "Some Psychological Evidence on How People Debug Computer Programs," *Int. J. of Man-Machine Studies* 7 (1975): 151–182.

BD80 Brooke, J. B., and Duncan, K. D. "Experimental Studies of Flowchart Use at Different Stages of Program Debugging," *Ergonomics* 23(11) (1980): 1057–1091.

GS84 Gilmore, D. J., and Smith, H. T. "An Investigation of the Utility of Flowcharts During Computer Program Debugging," *Int. J. Man-Machine Studies* 20 (1984): 357–372.

AJ85 Anderson, J. R., and Jeffries, R. "Novice LISP Errors: Undetected Losses of Information from Working Memory," *Human-Computer Interaction* 1 (1985): 107–131.

Ve85 Vessey, I., "Expertise in Debugging Computer Programs: A Process Analysis," *Int. J. Man-Machine Studies* 23 (1985): 459–494.

SSP85a Spohrer, J. C.; Soloway, E.; and Pope, E. "A Goal/Plan Analysis of Buggy Pascal Programs," *Human-Computer Interaction* 1(2) (1985): 163–207.

SSP85b Spohrer, J. C.; Soloway, E.; and Pope, E. "Where The Bugs Are," *Proceedings Computer-Human Interaction '85*, ACM, 1985, 47–53.

Ve86 Vessey, I. "Expertise in Debugging Computer Programs: An Analysis of the Content of Verbal Protocol," *Transactions on Systems, Man, and Cybernetics* 16(5) (1986): 621–637.

GO87 Gugerty, L., and Olson, G. A. "Comprehension Differences in Debugging by Skilled and Novice Programmers," *Empirical Studies of Programmers*, Ablex Publishing Corp., 1987, 13–27.

KA87 Kessler, C. M., and Anderson, J. R. "A Model of Novice Debugging in LISP," *Empirical Studies of Programmers*, Ablex Publishing Corp, 1987, 198–212.

SS87 Spohrer, J. G., and Soloway, E.,"Analyzing the High Frequency Bugs in Novice Programs," *Empirical Studies of Programmers*, Ablex Publishing Corp, 1987, 230–251.

KA88 Katz, I. R., and Anderson, J. R. "Debugging: An Analysis of Bug-Location Strategies," *Human-Computer Interaction* (3) (1987–1988): 351–399.

Ve89 Vessey, I. "Toward a Theory of Computer Program Bugs: An Empirical Test," *Int. J. Man-Machine Studies* 30 (1989): 23–46.

Ca89 Carver, D. L, "Programmer Variations in Software Debugging Approaches," *Int. J. Man-Machine Studies* 31 (1989): 315–322.

SJW90 Stone, D. N.; Jordan, E. W.; and Wright, M. K. "The Impact of Pascal Education on Debugging Skill," *Int. J. Man-Machine Studies* 33 (1990): 81–95.

AB91 Allwood, C. M., and Bjhorhag C-G. "Novices' Debugging When Programming in Pascal," *Int. J. Man-Machine Studies* 33 (1991): 707–724.

Eb94 Ebrahimi, A. "Novice Programmer Errors: Language Constructs and Plan Composition," *Int. J. Human-Computer Studies* 41 (1994): 457–480.

Index